The Unfair Trade

ALSO BY MICHAEL J. CASEY

Che's Afterlife: The Legacy of an Image

The Unfair Trade

How Our Broken Global Financial System Destroys the Middle Class

MICHAEL J. CASEY

CROWN
BUSINESS
NEW YORK

Published in the United States by Crown Business,
an imprint of the Crown Publishing Group,
a division of Random House, Inc., New York.
www.crownpublishing.com

Library of Congress Cataloging-in-Publication Data
Casey, Michael, 1967–
The unfair trade : how our broken global financial system destroys the middle class / Michael Casey.
p. cm.
1. Finance—History—21st century. 2. Economic history—21st century. 3. Middle class.
4. Income distribution. 5. China—Foreign economic relations. I. Title.
HG173.C42 2012
332'.042—dc23 2011047163

ISBN 978-0-307-88530-2
eISBN 978-0-307-88532-6

Printed in the United States of America

Book design by Jennifer Daddio
Jacket design by Michael Nagin
Jacket illustration by Justin Sullivan/Getty Images

10 9 8 7 6 5 4 3 2 1

First Edition

To Zoe and Analia

CONTENTS

Introduction: The View from James Street 1

Part One

THE RISE OF CHINA

1: Origins of Dysfunction: How We Got Here 31

2: Average Joes: Drowning in a Sea of Global Financial Liquidity 63

3: Virtue and Vice: The Savings and Debt Conundrum 98

4: The Long Reach: China's Insatiable Appetite 132

5: Race to the Bottom: Losers in the Global Economy 162

Part Two

THE RISE OF GLOBAL FINANCE

6: Global Finance Between a Rock and a Hard Place: Too Big to Fail *and* Too Big to Succeed 189

7: The Little Nation That Could: Cutting Bankers Down to Size 229

8: PIIGS and the Systemic Crisis: When Bond Vigilantes Get Their Dander Up 267

9: The Global Liquidity Machine 310

10: What Is to Be Done? Toward a Less Tumultuous World 337

Acknowledgments 365

Notes 369

Index 393

The Unfair Trade

INTRODUCTION

The View from James Street

I have a neighbor across the street in Pelham, New York, whose good humor, intelligence, and well-stocked collection of single-malt scotch make him an ideal companion with whom to mull over the world's problems. An avid and thoughtful reader, Scott would repeatedly tell me that he hoped my book would give him reassurance. He wanted to be convinced that, after the financial turmoil and political uncertainty that have characterized America's recent experience with globalization, eventually "everything is going to be all right."

Given the spectacular recent failures of the financial system I was writing about, Scott's request for optimism was a tough ask. Still, I did respond by laying out what I saw as some of the hopeful signs of progress that globalization has delivered. There was the fact, for example, that between 1990 and 2005 the number of people living on less than $1.25 a day dropped by 400 million, putting the world on track to far surpass the UN's Millennium Development Goal of halving the rate of extreme poverty between 1990 and 2015. Or there was the seven-year increase in life expectancy from 1990 to 2010, the 47 percent decline in infant mortality over the same period, or the 11-point rise in literacy rates to

84 percent for people age fifteen and over. The relentless advance of a 1.3-billion-strong China over that time disproportionately pushed up the aggregate results, but this newfound upward mobility is truly a global phenomenon. It has spread across Asia, Latin America, and Eastern Europe. Even sub-Saharan Africa, the forgotten continent, is posting gains, with growth rates averaging 4 percent over the past four years and social indicators in health, education, and general development all showing real improvements since 2000. On an international level, Adam Smith has been largely proven right: free trade and integration led to greater and more efficient production of goods and services for all.

Yet it's hard for Scott and hundreds of millions of Westerners like him to fully appreciate these advances. They associate globalization with disruptions to their lives and greater instability—and for good reason. In 2008, the world was thrust into a nauseating financial crisis, the likes of which had not been seen in eighty years. And just three years later, with a new crisis rocking Europe, it was facing another bout of financial turmoil, this one potentially even more destructive than the previous one. These crises have shown that many of the jobs created before them were transitory, especially in the bubble-economics sectors of financial services, real estate, and residential construction. In the United States, where inflation-adjusted data show household income dropping 7.1 percent from 1999 to 2010 and the median wage of male workers unchanged from 1968, inequality widened to levels not seen since 1928, the year that preceded the Great Depression. The top 1 percent of earners received 21 percent of the nation's total income in 2008, up from 9 percent in 1976, after having accounted for a whopping four-fifths of all income gains between 1980 and 2005. Globalization and the Internet have allowed U.S. labor productivity to increase on average about 3 percent per year since 1995, but the income gains from that improved efficiency have flowed almost entirely to the upper echelons of American wealth. Although everyone's life has been enriched to some extent by a greater abundance of affordable goods and by exponential developments in communications and medical technology, the majority has slipped enormously in relative terms.

Yet even that disparity could be rationalized into some concept of an improved overall quality of life if it weren't for a new element that these crises have introduced: a profound sense of uncertainty about the future.

I traveled widely to research this book, and from one continent to another I encountered people who'd lost their faith in political and financial institutions. I heard it from bankrupt homeowners in different parts of the United States, from underinsured laborers in southern China, from terrorized factory workers in Ciudad Juárez, Mexico, from rent-choked retailers in Hong Kong, from duped savers on the Channel Island of Guernsey, and from the unemployed of the Costa del Sol and Reykjavik. And it's not just among these hardest-hit cases. For the first time, an April 2011 Gallup survey showed that a majority of Americans—a society dominated by the middle class, to which Scott belongs—believed it was "very or somewhat unlikely" that their children would enjoy a standard of living better than theirs. Worldwide, this emotional reaction has manifested both in a backlash against the political establishment and in deep divisions within that establishment. It is reflected in the political advances of nationalist anti-euro movements in Finland and other parts of Europe, while the governments of the United Kingdom, Germany, Ireland, Greece, Portugal, the Netherlands, and Belgium all struggled to sustain parliamentary majorities. It is also apparent in the rise of both the U.S. Tea Party and the Occupy Wall Street movement, as well as in the uncompromising Washington partisanship that let the credit rating of the world's biggest economy fall victim to what looked to the rest of the world like a schoolyard brawl. The divisions that threatened to turn the 2012 U.S. presidential election into a bitter class battle stem from this discontent.

Yet the root cause of all this angst is neither global integration nor an insensitive free market. Rather, it's founded in an internationally inequitable and unbalanced mix of policies that have created perverse economic incentives and so have undermined the functioning of global market forces. This network of flawed policies distributes the spoils of integration unfairly, benefiting politically privileged elites and holding back everyone else. This is ultimately what has filled people's lives with uncertainty and instability. And given that these disruptions are directly correlated with the broad advance of globalization, it is hardly surprising that many now want the process of integration reversed.

My neighbor Scott has an appreciation of how the lives of many around the world have changed for the better, but as he puts it, "I can't think about that. I have to think about what globalization means to me, and I simply can't conclude that it is positive. If my job is outsourced, what can I do? I'm a midcareer manager with a wife and a nine-year-old daughter to support. There's no way to retrain me into something more competitive, more globally adept. I have to ask myself, 'How do things look from here, from James Street?' And they're not better. They're worse."

Who can dispute that viewpoint? Here's a decent, hardworking man who seeks the security of the status quo, not a bigger piece of the pie. He's not greedy. His greatest desire is to ensure that his child has the same opportunities he had. And how is that any different from me? My wife and I chose to live in Pelham because its schools offered the best we could afford for our daughters. So much for integrating with the world; Pelham isn't even integrated with neighboring Mt. Vernon and the Bronx, where incomes are lower, the schools have fewer resources, the crime levels are higher, and the life prospects for children are poorer. This is our deliberate choice. I can make all the high-minded analyses I like about the benefits of globalization, but my priorities are also based on what's best for my immediate family, on what happens at the local level. Don't we all view the world from our own versions of James Street?

Here lies the crux of the challenge ahead. Globalization is an unstoppable train. Even if we wanted to return to a world of protectionism and high tariffs, or if a political backlash led to the dissolution of the World Trade Organization (WTO), the modern intricacies of global supply chains make such a return nearly impossible. And yet the instinct to resist the disruptive changes that come with greater integration is strong. We all feel it to some extent and so unwittingly act as agents of the distorting policies that protect the dysfunctional status quo. It has always been so. Throughout modern history, technological change and the accompanying expansion in human capability have run up against an instinctive conservativism, leaving our social, political, and legal structures ill-prepared for these new realities. (Think of how ethical boundaries have persistently been challenged by scientific and medical advances over time—from Galileo to stem cell technology.) This, at its core, is what Europeans were grappling with as their debt crisis came to a crunch moment in late 2011. Their financial markets had computerized and globalized so rapidly that they now operated in an *international* sphere where time and distance were no longer a barrier to commerce. But their politics—and therefore the financial regulatory apparatus deployed to manage those markets—were anchored in older institutions that intrinsically protected *national* interests. This mismatch, a product of the same, innate resistance to sweeping change that Scott and I both experience, left Europeans inadequately prepared for the financial maelstrom into which they were hurled. Americans and other non-Europeans are by no means immune from such breakdowns either. As we will see in the pages ahead, tensions between forward-marching globalization and stagnating national politics are on the rise everywhere. My goal is to demonstrate how, in hanging on to a nonintegrated political status quo, we have failed to stop a powerful, globalized financial system from working against our common interest. In doing so, I hope to encourage readers to overcome this conservative instinct and push for reforms that steer globalization into the direction of a truly level playing field.

Even so, Scott's viewpoint demands attention: any serious attempt at reining in the power of global finance must first recognize the deep-seated human resistance to the changes this would entail. Such fear of the new is not something to be belittled or caricatured as backwardness. It is founded on nothing less than the dreams we hold for our children. We must give people reasons to hold on to such hopes. And yet it's fair to say that these will never be realized if we don't reform our broken global financial system.

In our quest to understand this dysfunctional system, we'll first take a visit to the Bund, Shanghai's elegantly restored colonial district, and gaze across the Huangpu River at the spectacular Pudong skyline on the other side. When I look at it—and quite likely if Scott were to do so—thoughts of Manhattan immediately spring to mind. It's not that Shanghai's business district looks especially like New York's. In fact, with the skyward-reaching spire of the Oriental Pearl Tower drawing the eye, the scene is reminiscent of Toronto, with its dominating CN Tower. But I can't help but compare it to lower Manhattan's skyscrapers. Why? Because both skylines are culturally entrenched symbols of what the future might hold, both for these two giant cities' inhabitants and for the countries to which they belong.

More than the White House or U.S. battleships, the preeminent icon of American power in the twentieth century was Manhattan's skyline. Then a group that detested that power sought to destroy the image itself. In the decade following the World Trade Center attacks, their efforts meant that a view of the cityscape could conjure painful feelings of loss, not progress. Compared to the speed with which Shanghai was relentlessly reaching for the sky, the long delays in the construction of 1 World Trade Center, aka the Freedom Tower, seemed to symbolize a decline in American power. (That a China-based manufacturer was awarded the contract to make the impact-proof glass enveloping the tower only seemed to rub salt into that wound.) On that same island eight decades earlier, and in the midst of an even bigger economic crisis, teams of immigrant construction workers took just one year to build the Empire State Building from U.S.-produced materials. That aptly named accomplishment staked America's claim on the twentieth century. More recently, however, the hole that the fallen Twin Towers left in the Manhattan skyline hinted that this claim wouldn't be renewed for the twenty-first century.

By contrast, Shanghai seems desperate for the world to know that China now possesses the all-conquering spirit that turns a nation into an empire. Especially at night, when some buildings run giant video displays down their facades while brightly lit barges float around like Christmas trees on the water, the Pudong skyline could have been lifted right out of the future. One can picture flying cars buzzing around the tops of its skyscrapers as if in a scene from *The Jetsons* or, more ominously, from the movie *Blade Runner.* Pudong was mainly farmland in 1990, when Deng Xiaoping flagged it as the site for a financial center that would lead his country into modernity. Now it represents the beating heart of Shanghai's rapid expansion, its ubiquitous construction cranes forming the vanguard of China's full-steam-ahead charge toward urbanization. No wonder Scott and millions like him fear that China is overwhelming us.

But like any symbolic reading, this assessment of the two cities misses the nuances of reality. With a bit more information, one can compose an equally compelling story that puts the two skylines in a symbiotic relationship. The industries that drive Shanghai and New York are interlinked via the trade and financial flows that arise within the China-U.S. economic partnership. The Shanghai of the twenty-first century was built upon the wealth generated by China's exporting colossus, which depends on consumers in the U.S. market. Because of China's exchange rate and monetary policies, as well as other rules that limit how much wealth trickles down to its 1.3 billion citizens, the export machine creates an ever-growing pool of dollar-based savings. A large part of those savings is commandeered by the People's Bank of China, which then transfers it to the U.S. government in return for its bonds. In an indirect but very significant way, that money helps sustain the securities trading businesses that keep New York's lights on. It's not for nothing that the city's real estate prices held up while homes across the rest of the United States plunged in value after the 2008 crisis. Nor should it be surprising that after $24 billion had been spent on reconstruction, the area around the World Trade Center was booming once the ten-year anniversary of the September 11 attacks came around.

Seen this way, Pudong and lower Manhattan are not adversaries but rather two halves of a powerful coalition. They are interdependent hubs in a Chinese-U.S. relationship that functions much like a single, fused economy—"Chimerica," financial historian Niall Ferguson calls it. But for all the wealth it generates, this is an inefficient international relationship, one that discriminates against different sectors of both countries' societies. Members of the prosperous business class in the bustling port cities along China's eastern coast—Shanghai, Shenzhen, Guangzhou, and Tianjin—are that country's biggest winners in this arrangement. Its losers are the poor and the lower middle classes from China's rural interior. Similarly, those most privileged by it in the United States are concentrated on or close to the two coasts: bankers in Manhattan, hedge fund managers in Greenwich, Connecticut, mutual fund managers in Boston, bond management firms in Los Angeles and San Francisco. America's losers, though, can be found throughout the fifty states.

This coast-versus-hinterland dichotomy in both China and the United States is exhibit A in our case for showing how the wide gaps in opportunities for people in different circumstances around the world reflect a fundamental failing in the structure of the global economy. As we'll learn, it all comes down to how policies set in Washington, Beijing, and other political capitals combine to create a dysfunctional global financial system that provides the biggest benefits to a privileged few while it subjects everyone else to uncertainty and instability.

Terry Gou has done extraordinarily well from this arrangement, not to mention from the weak exchange rate policy and the general pro-export orientation of China's economic model. Gou grew up poor in Taipei, but with a $7,500 starter loan from his mother in 1974 he rode the China boom to personal wealth of $5.7 billion in 2011, according to *Forbes*. Now the highest-profile member of a new breed of cross-Taiwan Strait businessmen, his company, Hon Hai Industries, better known by its trade name Foxconn, produces more of the world's consumer electronic products than any other. It has factories in ten locations in China and additional plants in six other developing countries, employing a total staff of almost 1 million. That's more people than are on the payrolls of Apple, Dell, Microsoft, Hewlett-Packard, Intel, and Sony put together. Indeed, Foxconn work teams churn out products for many of those marquee names. The reclusive Gou keeps his official residence in Taipei but he spends much of his time at Foxconn's Longhua manufacturing compound in Shenzhen, where workers assemble hot-selling items such as Apple's iPad and Nintendo's Wii consoles. He is a notorious workaholic and a penny-pincher, although he does find the time and money to do other things, including shopping for $30 million castles in the Czech Republic and pursuing his passion for tango dancing.

In 2010, Hon Hai Industries generated a staggering $95.19 billion in revenues, the vast bulk of it earned overseas. That's about $260 million a day, Terry Gou's own contribution to the money flows that prop up a dysfunctional world financial system. Until laws requiring exporters to repatriate their foreign earnings were relaxed in late 2010, these earnings and those of many other Chinese exporters would automatically return to China, along with billions more every day from thousands of other exporters, dollars that the fixed exchange rate policy of the People's Bank of China (PBOC) compelled it to acquire. Even after those changes, exporters such as Hon Hai continued to bring their earnings back into China, mostly because they knew the exchange rate was undervalued and destined to keep rising. At the time of writing, the yuan had risen by about 7.3 percent against the dollar in the eighteen months that had passed since the central bank ended a two-year policy of rigidly fixing the exchange rate and began making tiny daily upward adjustments to it. Then, at the end of 2011, with the global economy entering another slowdown, yuan inflows eased and sometimes even turned to outflows as investors speculated that the government would abandon the appreciation policy, just as it had during the recent global economic crisis. But although there were varying opinions about the yuan's fair value, analysts generally agreed that the Chinese currency was still considerably undervalued against virtually all of its trading partners' currencies. The fact that the PBOC added about $1 trillion in reserves during the period of appreciation was proof of undervaluation and therefore of a mercantilist policy that's deliberately intended to support Chinese exporters.

Intervention on such a scale has sweeping global implications. C. Fred Bergsten, the director of the Peterson Institute for International Economics, called it the "largest protectionist measure adopted by any country since the Second World War—and probably in all of history." There will come a time when the yuan is no longer considered undervalued, and a European or U.S. recession that hurts Chinese exports could hasten that moment. But the global distortions created by the interventions of the past decade will take many, many years to undo.

Fueling these distortions is a giant, endless circle of dollars that flows between China and the United States. It starts with the earnings that Chinese exporters such as Foxconn make when they sell their products to Americans. Those proceeds find their way to the People's Bank of China, which then sends them back to the United States, where they help create the credit with which Americans buy more Chinese goods and stoke the incomes of New York bankers.

Even though its power has waned slightly, the gargantuan Chinese export sector's revenues produced an average trade surplus of around $13 billion a month in 2011, or just under $750 million per business day. Those foreign earnings, along with inflows from approved foreign investors in land, plant, and machinery, as well as from any foreigner who can get around the government's strict capital controls to speculate on Chinese financial instruments, meant that many more dollars came into China than yuan were sent out. Only purchases by the PBOC, which relentlessly sold yuan in return for dollars, would prevent this perpetual inflow from pushing up the local currency's value beyond its tightly managed exchange rate target. To pay for those purchases without pumping new inflation-stoking yuan into the economy, the central bank issued yuan-denominated bonds to Chinese banks, which were flush with cash deposits drawn from China's enormous store of household and corporate savings. After effectively converting these savings into foreign currency, the PBOC then had to decide where to invest it overseas. By mid-2011, accumulated reserves hit $3.2 trillion as of September 30, 2011. There simply aren't enough foreign markets big or liquid enough to ensure that prices don't tip against such a central bank when it buys or sells, and that are legally stable enough to protect future transactions. Thus the PBOC typically, albeit reluctantly, steered most of its money into U.S. Treasuries, the bonds of the world's main reserve currency. Chinese foreign reserves fell slightly in the latter part of the year to end it at $3.18 trillion. This was partly explained by the burst of speculative outflows that occurred in December, but there were also hints before then that Chinese banks were being told to hold onto dollars rather than sell them to the PBOC. If it accepted those dollars, the Chinese central bank would have had to gorge itself even more on Treasuries, and by then it was suffering indigestion.

Central banks from other trade surplus countries, including the Bank of Japan, have had to make similar choices, but none has ever bought Treasury bonds as voraciously as China, which has in one decade trebled its reserves to far outrank any other country. As of September 2011, China officially owned $1.15 trillion of the U.S. government's $14.3 trillion Treasury debt. It also maintained massive holdings of debt issued by the now government-owned home loan agencies Fannie Mae and Freddie Mac. The true figures are likely to be far higher than these Treasury data suggest. Beijing's reserve managers are believed to disguise their purchases of U.S. securities—presumably so as not to show their hand and have the market work against their interests—by channeling their transactions through private banks and U.K.-based money managers. Suspiciously, the September 2011 Treasury data show Chinese holdings of Treasuries virtually unchanged from a year earlier, while those registered to U.K. residents more than doubled with a gain of $231 billion, exceeding that of any other country—even Japan, the other great reserves-owning behemoth.

While there are many other sources of demand for U.S. Treasuries, the marginal effect of China's purchases is so large that it can't help but support U.S. bond prices. That in turn keeps down the yield that investors earn on those securities. (By definition, yields move in inverse relation to prices on bonds and other fixed-income securities.) Over time, this has allowed the United States to roll over its enormous calendar of expiring debt at dirt-cheap borrowing rates—which hit a record low of 1.67 percent for ten-year bonds in September 2011. In effect, China is an enabler of America's debt accumulation and its steep fiscal deficit, which the Congressional Budget Office projected to reach 8.5 percent of gross domestic product (GDP) in 2011. The cross-Pacific savings flows—and, more broadly, the privilege of controlling the world's reserve currency—encourage political short-termism in the United States, which means that reforms urgently needed to bring down the country's long-term deficits are postponed. It was disturbing how little attention was focused on this international aspect of America's debt problem during the rancorous debt ceiling debate that resulted in the ignominious downgrading of America's credit rating by Standard & Poor's. A debate that was reduced to overly simplistic mantras—"taxes kill growth" from the right, "Social Security can't be touched" from the left—ignored the elephant in the room. America's debt challenges are inseparable from the problem of global imbalances.

The last thing a big investor like China needs is a future debt crisis in the market in which its holdings are concentrated. Yet by entering into what can only be described as a codependent relationship, Beijing is helping to foster the kind of U.S. fiscal problems it most fears. China cannot be blamed for an irresponsible budget process, but the fact is that the perpetual demand for U.S. government bonds created by its excess savings and managed exchange rate policy makes it easier for Washington to put off the hard decisions. Without China paying a high price for the United States' debt, Congress would have been forced into a reckoning over deficit reduction many years earlier. Just as high market interest rates on government debt will force politicians' hands on tough decisions—as with Greece, Ireland, Portugal, and Spain's adoption of tough austerity measures during the recent euro zone sovereign debt crisis—low rates tend to breed complacency. What's more, they encourage a willingness to take on debt across all of society. Since Treasuries are the benchmark for pricing every other form of credit, their rising prices and falling yields ripple through America's financial markets, pushing investors to seek better deals on higher-yielding debt securities. That brings down interest rates on other loans and creates temptations for borrowers. It also fires up the kinds of factories in which New York specializes: bond trading desks.

As the China-to-U.S. trade and finance cycle accelerated through the first eight years of the decade, the monumental international fund flow became the gasoline with which Wall Street's traders, salesmen, and financial engineers cranked up a prodigious new moneymaking machine. It was a marriage made in hell, as Chinese money, the fastest-growing source of U.S. finance, was taken in by America's underregulated, misincentivized financial sector and multiplied many times over into an explosion of excess credit. The profitable relationship meant that investment banks could promise the sky in salaries and so lure many of the sharpest young minds from around the world. Math graduates who might otherwise have discovered clean energy solutions at engineering firms ended up designing complicated new "securitized" and derivative products for banks to sell. Their inventions included the now notorious collateralized debt obligations (CDOs), into which were bundled thousands of home loans before they were chopped up into securities of differently ordered claims. In what seemed like financial alchemy, high-grade AAA-rated securities could thus be magically created from otherwise low-grade mortgages—all with a little help from ratings agencies, the able assistants of the Wall Street illusionists. It wasn't until 2008 that investors were reminded that there is no such thing as magic.

With demand from China's and other countries' central banks driving up the price of AAA-rated Treasury bonds—and thus pushing down their yields, or returns on investment—pension funds and other institutions whose charters required them to hold high-rated debt eagerly turned to these newfangled securities as substitutes. In the process, they delivered a river of fees to the Wall Street banks that designed them and to the ratings agencies that gave them their AAA stamp. As the CDO factory cranked up, it absorbed more and more mortgages into the securitization process, which freed up capital at the originating banks, allowing them to go out into suburban neighborhoods and recruit still more home loan clients. Most people saw it as a perfect, virtuous cycle that was fast-tracking the country to universal home ownership. Only as time went on did a few Wall Street insiders, their clients, and some savvy academics recognize that the system was a ticking time bomb.

Among the fortunes created by the young "quants" who fashioned these new instruments were those that accrued to Fabrice Tourre, to his employer Goldman Sachs, and to the firm's well-heeled clients. Tourre, a smart young graduate of the elite École Centrale Paris engineering school, joined Goldman at age twenty-two in 2001. He mastered the art of designing CDOs, as well some even more complex swap derivatives, and he was soon bestowed with the common Wall Street title of vice president. By the end of the decade, however, when an email to his girlfriend surfaced during a Securities and Exchange Commission (SEC) investigation, he'd become publicly known by a more notorious title: "Fabulous Fab." Written just before the financial crisis took root, his email read, "The whole building is about to collapse anytime now. . . . Only potential survivor, the fabulous Fab . . . standing in the middle of all these complex, highly leveraged exotic trades he created without necessarily understanding all of the implications of those monstrosities!!!"

The SEC used that message and a host of other data to file fraud charges against Tourre's employer. In a case that Goldman settled out of court for a record $550 million, the SEC charged that in 2007, right at the top of the housing boom, Tourre knowingly assembled complex "synthetic" CDOs whose derivative-based structure was founded on dubious mortgages, and then passed them off to naive investors as if they were low-risk securities. Meanwhile, the SEC said, a better-informed and more privileged client used the same investment vehicle, which Goldman had named Abacus, to place short-selling bets against the securities. Months later, that client, hedge fund manager John Paulson, made $1 billion for his Manhattan-based firm Paulson & Co. when waves of defaults started hitting the subprime mortgages inside the Abacus structure. It was a crowning moment in a year-long spree of bets against the housing bubble that earned Paulson & Co. a staggering $15 billion. Paulson himself took home $4 billion that year, catapulting him to sixth place on *Forbes* magazine's list of America's richest people. For his part, the then-twenty-eight-year-old Tourre earned a $2 million bonus. After paying a mere $4,000 a month in rent for his Greenwich Village apartment, Tourre could devote his winnings to other pursuits, including what his neighbors described as wild, all-night parties. Once the crisis hit, Tourre moved to Goldman's London unit. But after the SEC investigation broke in the spring of 2010, he was put on administrative leave. He continued to receive his salary and benefits while Goldman paid his legal fees in a case that was to leave the Frenchman, remarkably, as the only individual from all of Wall Street to be sued by the SEC on charges arising from the mortgage crisis.

While the elite businessmen and bankers who thrive off the U.S.-China relationship invariably reside in the big trade and financial centers on either country's coasts, the laborers and consumers who support the transnational enterprise often come from places farther inland. The way this deal has played out, it has left the skyscraping city as the victor and the hinterland as the loser.

Economic advancement does not come free. And in China, the heaviest price has been disproportionately paid by inhabitants of the rural interior and their single-child offspring, 220 million of whom have left home in recent years to work grueling shifts in coastland factories. These people, known as the "floating population" because they fall outside China's strict provincial system of residency, have their eyes on a brighter future. And eventually this may come to their children or grandchildren. But it need not be such a long, arduous path to prosperity. These people are better-off than they were in their villages, but that's not saying much. And throughout the boom of the past two decades, various discriminatory policies ensured that China's working-class majority has subsidized the well-connected minority that controls its export business. Due to a fixed, undervalued exchange rate, a set of rules that explicitly limit migrant laborers' access to education, health services, and social security, and a closed banking system, workers saw their purchasing power restrained and their investing options limited. Bereft of state support for retirement or health needs, these people and the relatives they leave behind are forced to save excessively, keeping their money on deposit at state-owned banks that pay very low government-mandated interest rates. This way, they contribute to a growing pool of funds that's used to finance the export machine at deliberately repressed interest rates. As Peking University professor Michael Pettis describes it, China's growth is built upon "the rape of household savers."

Industrious workers like twenty-one-year-old Xui Li (not her real name) sacrifice life, love, and family to save for the future while their employers become rich on their labor and their underremunerated savings. Born in a small village in Hubei province, Xui Li moved to Shenzhen in 2010, where, when I met her, she was working and living in the Longhua headquarters of Terry Gou's Foxconn plant—together with 300,000 others. Occupying almost an entire square mile, the sprawling, enclosed compound is a city unto itself. Inside, lines that would distinguish Xui Li's private life from her work life were blurred. Most of her waking hours were spent before a stream of semiassembled Hewlett-Packard printers, into which she snapped the internal belts that drive their cartridges. Putting in ten-hour shifts, she said her team assembled 2,400 separate units each day. She worked six days a week and earned 1,200 yuan, or about $200, a month. That amount was less than the standard Foxconn wage, but it was due to increase after she'd completed six months at the factory. Xui Li left the compound only once a week—on Sunday, her day off, which is when I encountered her among hundreds of young men and women streaming out of the entrance of the Foxconn headquarters in Shenzhen. She slept in a bunk bed in a female-only dormitory, ate virtually every meal in one of many cavernous cafeterias in the compound, and even spent her social time attending Foxconn-sponsored events. She wore the same uniform as everyone else, watched an internal Foxconn TV service, shopped at the company supermarkets, and got medical treatment at the compound's Foxconn hospital. Everywhere, there were banners and displays with slogans professing the benefits of working for Foxconn. Even the manholes were stamped with its logo.

Like cloistered nuns and monks, the staff in this compound was for many years shut off from the rest of the world and largely forgotten by the Western media, thanks to Hon Hai's strict control over access. Then, in 2010, a spate of thirteen suicides by workers who were jumping from the top floors of dormitory buildings suddenly thrust unwelcome attention onto this compound, prompting some foreign customers to ponder the *real* cost of the gadgets they buy. The victims' motives were not always made clear, although some left suicide notes apologizing to their families and suggesting a sense of failure in their ambitions. But others tried to speak for them, including the Foxconn worker who posted this statement on a blog after the twelfth suicide: "To die is the only way to testify that we ever lived. Perhaps for the Foxconn employees and employees like us—we who are called *nongmingong,* rural migrant workers, in China—the use of death is simply to testify that we were ever alive at all, and that while we lived, we had only despair."

Hon Hai's first response to the public outrage was to put nets above the concrete floor to catch falling jumpers and to request that workers sign a letter swearing not to take their lives. But it also went on a PR kick, hiring New York firm Burson-Marsteller to spruce up Foxconn's image. The company staged a rally at a stadium inside its sprawling Shenzhen campus to boost morale, with tens of thousands of employees paraded in "I ♥ Foxconn" T-shirts, while Gou personally sponsored tours for select journalists. (This controlled open-door policy lasted only a week or two. My own request for a tour and interview five months later was turned down.) In these media presentations, Gou announced plans to eventually let workers live independently outside the compound and, most significantly, he raised the basic monthly wage for Shenzhen workers from around $180 to $300 a month. Notably, however, he also vowed to start shifting more production to the interior, where wages are lower, to protect his profit margin, and to expand operations overseas. Xui Li said she'd been promised a job in Wuhan, nearer to her hometown, but her boss had been vague about whether she could keep the raise she was due and when the move would take place.

It's unclear whether these reforms will mean more freedom for people such as Xui Li. It's also unclear whether any of these changes will address what are likely the real reasons some of her colleagues chose to end their lives. It's quite possible that morale won't improve without a fundamental overhaul of a business model that hinges on squeezing as much production as possible out of a pliant and dependent workforce. Any student of Chinese history will find something eerily familiar in the way that Hon Hai's Taiwanese owner, sitting inside his own Forbidden City, treats his army of staff.

If we followed all the U.S.-bound iPhones, Dell computers, Nintendo consoles, and other items produced in Foxconn's Longhua plant and similar factories along the Chinese coast to their final destinations, we'd end up crisscrossing the entire landmass of the United States. Far more often than not, we'd end up in homes in the suburban areas that surround the country's towns and cities, the heartland of the American middle class. In these places we find the people who represent the American equivalent of the neglected hinterland of China. They too have paid the price for the dysfunctional U.S.-China relationship that enriches city-based elites in both countries.

Here, on Main Street USA, we find the backbone of the U.S. economy. Middle- and lower-income households fueled the boom of the past decade with their spending and then bore the brunt of the bust. They suffered most of the 8 million job losses and the 7 million home foreclosures since 2007. They contributed to the pension and retirement funds that purchased Wall Street's doomed CDOs and other toxic securities before the market tanked and their value plunged. Their taxes backstopped the $700 billion program to bail out the country's biggest banks and companies in 2008. They provided the soldiers who fought the wars in Iraq and Afghanistan. And even once the economy began recovering from the crisis, they continued to struggle as it failed to add enough jobs to keep up with population growth and kept toying with a return to recession. With home prices still falling, the jobs that disappeared—millions of them in construction—weren't coming back, and people's debts were still exceedingly burdensome.

Yet this suburban base remains vitally important as a market for Foxconn and other Chinese exporters. In 2007, the year before the financial crisis, households earning less than $150,000 a year accounted for 83 percent of all consumer spending in the United States. In that year also, Americans took on an additional $70 billion in new credit card debt and $1.14 trillion in mortgage loans to bring the total amounts outstanding to $942 billion and $14.6 trillion, respectively. That's a total of $131,000 per household. Without these debt-dependent consumers the international cycle of trade and finance would stop.

Among the tens of thousands of Hewlett-Packard computer components that have passed through Foxconn's Longhua plant's gates were parts that went into a desktop computer that found a home in Philadelphia. The machine was used to manage the accounts of John DeVlieger, an artist whose classic Italian-style murals were sought after during the housing boom by wealthy hedge fund managers in Connecticut and New York. DeVlieger's income was decent but unpredictable and the burden of legal fees and child support payments from a recent divorce left him short of cash. So in 2006 he decided to tap the equity he held in a small investment property in the working-class Philadelphia suburb of Upper Darby, where a single mother of three kids paid him $1,200 a month in rent. He'd bought the place for $100,000 in 2004, but two years later Ameriquest Mortgage, a loan originator, offered him a line of credit worth $148,500—virtually equivalent to the full appraised value. Given the thin equity buffer and his unpredictable financials, the adjustable-rate loan started with a high 8.5 percent rate and was deemed a subprime mortgage. It was immediately sold to Citigroup, which bundled it into a special investment trust for mortgage-backed securities bearing the acronym CMLTI 2006-AMC1. Whether or not DeVlieger knew that his loan was securitized in this way, he was oblivious to the fact that it brought him within one degree of separation from Fabulous Fab Tourre and his client John Paulson. For it was precisely Paulson's expectation that people such as DeVlieger would default that led the hedge fund manager to choose the CMLTI 2006-AMC1 trust as one of the ninety-two securities incorporated into the Abacus deal.

Soon the housing crisis and recession came. Not only did DeVlieger's art commissions dry up, but his tenant lost her job and fell behind on the rent. "She was in a real predicament. I couldn't kick her out. I didn't even try to," he said. "I tried to renegotiate the mortgage, but that didn't work. So my payments kept on ballooning. It was a house of cards." DeVlieger hung on until 2010, when he finally succumbed to foreclosure. And when the tenant got wind of that she stopped paying altogether. "She really had me over a barrel," he said. A perfectly decent tenant-landlord relationship was destroyed by the bubble created by Wall Street's illusionists. And the pain felt by these two people translated directly into pure profit for John Paulson. As soon as people such as DeVlieger started missing payments or seeking to renegotiate their loans, the price of the securities in the Abacus structure plunged, delivering unprecedented capital gains to the hedge fund manager who had made short-selling bets against them.

Many Americans now argue that people such as John DeVlieger got what they deserved. He and the millions like him who took on zero-down-payment and other high-risk loans should have known their limits and lived within their means, they will say. But while it's true that many borrowers acted irresponsibly, this point of view ignores the systemic factors that led mortgage lenders to provide such large, unaffordable loans and to the public delusion that viewed this as OK. DeVlieger, who had been a landlord for many years and "had always been pretty selective" about properties, wrongly assumed that real estate would always rise in price. But this "bubble thinking," as Yale economist Robert Shiller calls it, was shared by most Americans at the time. There were many causes of this collective breakdown of logic and this book will examine some of them, but the key point is to recognize that the causes of the crisis were *systemic,* that they stem from deep-seated structural problems and cannot be solely blamed on rogue financiers or overzealous borrowers. The system—that is to say, the global system—is dysfunctional, and if we don't recognize that and fix the policy framework that makes it that way, we will experience another equally severe crisis. This system is fixed in favor of a privileged few but is geared against people such as DeVlieger and his tenant, as well as the pension funds that bought the other side of Paulson's Abacus deal; they were the ones left holding the bag when the crunch came. They—and not the U.S. bankers, real estate brokers, and Chinese exporters who inflated the bubbles—paid the biggest price when the crisis made its inevitable arrival. People like them, the ordinary middle and working classes of America, China, and other countries, will pay for it again when the next crisis comes.

The divisions created by this discriminatory global system are not confined to the United States and China. The relentless growth of China's export machine is also feeding economic distortions elsewhere. Look no further than the destitute "peripheral" nations of the euro zone—Greece, Italy, Spain, Portugal, Ireland—all desperate to export their way out of a crisis that's roiling the entire global economy. Shackled to an overly strong euro, their producers are no match for the cheap products of China and the undervalued yuan, which traps them in a vicious cycle of sliding growth, rising debts, and, ironically, dependence on Beijing for financing. Few countries have ever put so many people around the world through so much change in such a short period of time as China has over the past decade. As it has grown, China has left distinct groups of winners and losers in its wake. Through a more or less random sampling of travel spots, this book will explore examples of each. We will see how workers in Perth, Western Australia, have earned riches they could never have dreamed of thanks to relentless Chinese demand for their state's minerals. But we'll also visit Ciudad Juárez on the U.S.-Mexican border, a town that has become the most violent city on earth in large part because its manufacturing industry failed to compete with the Chinese exporting zeitgeist that entered the U.S. market in 2001. The stark differences between such places illustrate the imbalances of a globalized world in which people's actions in one place reverberate to disrupt lives thousands of miles away. That world is an inequitable, unstable place in which great fortunes can be won or lost depending on how one is placed within it.

Such arbitrary divisions between the privileged and underprivileged are nothing new, of course. The luck of birthright has existed since feudal times. But according to one view of globalization popular for most of the past decade, they were supposed to be disappearing, at least in terms of equality of opportunity. Advanced telecommunications, faster transportation, and enhanced labor mobility, all backed by an improved framework of international law and free trade treaties, were said to be leveling the playing field for global commerce. The world was flat, declared columnist and best-selling author Thomas Friedman, describing a global economy in which nation-states were ceding power to a giant, free-for-all marketplace. According to the Friedman thesis, the winners would be those who sold products or labor of the highest quality and value for money, while those unable or unwilling to innovate, increase productivity, and ascend the value chain would lose. As governments ceased propping up favorite domestic industries, everyone would have to compete on those basic terms. This new hypercompetitive world would be tough, but it would not be discriminatory, and by encouraging a drive for productivity and innovation it would ultimately be a better place.

The global financial crisis and the starkly divided world of winners and losers that emerged in its wake dispelled this myth with brutal force. It showed that although goods, services, and capital markets have indeed gone global, the playing field is far from level—and precisely because of the distorting role played by a well and truly alive nation-state. Yet even as the financial crisis has exposed an alarming degree of fraud and corruption among those who rode the prior credit bubble to great wealth, pursuing the perpetrators won't in itself fix the problem. The issue here is the failure of our economic and political system, and for that we are all in some way complicit. We—that is to say, those of us with the right to vote, we who live in the wealthy democratic societies of the West—have let the few who thrive from this failing system use their financial resources to manipulate our electoral process and block any serious reforms to it. Until we destroy the scourge of money politics, our democracies will fall short of their rule-by-majority promise, ensuring that our societies become increasingly divided and economies more unstable.

According to the neoliberal dogma on deregulation and privatization that held sway after the end of the Cold War and informed Friedman's thesis, there was little wrong with the economic inequities that later propelled those who participated in the Occupy movement into the streets of the world's capitals. Wealth disparities were part and parcel of a more efficient free market system, one that was forcing the global economy into a survival-of-the-fittest process of evolution. By neoliberalism's own internal logic, if you intervened in that system, you would hold back the advance of human prosperity.

But this view failed to recognize that the "free market system" is not free at all. The global economy is unbalanced, fraught with massive distortions, inefficiencies, and inequities, most of which arise directly from government policies—sometimes from too much regulation, other times from too little. Each flawed policy is a problem in itself, but worse is the damage done by their misalignment with one another. A global matrix of mismatched, distorting policies lies at the heart of many of our economic problems. These distortions, and not some Darwinistic process that weeds out laziness or incompetence, are the major reason why in 2010 America's wealth gap was at its widest level in eight decades.

Yet few see this picture. Instead, many blame international inequities on supposed flaws in national character—on Americans' rampant consumerism or on the sloth of the Greeks and Italians. But while no one can dispute that Americans must learn to live within their means—indeed, circumstances are now forcing them to—or that Greece and Italy need structural reforms that ensure that hard work is rewarded, it's dangerous to view these countries' problems in isolation from the policy distortions that shape the global financial system. It might be easier to understand the crisis as some kind of retribution for an era of wanton excess, but such moralizing won't shape effective policy making. The solution requires a wholesale change in the way the global economy is structured. Without that, the arrival of a more frugal U.S. consumer will only add more hardship.

A good place to start is the price of credit, the mechanism through which America's and Europe's debt has ballooned. For too long, debt was mispriced. It was given too high a value by creditors, the corollary of which meant that borrowers paid too little. Yes, greed and naïveté contributed to the mania for U.S. subprime mortgages and for investment homes in places like Spain and Ireland, but the financial bubble would not have been possible without the fundamental mispricing of debt caused by the interplay of poorly designed policies from different governments around the world.

It's a central tenet of economics—and certainly one that the neoliberal reformers subscribe to—that if you mess with prices you undermine the market's capacity to allocate resources to where they are most needed. There are sometimes good reasons to intervene in that process and create positive incentives—to steer funds toward infrastructure, education, or health services, for example—but if price distortions happen on a systemic, economy-wide basis, the growing mismatch between demand and supply eventually produces a crisis. These price distortions can arise because government regulations favor certain industries and firms or, conversely, because a failure to enforce pro-competition regulations allows private monopolies to undermine the free market. Either way, we end up with perverse incentives so that people consistently make economic decisions that lead to suboptimal economic results for all. Case in point: the failure of the Soviet Union's centrally priced economy. Something similar happened to the entire world before the crisis. We had integrated our economies to an unprecedented degree, but by leaving in place all these misaligned policies, prices, and incentives, we misallocated resources and created an inherently unstable financial environment. Integration is indeed the route to prosperity, but it needs coordination to ensure efficiency.

In China, the undervaluation of the yuan, low interest rates, and savings-inducing social policies reduced the cost of entry into manufacturing and created an overwhelming incentive for Chinese businessmen to focus on exports rather than domestic consumers. In the United States, the overpricing of bank assets encouraged excessive risk taking, all because of the unspoken "too-big-to-fail" doctrine, with which the government implicitly guaranteed to bail out banks if they fell into trouble. This in turn left the U.S. economy dangerously dependent on a continued credit-fueled expansion in household spending. And in the euro zone, a similarly overprotected banking system operating under a one-size-fits-all monetary policy severely mispriced the value of government debt to stoke a credit boom that disguised the region's internal imbalances. To a large extent, these policy distortions can be traced to the twin trends that I've loosely grouped into the two parts of this book: the rise of China as a world economic force, and the emergence of a powerful, underregulated, and globalized financial sector. Together, these tectonic shifts have put the world economy off-kilter.

The imbalances have reached a point where the previous dichotomy, one in which China and other developing countries manufactured stuff and the rest of the developed world bought it, cannot last. As they gradually reduce their overinflated debt by selling assets in a multiyear "deleveraging" process, U.S. and European societies will inevitably face a continued slowdown in spending. These advanced economies' consumers are not the pot of gold they were for developing countries' producers and will themselves depend on exports to spur growth. To get the world back to equilibrium, then, policy incentives must change so that Chinese save less, Americans save more, and Europeans sort out their intra-continental savings and spending mismatches. If we fail to achieve this rebalancing, the eventual outcome could be devastating: trade conflicts, social upheaval, even revolutions and wars. In an era in which peaceful democracy appears to be ascendant, and where open trading systems are protected by the World Trade Organization, such conflicts might seem like distant prospects. But in the grand sweep of human history, they are common.

The problem is that no side will change on its own for fear that others will freeload. The only way forward lies in multilateral agreements reached through forums such as the Group of 20 developed and developing nations and the International Monetary Fund. Yet for national governments to engage with one another in this way, they too need to be properly incentivized. They will seek to change the status quo only if they are under effective political pressure do so—if ordinary people like you and me demand it.

Throughout my conversations with people affected by the financial crises of recent years, I encountered a profound, worldwide loss of trust in our political and economic institutions. The disturbing conclusion I draw from this is that we are losing faith in our collective ability to form governments that will represent the collective will of the people. That marks a depressing departure from the optimistic, if often misguided, utopianism of decades past. It also poses a serious threat to free market capitalism, a system that, for all its flaws, has until now proven to be the most effective in fostering and perpetuating human prosperity. A functioning capitalist system depends on people's trust and confidence: trust that the law will protect their contractual and property rights, trust in the currency in which they save, and confidence in a stable future. Without trust and confidence, people don't invest in risk-bearing assets. And that means that businesses are denied a flow of funding that's needed to permit growth.

In movements as disparate as Occupy Wall Street, the U.S. Tea Party, and the Arab Spring, we find evidence of people seeking to force political change for what they see as the better. And that should be encouraging. But for most of them, the focus is on attacking existing institutions rather than building better new ones. Equally important, few of these protesters are focused on what must happen at the international level. Our societies need to take that next step and do so in concert with one another. It's an enormous challenge, but if we don't find a way to collectively reform our broken global financial system, the next decade looks bleak.

You don't need to hear it from me. In the pages that follow, ordinary people will, like Scott, give voice to their fears, hopes, and dreams and so demonstrate how our existing global system is untenable. Taken together, their stories should also make it clear that, whichever way things go from here, we are all in this together.

PART ONE

The Rise of China

1

Origins of Dysfunction: How We Got Here

Richard Nixon was the accidental architect of our current global financial system. That makes him the ideal starting place for getting a grip on the dysfunctional nature of the world economy. In the late 1960s and early 1970s, outlays for the Vietnam War were playing havoc with the finances of the U.S. government. The trade deficit was expanding monthly as American consumers gravitated toward cheap new imports from Europe and Japan. A growing band of nervous foreign investors began exchanging their dollar reserves for gold, driving U.S. gold holdings down to dangerously low levels. President Nixon felt trapped by an economic juggernaut he could not control.

So, on August 5, 1971, Nixon gave a televised address to the American people. Its significance was likely lost on most of his audience, but it hit like an earthquake in the halls of the world's banks. Looking solemnly into the camera, the president began by speaking gravely about an "all-out war" waged by "international money speculators" against the United States. Then, as he vowed without a trace of irony to protect the dollar "as a pillar of monetary stability around the world," Nixon let it be known that he had instructed Treasury Secretary John Connally to suspend the dollar's convertibility into gold. With those words, the Bretton Woods system, a regime that had maintained global monetary stability since the end of World War II, was finished. The amount of dollars in circulation would no longer be backed by the requirement that the Federal Reserve hold the equivalent value in gold, an arrangement that had made the greenback an anchor for every currency in the world. Nixon described the measure as "temporary" and vowed to work with the International Monetary Fund (IMF) and America's trading partners to create "an urgently needed new international monetary system" that would ensure "stability and equal treatment." But these pledges proved impossible to fulfill. A year and a half later, the major currencies of the world had delinked from the dollar and were now free-floating. The end of the gold backing became permanent, and no coordinated global currency system was ever established again.

The "Nixon Shock," as it became known, had profound, far-reaching consequences. It allowed money and credit to flow more freely across borders, which meant that economic growth rates accelerated. But it also meant that financial volatility and instability rose dramatically and that financial institutions garnered more power. The dramatic end to the Bretton Woods system transformed the global economy, setting it on a path to its current unbalanced state.

Gold: Stabilizer or Straitjacket?

In freeing the Federal Reserve from the constraints of the gold pledge, Nixon unshackled the Fed's most powerful—and some would say reckless—instrument for economic pump priming: the power to create money. The same went for other central banks when their governments responded by delinking their currencies from the dollar. The world was catapulted into an age of fiat currencies, the legal tender that is backed not by some tangible asset but by the intangible concept of the public's confidence in the government. Three decades later, the true implications of that power played out in the unprecedented monetary measures taken after the 2008 crisis. It made possible the Fed's massive "quantitative easing" efforts, the bond-buying programs through which the Fed pumped trillions of fresh dollars into the U.S. economy in the years following the crisis. Those contentious monetary injections were hugely controversial. Rick Perry, the governor of Texas and a contender for the Republican presidential nomination as of this writing, called Fed chairman Ben Bernanke's action "almost treasonous" and said that he would be treated "pretty ugly down in Texas." But Bernanke and the Fed likely saved the U.S. economy from the ravages of a Japan-like cycle of deflation. Still, in driving down the dollar—which made other countries' exports more expensive—they also infuriated America's trading partners and contributed to inflation in oil and other commodities. The Fed's actions stirred up hard-core critics of fiat monetary systems and reignited one of the most fractious and emotion-laden debates of the economics profession.

The 2008 crisis led to an increase in the ranks of those advocating a return to the gold standard—by which its fans mostly mean something more populist than the Bretton Woods system, whose dollars-to-gold pledge applied solely to governments and did not grant individuals the same right to fixed-rate exchange of bullion for cash. These people argue that full gold convertibility lends stability to the monetary system by denying profligate governments the temptation to monetize their debts. Printing money is the easy way out, and a dangerous one, they say, since monetary expansion is inherently inflationary. The Weimar Republic, if it had been constrained by the gold standard, would not have become a byword for hyperinflation. Nor would there ever have been such a thing as a $100 billion Zimbabwean banknote, a denomination that bought just three eggs when it was released in July 2008. A proper gold standard makes such episodes impossible. Yet that does not make it a magic bullet for ending financial instability.

Central bankers are human and prone to both mistakes and political pressure. That's why some fiscal conservatives argue that we should limit these officials' discretionary power by tying the monetary base to the value of some external asset. And gold, they believe, has proven itself through time as the natural choice. Although it has only modest industrial uses and little intrinsic value beyond its aesthetic appeal, gold has a rare and pure atomic structure that bolsters the integrity of the metal and makes it perfectly fungible. It has been sought after as a store of value across cultures, national borders, and political systems. It was the currency of the realm in feudal kingdoms. Empires were founded upon the quest for it. Wars have been both fought over it and funded by it while those made homeless by such conflicts have used gold to ferry their savings to safer harbor. Southern Vietnamese refugees stuffed thin 15-gram "gold leaf" bars into their shoes or the lining of their clothing when they fled their homeland in the 1970s. European Jews who escaped the Holocaust put all their savings into transportable gold; so too did Palestinian refugees who strapped gold chains, coins, and bars to their bodies before Jewish soldiers expelled them from their homes during the 1948 Arab-Israeli War. Gold prices have always rallied when investors fear inflation or generally lose confidence in governments. As we'll see in Chapter 9, that's precisely why gold made a spectacular comeback in the wake of the 2008 crisis.

Still, in the globalized financial system that evolved out of the Nixon Shock, one in which automated, high-speed trading programs now place multibillion-dollar buy orders and then follow them up with equivalent sell orders milliseconds later, the efficacy of restoring a currency pact based on this alluring metal is questionable. Gold supplies are tiny relative to financial flows. Whereas average turnover in the foreign exchange market now stands at $4 trillion every day, the total amount of gold produced throughout history runs to only about 165,000 tons, enough to fill just three Olympic swimming pools. This scarcity makes the precious metal susceptible to hoarding. A gold standard would also leave governments overly focused on securing bullion supplies, a distracting priority for macroeconomic policy making. By the same token, countries blessed with large gold deposits would have an unfair advantage; extracting more of it would allow them the privilege of being able to expand their economies at no cost.

Given the massive international financial flows that technology has fostered in the age of globalization and because of the central role the dollar plays as the world's reserve currency, any U.S. gold standard would need to be internationalized via a system of gold exchanges so as to prevent financial imbalances from developing. But that would leave governments subordinating their domestic national priorities to the system's demands for automatic balancing. It seems doubtful that this would be tenable in the modern democracies of today. (The economic historian Barry Eichengreen has convincingly demonstrated how the advent of universal suffrage produced the strains that ultimately undermined history's only true international gold standard exchange, which existed from 1870 to 1914.) Here's why: when a country on the gold standard runs a trade deficit, its gold reserves decline automatically, which according to the strictures of the system requires that it raise interest rates to attract foreign capital and restore its depleted gold reserves. But if that happens during an economic contraction, this brake on growth can have a brutal impact on people's lives. (Greece subjects itself to the same under the de facto "gold standard" of its economy's peg to the euro.) Over time, the international system balances itself out as growth returns to the affected country. But in the short term, the forbidden tool of devaluation looms temptingly, a solution that's easier to administer politically as it shares the burden with foreigners. It's hardly surprising that on that evening in August 1971, Nixon, who fundamentally mistrusted multilateral institutions, cast blame on shady foreign "money speculators."

What is most lost in this age-old debate, however, is the fact that the rigid system preferred by goldbugs has historically failed to deliver the holy grail of permanent financial stability for the same basic reason that fiat currency regimes have failed: governments face overwhelming national political pressures that prevent them from coordinating policies internationally. Without the giant imbalances in trade and capital flows that arise from misaligned policies, and without the politically untenable outflows of jobs and price pressures that come with them, either the gold standard would survive or economies would be sufficiently stable that there'd be no need for it. Either way, the conclusion is the same: we desperately need to improve international cooperation between governments.

Currencies Go Topsy-Turvy

Nixon's bold currency move ended one problem but created a host of others. The sharp drop in the dollar and the world's sudden immersion in a system of floating exchange rates wreaked havoc with international contracts and drastically shifted the terms of trade between countries. It especially posed a threat to the newly amalgamated European Economic Community, forcing its members to take steps to align their currencies. These measures would eventually lead to the ultimate manifestation of continental monetary union: the euro.

As currencies realigned in the wake of the Nixon Shock, so too did the prices of every asset affected by them. The immediate impact was a collapse in world stock prices. Although the devaluation initially gave a big boost to the U.S. economy, which grew rapidly in 1972, things turned sour in 1973 once the pound, the yen, and the Deutschmark were all fully floating against each other. That year delivered one of the worst bear markets in global stock market history. By the time prices stabilized in December 1974, the Dow Jones Industrial Average had lost 47 percent of its valuation. London's FTSE 100 index dropped by 73 percent, as Britain's exporters lost money on the back of a stronger pound and as its internationally active banks were blindsided by rising global inflation.

The suspension of dollar convertibility into gold landed in a period of intense geopolitical tension. Most notably, the Organization of Arab Petroleum Exporting Countries hit financial institutions with the economic equivalent of an atomic bomb. OAPEC's 1973 oil embargo produced an exponential increase in energy prices and drove up the prices of virtually everything. Since it coincided with a decline in the now floating dollar, this inflationary surge meant that demand for U.S. bonds fell, which in turn led to higher borrowing costs. This toxic environment produced stagflation, an unprecedented combination of unemployment and inflation, which stuck around for the rest of the decade. It was not an auspicious beginning to the post–Bretton Woods era.

The end of the dollar-gold peg also introduced the concept of foreign exchange and monetary policy risk to the boardrooms of multinational companies, spawning whole new businesses for financial institutions: currency and interest rate hedging. In 1972, the Chicago Mercantile Exchange launched trading in foreign exchange futures, contracts that would allow companies to lock in the price of a currency over time. The demand for new forms of financial insurance also gave rise to trade in options, instruments that give the purchaser the right but not the obligation to buy or sell a currency, commodity, or financial security at a predetermined price. Economists Fischer Black and Myron Scholes then gave the industry a big boost by introducing a sophisticated valuation model for these complex derivative instruments. Enhanced later by the collaboration of a third economist, Robert Merton, the Black-Scholes model meant that options could now be easily bought and sold on secondary markets. But while the three academics' ideas brought an appearance of certainty to a financial sector where prices previously had been based on guesswork, their legacy is not all rosy.

The Black-Scholes model created the illusion that risks of all kinds could now be traded out of existence when in fact the model was unable to incorporate the rare but real prospect of extreme movements in the price of the underlying security—"tail risk," as market practitioners call it. As the use of derivatives grew, this overconfidence would produce some famous failures in the 1990s: the collapse of the 233-year-old Barings Bank in 1995 due to the speculative trading of a single trader, Nick Leeson, and then, amid the subsequent Asian crisis, the downfall of the giant hedge fund Long-Term Capital Management in 1998. LTCM's demise was all the more notable for the fact that its directors included none other than Myron Scholes and Robert Merton. The year before, the pair had shared the Nobel Prize in economics for their work on options pricing. Even after that spectacular failure, investors would repeat the same essential mistake over and again, wanting to believe that innovation had somehow killed risk. The consequences in 2007–8, as we now know, were devastating.

In contrast to financial institutions, U.S. exporters initially welcomed this new era of weak dollar exchange rates. Exports went from a healthy average annual rate of 7 percent in the 1960s to a 17 percent annual pace of growth in the 1970s. Even after adjusting for yearly average inflation of 7 percent, this decade-long expansion delivered hefty profits to U.S. companies. But these data were misleading. Most of the gains were the result not of a real pickup in productivity or innovation but of a mathematical extension of the exchange rate adjustment, which made U.S. goods cheaper and boosted the value of foreign earnings when expressed in dollar terms. After years of operating under a fixed currency system, U.S. companies weren't used to distinguishing between real returns and exchange rate gains. And even with the expanded availability of options and futures contracts, very few U.S. exporters employed hedging techniques. While the dollar was falling to your advantage, the thinking went, why would you want to hedge away that profit?

Come 1979, these firms got a rude awakening as six-foot-seven-inch Paul Volcker barged his way into world financial markets when Jimmy Carter appointed him Federal Reserve chairman. Vowing to break the back of inflation at all costs, he sharply jacked up interest rates. This triggered a steep recession in 1981, but it also encouraged the world's increasingly swift-moving fund managers to steer their money into higher-yielding U.S. bank deposits, which drove up the dollar. Big U.S. exporters such as machinery producer Caterpillar were hit with hundreds of millions in losses.

As the dollar strengthened while Japanese cars, electronics, and other goods took over world markets, its value against the yen became a contentious topic. This is when the U.S. trade deficit, now a permanent feature of the American economic landscape, became entrenched. Alarmist talk of a trade war grew. So at the end of the summer of 1985, finance ministers from the United States, Japan, France, West Germany, and Great Britain met at New York's landmark Plaza Hotel, overlooking Central Park, to address the problem. The outcome was the Plaza Accord, an agreement to weaken the dollar by having the countries' central banks jointly intervene in currency markets. In a reminder of the power governments have to dictate financial valuations on a global scale, foreign exchange traders immediately took heed of the warning that they would lose money if they kept buying dollars. By February 1987, the greenback had depreciated so far that the same governments gathered again in Paris to sign the Louvre Accord, aimed at halting its decline.

These ad hoc interventions, coupled with the success of Volcker's bitter monetary medicine, created the impression that even in this unpredictable post–Bretton Woods era the world's financial authorities would keep monetary valuations sufficiently in line for investors to confidently place bets on stocks, bonds, and business ventures. Inflation had by then all but disappeared, restoring predictability to prices in a way that made it easier to invest funds over the long term. The so-called Great Moderation had begun, and although it was accompanied by periodic financial turmoil—highlighted by the brief but severe stock market crash of October 1987 and the U.S. savings and loan crisis—it meant the overall global economic mood shifted into a decidedly more optimistic mind-set. An upward progression in business and investor confidence would continue for years afterward, as an almost religious belief in the supposed rationality and benefits of unfettered free markets became entrenched.

This trend had its roots in the West, but it would eventually spread to the developing world and so fundamentally transformed the global economy. Yet to get there, big changes had to happen on the geopolitical front. The Cold War had to be resolved if the poorer nations of Asia, Latin America, and Eastern Europe that had been torn apart by ideological divisions were to be brought under the tent of global capitalism. Events in Berlin two years later would provide a symbolic rupture allowing that process to come about. However, the beginning of this parallel political liberalization can also be traced back to Richard Nixon and his engagement with the one developing country that would, decades later, single-handedly redefine how the global economy functions.

A Giant Stirs

One year after he turned the foreign exchange world upside down, Nixon's second big contribution to the modern world economic order came with his visit to Beijing. Mao Zedong, who had been confined to a sickbed only nine days before Nixon's visit, greeted the U.S. president with an outstretched hand, making for a historic photo op. The two countries still had much work to do to set aside past tensions, but with Nixon recognizing China's interest in a "single-nation" solution to its dispute with Taiwan, a mutual understanding was established and the path was set for more open bilateral trade. For Nixon and his national security advisor, Henry Kissinger, the moment provided a powerful strike in America's Cold War struggle against the Soviet Union, which suddenly looked cornered. But for China, it was an international coming-out. Mao's tyrannical regime remained entrenched until he died four years later, but the symbolism of his communist nation's rapprochement with American capitalism presaged a more open economy in the future. It helped clear the way for the reformist Deng Xiaoping to claim power in 1978. A year later he normalized relations with the United States and launched a centuries-overdue process of modernization.

Deng's "four modernizations"—in agriculture, industry, science and technology, and the military—were aimed at his goal of "socialism with Chinese characteristics." It was the liberalization strategy of a gradualist. China continued to centralize political control but encouraged local authorities to make their own modest reforms at the regional level. Deng could see the rapid advances being made in Japan and Taiwan, two countries whose brand of capitalism also incorporated a heavy dose of central planning. He knew that he too had to unleash the entrepreneurial zeal of his people in a choreographed way.

Deng was remarkably successful. Peasants could now till a portion of their own land for profit, dramatically improving crop yields and encouraging some in rural communities to branch out into business. Then, with Deng provocatively announcing that China should "let some people get rich first," a capitalist class was created from scratch as new sectors were opened to private enterprise. Yet the state maintained tight restrictions over political activity—as was made clear during the 1989 Tiananmen Square crackdown—and took a slow, gradual approach to liberalization. As this process continued through the 1980s, it prepared China for an unprecedented pace of economic development after 1990, when for two decades it would run an average annual growth rate of 9 percent. In so doing, this giant nation transformed the global economy.

As China emerged from the cocoon it had occupied since its humiliating defeat by Great Britain in the Opium Wars of the mid-nineteenth century, big changes were also happening in the land of its old colonial adversary. Margaret Thatcher, Britain's "Iron Lady," came to power in 1979, and her Conservative government set about undoing the quasi-socialist structure of the U.K. economy. She privatized state-owned industries, sold off coal mines, broke up unions, and generally extracted the government from the economy. In 1986, the "Big Bang" financial reforms were introduced, including an end to a ban on stock brokerages performing banking services. The change gave British banks a chance to grow in scale. They became world leaders in capital markets, which were starting to challenge commercial bank lending as the driving force behind global financial flows. To this day London handles far more foreign exchange and cross-border bond deals than does New York.

It would take thirteen more years of heavy lobbying by U.S. banks for Congress to follow suit with the repeal of the Depression-era Glass-Steagall Act, which had prohibited mergers between investment banks and their commercial counterparts. But the international ramifications of the 1986

U.K. banking reforms were profound nonetheless. Foreign institutions started setting up their own combined investment and commercial bank subsidiaries in the United Kingdom, which set the stage for the global mega-banks whose gargantuan size would later pose a systemic risk to the world economy they came to dominate. "Too big to fail" would not enter the lexicon until late in the first decade of the 2000s, but the problem had its beginnings in London in the mid-1980s.

As the reforms turned the United Kingdom into a financial powerhouse, the British regained a role on the international geopolitical stage. Wielding this newfound clout, Thatcher threw her weight behind Ronald Reagan in his battle with the Soviet Union. With the United Kingdom's unwavering support, the United States spent heavily on military spending throughout the 1980s, a fiscal extravagance that flew in the face of Reagan's small-government reforms in other sectors of the economy. The ailing Soviet regime could not keep up, and by the end of the decade it was dying, led by the collapse of its communist allies in Eastern Europe. In the fall of 1989, as East Berliners drove their sputtering Trabant cars into the glitzy neon wonder on the western side of their city's reviled wall, the message seemed clear: global capitalism was triumphant, the superior ideology.

It was a great moment for the cause of human freedom, but for Europe it created another challenge, one that had both economic and geopolitical ramifications. The reunification of Germany would restore its status as Europe's undisputed economic powerhouse. Understandably, given the continent's wartime history, that prospect made other members of the European Union (EU) nervous, especially France. They decided to seize the initiative while Germany was still grappling with the heavy cost of reunification and bind it into a more lasting relationship with the rest of Europe. So in 1992, foreign and finance ministers from twelve countries agreed to turn the European Community into the European Union. With the Maastricht Treaty, named for the Dutch city in which it was signed, they set rules for fiscal deficits and debt levels and, fatefully, laid out a path for the introduction of the euro. By 1999, Germany would be bound to France via a monetary arrangement that would also include Italy, Spain, the Netherlands, Ireland, Belgium, Portugal, Finland, Austria, and Luxembourg. More than ten years later, with the euro zone having added seven new members but now struggling to adjust its disparate political structure to the stringent market demands that come with monetary union, it is worth remembering that the crisis-prone euro began as a political project.

Beyond these tangible, substantive effects within Europe, the end of the Cold War also prompted a sharp rightward shift in the world political pendulum. The woeful failure of communism and of the blinkered ideologues who supported it was seen as vindicating the extremists at the other end of the spectrum, the advocates of pure laissez-faire free market capitalism. Despite repeated episodes in which investors had demonstrated their capacity for irrational, herdlike behavior, advocates of the efficient-market hypothesis took this as the ultimate victory. Their central idea, that markets are rational and when left entirely alone will always provide the most efficient allocation of capital, had been developing over the course of the twentieth century. But it wasn't until the 1980s came to a close, with television cameras capturing dramatic scenes of communist regimes tumbling across Eastern Europe, that die-hard believers in this theory had a compelling image with which to sell the idea to the rest of the world. Unfortunately, this burst of new branding did not make the idea itself any less flawed, as we learned at great cost two decades later.

The Human Side of Boom and Bust

Market ideologues became ascendant in the think tanks of Washington, and their policy prescriptions became dogma, in both developed and developing countries. Over the next ten years, the financial sector was aggressively deregulated in the West. The trend reached its climax in 1999 with the repeal of the Glass-Steagall Act, a move that created irresistible incentives for investment banks to turn the once-staid commercial banking business of mortgage lending into a high-return, high-stakes profit center inside their risk-driven trading floors. This was followed in 2000 with the exemption from regulatory oversight of the rapidly growing market for customized over-the-counter swaps, tradable contracts in which one party is paid to assume the risk that some adverse event, such as a bond default or an interest rate increase, hurts the other's investment position. Financial institutions were in effect given the government's blessing to enter into countless deals whose terms were hidden from view, giving rise to a giant, cloaked network of intermingled contingent liabilities. The global notional value of outstanding swaps grew from $70 trillion in 1999—after having been nonexistent a decade earlier—to a whopping $708 trillion by mid-2011. Inside that pool of interconnected loans lay the risk of cascading bankruptcies if some external event triggered a wave of self-perpetuating payments. It was a systemic time bomb, and along with the investment bank bubble in mortgages it would burst in the financial chaos of 2008.

In developing countries, the so-called Washington Consensus became a template for sweeping reforms emphasizing privatizations, fiscal discipline, liberalized trade and foreign investment, competitive exchange rates, export-oriented policies, and market-based interest rates. Much of this was constructive for the global economy in the aggregate, which would show unprecedented growth over the next two decades—and for former communist regimes, it was certainly an improvement from a system that killed the incentive for personal advancement and innovation. But the new model also generated excesses and a boom-bust cycle of financial instability that would become more severe as time went on and as risks built up in the global financial system.

The deregulation drive inside countries coincided with a massive overhaul of the world's trading rules. The Uruguay round of trade talks cut tariffs on countless manufactured goods and created the World Trade Organization, the new policeman of world trade. It was an impressive show of global unity—one that, unfortunately, could not be repeated. But by 1994, after the North American Free Trade Agreement had been signed by the United States, Canada, and Mexico, the gains in global integration were palpable, and international commerce got a lift. By 2000, total world merchandise trade had almost doubled from its level a decade earlier.

Initially, export-oriented Asian nations were the biggest winners in the post–Cold War embrace of global capitalism. Their rapidly expanding economies became magnets for foreign investment. A flashy nouveau riche emerged in cities such as Bangkok and Taipei, showing a conspicuous preference for BMWs, Johnny Walker Black Label scotch, and Mont Blanc pens. Yet much of this wealth creation was illusory, as it was exaggerated by actions taken by Asian central banks. Here again was a case of global imbalances induced by policies that distorted prices and created misplaced incentives. While the dollar and other major currencies of the world continued to freely float against each other, the Asian monetary authorities committed themselves to fixed exchange rate regimes. They vowed to intervene in the market if their currencies moved outside a preordained range against the dollar. At first, these seemingly predictable exchange rates gave local banks a sense of stability, as it meant less volatility in their foreign exchange exposure. That in turn gained them easy and relatively cheap access to foreign currency loans, which fed into a treadmill of unsustainable investment- and construction-led growth. This fluid credit flow fueled a bubble in real estate and other asset markets until early July 1997, when the devaluation of the Thai baht set off a chain of events that would bring down this house of cards. As the pegged currencies of Asia and other emerging market regions toppled like dominoes, the world financial system went into a tailspin.

I lived in Jakarta in the mid-1990s and saw firsthand how all this played out. When I left in June 1997, few thought Indonesia's economy, then going like gangbusters, was teetering on the edge of an abyss. But less than a year later, the country found itself in a political maelstrom as the Indonesian rupiah went into free fall. Its peg to the dollar had become the next line of attack for speculators after they finished breaking the South Korean won. This fomented a crisis that forced President Suharto, the dictator who had reigned over a crony capitalist economy for thirty-one years, to accept a $43 billion loan from the IMF. The deal came with tough conditions: high interest rates, an end to gasoline subsidies and other government interventions, and fiscal belt-tightening. These austerity measures kicked in right as the economy was descending into chaos. The net result was a breakdown in public confidence and social order that would bring an end to the Suharto regime.

Eleven months after leaving a growing economy that was drawing in a steady stream of businessmen and investors, I found myself on a near-empty Boeing 747 from London to Jakarta. When I arrived at Soekarno-Hatta International Airport, I saw a mass of anxious Indonesians clutching hastily packed boxes. It was an exodus of fear. President Suharto had resigned a day earlier, the culmination of ten days of a violent outpouring of bottled-up fury, much of it directed at members of the country's ethnic Chinese minority. The financial chaos had exacerbated deep-seated ethnic tensions as indigenous Indonesians turned on the Chinese, traditionally key actors in the country's merchant class, as scapegoats for Indonesia's economic ills.

A friend, Reuters reporter Jim Della-Giacoma, penned a haunting personal reflection on what he saw, including this account of a scene in Glodok—the city's unofficial, ramshackle Chinatown—where local Chinese shop owners and their families were knifed by gangs of marauding youths while their stores were looted and torched: "As I dictated my story standing next to a tray of charred meat, the stench of the burnt flesh even overpowered the lingering smell of burnt plastic. I rate it as one of the most disconcerting smells I have known in my 32 years, a distant cousin of the familiar aromas of cooked livestock we associate with Mother's cooking or Father's barbecue. One man told me the charcoal and yellow pieces, on which flies now hopped back and forth, were not human but meat salvaged from the supermarket. I could have carried on the fiction if not for the unique smell and unmistakable shape of a human hand complete with wristwatch being one of them."

Events such as these offer a poignant reminder of how human lives can be profoundly affected by financial policy making. Until a crisis such as Indonesia's in 1998 or America's ten years later hits, most people have no idea how they might be affected by such things, and even after they've been blindsided by its effects, they remain confused and mistrustful. The fact is, a straight causal line can be drawn from Asian central banks' distorting currency policies through to the economic imbalances they created, then on to the Asian financial crisis and finally to this orgy of violence in Indonesia. Sadly, the line didn't stop there. Contagion from the financial upheaval spread around the world like a virus, as the cycle of competitive devaluations spiraled wider. Fixed exchange rates everywhere came under attack as each country's exporters felt the competitive challenge from Asia's newly weakened currencies and as prices for the commodities produced by many developing countries plummeted.

The lesson for the governments of Indonesia, Thailand, and South Korea, as well as for Russia, Brazil, Argentina, and other countries rocked by what was dubbed "the Asian financial crisis," was that they had let their currencies get too high and had held too few reserves against them. The same lesson was embraced by an observant China, which had resisted the competitive devaluation pressure from its neighbors and maintained the yuan's peg to the dollar—earning kudos then for a policy that would later draw criticism. From then on, the central banks from Asia's export-driven economies would deliberately buy up foreign currency assets, both to keep their own currencies weak and to maintain a buffer of reserves. And since the dollar was just as entrenched in its role as the international reserve currency as it had been in the Bretton Woods era, their buying activity would focus on U.S. assets. With this deliberate policy of reserve accumulation, Asian savings were delivered en masse to American borrowers. The great financial transfer of our age was under way.

Buyers of Last Resort

Throughout these crises, the U.S. economy had powered along relentlessly, seemingly unfazed by the turmoil in Asia. It was the age of the

Internet boom and the instant, twentysomething multimillionaire. These new, young winners seemed to spring out of nowhere as a steady flow of dot-com companies launched initial public offerings to which investors swarmed in search of the next Microsoft. Such easy wealth flowing to computer geeks made it seem as if anyone could become instantaneously wealthy. The wild, breathless finale of a decade-long bull market rally swelled American workers' 401(k) accounts and inflated their sense of wealth. And as this bolstered their confidence, they expressed it in that all-American way: they spent money.

This is how, in the late 1990s, the United States entrenched itself as the world's most important consumer market. While everyone else was beset with financial difficulties, Americans kept digging deeper into their wallets and purchasing goods made elsewhere. They became the world's "buyers of last resort." As the country stocked up on foreign-made clothes, appliances, and toys, Americans' personal savings rate, which had averaged 7 percent of disposable income in 1991, dropped to an average of 2.7 percent in 2001. Simultaneously, the U.S. trade deficit went from $31.1 billion in 1991 to $108 billion in 1997 and then exploded to $364.4 billion in 2001. The relentless spending binge pulled the rest of the world out of its doldrums and at the time was seen as part of a healthy, symbiotic relationship. Just as Asian exporters were lifted by U.S. purchases, so too did the U.S. economy benefit from the weak currencies left over from the Asian crisis, which drove down the cost of foreign imports, boosted American households' purchasing power, and suppressed inflation.

The flood of cheap goods from Asia amplified globalization's already widespread disinflationary effect on prices. When combined with the rapid expansion of the Internet, the development of sophisticated new purchasing and inventory management systems, and the rollout of various business-to-business software technologies, a virtuous cycle of productivity enhancement was put in motion. Suppliers in Asia and other developing regions started advertising their wares online, allowing U.S. buyers to bargain-shop from anywhere in the world. Companies such as Walmart hooked their automated purchasing systems into a globalized system. And although this meant U.S. jobs went overseas, sowing the seeds for what would become a deep malaise in the labor market a decade later, the benefits of these low prices seemed then to outweigh the costs. With the financial services and information technology sectors booming, the jobless rate got as low as 4 percent in 2000—a figure that was, for all intents and purposes, the equivalent of full employment.

Something odd was happening to the U.S. economy. After an almost decade-long boom, it should by then have been subject to inflationary pressures, with the Fed starting to put the brakes on with higher interest rates. But consumer prices grew on average through the 1990s at a benign annual pace of around 2.8 percent and even decreased during the high-growth period at the end of that decade. Fed chairman Alan Greenspan concluded that a paradigm shift had occurred. He and others called it the "New Economy," one allowing for faster and longer noninflationary growth periods of low unemployment. Logic held that this New Economy could accommodate easier monetary policy for longer. So that's what Greenspan administered. In the twelve months ending in February 1995, the Fed progressively increased its target federal funds rate to 6 percent. But throughout the rest of the 1990s, the rate never got higher than that, even as the stock market soared and the U.S. economy's jobs- and wealth-creating machine went into overdrive. For some time, this supportive posture looked like an exceptionally good call. Greenspan was lauded as a genius, or as *Washington Post* reporter Bob Woodward described him in the title of a hagiographic account of the Fed chairman's leadership, a maestro.

Until the more recent financial crisis, a cultlike status of infallibility gathered around Greenspan. Normally feisty congressmen from both sides of the aisle who'd famously grilled other public figures in the House or Senate would go soft whenever the Fed chairman made his occasional appearances on Capitol Hill. This adulation was not helpful: it created the sense that sound stewardship of the U.S. economy could be delegated to this sagelike figure and that all the federal government needed to do was get out of the way. Once again, the illusion of perfect control over risk was the problem. In hindsight, one man could not alone comprehend and manage the vastly complex changes then coursing through the global economy. Errors would inevitably be made. Big ones.

Perfect Storm

The party soon ended when a decade-long bull run in equities came to a screeching halt in 2000. After peaking on March 5 at 5,132.52—more than double its value from a year earlier—the Nasdaq index, heavy on tech stocks and dot-coms, lost a staggering 38 percent of its value over fifty-six trading days. And by September 2002 it had fallen by 78 percent from its peak. Initially, the Fed did nothing. Undoubtedly relieved that the market was finally correcting itself, the Fed even raised its federal funds rates to a new high of 6.5 percent in May 2000. But as the destruction of paper wealth infected the rest of the economy, the Fed reached for its monetary toolbox. In early 2001, with a recession taking hold, it started cutting rates in gradual increments until September 11, when the carnage in lower Manhattan from the World Trade Center attacks spurred a giant new liquidity response. On September 17, Greenspan's team cut its target rate from 3.5 percent to 3 percent and then progressively lowered it over the course of the rest of the year to 1.75 percent. Meanwhile, the new administration of George W. Bush slashed taxes on income and capital gains to stimulate the economy. In so doing, it wiped out the fiscal surpluses of the preceding Clinton years and set the government's budget on a path toward the giant $1.5 trillion deficit that would haunt it at the end of the decade.

The economy recovered from the terror attacks more quickly than many expected. But the Fed still waited until the end of 2004 to take its target rate back above 2 percent and then only incrementally increased it to a peak of 6.75 percent by June 2006. In hindsight, it looks like the Fed cut rates too low in the first place and then took too long to raise them again. By then, the rest of world was overrun with financial liquidity—much of it emanating from the savings stockpiled by a booming China and other emerging market economies—while equities, bonds, and real estate markets were reaching new, lofty heights. The symbol of this new era was the "McMansion," the breed of cookie-cutter five- or six-bedroom homes that popped up like giant mushrooms in the cul-de-sacs of housing developments across the country. The property markets of growing cities such as Las Vegas, Phoenix, and Miami were especially hot. And yet the Fed resisted raising rates, even as the Bush administration vastly overspent beyond a newly reduced tax base, pumping money into the economy via outlays on the Iraq war and drug credits for Medicare recipients. The combination of low interest rates and gaping fiscal deficits was a recipe for economic imbalances.

The trends were decades in the making, traceable back to Nixon's dollar gambit in 1971. Lenders were doing everything and anything—from taking crazy risks to committing outright fraud—just to keep the money flowing down the financial chain to an ever wider group of homeowners. That way they could satisfy their shareholders' persistent demands for returns that matched those of their peers in the financial sector. Meanwhile, mortgage buyers Fannie Mae and Freddie Mac fueled the economic distortions that critics of these two privileged institutions had long predicted. The two government-sponsored enterprises were privately owned, but because they were a creation of Congress and had a mandate to reduce home loan rates, they carried out their mortgage-buying operations with what was widely assumed to be an implicit government guarantee. That gave them an inherent competitive advantage over other lenders when it came to financing. (Later, the nationalization of the two firms in the midst of the 2008 crisis provided ex post facto proof of this assumption.)

Fannie and Freddie had always played vital roles in driving down mortgage rates and thus in making home loans more affordable. But in the 2000s their buying accelerated, thanks to a policy drive to expand home ownership that landed in the middle of the global liquidity boom, delivering to the two firms a steady stream of investors eager to buy their "guaranteed" bonds. In 1995, the Department of Housing and Urban Development, which had taken a regulatory oversight role for the two mortgage buyers three years earlier, agreed to let Fannie and Freddie buy mortgages that had been issued to subprime borrowers—those whose low income-to-assets profile did not qualify them for conventional loans. While HUD expected the two agencies to use strict lending standards before it purchased such loans, once the next decade's global liquidity boom worked its way into the U.S. housing market, their lending in this category expanded rapidly. By 2006, subprime loans accounted for 20 percent of all Freddie and Fannie mortgage purchases.

By then, a worldwide hunt for yield was under way among conservative bond market investors who wanted to park their money in "safe," highly rated, yet profitable securities. The yields on U.S. Treasury bonds—a measure of investment return that always moves inversely to price—had become unattractive as the central banks of China, Japan, and other Asian saving nations gobbled up these "risk-free," "benchmark" government instruments. So bond investors went farther out along the risk curve. Next in line—in terms of higher yields in return for incrementally more risk—were the "agency bonds" of Fannie and Freddie. But the implicit government guarantee—one that central banks such as the People's Bank of China even recognized—meant that their yields also fell to levels only marginally higher than their Treasury bond equivalents. Essentially there was too much demand for low-risk investments and too little supply.

As we learned in the introduction, Fabrice Tourre and his fellow "quants" provided the solution to this problem with their AAA-rated mortgage CDOs. Helped by myopic ratings agencies and cheered on by Greenspan and other officials blinded into believing that Wall Street's financial innovations had solved the age-old problem of managing risk, the CDOs and the credit machine they unleashed inflated a tremendous bubble. As lending standards plunged, a mania for housing spread its way across the economy and into the outermost reaches of the housing market.

Global financial forces and the irrational collective behavior that they fostered provided the fuel for the crisis that would soon follow, but the fault for not containing it still lies heavily with U.S. regulators and policy makers. After all, many other countries mostly avoided the housing crisis. Canada's housing market saw virtually no price impact, but that was because its government banned home loans with anything less than a 20 percent down payment. It is inconceivable that the Bank of Canada would have produced a document that offered even qualified endorsement of the risky adjustable-rate mortgages that were described in a Federal Reserve–published consumer handbook in 2007, one that purported to help U.S. buyers weigh the pros and cons of different types of mortgages. Clearly, the Fed was an integral part of the problem. It played a critical role in encouraging the gross mispricing that would bring the financial system to its knees a year later.

In big parts of Europe, meanwhile, a similar trend in prices and credit occurred, but for different reasons. The same global liquidity flood was sloshing into European markets, and its bubble-creating power was amplified by a giant new innovation of their own: the euro. As countries made preparations for the European single currency's introduction in 1999, the borrowing costs of peripheral euro zone nations such as Italy, Greece, Ireland, and Spain plunged. Once they abandoned the lira, the drachma, the punt, and the peseta, the governments of these countries would no longer pay a big borrowing premium over what Germany and other stable northern European nations paid on their bonds, investors reasoned. In just four years, Italy's ten-year sovereign bond yields went from a 1995 peak of 13.75 percent to 3.5 percent at the euro's debut. There they stayed for the next nine years. The same massive credit windfall was enjoyed by Greece, Spain, Ireland, and Portugal, with different effects in each. In Greece it allowed the government to spend lavishly on an extensive welfare state and to rack up untenable fiscal deficits. But in Spain and Ireland, the benefits flowed to private sector banks, which created a giant mortgage lending system that previously had not existed, fueling an unprecedented borrowing and construction binge.

This was another case of gross mispricing and misplaced incentives. With the benefit of hindsight, we learned during the sovereign debt crisis that the credit risks in these peripheral euro zone countries had not diminished to anywhere near the level that bond prices had assumed during the euro's early years. The advent of the euro and the end to seventeen legacy currencies was supposed to make capital markets more efficient across Europe, freeing up lending for businesses and industry. It achieved that to some extent, but mispriced credit rates also steered money away from productive industries and instead into construction and real estate. This is one reason why Ireland, which had been the poor man of Europe two decades earlier, ended up with the highest concentration of home ownership in the world. It's also why the Irish government had to call on the EU and the IMF to fund a $50 billion bailout of its banks in 2010. The country's fiscal deficit that year ran to a whopping 30 percent of GDP. Meanwhile, contagion—a concept last seen in Asia ten years previously—began working its way into the economies of Greece, Portugal, Spain, and eventually Italy. By 2011, the equivalent of a continent-wide bank run was raging like a wildfire through the region's financial system and stoking a full-blown crisis that threatened to destroy the euro as a common currency.

Codependence

As if in an alternate universe, emerging markets had a profoundly more positive experience with globalization. Developing countries, especially Brazil, Russia, India, and China—dubbed the "BRICs" by Goldman Sachs chief global economist Jim O'Neill in 2001—came into their own in the first decade of the new millennium as they embraced orthodox free market policies and tapped into the opportunities of an ever-broadening global marketplace. While advanced countries threw all their eggs into a basket dominated by finance and services, these emerging market economies went from strength to strength, creating new manufacturing and service industries while rapidly improving the quality and sophistication of their output, enabling them to climb the technology ladder that would add value and increase earning power. Between 2000 and 2008, some 30 percent of total world growth was generated by the four BRIC countries, up from 16 percent in the previous decade. Across the emerging market world, hundreds of millions of people were added to the ranks of the middle class as both income and spending levels rose at a rapid pace.

But it wasn't all roses for the developing world. This was also a period of extreme movements in commodity prices, which led to food and energy inflation and so fueled divisions in societies. Producers of crops and resources profited, but the urban poor in many places eventually found their disposable incomes squeezed by the higher prices. In some cases, this led to political upheaval, most notably in Egypt, Tunisia, Libya, and other Middle Eastern countries that experienced the "Arab Spring" in late 2010 and into 2011.

Ultimately, these disruptions can be traced to the distorting policy imbalances that developed within and between countries as the global financial expansion unleashed by the Nixon Shock of 1971 reached its zenith in the latter part of the 2000s. And it's impossible to grasp the nature of those policy effects without comprehending the relationship between the United States and China, the behemoth of the BRICs. Starting with Nixon and Mao's icebreaking moment, the two giant countries' relationship would grow into an economic pairing of a kind the world had never seen. Once the new millennium had begun, their economies had acquired a deep interdependence—one could equally say codependence. The American consumer market provided the means through which China, with its export-oriented economy, could clock the fastest sustained rates of development in history. And China, meanwhile, provided the cheap goods needed to sustain the American way of life, as well as the finance to pay for it. Yet the relationship also produced a wholesale relocation of economic activity from one side of the Pacific to the other and a destructive deflationary trend in the United States, both with painful consequences.

At this time, China established itself as the undisputed manufacturing center of the world, and it seemed to be on a mission to produce every fabricated thing that the world consumes. What first began with a focus on low-wage labor-intensive industries—textiles, toys, plastic housewares—grew to include almost the full range of consumer electronics and then beyond that to a growing list of increasingly sophisticated products. During the twelve months ending in December 2010, China's capacity for many clean energy products such as electric cars and solar panels exceeded that of any other country, its Tianhe-1A was declared to be world's fastest supercomputer, and its one-year-old Guangzhou-to-Wuhan bullet train became the world's fastest passenger train in service. Much of this spectacular advance was possible because of efficiencies provided by China's overwhelming pool of low-cost and highly productive labor. But that pool could not have been tapped if it hadn't been for the ongoing program of political and economic reforms aimed at creating Deng's "socialism with Chinese characteristics."

Meanwhile, developments in the United States were also inexorably steering businesses toward China. An information technology boom that had opened up business to greater competition generated a constant feedback loop of rising productivity—essentially the capacity to produce more stuff for less money. That was good in principle, but it also meant that firms with costly operations at U.S. sites, with local workers earning American wages, faced an unrelenting competitive challenge. The only way to survive was to drive down costs, and for many that meant moving to China. Either they shifted parts of their own production overseas (offshoring) or let foreign suppliers do the work for them (outsourcing).

The technological changes that drove firms to this solution also facilitated it. When it was let loose on business transactions, the Internet and communications revolution led to quantum leaps in the efficiency with which goods could be produced overseas and brought to market. Just-in-time inventory management systems, the Net-based integration of computer systems, and advances in scanning equipment combined to permit goods with bar codes to be monitored all the way along their international supply chains with nearly perfect accuracy. That visibility and certainty sharply reduced the amount of inventory firms had to carry in their warehouses, delivering monthly cost savings and permitting companies to operate with longer factory-to-warehouse shipping times, which in turn allowed them to seek out cheaper suppliers in far-off locales.

As these systems developed, they were rapidly rolled out overseas. China's computing, telecommunications, and general networking capacity grew by leaps and bounds, with its broadband subscribers growing from 10 million in 2000 to 120 million in 2010 and its cell phone usage surging from 100 million to 824 million. Having passed European nations, then Japan, and finally the United States, China is now far and away the biggest user of both services. No longer was the Asian country too far away or too unpredictable to be a feasible manufacturing base. With the ease of a mouse click, purchasing managers could now monitor the passage of their goods as they went from the factory line in Shenzhen to the shipper in Hong Kong to the distribution depot in Long Beach. Along with improvements in shipping and loading speeds, video conferencing, international accounts management, and other services, these advances led company after company to see China as their preferred escape from the relentless cycle of productivity-competition challenges.

Yet for all these seismic shifts, China couldn't become the exporting colossus we now know without the official imprimatur of the world trading community. That's why its 2001 accession to the WTO marked a key inflection point for the global economy. The U.S. government's role in that status change cannot be understated. It took Washington's approval to win over the remainder of the WTO's wary membership. And in reaching that decision, the United States helped reshape the entire Chinese economy in a way that would have lasting impact on its own producers.

According to Charlene Barshefsky, the former U.S. trade representative who oversaw the marathon negotiations throughout both terms of the Clinton administration, China's leaders began the process in ignorance of what was required of them. "After the first year of talking with them [1993], it was clear to me that (a) they never understood what entering the GATT [General Agreement on Tariffs and Trade] and then the WTO would mean for their economy in terms of breadth or depth, and

(b) their leadership had no idea what would be involved in terms of political and economic decision making," recalled Barshefsky. So in 1995 she handed her Chinese counterparts a road map to the WTO—a nine-page, single-spaced document outlining a major overhaul of China's basic economic and legal structure so as to bring it into line with market-focused Western norms. "This was a document that was designed to galvanize the leadership so that there was no misunderstanding . . . that they would have to make fundamental changes to their economy of substantial scope, governing all goods, all services, agriculture, and basic rules," Barshefsky said.

An experienced Washington trade litigation lawyer whose trademark look was defined by a set of colorful scarves, Barshefsky was nicknamed "Stonewall" for her unbending approach to negotiations and her prodigious stamina. Here she was up against an equally tough counterpart: trade minister Wu Yi, the "Iron Lady of China." Wu, who later became vice premier, was known for her charm, steady resolve, and reputation as a straight talker. On paper, it was Barshefsky who won this battle. The United States made no major concessions to China, even if in 2000 Congress finally granted China what it needed to enter the WTO: permanent-normal-trade-relations status. This put an end to the annual routine of Beijing having to lobby for a renewal of its most-favored-nation status. Yet it was no more than the same rights the United States granted to nearly every other country. And to achieve that, China had to make profound changes. Following Barshefsky's road map, its government had spent the preceding five years making sweeping reforms. It shut down many state-owned enterprises, redrew its legal code to incorporate U.S.-style notions of intellectual property rights, and modernized its antiquated, bad-debt-riddled banks. You could say it submitted to an American nation-building plan.

Still, China undoubtedly got what it wanted out of the WTO. With the opening up of new markets for its exports, China's already rapid pace of economic development accelerated to unprecedented speeds. Thus the communist regime could keep its pact with the Chinese people: it produced jobs and income growth, and they accepted its authoritarian rule. For a time at least, American workers did well out of the deal too. Although it meant they were priced out of a host of new job sectors in the global economy, the new inflow of low-priced Chinese goods allowed them to sustain the lifestyle they'd become accustomed to, while the cheap credit that China helped to subsidize generated employment in finance, retail, and construction. Sad to say, the 2008 crisis proved that many of those jobs were temporary. The debts, in contrast, stayed on.

In 2007, economic historians Niall Ferguson and Moritz Schularick labeled this relationship "Chimerica," encouraging people to think of the United States and China as a single, fused economy that accounted for a quarter of the world's population, a third of its GDP, and over 60 percent of world economic growth between 2002 and 2007. "West Chimericans are wealthy and hedonistic; East Chimericans are much poorer," they wrote. "But the two halves of Chimerica are complementary. West Chimericans are experts in business administration, marketing and finance. East Chimericans specialize in engineering and manufacturing. Profligate West Chimericans cannot get enough of the gadgets mass produced in the East; they save not a penny of their income and are happy to borrow against their fancy houses. Parsimonious East Chimericans live more humbly and cautiously. They would rather save a third of their own income and lend it to the West Chimericans to fund their gadget habit—and keep East Chimericans in jobs." Under this arrangement, Ferguson and Schularick said, "East Chimericans generate massive trade surpluses which they immediately lend back to West Chimerica"; this in turn "depresses the key long-term interest rate in West Chimerica" and sustains a boom for "financial and real assets in West Chimerica and its satellites."

If this sounded like a marriage that was too good to be true, it was meant to. The term "Chimerica" was also a reference to a chimera, the authors said, the monstrous two-headed beast of Greek mythology. And near the end of the decade, that beast's frightening potential was unveiled as the financial crisis wreaked havoc on the world. The biggest fall was felt by the United States, where jobs were slashed and home prices plunged. By 2010, people's attitudes about the relationship had turned negative. A survey by the Pew Research Center found that 46 percent of Americans thought increased trade with China had been bad for the United States, against 45 percent who saw positive effects. The House passed a bill that would compel the U.S. Treasury to impose punitive tariffs on Chinese goods in retaliation for "currency manipulation," and while the Senate rebuffed that one, it resoundingly approved its own bill a year later, only to have the newly Republican-controlled House reject it. During the 2010 midterm election campaigns and the 2012 presidential campaigns, candidates produced ads that charged their incumbent competitors with having voted to send jobs to China or that otherwise sought to make themselves out as "tough on China." China no longer had to worry about having its most-favored-nation status renewed, but it had also become most-favored bogeyman among scapegoat-hunting U.S. politicians.

U.S. anger is justified. In 2001, China committed to free trade, yet as we'll learn in Chapter 3, it continued various distorting policies that gave unfair advantages to its exporters. The state deliberately sets interest rates low while keeping its currency artificially weak and limiting the yuan's convertibility. It also curtails workers' organizing power and restricts their welfare benefits, a stance that compels them to save for the future, which provides an even bigger pool of cheap finance for industrialists. The government's centrally planned infrastructure projects are often pursued in the service of exporters and prioritize "indigenous" products through procurement protocols, which foreign patent holders say results in the pirating of their technology. Under its program of special economic zones (SEZs), China built entire cities from scratch—such as Shenzhen, which now has a population of 10 million—to attract foreign investment into exporting facilities. It has dished out cheap land to favored developers, often forcibly confiscating it from existing inhabitants in a way that would be impossible under Western laws dealing with civil rights and property ownership. All this has made it possible for big manufacturers to set up in the exporting coastal regions and has facilitated the biggest mass migration in history. By government design, more than 200 million people have moved from poor rural areas into the coastal regions, their bodies absorbed into the machinery of the Chinese exporting superstructure. Even after following Charlene Barshefsky's road map, China's economy is still subject to central planning and its one-party political system remains highly authoritarian. With wages and other costs rising in the post-crisis period, the country's entire model is now in question.

Yet the other side shares blame for the imbalances. China's excess savings and currency policies generated the capital that flowed to the United States, but America's dysfunctional financial system steered it into the least productive areas. The United States failed to improve vital social and physical infrastructure, partly because of political divisions at the federal, state, and local levels, but also because the housing boom consumed the financial, material, and human resources that might otherwise have gone toward better transportation, education, health care, and energy. Poor-quality infrastructure makes production less efficient, another reason why the United States couldn't match China for jobs. (It's worth noting that Germany's high-end infrastructure allows it to compete as a major manufacturing exporter, even with wages far higher than China's.) And China itself is compromised by the deterioration in America's financial position, which leaves its loan of more than $1 trillion to the United States looking vulnerable. It must keep financing the U.S. government because if it started dumping U.S. bonds, it could precipitate a price collapse. Yet in maintaining the flow of financing, it perpetuates a dangerous codependency.

In essence, the global crisis stems from Americans having enjoyed too much of a good thing for too long—and from the structural factors that left them ignorant of the risks. The rally in asset prices, stoked by Chinese financial flows, left the average Joe with no historical reference for gauging the dangers of spending beyond his means. How could he comprehend that the constant advance in stock and home prices had to end, or that they were sucking up money that might otherwise have helped make his country a more attractive place to employ people? How was he to know that global imbalances were distorting the value of his home and his retirement assets? The gains were repeating year after year, so how could he imagine they would end?

But end they did. In the fall of 2008, the average Joe got a massive wake-up call.

2

Average Joes: Drowning in a Sea of Global Financial Liquidity

Meet Joe Bonadio, a victim of the international liquidity boom that left the American economy in a paralyzing debt trap. As a single, fifty-one-year-old man with no kids, Bonadio might not seem like your typical middle-class American. He never went to college and has never worked in a factory or an office. And he has spent the bulk of his adult life self-employed as a professional drummer, not exactly a common occupation. Still, in many ways, Bonadio's financial experience during the first decade of the twenty-first century was archetypally mainstream. For most of those ten years, he averaged about $75,000 a year as he hired out his services to other musicians and producers. It wasn't a huge income and it came in fits and starts, but he owned his own home and by juggling three credit cards he could manage the cash flow well enough to sustain a comfortable existence. Yet because of the sweeping shifts in the global economy outlined in the previous chapter, he ended the decade on the edge of bankruptcy and with a chastened view of his financial well-being—not unlike much of the American middle class. In that sense, Joe Bonadio is your average Joe.

Bonadio's story is a starting point for understanding how millions of

Americans have had their lives profoundly affected by a teeming Asian country that most have never visited. To them, China remains distant, mysterious, and culturally inaccessible. And yet, as the producer of the material goods that fill their houses and a key source of the credit with which they purchase them, that country has defined their lives in critical ways. The average Joe is oblivious to the fact that China and its hard-working, hard-saving citizens have both indebted and enriched him.

Man vs. Bank

Ever since he lied to his parents about taking a year off from studies and moved to New York, Bonadio has made a living out of music. Now recognized as one of the best recording session drummers in the New York area, he has added drum tracks to singer-songwriters' solo albums, collaborated on movie soundtracks, toured the United States with performers such as Marc Cohn of "Walking in Memphis" fame, and put percussion to advertising jingles. "I don't care what music I'm playing; I'm happiest when I'm sitting at my drum kit," he told me. "And most of the time, it always seemed like the work just came on its own, through recommendations and people wanting to use me. It came from the telephone and it seemed like the phone always provided."

But all that changed in late September 2008, after he returned to New York from a recording job in Los Angeles. "I came home and there were no calls. The phone had just stopped," Bonadio said. He didn't know it then, but he had become collateral damage in the Lehman Brothers collapse, one of millions whose livelihoods were immediately put in jeopardy as businesses responded to the ensuing credit crunch by cutting expenditures where they felt they could. Bonadio never thought of his services as a discretionary spending item, but others clearly did.

The phone stayed silent for months, forcing Bonadio to dig into his savings and build up debt. As the financial crisis tentatively wore off in the middle of 2009, a trickle of work came in, but it paid far lower fees per gig. It wasn't enough money to cover his mortgage, home insurance, car payments, and credit card bills, let alone his general living expenses. Part of the problem was that he was no longer competing for work merely with other drummers. Due to the same digital revolution that had transformed business models and powered globalization, Bonadio was now up against downloadable MIDI files and drum machines that were increasingly being produced at low cost in China. And although a live drummer gives drum tracks a more realistic feel, when ad agencies were slashing their budgets they sought cheaper options.

This shift by Bonadio's clients toward electronic percussion matched a pattern seen across the U.S. business sector, which moved aggressively during the crisis to protect shrinking profit margins as revenues shrank. Unlike in previous recessions, businesses now had a plethora of low-cost suppliers available worldwide, thanks to the twin trends of digitization and globalization, which had advanced relentlessly during the preceding decade. The driving force in that process was China, for although it wasn't the only source of cheap goods and services, the Asian giant set the pricing standard for almost everything. As U.S. firms fought for their survival by outsourcing, markets everywhere began to benchmark to the "China price." (More on this later in the chapter.)

While Bonadio's income faced competition from drum machines, his outgoing payments were being forced higher by a different kind of innovation, one that he adopted in March 2006: an interest-only mortgage. The existence of financial "innovations" such as this can also be partly linked to the rise of China. At that time, at the peak of the housing loan bubble, a record influx of excess savings was flowing into U.S. financial markets from the Asian giant, as well as from Japan, South Korea, and other Asian exporting nations. That was driving up the price of tradable mortgage securities, which by definition meant that their yields—a measure of expected return for bond investors—were falling and in turn forcing down the benchmark lending rate for home loans. That put banks and other institutions' profitability under pressure and gave them an incentive to deliver mortgage products with higher interest rates. By then, virtually every lender in the country was pushing exotic loans out the door to higher-risk borrowers, all so as to satisfy their shareholders' demands for returns that could match or beat those of their peers. Along with millions like him, Bonadio was swept up in this zeitgeist.

After inheriting a small amount of money upon his father's death, the drummer followed his brother's advice and signed up with a personal financial advisor from the Merrill Lynch branch near his gym. Three months later, the advisor phoned with a "really good deal." It entailed placing a new seven-year, interest-only mortgage on his home in Mt. Vernon, just outside New York City, and upping its principal from the $235,000 that he then owed to $318,000. The monthly payment was higher than the interest-plus-principal payments on the existing, smaller loan, but the rate was lower and Bonadio could use the added cash to both pay off high-interest credit cards and keep a buffer to tide him over in difficult months. In good months, he could freely make bigger payments to knock down the principal, but in bad months he wouldn't have to meet those demands. Bonadio's advisor reasoned that this flexible structure was more appropriate for his client, given his shifting monthly income. Moreover, his home had been appraised at $625,000, more than double the $245,000 he'd paid for it ten years previously. Bonadio had some doubts about taking on a loan that would mature in just seven years without any fixed principal payments, but he trusted the man on other end of the line. "He was my financial advisor," he said. "He was helping me invest my money. So I said OK."

By the end of 2009, Bonadio felt nothing but anger toward his Merrill Lynch advisor. With his income a fraction of what it was, the burden of making interest-only payments on a giant loan falling due in just three and a half years was a source of extreme stress. "I now had more money owed than I could pay, and I didn't know what to do," he said. "My fear had risen to an amazing level, because when you have a lot of time on your hands, and when one of the things that are really concerning you is finance, you watch the business channel. And all those channels did, for basically a year, was to spread flames of fear about how we are in a lot of trouble." Bonadio had long since blown through his cash buffer, and although he'd made some principal payments he still owed $309,000 on the home loan and had racked up an additional $50,000 in credit card debt. The value of his home, meanwhile, had followed the rest of the U.S. real estate market lower and was now estimated at just $350,000. With those numbers, there was no way he could refinance the mortgage. Bankruptcy looked almost inevitable. He had to find a way to work out a deal with his creditors. And the first place to start was with the credit cards, where he was stuck in the pernicious grip of compound interest.

Bonadio started responding to radio ads from one of the few growth industries of that time: debt settlement services, which promised to negotiate on debtors' behalf and cut their debts in half. But he found that each carried an onerous up-front payment, a system that was later restrained by a law introduced in 2010. These firms demanded 15 percent of the total debt owed and would not start the process until sufficient funds were stashed in escrow to cover their fee. Bonadio's view, quite reasonably, was that the negotiators should be paid a percentage of what they *saved* him, not of what he owed.

After encountering a dozen companies with the same up-front fee structure, he stumbled upon the Consumer Recovery Network. Not only did it charge an after-settlement fee based on money saved, it also offered the option of a one-off $999 payment for a set of instructional CDs that would teach him how to manage the negotiations on his own. Comforted by CRN's promise to treat the $999 as a down payment on its 15 percent performance-based advisory fee if he later wanted its help, Bonadio plunged into the do-it-yourself route. It was an eye-opening experience, prying open a window into the ruthless strategies that big banks use with the multitudes of cash-strapped debtors that the crisis had left in its wake.

As Bonadio quickly learned, a customer who falls behind on a credit card payment soon gets a phone call. At first it is a friendly reminder that the account is overdue. If that doesn't prompt a payment, there will soon be more calls, occurring more frequently. Bonadio says that at one point he was receiving between forty and fifty calls a day from his three banks.

Typically the calls are recorded messages, but if the recipient responds, a human being jumps on the line to suggest that the minimum payment be made. If the customer says he won't or can't make the payment, the bank representative will warn about a deteriorated credit rating and the perils of bankruptcy. At that moment, many debtors relent. In so doing they hand the bank a victory at their expense.

Here's why the banks win: Based on the universally applied 29.9 percent default rate that Bonadio was paying on his credit card debt, it would take forty-four years of minimum monthly repayments to pay back the $54,000 total. By then he would have paid an additional $130,000 in interest. In contrast, because of the front-loading effect of the interest paid when the loan was at its largest, the banks would have earned back the entire amount in just three and a half years.

What the bank desperately wants to avoid is a six-month cut-off date. If payments aren't received by then, it must write off the entire loan on its balance sheet, recognize the loss, and then fight with other unsecured creditors over what could be a measly payout from a drawn-out bankruptcy. That's why it resorts to the telephone equivalent of saturation bombing during the first ninety days. "They know what's going to drive you nuts and that you are going to give them $60 just to shut the phone up," said Bonadio. If just one of those calls hits its target and prompts a minimum payment, the clock kicks back to six months and the bank is in the clear. But if the customer reaches the fourth month with no payment, the game changes. Out of the blue, a settlement letter will arrive from the bank, offering to accept perhaps 50 or 60 cents on the dollar. The savvy debtor will politely demand something more generous. And the bank, weighing the cost of a lower settlement against that of a charge-off, will routinely concede. In Bonadio's case, he settled with Citibank, JPMorgan Chase, and Bank of America for an average 31 percent of the total, a saving of $37,379.

Most debtors cave in to the banks' phone call attacks, however. Spread across millions of households, their capitulation has far-reaching negative consequences for the broader economy, especially during tough economic times, as it means that millions of conscientious borrowers unwittingly condemn themselves to a state of perpetual indebtedness. Even when the banks claim to be working out a deal to get their clients back on their feet, it's not clear that the clients are the ones being best served. Two of the banks involved in Bonadio's case—Citigroup and JPMorgan Chase—responded to my requests for comment about it by assuring me that they never work with debt settlement companies and instead encourage customers to consult licensed, not-for-profit credit counselors. That stance would steer debtors away from the sharks, but it would also deny them help from outfits that achieve bigger take-home settlements, such as the Consumer Recovery Network.

Bonadio is one of the few who outwitted the system. Why? Not because of his steely resolve, but rather thanks to the help of yet another digital innovation: caller ID with ring controller. With that little box, he could program the phone to not ring whenever calls came from a number associated with one of the banks' debt collectors. The machine, he says, kept him sane. It also gave him the detachment and time with which to watch how the banks approached problems such as his and to better comprehend their modus operandi. That perspective embittered him. "I'm not a religious person," he said, "but it is as if Satan said, 'I want to be on earth,' and God asked him, 'What are you going to be?' And he said, 'I'm going to be a bank.'"

Bonadio's demonizing of the banks won't resonate with all Americans, especially those who believe that people like him were just paying the price for spending money they didn't have. But to spin that kind of simple morality tale out of the worst economic crisis in eighty years is to ignore the global financial forces that led to it, forces that overwhelmed the U.S. economy. In the years of hyperglobalization that preceded it, the ever-expanding trade surpluses in the exporting nations of the developing world created a glut of savings that flowed into the U.S. financial system. So while American competitiveness quietly declined, threatening jobs and undermining Americans' capacity to repay their debts, the inflows of foreign money left banks and other financial institutions flush with cash, money that was so cheaply obtained it was begging to be lent out. As competition for borrowers heated among these cashed-up lenders, they expanded their provision of increasingly risky loans. For sure, homeowners such as Bonadio should have been judicious in assessing their offerings, as should have the banks in the way they viewed their clients. But at that time, economists across the country were spouting the mantra that housing prices could never fall, and Federal Reserve officials were lauding the flexible new lending programs. In this climate, the proliferation of "affordable" subprime loans seemed perfectly rational. Such was the power that the international liquidity boom had on the collective psyche.

By far and away the biggest source of that mind-altering flow of global financial liquidity was China, which just happened also to be the biggest foreign threat to American manufacturers and their jobs. Between 2001 and 2008, China's foreign reserves exploded from $400 million to roughly $2 trillion—an increase unprecedented in world financial history—and the bulk of that was steered into U.S. bonds, rocketing the country into first place as America's biggest creditor. That financial expansion, a direct outcome of a pro-exports exchange rate policy, coincided with the loss of 1.8 million American jobs to China, according to state-by-state estimates by the Economic Policy Institute, a left-leaning Washington think tank. Yet at the same time, China's ever-expanding array of cheap goods was allowing indebted Americans to maintain their standard of living as the debt bubble inflated around them.

Joe Bonadio's life was profoundly affected by this international relationship, although like most Americans he never realized it. His problems began as his skills were made redundant by drum machines and software that were increasingly produced in China. His no-interest loan was financed by Merrill Lynch, one of the beneficiaries of the China-led global liquidity boom until its accumulation of toxic assets forced it into a shotgun marriage with Bank of America. And yet one could argue that the power he found to win the battle with his bankers also came from China, since that it is where the caller ID with ring controller was made.

Tracing the origins of that device will give us a window into the lives of the human beings on the other side of the Pacific caught up in this international financial juggling act. For a small, unimposing machine, the caller ID with ring controller packs a powerful backstory, that of a man whose life reflects an often overlooked factor behind the sweeping economic shifts of our time: the human capacity to overcome adversity and strive for a better life. It's a story that's filled with the tension this force generates inside China, where an authoritarian regime struggles to harness it without jeopardizing social stability. It's also one in which the United States and its libertarian principles play a direct protagonist role. Indeed, the story of the little machine attached to Joe Bonadio's telephone is a uniquely Chimerican tale.

A Chimerican Tale

The device that protected Joe Bonadio's sanity sprang out of a moment when China sank into a state of collective insanity. It was 1967, and Fang Xiyuan, a young man with a knack for mathematics, was on the verge of completing a master's degree at Shanghai's Fudan University. That same year, Fang also joined a group opposed to the "Gang of Four," the leftist cabal led by Mao's wife, Jiang Qing, that was garnering control of the Chinese Communist Party's political organs. That action meant that in 1970, with China gripped by the Cultural Revolution, Fang and his close friend Ma Peijun, a physics major, were dubbed as "counterrevolutionaries." Their academic careers were over. Ma was shipped off to a factory, and Fang was ordered to work as a cleaner.

Then, three years later, as the purges of intellectuals widened, the authorities decided that Fang needed more rigorous indoctrination. He was sent to a reeducation camp on Chong Ming Island, just north of Shanghai, where he was supposed to learn to live like a peasant. He was there for almost four years, with very little to entertain himself other than a dog-eared copy of Darwin's *The Origin of Species.* "We slept ten to sixteen people at a time in a single room with no water and no bathroom inside a hut made of bamboo and rice grass. When it rained, water would drop down onto my bed," Fang recalls. "I did all kinds of farmwork. There were no machines; everything was by hand. I planted rice, corn, wheat, and vegetables. I also had to clean the restrooms, putting people's excrement and urine into a 120-pound dung tub and then carrying it 400 to 500 meters to the crop field."

The Cultural Revolution ended in November 1976 after Mao's death sapped Jiang Qing's gang of its power. Fang and tens of thousands were released from the torment of the reeducation camps. Still, it wasn't until Deng Xiaoping had outmaneuvered the leftist factions of the Communist Party in a two-year jostle for power that this young, intelligent man would be brought back into productive service. As Deng introduced his sweeping reforms, Fang was reinstated at Fudan University, taking on a job as a mathematics instructor. Fang also got to revive a bond with his old friend Ma Peijun, forging a lasting relationship that Fang would call upon decades later to help him turn an idea for a new telephone gadget into a marketable product.

He was now free from the camp, but the years of hard labor had bred in him a visceral hatred for the Chinese Communist Party and a yearning for more complete intellectual freedom. Fang longed to leave China, and an opportunity arose after Ronald Reagan's historic visit to China in 1984, the first by a U.S. president since Nixon's. Reagan signed a cultural exchange accord with Premier Zhao Ziyang, which meant Fang could apply to a graduate program in the United States. To his delight, he was accepted into the University of Connecticut to study for a PhD in mathematics. In 1985, he moved his wife and young daughter to the university town of Storrs and into a completely new life.

Fang was immediately smitten. With his eight-year-old daughter rapidly learning English and acclimating to this new culture, he was convinced early on that he would not return to China. Four years later, he tuned in to CNN to watch the protests at Tiananmen Square and the subsequent massacre, viewing scenes that his colleagues in Shanghai would never see and cementing his determination to stay in the United

States. And as luck would have it, President George H. W. Bush responded to those events by granting temporary visa extensions to Chinese nationals living in the United States. Then, in 1992, that arrangement was made permanent with the passage of the Chinese Student Protection Act, which provided 55,000 green cards to Chinese who'd entered the country before April 2, 1990. James Fang, as Fang Xiyuan was by then calling himself, now had a path to U.S. citizenship.

After graduating in 1990 with a dissertation on risk theory, Fang wanted to start a business, to live out the great entrepreneurial promise of the capitalist society he now called home. So he bought a photo processing store in Meriden, Connecticut. The business struggled, but it provided the inspiration for the product that would later help Joe Bonadio settle his debts with his banks. "I was always getting annoying phone calls from telemarketers trying to sell me something," explained Fang. "So I kept on thinking, 'Is there a way I could design a product that could deal with this problem?'" He was so determined to bring this idea to fruition that he sold his business in 1997 and took a two-year computing course, which landed him a job at a consulting firm, Computer Science Corp., at the height of the dot-com boom. There, he worked on the software design for his product on the side and founded JF Technical Developing Co., securing patents for his caller ID with ring controller.

The only source of capital for the project was Fang's meager savings. When he looked for programmers to do the tedious work of engineering the unit's operating system, he found he couldn't afford American engineers. The solution was obvious but symbolically powerful. He called his old friend Ma Peijun and asked him to find programmers in Shanghai and a manufacturer to assemble the device. Ma's own import-export company would then handle shipping logistics for the finished product. James Fang had come full circle. At the beginning of the twenty-first century he was hitching his future to that of a city in which he had personally lived out one of the most tumultuous moments of the previous century.

Production began in 2003. Storing the incoming shipments in the garage of his home and cutting out middlemen by running the business from a basic website, he has garnered sufficient but not spectacular revenue. Selling at around $80, the product has mostly sold to senior citizens, who use it to block out persistent telemarketer phone calls. Early on it was clear that this business was never going to deliver enough money to sustain him, so he looked for work. He discovered there were jobs in the one sector of the Connecticut economy that was booming in the mid-2000s, all on account of the cash generated by the credit boom: gambling. Fang took a job as a supervisor at the giant Foxwoods Casino and Resort run by the Mashantucket (Western) Pequot Tribal Nation and then later moved to the Mohegan Tribe's nearby Mohegan Sun Casino. Although it suffered big losses in the 2008 crisis, much as Las Vegas's casinos did, the Mohegan Sun was tapping a new, lucrative client base for which Fang's language skills came in handy: high-rolling Chinese gamblers.

Tables Turned

For this rapidly growing new clientele, the casino could thank the economic miracle that occurred during Fang's absence from his homeland. While China's 2009 income per capita was only around $3,700 in nominal terms, far below the United States' $46,000, its rapid development had brought outsized benefits to higher-income earners, the kind who travel and spend big at baccarat tables. In 2009 alone, China added 112,000 new high-net-worth individuals (HNWIs) to its ranks, according to a report by Merrill Lynch and consulting group Capgemini. That took the total number of HNWIs to 477,000, putting China in fourth position after Germany, Japan, and the United States. (In Wall Street's interpretation, an HNWI is someone who has $1 million of investable net assets, excluding his primary residence.) The inequality of China's wealth is skewed even more at the top end of the scale: *Forbes* reported that China had 115 billionaires in 2011, placing it second in the world after the United States' 412.

Fang's old counterrevolutionary buddy Ma Peijun has benefited from this trend. His Shanghai-based exporting company, Credy Industries, has grown from strength to strength, bringing him a prosperity that he and Fang never dreamed of in their youth. He has ridden Shanghai's spectacular property boom, in which apartment prices rose more than 150 percent between 2003 and 2010. Fang, by contrast, has jumped from job to job and had bad luck with real estate: He spent $200,000 on a house in Norwich, Connecticut, in 2007, not long after Joe Bonadio took out the interest-only mortgage on his home just two hours south. Like Bonadio's, Fang's property has lost more than a third of its value. "Now, [Ma] is much richer than I am. In the United States you can buy a new house for $150,000, but in China it will cost you twice as much. So you have to be much richer to live there," Fang said. "I can't afford to buy an apartment in Shanghai now, but I can buy a house in the United States. So much has changed."

Although property analysts say Shanghai's unique financial and geographical circumstances make it a poor proxy for the broader trend of real estate across China, that's little comfort to Fang, who is eager to buy in his old home city, despite his bitter past. The problem is that Chinese state policies and foreign capital flows are working against him. Shanghai's prices have been pulled upward by the meteoric growth inside Pudong's 208-square-mile special economic zone, which gained privileged rights to develop a foreign-financed financial district in 1993. Like any real estate boom, this one is the product of a tug-of-war between finite space—as defined by boundaries of the Pudong SEZ—and big inflows of money. The earnings generated by exporters benefiting from China's weak exchange rate must go somewhere. But capital controls prevent those profits from being invested overseas, and because of the very low benchmarks fixed by the People's Bank of China, it is not worth depositing that money in a bank paying interest rates below inflation. So it flows into property. This confluence of factors explains why some wealthy locals have purchased Pudong apartments for $10 million. It gives one pause to think that this is happening inside the same city where, forty years earlier, a cabal of leftist extremists carried out a crazed strategy for ending social inequality, one that aimed not at lifting people out of poverty but rather at bringing James Fang and others down to the level of the peasant.

Although Fang is now heavily invested in China's success, his experiences there leave him wary of it. He still has faith in the United States' superiority. "There is a property boom [in China], but everything is now stable in the United States. In China, they won't let the prices go down, but they have to so that people can afford them." He believes China is losing its competitive edge in labor-intensive industries to Vietnam and other low-wage centers. The real challenge for his homeland, he says, is to become an innovator and push itself up the value chain to maintain profit margins and jobs—something Chinese officials are very keen to achieve and that various Western businessmen and economists expect to happen. But Fang doesn't see it as likely. China's economic model is too dependent on cheap labor for it to take on the value-added economies of richer neighbors such as Japan, Taiwan, and Korea, where labor is expensive but also highly skilled, he says. And the components inside his own product, the caller ID with ring controller, capture the essence of the problem.

Fang demonstrated this disparity when I met him in Shanghai during his annual visit to the city in 2010. He took me to a giant, multistory wholesale electronics bazaar where he purchased parts for his product. There, rows and rows of stalls display their offerings as if in a candy store: trays of tiny colorful components needed to complete the circuitry in different electronic gadgets. The most sophisticated items, displayed under locked glass countertops, are the integrated-circuit microprocessors, into which hundreds of microscopic transistors and other tiny semiconductor devices are squeezed onto half-inch silicon wafers. Otherwise known as IC chips, these are the brains of any computerized appliance, handling all the critical computing functions. They are also by far the highest-priced components. And when you look at their labels under the glass table tops, you find they are made in Japan, Taiwan, Korea, and other countries where labor costs are high. In Fang's case, he uses a U.S.-made IC chip that costs him around $2. All the other, far less sophisticated bits and pieces needed for the caller ID with ring controller—the lengths of copper wire, the plastic circuit board casings, the capacitors, resistors, inductors, and various other components for managing the electrical current through a circuit board—are made in China. Most of these were displayed in open wooden trays into which customers could put their hands. Their price tags showed them selling for a few cents each.

A key question for the future of the global economy hinges upon whether China can go from producing these secondary parts to highly sophisticated items such as the IC chips. Microchip producers such as America's Intel, Japan's Toshiba, and the Taiwan Semiconductor Manufacturing Company jealously guard the intellectual property in their products. They have so far managed to keep low-cost mainland Chinese manufacturers out of the field. Still, many believe that the microchip industry—and numerous other high-tech sectors—will soon go China's way. In 2010, U.S. businesses began to complain that China was unfairly fast-tracking this process by disadvantaging foreign producers via its "indigenous innovation policy," which requires government agencies to prioritize Chinese-made technology in their procurement. This comes on top of their frequent complaints about rampant piracy of intellectual property in China. Throughout the year, as China announced a string of new technological achievements, including the unveiling of the world's fastest supercomputer, talk was running high about the prospects of it eventually leading the world in high-tech innovation. Having taken all the manual labor jobs, China seemed to be on the verge of stealing all the brain jobs too. Would there be anything left for Western workers to do?

Yet the driver of China's economy is still its giant pool of cheap, industrious labor. If the relative costs of that labor rise—through either wage hikes, higher administrative expenses, a loss of efficiency, or an appreciation in the yuan exchange rate—the economy faces a difficult competitive challenge. China's leaders live in mortal fear that the growth of the past two decades could halt, leaving millions of young people jobless and ripe for another Tiananmen Square–like uprising. With social cohesion given such high priority, they are wary of unwinding their pro-manufacturing, pro-export policy base, even as other countries criticize them for fomenting global financial imbalances. Yet in sticking with this model, China could be limiting its future development. A system that places the employment of manual labor under an authoritarian hierarchy of command is less likely to encourage the outside-the-box thinking that drives innovation and growth in countries such as the United States.

The caller ID with ring controller's global journey from idea to product demonstrates this dilemma. The original concept came from Fang, a naturalized American citizen living in Connecticut who was educated in a U.S. institution. And although he outsourced the basic code-writing process to a few young Chinese software engineers, the core design of the gadget's computerized functions is also his. Likewise, its IC chip "brain" is made in America. Yet to transform the idea into something marketable back in the United States, low-cost human hands are needed. These Fang finds at the Shanghai Dingling Electric Co., where young women are paid to snap and glue together the chips, transistors, wires, and casings he purchases at the Shanghai electronics wholesaler. These women belong to a giant multitude of people who have moved from the poor rural villages of inland China to factories up and down the country's eastern coast. Their hands are the foundation of the Chinese economic miracle. If it weren't for them, Chinese factory owners, exporters, and middlemen wouldn't be buying multimillion-dollar apartments in Pudong or taking gambling vacations in Connecticut.

Wang Shen Ju

Fang and Ma Peijun's daughter Maggie Ma, who has managed Credy Industries since her father's retirement, took me to visit Shanghai Dingling's facility in a dusty neighborhood about an hour's drive from the city center. Dingling's owner, Ma Ren Yuan, gave us a tour of the assembly line. There I met the people who made sure that a cash-strapped drummer on the other side of the world could afford a little machine that helped him outwit his debt collectors.

We entered a room with about thirty young women sitting at benches in two lines, each wearing a lime-green uniform. That day they were working on a job contracted by Shinco, a Chinese maker of air conditioners, whose ductless split units had recently been introduced to the U.S. market. Each was working with a different component to be snapped onto a printed circuit board, giving the air conditioner its electronic nerve center. We stopped to talk to the first on the line, Wang Shen Ju, who was wielding a pair of pliers in front of a pile of small yellow plastic squares, each with a pair of two-inch pins sticking out of it. The plastic squares, I later learned, were EMI suppression capacitors, which cut out electromagnetic interference and thus prevent the annoying buzz that sometimes comes from electrical circuits. It was her job to snip the ends off the metal pins so they'd fit into their designated slot on the circuit board.

Snip, snip . . . snip, snip . . . snip, snip. Thus Wang continued, picking up capacitors one by one and cutting their two pins down to size. She had a bag of 1,000 in front of her that she had to finish. And as she kept snipping, she answered our questions, never once stopping or looking up to see my face. As I spoke through a translator, with her boss standing nearby, it was extremely difficult to get a conversation going, and I found myself awkwardly resorting to simple, closed-ended questions.

How old was she? "Twenty-five." *Snip, snip.*

Where was she from? "Anhui province." *Snip, snip.*

How long had she been working here? "Just over a year." *Snip, snip.*

When had she moved to Shanghai? "In 2005." *Snip, snip.*

Had she been recruited in Anhui for a job, or did she find one when she arrived? "I came here first." *Snip, snip.*

How much did she earn? "About 2000." *Snip, snip.*

How many hours a day did she work? "Eight hours." *Snip, snip.*

Did she miss home? There was a short silence. "Yes."

We walked down the line, talking to the women as they snapped capacitors, resistors, and inductors into the circuit board. Each conversation was the same: the worker looking down, continuing her task, giving short, single-sentence answers. Their ages ranged from eighteen to twenty-five, and half seemed to be from Anhui, an inland province due west of Shanghai, with the other half from Hubei, which was farther west from Anhui. I learned that most of them lived in dormitories not far from the factory, and that they'd all come to Shanghai on a whim, looking for work.

To economists and policy planners, these women with their faces turned away from me are statistics. They belong to the biggest migration in human history. According to official estimates, in China some 221 million people—two-thirds of the entire population of the United States—are living outside their home province, mostly because they have moved in search of work from an inland rural area to a manufacturing hub on the coast. Another 300 million are expected to make the same trek over the next three decades. These migrants form China's "floating population," so called because they live outside the parameters of the *hukou* residency system that formed a centerpiece of Mao's command economy. A person's *hukou,* a form of internal passport, is determined by family history and birthplace, and in theory is supposed to stay with that person for life. Although it has been made more flexible over time, the system continues to make a permanent distinction between a rural resident and a city resident and so hinders a migrant's economic rights. Typically, a city government will refuse public services to anyone without that city's *hukou.* That means that up to a quarter of China's population, and the poorest sector of it, cannot get state schooling for their children in the cities where they live. They are also denied public housing, health benefits, and social security.

In a few cities, Shanghai included, these rules have been relaxed, giving migrants a somewhat better deal. And there is widespread acknowledgment within China that the *hukou* rules need to change nationwide. But because of the drain this would impose on the public purse and because the provincial public services system is highly decentralized, very few reforms have been made. Meanwhile, as the migrations continue, the discrimination deepens. The wealth gap between relocated country folk and birthright-privileged city dwellers grows, taking nominally communist China ever further from its egalitarian ideals to create one of the most unequal societies on earth.

There are now two Chinas, both of which a visitor to Shanghai can encounter with little effort. One China is represented by the city's rising nouveau riche. On the weekends they can be found on Nanjing Road, Shanghai's premier shopping district, which is graced with outlets for high-end luxury brands such as Tiffany's, TAG Heuer, Swarovski, and Lancôme. They might spend their evenings sipping flavored martinis at the chic new bars on the rooftops of the Bund's gorgeously renovated colonial buildings, from which they can gaze upon the space-age neon marvel of Pudong. In the second China, we find people such as Wang Shen Ju, cursed by her possession of a rural *hukou,* living in a cramped dormitory near the factory in which she works. She spends her days repetitively snipping metal pins from countless identical pieces of plastic and her evenings missing home.

Wang and the more than 200 million people like her have taken this option because it is more lucrative than staying put in their villages. In a material sense, their lives are markedly better than they were, as are those of the families back home who depend on these workers' remittances. Only a deluded believer in the Maoist dogma of the Cultural Revolution could argue otherwise. And yet, in relative terms, Wang and the rest of the floating population are struggling to improve their bargaining position within the Chinese economy. Denied the basic welfare backstops that the *hukou* system affords city dwellers, they can't afford to take the risks others take in search of better jobs—such as taking the time to learn a trade. That keeps their wages down and works to the advantage of employers that depend on cheap, unskilled labor. Along with other state-sponsored incentives, including the weak exchange rate, the system entices investment into industries geared toward low-cost, low-value-added, labor-intensive work.

Once again we find a policy-induced mispricing, in this case of the main input in the production process: labor. It ensures that capital is misallocated into China's for-export manufacturing industry and diverted away from investments in industries with higher-cost labor whose development could spawn a more self-sufficient, consumer-led society. What's more, the discriminatory system contributes significantly to China's almost 40 percent savings rate. Without proper insurance for their health and retirement, people such as Wang are compelled to save. Unable to enter the property market, they put their money into Chinese banks paying negative real interest rates. These funds provide a cheap source of capital for Chinese businesses in the manufacturing and export sector, or for property speculators. Along with the savings of more well-to-do Chinese city dwellers, this money also finds its way into a global pool of cheap finance. It enters the same international slush fund that ultimately helped a Merrill Lynch mortgage lender provide a cheap, interest-only loan to Joe Bonadio in 2006. These workers' savings are the foundation of the world's economic imbalances.

Most of the tasks performed by these citizens of the second China are characterized by tedious monotony. For someone privileged enough to earn his income in a field that encourages creative thought, it seems unfathomably boring. But it is no different from working-class environments across the world—I saw a thousand seamstresses in a cavernous factory in Jakarta carrying out the same sort of repetitive activity. And who's to say the workers at Shanghai Dingling Electric Co. aren't better-off than, say, the Mexican migrants who spend their days hunched over strawberry fields in California or packaging beef in the slaughterhouses of Nebraska? The harsh reality of the global economy is that the poor and underprivileged do jobs we lucky white-collar workers can't even conceive of doing. But what makes the Chinese role in this system so significant is its scale. It is much more than merely the adoption of a weak currency; it is the presence of millions of needy young people willing to work very hard for comparatively little money. The masses of young Chinese men and women who spend their days, or nights as the case may be, snipping pins, threading pieces of leather, or snapping bits of plastic together—they are the true backbone of the global manufacturing system.

From what I gathered, Ma Ren paid the women on his assembly line

2,000 yuan a month, or $300, for a forty-hour week. Compared with the approximately $300 a year earned by rice farmers in these migrants' home villages, it's a big improvement in living standard. It's also a significant advance in working conditions compared with those of factory workers in the giant manufacturing zone that rings the Pearl River Delta, farther south. Unskilled workers there frequently told me they were entitled to a forty-hour-a-week base salary of around 1,200 yuan a month. And although they'd usually take home more than that because they typically worked sixty hours a week, it was often a struggle to get employers to honor overtime benefits for those additional twenty hours.

For the most part, Ma Ren's more generous terms are explained by Shanghai laws, which set the highest minimum wage in the country to match its cost of living. But when translated into dollars and compared to his competitors in the United States, he is paying his staff peanuts. As we've seen, that's a direct outcome of a discriminatory system that weakens laborers' bargaining power. Also because of that system, Ma Ren is under no obligation to provide his workers with health care or many other benefits considered routine in the West. He makes no contribution to their retirement accounts or to a workers' compensation fund, and pays no other payroll taxes. And this is at the same time that he and all other export-focused businessmen operating in China benefit from low interest and exchange rates, both of which are mandated by the central bank and made possible by the excessively inflated savings rates of the working- and middle-class populations. Together, these policy-induced conditions give Chinese producers a powerful competitive advantage over producers in other countries and form the basis for a global deflationary force known to manufacturers everywhere as "the China price."

"I'm Not Buying"

"I'm sorry. If you can't get me the China price, I'm not buying."

That, roughly put, is what manufacturers the world over now frequently hear from their business customers. It is an ultimatum, one in which the bargain for the recipient is economic survival. When played out on a global scale, it has a profound downward effect on prices. It drives down costs everywhere, helping to spur big productivity gains for many companies. But it is also why millions of factories worldwide have shut their doors over the past two decades and why tens of millions of jobs have disappeared. For U.S. manufacturers wishing to keep their operations in the country in which they were founded, the China price presents them with a painful choice.

The dilemma has been a factor in business decision making for a number of years, but the China price effect grew to extremes in the latter part of the past decade. In fact, its most pernicious impact was felt in the aftermath of the 2008 crisis, when it was a drag on the U.S. economy's ability to restore healthy economic and employment growth. In effect, the China price sapped U.S. policy makers of their power to influence the direction of the U.S. economy even as they took extraordinary measures to stir it back to life.

Led by Ben Bernanke, whose doctoral work on the policy mistakes of the Great Depression convinced him that the Federal Reserve had to pull out all the stops to keep the economy growing, the Fed started buying Treasury bonds and mortgages in the open market. Through these transactions it pumped a staggering $2.35 trillion worth of new money into the economy in the two and a half years to mid-2011. Meanwhile, the Obama administration unleashed the American Recovery and Reinvestment Act, a fiscal stimulus program worth an unprecedented $787 billion. These efforts prevented the economy from falling into the same deflationary trap that grips Japan's economy, where an endless pattern of declining prices encourages consumers to postpone purchases and perpetuates a self-fulfilling process of shrinking income and economic stagnation. But given the amount of firepower directed at the problem, it is striking how weak demand continued to be, how few jobs were created, and how little pricing power businesses had. Three years after the Lehman Brothers crisis, unemployment was holding near three-decade highs above 9 percent, while core inflation—a measure that strips out volatile food and energy prices—remained below the Fed's 2 percent target rate.

These statistics speak to a failure to close what economists call the output gap, the difference between excess production and the newly reduced level of demand. In a normal economic recovery this gap is closed quasi-automatically, via the magic of the inventory cycle. Firms first respond to the collapse in demand by running down their inventories, but as those stocks reach unsustainably low levels relative to sales they start ordering again, which in turn leads to a revival in production at factories, fresh job creation, higher aggregate income, and a restoration of business pricing power. Following the crisis of 2008, however, the cycle either stopped working or took much longer to play out. The most common explanation for this was one backed up by research from economists Carmen Reinhart and Kenneth Rogoff, who demonstrated that recoveries from unemployment declines caused by financial crises have through history occurred at a slower pace than those following the plain-vanilla recessions that stem from the natural boom-and-bust rhythms of the inventory cycle. Reinhart and Rogoff argued that the United States and other developed economies faced five to ten years of slow growth because of the giant overhang of debt leftover from the credit bubble. Before recovery could begin, they and others said, consumers, businesses, and eventually governments first had to "deleverage," so as to lower the amount of debt they held compared with their assets. And the only ways to achieve that were by cutting back on spending and by selling assets, the latter occurring in the housing market through a wave of foreclosures. Both responses put downward pressure on prices and income. This could be thought of as a long financial hangover, the price paid for having binged on too much debt before the asset bubble burst. It meant that demand would take a lot longer to rise to the level of productive capacity and that the market's incessant search for economic equilibrium could be achieved only by more cuts in both prices and output.

I brook no issue with the debt hangover thesis. A big part of this book is dedicated to examining the lasting damage that the credit bubble has wrought on Western economies. The problem I have is that people who cite it tend to understate the equally important role played by globalization in this process. Any analysis of the post-crisis environment that ignores the context of the global economy, in which manufacturers in emerging markets play an outsized and highly influential role, is incomplete. Business activities are so comprehensively globalized that it is impossible to look at what happens to the United States in isolation from what's happening in places such as China. In 2009, the U.S. economy was facing not so much a domestic output gap as a global one. And the concept of the China price gives us the means for understanding how it works.

Once the crisis hit, U.S. corporate executives did two things to protect their shareholders' businesses: they laid off workers at a pace not seen for seven decades, and they spread their operations as far globally as they could to find the cheapest supplies and services. Inevitably, a new wave of businesses set up operations in China at this time, where they were also drawn to the tantalizing prospect of new sales.

For the biggest American companies, the strategy worked. Research by Fidelity Investments' Market Analysis, Research and Education group showed that operating profits for companies in the S&P 500 index rose more than 100 percent year-on-year in both the third and fourth quarters of 2009, with more than 80 percent exceeding analysts' forecasts. David Bianco, then a Bank of America Merrill Lynch strategist, calculated that by 2010, 40 percent of S&P companies' profits came from overseas, which meant an even greater contribution in terms of earnings growth, given how much faster the rest of the world was growing than the United States. The cost cutting—as well as Bernanke's gift of cheap money—was a key reason the same S&P index of share prices rose a whopping 23.4 percent over the course of 2009 and a further 12.8 percent in 2010. And in turn, it helped Wall Street make record profits of $55 billion in 2009 and to pay out bonuses of $20.3 billion. (The bonus pool might have been a record too if not for scandal-plagued Goldman Sachs, which opted for the political tactic of lowering its payments despite a phenomenally profitable year.) The spillover effect continued into 2010, when Wall Street firms posted profits of $27.6 billion, their second-highest total on record, and paid bonuses of $20.8 billion, the fourth-biggest amount on record.

As big public corporations' numbers quickly improved, each company's shareholders demanded the same results, forcing more and more Americans into the ranks of the unemployed. In November 2009, the jobless rate hit a twenty-six-year high of 10.2 percent. One reason for that stark divergence is that the small businesses that account for more than half of all U.S. employment were caught in the competitive trap unleashed by the bigger guys' relentless cost cutting. They had far less capacity to cut staff or outsource their operations overseas and no capacity to raise prices. If their competitors were now getting the China price from their suppliers, then they would have to do the same. The alternative was bankruptcy.

The deflation threat that Bernanke had to battle was thus a global one. It would take a giant increase in Chinese consumption or a similarly large decline in Chinese production before the United States would reach equilibrium. And since Beijing was taking only incremental steps at best to achieve the first of those goals, this was going to be a long, drawn-out process. In the meantime, the Fed's monetary injections, unprecedented as they were, would have only minimal effect. They helped large companies issue low-interest bonds, which in turn allowed Wall Street banks to rake in big underwriting fees, but they did very little to help small and medium-sized companies. Even with the base rate at zero, banks were unwilling to lend to them in an economic environment in which domestic demand refused to pick up and jobs were going overseas. The Fed's policies, in other words, were doing virtually nothing to help the little guys. As Keynes would have said, Bernanke was pushing on a string.

Federal Reserve officials tend to take a sweeping, macroeconomic view of things. They can't tailor monetary policy to suit the interests of a particular community, let alone those of a specific firm, much less an individual person. Yet the boundaries of the job are also confining: by definition, they are accountable solely for the macroeconomic performance of the domestic U.S. economy. Bernanke doesn't answer for Germans, Indians, or South Africans. (That's not to say that the Fed's policies don't have a major international impact—as we'll see in Chapter 9—or that the world's central bankers don't at least try to coordinate policies.) And yet what the China price dilemma demonstrates is that the forces now dictating U.S. inflation and employment are both global and local and thus outside the purview of this institution upon which we've come to rely. These economic ills are the outcome of an international drama, one that doesn't so much play out in the halls of the United Nations or the International Monetary Fund as in the lives of the people working at firms such as Dingling Electric in Shanghai and Electropac, a maker of printed circuit boards in Manchester, New Hampshire.

The Great Reset

Printed circuit boards, or PCBs, whose intricate signaling networks are vital to the functioning of almost any electronic product, are a mostly unseen but fundamental element of our modern, gadget-filled lives. They are also very much part of the American high-tech success story. These days, the vast majority of PCBs are made in China—the PCB that Dingling Electric workers were passing down the assembly line was manufactured in-house, for example—but as recently as the early 2000s, U.S. manufacturers still did a roaring trade in them. When the Internet boom combined with the Y2K corporate technology overhaul in the lead-up to the year 2000, demand for PCBs grew at a breakneck pace. And after Y2K passed uneventfully, the momentum created by the related upgrades at IT departments sustained the industry for some time.

As a result of this boom, Steven Boissoneau found himself at the peak of his income-earning capacity in 2001. He was then the vice president of Electropac Co. Inc., a printed-circuit-board maker founded by his father, Raymond Boissoneau. As the digital age came upon the world, the family-owned firm went from a company of a dozen or so employees at its founding in 1976 to one of 476 staff in four different locations across New England and Canada, with combined sales of $50 million a year. Shortly before then, Electropac had even acquired a symbolic badge of success: a corporate jet. Yet Steven Boissoneau had inherited a conservative blue-collar ethos from his father, and he was frugal with his money. Although he and his wife, Elena, had been talking for years about investing some of their savings in a horse farm, one that their horse-loving second daughter, Korie, could manage after she finished her studies in equine science at the University of New Hampshire, they constantly balked at the commitment. But then came the terrorist attacks of September 11. Steven Boissoneau, like most Americans, experienced a deeply personal reaction. In his case it prompted him to stop dithering on the farm purchase. "The emotional reality sank in," he said, "that sense that if you don't do it today, when will you do it?"

Eight years later, Boissoneau had lost the farm. He had also lost the home he'd bought in 2003, and he no longer owned a car. He was renting a small one-bedroom apartment just across from the Electropac plant in Manchester, New Hampshire. Yet even that cut-price rent couldn't keep him off the financial skids. The $1,600 monthly unemployment check he was receiving was barely covering his wife's $1,500-a-month prescription for a painful medical condition. When I met him in January 2011, he was weighing filing for bankruptcy. The fifty-two-year-old factory manager had become the victim not of his own imprudent spending but of a set of sweeping global forces that had turned his family's business upside down, forces that he simply could not control. By his and his father's telling, Boissoneau's financial fate was the result of three conspiring factors: profound technological change, the inexorable rise of Chinese manufacturing, and corporate America's willingness, as the younger Boissoneau put it, to "cannibalize itself."

The financial crisis was a brutal blow for Electropac, stripping it of 70 percent of its revenue flow in late 2008 and early 2009. But the bigger global themes that played out before and after those tumultuous events had a more lasting and damaging effect. Two years before I met Steven, Raymond Boissoneau had given his son the uneasy task of overseeing the wind-down of three of Electropac's four factories, two in Canada and one in Londonderry, New Hampshire. And yet even after those buildings had been shuttered and the Manchester staff cut back to a bare-bones forty-five, even as global demand for PCBs in telecommunications and high-tech medical gear recovered sharply from the crisis, and even after Raymond, who was still the president, had foregone his salary, a final sacrifice was still needed. "It was either me or it was Electropac," the younger Boissoneau said. "Either I took the losses or Electropac took the losses. There were no options." So the son of the founder quit the company around which his entire adult life had rotated.

Electropac's rise and fall is a case study in American innovation becoming a victim of its own success. Throughout the second half of the twentieth century, the PCB industry was beholden to Moore's law, the trend in computing observed by Intel cofounder George Moore whereby the number of transistors that can be placed on an integrated circuit doubles every two years. That law has pretty much held true for half a century, producing an exponential expansion in computing power and dramatically reducing the price of computers. It explains why the 2-gigahertz chips now used by the most advanced smartphones are a thousand times more powerful than the 2-megahertz computer that guided Apollo 11 to the moon in 1969. As computers advanced, they further facilitated the design and construction of even more powerful IC chips, creating what economists call a positive feedback loop, a virtuous circle in which innovation gave rise to further innovation.

What was true for computing was true for its cousin the PCB industry. As computing power improved, the precision with which printed-circuit-board makers could design and integrate circuitry into their products kept expanding at a rapid pace. The increasingly sophisticated circuit boards improved not only their customers' machines but also their own tools, thus allowing them to create even more advanced products. What looks like a single circuit board of, say, a tenth of an inch will now contain many layers of complicated circuitry, each printed onto a separate copper laminate sheet that's melded to the others. Multilayer PCBs can now run to forty layers, a level of complexity that was inconceivable in Electropac's early years, when its staff used mechanical drills operated with foot pedals to create the board. The problem for the industry is that this ever-expanding computing power has turned a once high-tech, specialized production process into something that can be easily and relatively cheaply replicated. Although the products themselves are always customized, the process has been commoditized, which in turn means it has become exportable. Once the industry reached a critical point of efficiency, it could be transferred to lower-cost locales, such as China. This is what happened at frightening speed between 2001 and 2010, a period that Steven Boissoneau refers to as "the decade of damage."

The other factor that drove this trend arose from the workings of the U.S. stock market. In the 1980s, amid what was then the IBM-led computing wave, and as manufacturers of all stripes began changing their production models and contracting out tasks they'd previously performed in-house, PCB makers enjoyed sharp expansions in demand. As they grew, their hunger for capital grew too, leading many privately held companies to take themselves public. They were now answerable to a more detached, profits-focused group of shareholders and inclined to seek big volumes rather than develop specialized customer niches. When a "hiccup" occurred in the PCB industry in the early 1990s, as Raymond Boissoneau described the impact that the era's recession had on an unsustainable buildup in telecommunications equipment stocks, shareholders demanded growth by other means. A "big acquisition grab" began in which "the volume guys started to feed off each other," Steven Boissoneau said, citing as examples industry leader Hadco's purchase of Zycon in 1996 and Sanmina-SCI's subsequent takeover of Hadco in 2000. "They started wheeling and dealing, to pick each other apart. They would buy the other guy's square footage and they'd liquidate, close down that square footage but keep the book of business," he said.

Yet while this consolidation proceeded, so too did the offshoring and outsourcing of business to Asia—first to Japan and Taiwan, and later to China. So although the domestic base of factories was shrinking, the number of low-cost competitors for these U.S. firms was bigger. "There are now about 300 PCB manufacturers left in the United States, but it's times thirty in terms of how many people are actually selling the product. You went from having 600 competitors in the 1990s to now having 10,000 competitors," said the younger Boissoneau. So by the time the Y2K boom ended, "a lot of those bigger guys got caught offside. They thought that the consolidation would help them shore up business, but at the same time there was this shadow increase in competition from outside."

As a privately held company, Electropac was mostly immune from shareholder pressure, but it could not as easily withstand the pressure from its customers. Throughout the 2000s, the company began receiving annual letters from its bigger customers demanding price cuts of 5 to 10 percent if it wanted to continue its contracts. And this was before the global financial crisis, when the economy was supposedly healthy. In essence, the entire U.S. manufacturing base had shifted its focus to China, where it seemed almost anything could now be produced at markedly lower cost. Not only were the PCB makers moving there, but everyone along the supply chain was either doing so or being held to cost standards as if they'd done so. In order to keep shareholders happy and survive competitive pressure, each business would demand the China price from its suppliers. Even for Electropac's remaining clients—those who believed for various reasons in retaining a portion of locally sourced parts—this pricing benchmark has become standard. "It has changed how you value your product and your services," Steven Boissoneau said. "Many times when you quote your price domestically it is compared to China quotes. And then they'll do the math on whether it is worth it for them to even place a small order domestically. . . . What has been lost completely is the concept of domestic value, of what it really takes domestically to produce."

It is not just in quoted prices where this imbalance arises. Customers now demand 90- to 100-day payment terms, said Boissoneau, even big, cash-rich companies such as General Electric that can afford to make payments earlier. "They do not hold the Asian markets to the same standards that they hold the domestic markets . . . and yet the pricing standard is established there," he said. "When you have a Fortune 500 firm expecting tier-3 suppliers to provide 90- to 100-day payment terms for products and services delivered to them, how are domestic companies supposed to survive?"

This brutal price competition reached a new degree of intensity after the financial crisis. At that point, mere survival became the priority of every player in the market, and the China price was a way to ensure that—at least for buyers. "They talk about the 'reset,' and I think that's a great word because that was the ultimate reset," Steven said. "The ones that were on the fence—you know, the 'good fight' guys, the companies that were sticking it out—they too had to reset their prices. All other options were taken off the table at that point. You either did this or you didn't survive."

And yet survival for some meant the death of others. It wasn't just the layoffs by Fortune 500 companies that drove the unemployment rate above 10 percent; it was the collapse of small family-run manufacturers whose customers would no longer buy items at prices that kept them in the black. Remarkably, Electropac did not add its name to the obituaries. It survived this onslaught, albeit in a much reduced state, through a mix of pragmatism, cost savings, creative relationship building, and "stubbornness," said Raymond Boissoneau. For now it means that a rich manufacturing history remains intact, one that's laid out in a little museum inside Electropac's administrative headquarters and last remaining plant, a building that was a shoe factory in the early 1900s, when Manchester was the center of the booming northeastern clothing industry. It is now one of the few old red-brick millhouses not to have been refurbished and turned into loft-style apartments or office space. As he faces the future, Raymond Boissoneau recognizes that selling the building to a developer will be his financial backstop. But he is determined to keep alive the family-owned and -run firm that he built from scratch. He has effectively tied himself to a company that is the ultimate expression of an American rags-to-riches journey, one in which four generations of Boissoneaus have worked, including his own father. And yet the price for Raymond's determination to stand up to the China price is high.

As Raymond, Steven, and I walked through the spacious building in January 2011, vast sections of the place were breezy and cold, the heat having been rationed to vital areas. Large parts of the shop floor were no longer functioning, and a massive warehouse of spare parts on the top floor sat idle. Electropac's ruthless cost-cutting helped return its books to the black in June 2011. But according to Steven Boissoneau, that result wouldn't have been possible if Electropac hadn't also recently started accepting commissions for passing certain orders that it couldn't profitably complete to cheaper manufacturers in Zhu Hai, China. In fact, this brokering business is the only part of the firm's operations that makes a pure profit. It's a twisted situation: the outsourcing phenomenon that tore apart this company's domestic manufacturing model is now helping to pay the salaries of the U.S.-based workers who are supposed to be keeping that model alive. Given the increasing ease with which customers are cutting out middlemen in global contracting, it's not clear how long this hybrid model can survive. "One year, two years, three years down the road, it is not sustainable," said Steven.

After leaving the company, the younger Boissoneau began exploring relationships with other manufacturers, hoping to use his knowledge to help them keep their facilities running in the United States. He focused on the apparel business. What he found were firms in desperate conditions, including a maker of high-end leather coats operating out of a factory with no windows in the midst of a freezing Massachusetts winter. "They've gone through an entire decade of damage, and the people are scarred, I mean really scarred," Boissoneau said of the clothing companies he visited. "You can just see the wounds from what's happened, how badly these individuals have been hurt." After concluding that there was nothing he could offer to improve these firms' outlook, Steven Boissoneau was at the time of our meeting considering an expatriate job for one apparel company's operations in El Salvador, a move that would mean uprooting from the town and the company that has been the center of his life. "This is what I'd been groomed for my entire life," he said of what was supposed to have been his "destiny" at the helm of Electropac. "I'm now fifty-two years old. I can't wait for the politicians or the government to change the playing field. I can't wait for the industry to come back. I tell you what, though: the last three years were the toughest years of my life. . . . What was shocking to me and disheartening was what American companies were doing to American companies—the disregard for the supply chain, for the human beings, for the investments, for the time served, for everything. The value system virtually no longer exists."

By comparison, the older Boissoneau sees a certain inevitability to what has happened, viewing the industry's shift to China in light of the migration of manufacturing from Europe to North America that fueled U.S. industrialization in the late nineteenth and early twentieth centuries. "They are taking a page out of U.S. history," he said. It's a surprisingly come-what-may view for a man who's seen his company ripped apart by globalization. This viewpoint would find sympathy among those who cited Joseph Schumpeter's famous "creative destruction" phrase to describe the seemingly unbeatable strength of U.S. capitalism in the 1990s, when globalization seemed like an indisputably positive, disinflationary force. In the abstract, there's still nothing wrong with that description of how capitalism achieves efficiency, and it's an accurate portrayal of how Electropac's industry functions. Creative destruction has been the modus operandi of PCB makers throughout Raymond Boissoneau's career. No one can deny the profound advances in efficiency, sophistication, and cost-effectiveness that have transpired as producers have battled perpetual and increasingly global competition.

The comforting part of the otherwise scary idea of creative destruction is that there's supposed to be something with which to pick up the broken pieces after the destruction has taken place. In the low-unemployment phase of the 1990s, Americans convinced themselves that this came by way of higher-paying creative jobs, as typified by the success of dot-com start-ups. And during the housing bubble, construction, real estate, and finance jobs served as an offset to the constant outflow of manufacturing employment. But after the crisis, with only 140 million Americans employed in any job at all—less than half the population—the creative part of "creative destruction" was harder to pinpoint.

In aggregate, all citizens of the world are better-off for the PCB industry having been driven to new heights of innovation by global competition. World productivity is higher, and there's a greater array of affordable goods on offer for all. There's even a net increase in jobs when China and the United States are taken together. But since the losses and gains are not shared equally across geographic areas, the inherently localized nature of our political systems means that governments in losing places such as the United States have a hard time reconciling those losses with their constituents. The political backlash from manufacturing job losses was minimized in the years before the 2008 crisis because there appeared to be benefits to Americans in the global shifts of the time. But the case for globalization is now harder to make, as valid as it might be. There are a lot of people who feel like Steven Boissoneau. "I don't want to resort to tariffs just yet, but again if you are the largest consuming nation on the planet, that is your advantage," he said. "We should be saying, 'What can we do for ourselves first?' And this is maybe a case of me stepping away from globalization, from the global initiative, but you know, we want to be one nation within the globe. And the people on the shop floor are asking how this all impacts them. I don't think it's all about what they can buy, but the total quality of life."

It's hard to see how Boissoneau's suggestion that his country privilege its own manufacturers over China's is doable without some sort of protectionist mechanism that limits Chinese imports. And since his views are hardly unique, such ideas now stand as a major challenge to the global economic system. If a tit-for-tat trade battle with China escalated into all-out commercial conflict, perhaps with Beijing retaliating against U.S. tariffs by withdrawing its currency reserves from U.S. assets, it could have unforeseen and devastating consequences for the world. Yet the losers in the great global imbalances of the post-crisis era, such as the Boissoneaus, have a compelling case, and if things don't improve in the United States, their voices may gain enough prominence to enforce a step away from free trade. In pointing out that the problems that he and countless others face stem from choices made by Americans—by his competitors, by his customers, by his political representatives—the out-of-work factory manager also offers a valuable reminder that when we talk about the "threat from China," we are talking about a global system to which we have all acquiesced. China cannot be demonized on this issue any more than can the owner of a struggling PCB maker who chooses to enter the brokering business to keep his company afloat. The solutions to the problems of Electropac and other American manufacturers are not simple—rampant protectionism is not one of them—and they most certainly won't be uncovered if we concentrate blame on one country and fail to recognize our common responsibility for a global system that gives rise to them.

Even so, China's policy framework is a central issue. We'd ultimately all be better-off if China let market forces dictate the price of its currency, its credit, and its labor, and if it didn't pursue policies that drive down the costs of its goods, generate excess savings, and turn it into a giant global financier. It is true that China's current economic policy model helps Americans and other foreign consumers satisfy their desires for material things, and in that sense the rest of the world implicitly endorses it. Yet the destructive codependent relationship that has formed around this model wipes out companies such as Electropac and generates the disruptive global money flows that bring people such as Joe Bonadio to the brink of bankruptcy. At the same time, the model has allowed the Chinese economy to grow prodigiously over the past two decades. That has brought prosperity but, as the following chapter demonstrates, it has also created stark economic and social imbalances inside and outside its borders. The big question is whether those distortions will diminish in an orderly fashion or whether it will take some crisis to force change in China, a crisis that would pose a threat to the entire global economy.

3

Virtue and Vice: The Savings and Debt Conundrum

The global imbalances problem that economists and finance ministers obsess about might sound like an arcane subject, but it can be broken down to a fairly simple dichotomy: Americans spend too much and Asians save too much. One problem with putting it that way is that to most people it sounds like only one side needs to change its ways. Across cultures, debt is seen as a vice, savings as a virtue. This is a simplistic view, however. The global economy would seize up if credit stopped flowing, an outcome that we got a taste of in the six months after the Lehman collapse. Niall Ferguson has convincingly argued that human progress through the past millennium was in large part driven by the advance of lending and thus, by extension, borrowing. In fact, rather than saying they spend too much, one could equally say that net-borrower countries such as the United States produce a surfeit of investment opportunities so that net-savings countries, which have too few of them, have somewhere to make a return on the excess funds they have lying around. The United States has drawn trillions of dollars from the latter group's pool of excess funds over the past thirty years, and although that process has now clearly gone too far, it's worth noting that it financed a period of significant prosperity.

But if debt can be a virtue, could savings ever be a vice?

If there's a testing ground for that hypothesis, it's China. The most populous nation on earth has one of the highest saving rates in the world, estimated at between 25 percent and almost 40 percent of disposable income in 2010, depending on which government statistics one follows. When you lump in the savings of businesses and government entities—within which a disproportionate amount comes from hundreds of thousands of state-owned enterprises, whose preference is to hang on to their profits rather than pay dividends to the government—the total reaches more than 50 percent of GDP. In other words, China as a whole saves more than half what it earns. With such numbers, you end up with an unfathomably large rainy-day fund, one that's growing by trillions of yuan every year. In the year ending June 2011, household deposits alone rose 17 percent to 33.7 trillion yuan, or $5.2 trillion, more than the combined GDP of the three other BRIC countries—Brazil, Russia, and India.

In squirreling away that money every year, mom-and-pop Chinese, in concert with all those government-owned firms that withhold money from taxpayers, offer the private business sector an astoundingly large pool of finance to draw upon. That allows the government to fix borrowing rates at levels close to inflation. It amounts to a giant financial subsidy, and when combined with an artificially weak currency it lets the country's exporters sell their products cheaply enough to grab an overwhelming market share in foreign markets such as the United States. This in turn results in a persistently large surplus in China's current account—a measure both of the nation's total receipts and expenditures with the rest of the world and of the degree to which its citizens' excess savings must flow overseas in lieu of domestic investment opportunities. Meanwhile, the United States runs a mirror image on *its* books: its household savings rate is one of the lowest in the world, and over the past decade it has consistently run a current account *deficit* of between 3 and 6 percent of GDP. By default, the United States must borrow from overseas the amount by which its domestic savings fall short of its spending and investment needs. In this way, the world's two biggest economies feed off each other. Notwithstanding a modest diminishing in these imbalances since the crisis, the basic dichotomy remains intact: every year Chinese families put aside a third of their income and in so doing fill up the fount from which American families finance their spending.

For many years, this relationship generated hidden distortions as the excess Chinese savings helped fuel the U.S. housing bubble. Once the tumultuous events of 2008 came around, this asymmetric bilateral relationship came upon its reckoning. Americans now have to save more and must keep doing so for the foreseeable future—as must Europeans while they struggle to get their debt crisis under control. But their efforts at frugality will be for naught if Chinese consumers do not do their part and spend more. It's up to them to purchase a bigger share of a global oversupply of goods. Without that shift, this global glut will produce deflationary pressure, stagnating profits, and anemic jobs growth around the world. We need China to change quickly, and that's far more easily said than done.

Here's the problem: Without U.S. and European consumers to keep its export machine running, China has ramped up investment in infrastructure, housing, and factory construction to sustain growth and create jobs for millions of new job seekers each year. But that strategy has become a treadmill, one that is increasingly difficult to stop. If China halts the investment flow too suddenly, it will leave a vacuum of demand, doing grave harm to its own economy and that of the rest of the world. But if it stays on the treadmill too long, overly delaying its transition to a consumer-led economy, an even bigger bubble of overcapacity will develop, fomenting financial risks for all of us.

All this comes down to China tackling its high savings rate. But before we address that, we must try to comprehend its underlying causes. How indeed do Chinese, who are significantly poorer on average, manage to save so much more than the comparatively rich citizens of the United States? Popular explanations often follow cultural stereotypes and contain a moralistic message: Chinese are depicted as prudent, thoughtful planners while Americans are viewed as impatient hedonists. And yet in the modern, rapidly growing China, displays of ostentatious spending are now commonplace at various levels of society even as the country's savings rate has increased. The propensity to save may, in fact, have much less to do with culture and more to do with the structure of the Chinese economy. To some extent, it is a simple by-product of rapid economic expansion, which generates income growth at a rate faster than people can increase their spending patterns. But China's savings rate is much higher than even that phenomenon would suggest, which inevitably leads to the conclusion that it stems from the incentives to save built into the framework of Chinese policies. Much as a low price for credit is the main driving force behind Americans' high level of borrowing, Chinese families are driven to save by the *high* price they pay for *not* doing so. This "price" is defined by the various contingencies for which millions must prepare: for retirement, for health care, for education, for loss of income from injury, and, as we'll learn, from men having to attract a bride in a land where social engineering has left a shortage of females. In other countries such costs are at least partly insured by the state, guaranteed by employers, or simply nonexistent. China's globally distortive high savings rate is largely a function of domestic policy. Because of that, an elite few are advantaged by access to a captive pool of cheap financing while the vast majority are trapped by the limited options available to them.

China didn't always save this much; in the early 1990s, household savings were about 15 percent of disposable income, at a time when the U.S. rate held around 7 percent. The doubling in Chinese household saving since then coincides with the surge in export-driven manufacturing and the massive migration of poor rural Chinese. The hundreds of millions of migrants who've flocked into coastal cities to earn a living in factories are a key motor behind the savings growth. We'll let their stories explain why this is no longer a good thing for China or the world as a whole.

Ruan Libing

In 1980, the Chinese government named Zhu Hai, a city on the southern side of the mouth of the Pearl River, as one of four new special economic zones where businesses would get various incentives. These included special tax breaks aimed at attracting export-oriented foreign investment and the right to repatriate foreign currency through those zones. Along with two other SEZs set up in Guangdong province at that time—Shenzhen, on the northern side of the river mouth, and Shantou, on the coast to the south—Zhu Hai was chosen because of its port and its proximity to the British-controlled entrepôt of Hong Kong. Although it never quite reached the dizzy heights of Shenzhen, which benefits from its land border with Hong Kong, the liberalization brought rapid growth to Zhu Hai and an influx of investment by foreign companies. Special incentives were later rolled out for other cities dotted around the Pearl River Delta, including the provincial capital, Guangzhou, and its satellite cities Foshan and Dongguan, incorporating some 120 million people into a zone that would become the world's manufacturing hub for consumer goods.

Zhu Hai continues to be an important part of that hub. In addition to the SEZ incentives, the allure of Zhu Hai for investors has been the same as that for the rest of the Chinese coast: a self-perpetuating inflow of young, able laborers from the countryside. To talk to some of these workers, I walked through a rabbit warren of apartment buildings and small, family-run workshop businesses, climbing the stairs in a stark, Soviet-style building to an eight-by-ten-foot room with a double bunk inside it. There I met Wu Guoseng and Wu Xinfeng. As members of the technical staff at Zhuhai Raysharp Tech Co., the two Wus were lucky: they were only two to a room in their company-sponsored living quarters. Workers in operations, such as Wu Guoseng's fiancée, Huang Rong, had to share with three others. But there was nothing any of them could do about the incessant noise. A factory making wire coils underneath their building ran twenty-four hours a day, producing a constant din of thwacking and grinding sounds.

When we met, Wu Guoseng earned 1,900 yuan a month (about $283 at the time), working 8:00 a.m. to 5:00 p.m. six days a week at Raysharp, a maker of DVRs for closed-circuit security cameras. His fiancée, Huang, whom he had met during a trip to his village in Hunan and had convinced to join him at Raysharp, earned about 1,200 yuan ($179). She worked a night shift from 8:00 p.m. to 5:00 a.m., also Monday to Saturday. Sundays were the only time they got to spend together, and at that point Huang was often too tired to go anywhere. They rarely ventured outside of the zone of their living quarters. But at least that meant they could save money. Even on this meager income, Wu Guoseng was putting enough aside to confidently plan a family with Huang. Meanwhile, his roommate was an example of the possibilities up the ladder. As a member of the research and development team, Wu Xinfeng earned 2,500 yuan per month, an income of about $4,500 annually at that time. When I told him that I thought an R&D officer at a similar company in the United States could easily earn $100,000 a year, he looked at me and shook his head. "I don't believe you," he said. I asked him what he'd do with such money. He shrugged. "I don't know. Spend it, I suppose." And then he added, "But because I don't have such money, I have to save."

A region of people who think like that does not make for an attractive market in which to sell goods. But it's a great place in which to make stuff to sell elsewhere. And that's what underpins the economy of Zhu Hai and other parts of the Pearl River Delta, where international companies have come en masse to tap the cheap wages and industrious work ethic of people such as Wu. Few have done so more aggressively than Walmart. The giant U.S. retailer began operating in China in 1996; ten years later its annual imports from that country stood at $26.7 billion, equivalent to 12 percent of the entire U.S. trade deficit with China at that time. "If Wal-Mart were a country," writes economic analyst Zachary Karabell, "it would have been China's sixth largest export market." The company's outsourcing to China is seen by its critics as a direct loss of U.S. jobs. Walmart's trade deficit with China alone eliminated nearly 200,000 U.S. jobs between 2001 and 2006, according to one estimate. The jobs that

Chinese workers take in their place don't come with nearly the same benefits or job security.

At the age of twenty, Ruan Libing took a job with one of Walmart's suppliers in Zhu Hai, Elec-Tech International Co. As a newcomer, and with only a few days' training, Ruan was given the ten-hour night shift on a big upright machine that stamped molds for a model of electric can opener marketed by the U.S. retailer. He had a quota: 1,500 molds for each shift, around three a minute. Just three nights into the job, working amid the raucous noise of the machines, he reached out to remove some debris he'd spotted on the plates. But in so doing he disrupted the delicate balance between the two pedals at his feet and the levers in his hands. In response, the stamping mechanism slammed down onto his left hand, leaving it hanging with one finger in place. A few hours later, after he'd passed out from the pain en route to a local hospital, a doctor opted to amputate.

When I met Ruan, he was sharing space at a friend's tiny apartment outside Zhu Hai's city limits, less than a mile away from where the accident had taken place a year earlier. A diminutive, soft-spoken young man, he mostly kept the stump on his left arm in the pocket of his jeans, as if embarrassed for the world to see it. A prosthetic hand provided by China's social security agency was too heavy and uncomfortable to use, he said. He was in limbo, unable to return to his village and unable to work, hoping only that a lawyer who'd taken on his case would get the company to increase its 90,000-yuan compensation. Without a hand, he would likely never work again. That money, plus a 20,000-yuan payout from social security—about $16,400 in total—was supposed to sustain him for the rest of his life.

What he most feared was his family's reaction. Ruan's parents were illiterate and both over the age of fifty, earning a mere 500 yuan a year. They were counting on their son's remittances to sustain them and to help restore their house, which had been all but destroyed in an ice storm in 2007. His father suffered from a severe stomach ulcer and had not been able to afford surgery. He was also prone to drinking, which only made his illness worse. Ruan couldn't bring himself to tell them what happened. Two months of agonizing fear went by until he finally summoned the courage to tell his cousin, Ruan Xiaolu, what had happened. She proved to be a godsend.

Xiaolu immediately phoned a friend she'd met when she worked in Shenzhen, a New Zealander who she thought would know what to do. He referred Ruan's case to China Labour Bulletin (CLB), a Hong Kong–based advocacy group that saw in it a way to expose the inadequacies in China's compensation system. CLB's interests lay in pursuing justice and legal reform. But the case for reform is also supported by economists. That's because the compensation law as it is written produces misaligned economic incentives in terms of both employer and employee behavior—including adding to people's propensity to save.

CLB found Ruan a lawyer, who managed to get a district judge to hear the case, making it the first in China where the judiciary had addressed a compensation claim of this kind. The claim was rejected, but Ruan's lawyer immediately appealed. Meanwhile, another Hong Kong not-for-profit group found that six other former employees of Elec-Tech had lost their hands. It called on Walmart to take action against its supplier, and the retailer responded with a surprise audit that uncovered fifty-five separate injuries in one year at Elec-Tech. It also learned that half of the stamping machines were not equipped with infrared detectors and other safeguards.

In the meantime, Ruan's puny compensation—the equivalent of 200 yuan, or $30, a month for the rest of his life—was causing great angst 1,000 miles to the north in a little village called Rowing Boat. To get to his hometown in the interior of Hunan province takes a whole day and night on one of the buses that ferry migrant laborers around China's countryside. Luckily, I had an alternative: the fastest passenger train in the world, the Guangzhou-to-Wuhan railway. With a top speed of 244 miles an hour, it is faster than any similarly configured Japanese or European train in service. To ride on it en route to a village that seems locked in feudal times is to give oneself historical whiplash. For the first leg of the journey, a two-and-a-half-hour trip from Guangzhou to Changsha, we rode in silent comfort as the speedometer above the cabin door ticked up to 350 kilometers per hour. Outside, rural Chinese villages surrounded by paddy fields whooshed past, offering an idyllic tableau from the window. In Changsha, we took a half-hour taxi ride from the bullet train's out-of-the-way station to the central bus terminal, where we were greeted by a giant golden statue of a waving Mao. A three-and-a-half-hour bus ride to a town called Longhui followed, before a one-hour taxi ride along a potholed route to Rowing Boat. It took twice as long to travel the 200 miles from Changsha to our final destination as it did to travel 500 miles on the high-speed train from Guangzhou.

The contrast between the two Chinas evident throughout that journey was given a final accent upon our arrival in Rowing Boat, which sits on a meandering stream with scraggy rice paddies terraced along its banks. As we walked through the township to the stares of locals, while dogs, chickens, and ducks darted around our feet, the place seemed almost entirely limited to old people and young, barefoot children. The middle generation was missing. Its members had left to work in the cities of the coast, I was told, leaving their kids in the care of grandparents. Some of the residents lived in little traditional gray peasant cottages with pitched tile roofs; others were in brand-new two-story homes with shiny white tiles and balconies, monuments to the remittances that flowed into the town from this absent piece of the community.

We were met by Ruan Xiaolu, who took us to meet her injured cousin's parents. They were living in a relative's cowshed because work on their damaged home had stalled for lack of money. Ruan Libing's father emerged, smiling nervously, a dark-skinned, weathered man with red betel nut stains on the few teeth he had left. Now in his late fifties, Ruan Kaigui had spent his entire life farming rice in the paddies nearby. He had married late in life, as his stomach illness and other ailments made it difficult to find a bride. He finally settled on Liu Xiemei, whose developmental disabilities had similarly hindered her search for a partner. And now, sitting on rickety wooden milking stools in a dusty yard, they explained that the same issue had worried them about their son, Libing, since his accident: they feared he would never find a bride. "We cried for a week nonstop when we heard the news," said Ruan Kaigui, who conceded that he had started drinking again. "Our only hope lies in getting more money for him. That way we can build him a house. And with a house, he might be able to get a girl."

Libing's marital challenges speak to a wider problem in Chinese society, one that also contributes to its high savings rate. With the number of boys born now exceeding by 20 percent the number of girls born, millions of Chinese men find the hunt for a bride to be an emotionally draining obsession. In the opposite of India's dowry tradition, Chinese families of young males will scrimp and save to come up with a bride price, a practice that has given rise to a new breed of female con artist: the runaway bride who disappears with her money after the nuptials. It can all be blamed squarely on the one-child policy in place since 1978, which has promoted a flood of gender-based abortions by parents seeking male heirs, a mismatch that has effectively mispriced marriage.

Shang-Jin Wei, an economics professor at Columbia Business School, found that Chinese households with sons saved more on average than those with daughters and that this difference was accentuated in regions where the male-to-female ratio was most skewed. Those same regions also saw a bigger housing price increase than others that had comparable income levels but less of a gender mismatch—presumably a sign that bride-seekers felt more compelled to display the trappings of a dwelling when eligible women were scarce. "From an individual household's viewpoint, when the competition for a marriage partner is tough, it cannot afford to save less than its competitor," wrote Wei in a column for *Forbes* magazine. "I call this effect 'keeping up with the Zhangs.'" He notes that the doubling in China's savings rate from around 16 percent in 1990 occurred over two decades in which the one-child-policy generation began to come of age.

In the end, Ruan Libing was given a slightly better chance of affording a bride than he'd first feared. For that he could thank both his lawyer and the publicity generated by his case. While Hong Kong journalists reported the Walmart investigation, Elec-Tech relented and agreed to an out-of-court settlement worth an additional 130,000 yuan, or $19,000.

Case closed? Hardly. The money available for the rest of this young man's life remains ridiculously small. And as Walmart's own inquiry found, blame lies with a grossly negligent employer. Clearly, China's compensation law needs an overhaul, so that companies have an incentive to look after their workers. Additionally, a more realistic worker compensation scheme would help reduce the savings rate. The threat of an accident like Ruan's one day hurting workers' income-earning potential is another factor—along with the *hukou* system's restrictions on health care and social security, and the bride price—behind China's excessively high savings rate, economists say. Two months after Ruan Libing's settlement, the state council approved an increase in the amounts that employers had to pay under different injury or death scenarios, but the change was modest and the same one-size-fits-all approach was maintained without any adjustments for employer negligence. Meanwhile, hopes that the government would modernize the compensation system via the country's twelfth five-year plan proved ill-founded, as the National People's Congress concluded in March 2011 with no hints of concrete reforms to workers' rights. That's a pity; reform would generate international benefits. Not only would it encourage less precautionary saving and so help to chip away at the world economic imbalance, but it could also open doors for U.S. insurers and other institutions that have long pushed for China to open its financial services market. With their actuarial expertise, these firms could design a robust system that would give workers peace of mind, incentivize employers to improve their work conditions, and reduce factory downtime.

One would hope that the foreign buyers of these firms' products would exert pressure for change. But although Walmart responded swiftly to the Elec-Tech case and showed concern for injured workers' welfare, the company's formal set of ethical standards suggests that it ordinarily remains indifferent to the host country's labor laws. In an email detailing the steps Walmart had made to improve worker conditions at the Zhu Hai plant, spokesman Kevin Gardner steered me toward its "Standards for Suppliers" code of conduct. The text in that eleven-point code, with headings such as "compliance with laws," "voluntary labor," "environment," and "financial integrity," makes clear that the most important ethical consideration for a Walmart supplier is that it abides by local laws. And the problem in this case was that although Elec-Tech may have been outrageously reckless with safety, its less-than-generous compensation payout was fully legal.

That said, this woefully unequal relationship between Chinese workers and their employers is becoming better balanced, even if it is happening very slowly. Change is coming in an organic, unplanned way, which is good for workers' rights but poses a challenge to a state-designed system that is struggling to shift from a low-cost manufacturing base to a more advanced economic model. Most important, there has been an exponential improvement in access to information for a generation of migrant workers. Ruan's cousin Xiaolu, the one member of the family who had the wherewithal to find a lawyer, is a case in point. At age fourteen she moved to Shenzhen against her parents' wishes and found work on an assembly line making baby strollers for the Italian brand Chicco. From that start, she eventually wound up working as a travel agent. With her sophisticated glasses, bob haircut, and impressive command of English, Xiaolu—or Lu Lu, as she likes to call herself—cut a striking image in a town filled with aging peasant farmers. She had come home to raise her son, to whom she had given the English nickname "Charlie." Once he reached twelve months, she planned to return to Shenzhen with her husband. Charlie would stay in the village with his grandparents so that he can attend school, but eventually she wants him to study abroad and become a lawyer. It's a vision of the future far removed from that of the generation above her, a gap that was brought home when I asked her uncle and aunt, through my translator, whether they thought the Chinese compensation law applied to their son was fair. Xiaolu interjected in English: "They can't answer that question. They have no idea what the law is."

Managing the Jobs Machine

The educational advances achieved by people such as Ruan Xiaolu are at once a measure of China's success and a direct challenge to the economic model that has fueled it until now. The demands that such people make could be the trigger that knocks China off its growth treadmill and provokes a crisis. Until recently, the country's growth model was built on the constant migration of country folk such as Xiaolu to glitzy coastal cities such as Guangzhou, Zhu Hai, and Shenzhen, where they provided a vast pool of efficient labor. Urbanization created economic efficiencies by bringing human resources closer to the point of production and by unleashing positive network effects as it concentrated labor and customers in one place. But the model also depended on these people submitting to a system that denies them the same rights as their compatriots who were born in the coastal manufacturing cities, a system that forced them to save excessively, kept them unorganized, and stymied their efforts to press for higher wages. Now, these increasingly better-educated migrants, most of whom are in their twenties and early thirties, are for the first time finding empowerment in the tools of modern communications—in smartphones, Internet forums, and email. They are better informed about what's provided at different workplaces and so can lobby for higher pay, safer work conditions, and more generous benefits from their employers. Like Xiaolu's cousin Libing, they can also find legal representation to press for fairer treatment against wrongdoing by an employer. In the knowledge that their workplaces are becoming more technologically sophisticated as Chinese producers seek to move up the value-added chain and as foreign purchasers become more demanding, skilled workers are finding that their bargaining power is enhanced.

This rising power of labor, albeit still severely curtailed, is a natural progression for any rapidly developing country. But it will pose a serious challenge to the Chinese government's existing economic strategy and to the export industries that have coalesced around it. Higher wages eat into firms' profit margins, and with the yuan gradually rising in value, the combined impact on their international competitiveness is significant. Exacerbating and accelerating this problem is inflation, which has become an unwelcome by-product of China's relentless investment- and cheap-credit-led growth in the post-crisis years. Rising prices put upward pressure on business costs, including wages, and so further erode manufacturers' competitiveness. They also foster discontent among the masses of exploited workers, something the government fears deeply. Until a nervous government stopped publishing the data, its measure of "mass incidents"—a euphemism for strikes and other illegal gatherings of more than fifteen people—rose from 8,600 in 1993 to 90,000 in 2006. A Hong Kong newspaper reported Communist Party sources as saying that the figure surged to 127,467 incidents in 2008, and there is strong anecdotal evidence to suggest that higher consumer prices, exploitative employment practices, and corruption helped stir up even more such incidents after that. In the summer of 2010, for example, while Foxconn grappled with suicides at its Shenzhen plant, clashes between workers and security guards broke out in Honda, Toyota, and Sanyo factories across Guangdong province. In this tense environment, and amid mounting labor shortages in key industries, employers gave in more readily to wage demands. So did local authorities. In two successive increases in the second half of 2010, Guangdong province jacked up the minimum wage in the capital city of Guangzhou 40 percent to 1,300, or about $200. While such wage gains will be welcomed by labor rights advocates, who frequently point out that Chinese workers are prohibited from joining unions other than the state-run All-China Federation of Trade Unions, they also suggest the end of the cheap-labor stage of China's economic development. They will make it very hard for the country's exporters to compete against cheaper locales such as Vietnam across a range of labor-intensive industries. Such is the ruthless logic of globalization.

The challenge to competitiveness could make the government reluctant to repeal policies that keep labor cheap and compliant, including the *hukou* restrictions. But the truth is that China's economy needs to go in the opposite direction. It must break with the old model of curtailed labor rights, a weakened currency, artificially low interest rates, and exclusive customs and tax breaks for special economic zones, all of which have encouraged overinvestment in low-cost, export-focused manufacturing industries on the coast. China needs to move further up the value-added chain to develop homegrown high-tech industries that are less sensitive to labor cost competition. But while it is achieving that on many levels, it struggles to build brands of its own, leaving its U.S. and European corporate customers extracting large amounts of value from the supply chain even though the bulk of the production is done in China. And as it moves beyond being an outsourced assembly line to foreign brands, China also needs to focus its energies inward and become more of a consumer economy, less of a savings economy. In a win-win arrangement, the world would see a reduction in its destabilizing imbalances while China would break the insidious trap of rising costs and wage demands. It all depends on ending the incentives for people such as Ruan Libing to squirrel their money away.

The government knows it must engineer this sweeping economic transition sooner rather than later, but the challenge is to get the timing right. The authorities fear that if the export-oriented industries that thrive on the current model of low costs and high savings are disrupted too abruptly they will cut off a vital source of job growth. Every year, China must create enough jobs for 10 to 15 million young people entering the workforce. In the previous five-year plan, the government estimated it needed an annual growth rate of 8 percent to fulfill that task, and it surpassed that target with impressive regularity. The question is whether it can replicate that performance. These employment pressures will eventually ease—and ultimately morph into the opposite problem—when China's one-child generation approaches retirement. But before then they are likely to get even more intense. Yu Faming, director of the Employment Promotion Division under the Ministry of Human Resources and Social Security, has said China will need to create 25 million new jobs annually during the five-year plan that began in 2011.

Faced with this imperative, China responded rapidly to the plunge in its exports that occurred as the financial crisis began to strangle the global economy in the fall of 2008—an event that threatened to flush millions of unemployed youths into the streets. Within two months after the Lehman collapse, it unveiled a colossal $584 billion stimulus plan—much to the envy of Barack Obama and other world leaders, whose programs not only were far smaller in per-GDP terms but also required many more months of negotiation with their legislatures and local governments. In achieving this, Beijing had an ace up its sleeve: the country's army of diligent savers, who essentially financed the economic recovery effort. By directly ordering banks to unleash credit, the government marshaled the domestic savings pool so that it would finance investment and purchases of big-ticket goods. Thus China efficiently shifted the jobs-creating burden away from the exporters and onto the contractors, engineers, builders, and others who now occupied the vanguard of a nationwide construction boom. Underneath, however, it merely swapped one problem for another. Without there being a matching increase in demand—either overseas or domestically—to pick up the slack created by all this new production capacity and infrastructure, the cycle of investment would eventually run out of steam. And at that point, the excess slack in the economy would translate into income and job losses—such are the immutable laws of the business cycle. With its stimulus strategy, China simultaneously exposed both the short-term advantages and the long-term disadvantages of a centrally controlled economic system.

On the positive side, the socialist state's unique command of the economy helped it stimulate recovery far more quickly than the Obama administration ever could. This was most profoundly seen in its control over the country's financial system, through which it rapidly expanded bank credit. Although the four biggest Chinese banks have been partially privatized—such that American households now have indirect stakes in them via mutual funds—they are compelled to follow the lending instructions of the People's Bank of China. According to the PBOC, Chinese banks issued a whopping 9.6 trillion yuan ($1.5 trillion) in new loans in 2009, double the amount of credit growth in 2008, and added a further 8 trillion yuan in 2010. (By comparison, total bank credit outstanding at U.S. commercial banks shrank over the course of those two years.) One result of this was that Chinese customers bought 13.6 million cars in 2009, turning their country into the biggest auto market in the world, and then clocked up 18 million more purchases in 2010. A boom in property sales also ensued, sending prices soaring in Shanghai and other cities. And most important, there was a splurge in capital spending by provincial and municipal governments, which ramped up housing and other construction projects in anticipation of the government's "Go West" campaign, which sought to shift areas of production—and the people these would employ—away from the more expensive coastal areas into places where wages and other costs weren't so high.

But this frenetic activity also exposed the Chinese system's weaknesses. Without a market mechanism for disciplining the allocation of resources, excesses quickly appeared. By 2011, Chinese companies listed on local and foreign stock exchanges had plunged amid a string of accounting scandals, which delivered big losses to various speculators, including hedge fund manager John Paulson, and raised broader concerns about the quality of Chinese data. Armed with such concerns, some hedge funds began employing the same kind of über-bearish strategies that had given Paulson such big profits in his bets against the U.S. housing market, and targeted them at China. Believing that the surging investment machine was creating an economy-wide bubble, they put on trading bets that would profit if China's economy—and by extension its asset markets and those of countries that depend on it—hit a rough patch. As of the time of writing, they were still a minority, with most economists still upbeat about China's future. But it's not hard to believe these pessimists have a point. From various angles, China does look like a bubble.

"Dubai Times a Thousand"

To travel overland in China these days is to be greeted on the outskirts of every city with rows and rows of new apartment complexes and other mega-sized developments. Some of the more extreme projects have been slotted into the bears' PowerPoint presentations as they make their "sell China" pitches. A favorite of theirs is the district of Kangbashi, in Ordos, a wealthy coal-mining city in Inner Mongolia. A ghost town before it was even populated, Kangbashi was built from scratch with homes and office buildings to accommodate a million people. After five years of breakneck construction, the district was completed in 2008. But as of mid-2011, it remained almost entirely unoccupied.

The new Guangzhou South railway station, where I boarded the high-speed train to Changsha, is another example. Approached from a highway, the terminal stands as a hulking tangle of steel on the horizon, much like a modernist international airport or an Olympic stadium. Massive steel beams curved to look like giant banana peels hold its roof across 118 acres and five separate floors, most of them covered with silvery ceramic tiles. What was most striking to me, especially in a country where it's almost impossible to escape crowds, were the vast open spaces inside. In fact, with many Chinese unable to afford the fare, there seemed to be almost as many employees as passengers inside, most of them in blue uniforms busily dusting, sweeping, and polishing sections of floor that no feet other than their own are likely to touch. There were twenty-eight platforms for a schedule that was then running no more than four trains an hour, all bound for the same destination. The station cost $1.8 billion, and it's just one of eighteen such structures along the 700-mile route, many oddly situated far from their city centers. Extensions to the railway have since been built between Wuhan and Shanghai and then on to Beijing. In 2009 alone, China invested $50 billion in this high-speed rail network, more than the entire budget for highways, mass transit, and railways included in the American Recovery and Reinvestment Act that same year. It has earmarked $298 billion in total for the national network. The mind boggles to think how this investment will ever pay for itself. Indeed, as early as 2011, doubts were growing over the Chinese Railway Ministry's ability to repay its debts. Investors dumped the Ministry's bonds after a crash that killed 40 and injured 191 exposed the shortcuts it had taken with imported switching technology, forcing it to cut back on services. The government tried to fix this financing challenge by cutting taxes on income earned from railway bonds, which succeeded in boosting demand for them but also drew finance away from other, worthier recipients of funds that were denied this special incentive. A year earlier the railway had been a symbol of China's rapid growth and growing clout on the world stage. Now critics used it as a metaphor for the failings of a centrally planned economy where an artificial price for money—defined in terms of the exchange rate and interest rates—creates incentives for overinvestment and a misallocation of resources. "Manipulate enough prices and before you know it, the bullet trains, sans passengers, are streaking from empty city to empty city past idle steel mills and untenanted shopping malls," says Jim Grant, editor of *Grant's Interest Rate Observer,* a particularly outspoken China bear.

Much of the manic construction effort, especially in the residential sector, is contracted at the municipal or provincial level, where local governments are under pressure from the central government to maintain high levels of growth. If we are to believe the numbers—that is, if we ignore the doubts about Chinese financial reporting standards fueled by the 2011 accounting scandals—those provinces have had striking success in achieving their mission. All but one of China's twenty-two provinces and four direct-controlled municipalities recorded growth higher than the 8 percent target Beijing set for the country in 2010. Construction mecca Chongqing had the second-highest growth rate, 14.9 percent, surpassed only by the port city of Tianjin, which grew at 16.5 percent as it processed the arriving shipments of raw materials used to feed the construction activity in places such as Chongqing.

The bears argue that this top-down approach to "meeting the number" creates a temptation for municipalities to keep erecting buildings to spur growth, even though by leaving them unoccupied they are eating up investors' capital. A posting on the popular financial blog Zero Hedge detailed accounts of eleven landmark Chinese buildings, including hotels, apartment blocks, office towers, and a Shanghai overpass, that were demolished a few years after their completion. This cycle of demolition and reconstruction, it said, is the untold story of the 2 billion square meters of new building space that China adds each year and for which it consumes about 40 percent of the world's concrete and steel supplies.

Inevitably, this much construction dislocates tens of millions of people as provinces entice or force residents to give up their homes. With so much development income generated by this activity, abuses of power are commonplace. Land expropriation is the biggest source of corruption charges filed against local party chiefs and a constant catalyst for "mass incidents." In 2010, a website known as the "Blood House Map," which reported on violent expulsions around the country, became a hit among Chinese Net surfers.

Then there's the core question: how do the provinces pay for all this? In many cases, land is the only worthwhile asset local governments have. They mortgage it to pay developers, all with the hope, but not the guarantee, that they will make their money back in sales of units. Such sales were by 2010 accounting for more than 40 percent of many provincial and municipal governments' revenues. Although the local authorities insist that they use these inflows for capital spending and not to pay for services such as schools and sanitation, there's a risk that they will develop an economic dependence on this cycle of borrowing, land development, and real estate sales.

In mid-2011, the central government announced that total municipal debt stood at $2.2 trillion. The loans were sitting on the accounts of "special investment vehicles," or SIVs—the same kind of opaque, off-balance-sheet entities that Wall Street banks used to build their hard-to-count stock of toxic mortgage debt in the 2000s. In this case, there's no implied too-big-to-fail guarantee for the borrowers; it's a given that most local governments will be bailed out by the central government in Beijing if they face default. The upshot is that China's true debt-to-GDP ratio stands at about 60 percent of GDP—three times the benign 22 percent level cited by the IMF. Although that's still well below the near-100 percent levels of the United States and the troubled nations of Europe, it represents an extremely rapid growth in debt of dubious quality. And according to Victor Shih, a political scientist from Northwestern University who brought this provincial borrowing to the world's attention, its true size was likely closer to $3 trillion and rising at the time of the official announcement. That's enough to wipe out the country's foreign reserves. Local governments will have to sell "lots and lots of land every year for years to come" just to pay interest on this debt, Shih says. "To the extent that there is a real estate bubble today, it must continue for local governments to remain solvent." But the worrying thing, he adds, is that "you have to think that this growth in real estate and land prices must slow or reverse at some point." Sure enough, prices did turn lower in the second half of 2011. With home sales grinding to a virtual halt, thirty-three out of seventy cities registered price declines for the year.

Shih's critics contend that the central government has plenty of resources to manage a debt problem in the provinces—including its $3 trillion war chest of foreign reserves—and that fears about the risks to Chinese banks holding the debt are equally overblown since their balance sheets were cleaned up after a banking crisis in the 1990s. What's more, bubble-like price trends remain concentrated in wealthy cities such as Shanghai, while only about 50 percent of home purchases are paid for with mortgages. But the threat is less financial than it is economic. If Beijing must create 25 million jobs annually over the next five years, it will be tempting for local governments to maintain the cycle of borrowing and building to keep growth in the 10 percent range. But when it's clear that demand isn't high enough to sustain it, the investment treadmill will have to slow, probably dramatically. And that poses serious risks to the Chinese economy and, by extension, to the rest of the world.

As we've discussed, the way out of this trap is for China to reduce its savings rate and become more of a consumer society. But the greater the dependence on investment—which has accounted for half of the 8-to-11 percent growth rates achieved over the past decade—the harder it is to engineer a gradual, nondisruptive departure from that model. And as of late, things have been heading in the wrong direction: investment accounted for a whopping 50 percent of China's economy in 2010, having rarely been below 40 percent through the prior decade. "Nobody's ever done more than 33 percent [investment to GDP] for nine years, and China is well on the way to blowing away all those records," says Jim Chanos, the founder of hedge fund Kynikos Associates and perhaps the most prominent of the China bears. Chanos, who came to fame for predicting the collapse of scandal-ridden Enron Corp. in 2001 and made a lot of money shorting that company's stock, retook the spotlight in 2010 by declaring that China would be "Dubai times a thousand," a comparison to the property collapse and financial crisis that hit the Arab emirate that year. He has placed negative bets on various properties, companies, currencies, commodities, and other assets that have gained due to China's boom. For the first year or so, the strategy did poorly as China continued to grow, but Chanos is unwavering in his argument that the country's boom must eventually falter. He argues that China is on an input-led growth path similar to the one Southeast Asian nations were on in the 1990s, when they pursued the "Asian development model." As economist Paul Krugman predicted in a prescient 1994 paper, that process ran out of steam and led to the Asian financial crisis in 1997 because there wasn't enough final demand to soak up the output that was consistent with such high levels of investment. Peking University economist Michael Pettis likes to say that "China is the Asian development model on steroids."

Whereas consumption accounts for 70 percent of the U.S. economy, it represents only a third of China's. And although the consumer market is growing, it's trailing far behind the rate of investment growth. This ever-expanding productive capacity inevitably produces a giant surfeit of consumer goods with insufficient local demand to absorb them. Much as its Southeast Asian neighbors did in the 1990s, China relies on big-spending Western customers to buy up the surplus. Until 2008, that strategy worked like a charm. But when global trade collapsed with the crisis, the flaws in the model were exposed. So what did Beijing do? It doubled down its bets. With one hand it deployed stimulus to pump investment into capital projects, and with the other it propped up the export base, most significantly by freezing its exchange rate at an undervalued level.

Because the frenetic construction effort demanded ever more imported building materials, China's trade balance underwent a sea change in this period. By 2010 China was importing almost as much as it was exporting. The incoming goods were mostly commodities or industrial machines while the country continued to export ever-larger amounts of consumer goods. In came natural gas, copper, iron ore, and construction cranes; out went clothes, toys, and electronics. This did nothing to help manufacturers in the United States. And since the U.S. and European markets were not growing quickly, the fundamental question then, as now, was this: if China can't sell enough of its own goods, where will it find the money to acquire the materials it needs to perpetuate its march toward industrialization? As we'll see in the next chapter, China's race to industrialize is already driving up the price of the stuff it needs and making that process a more costly exercise.

Despite all the talk of developing an internal market, China's jobs machine is still very much structured around its role as a consumer goods exporter. That's why the exchange rate policy is still so tightly managed. By freezing the yuan at 6.80 to the dollar in August 2008, just as the global crisis was taking root, and abruptly halting a policy of gradual appreciation that had seen the yuan's value rise by 20 percent since July 2005, the People's Bank of China offered direct stimulus to its exporters at the expense of foreign producers. Once markets recovered in March 2009 and the dollar commenced a long, drawn-out decline against its counterparts, the yuan's peg to the sinking U.S. currency brought increasing financial distortion to the world economy.

As dollars that normally would have pushed a floating currency higher flowed into China's booming economy, the central bank bought them up at a frantic pace to keep the 6.80-to-the-dollar peg in place. Offering a direct signal of undervaluation, China's reserves surged 23 percent in 2009 to $2.3 trillion, money that it mostly invested in U.S. Treasury bonds and with which it helped the U.S. government finance the biggest budget deficit in its history. In June 2010, the government relented and let the yuan gradually appreciate at an annual rate of about 5 percent. But given how rapidly the Chinese economy was growing, this was too little too late. In fact, in the following twelve months, the dollar dropped 10 percent against a trade-weighted basket of currencies, which meant the yuan actually fell against the euro, the British pound, the Australian dollar, and other key currencies. Even after a rebound in the dollar in the second half of 2011, the yuan's global misalignment remained profound.

In deliberately curtailing the yuan's ascent, China infuriated producers in other countries, where it spurred talk of a "currency war." But it also brought a host of domestic problems that worked against the long-term goal of transitioning to a consumer society. It undercut Chinese citizens' purchasing power as it made imports more expensive. In essence, by fixing or semifixing its currency to its U.S. counterpart, China adopted the Fed's hyperloose monetary policy, a recipe for inflation, which in China spiked from close to zero in 2009 to 6.5 percent in July 2011. Near-zero interest rates might have been appropriate for an economy toying with a double-dip recession, with 9 percent unemployment and a threat of deflation, but it was hardly what the doctor ordered for one growing at more than 10 percent. It naturally created excess liquidity, and because the government intervened in certain industries to keep retail prices down—especially in energy and certain food products—the money just pushed up prices even further in other sectors. China was facing both consumer and home price inflation risks.

The crawling currency peg made China a magnet for the dollars unleashed by the Fed's quantitative easing programs. The idea of a guaranteed exchange rate increase only sweetened the appeal of investing that money in Chinese assets such as real estate. Although the flows were somewhat blocked by the country's capital controls, which ostensibly bar cross-border movements of money other than those related to imports or exports, the magnitude of fresh dollar liquidity was such that large amounts of money came in through the back door. (One common method is to overstate the value of bulk import orders for which the buyer needs foreign currency—a ruse that's relatively easily constructed when dealing in bulk commodities.) The PBOC had to absorb most of those greenbacks lest they drive up the value of the yuan beyond its pegged value. It thus accumulated $1 trillion in reserves during the twelve months to June 2011, paying for it with bonds rather than cash so as to avoid increasing the money supply and creating even more inflationary pressure. In those transactions, which it mostly conducts with the four biggest banks, the PBOC requires those institutions to accept interest rates far below inflation even as they place an ever-growing quantity of the bonds on their balance sheets. In a free market setting, this constant loss-making proposition would have caused the banks to collapse, but under China's centrally controlled system the solution is easy: the government simply mandates an artificially low deposit rate *ceiling* and a sufficiently high lending rate *floor* to assure the banks of comfortable profits in their dealings with the private sector. The cost of such price manipulation must be paid by someone, of course. And in this case it is borne by depositors, whose savings do not earn enough interest to keep up with inflation.

The PBOC had no choice but to continue with this awkward balancing act because if it paid higher rates on the debt owed to its banks it would not earn enough money on the other side of its ledger—its foreign reserve investments—to protect its own balance sheet. After all, most of its assets were either lodged in low-yielding Treasury bonds or sitting in crisis-prone euros. In both case, their assets were threatened by the worrying fiscal and currency risks. It wasn't exactly a glimmering portfolio.

For this and other reasons, the PBOC lobbied for faster currency appreciation, which would get it off the intervention cycle and slow the growth of its unwieldy balance sheet. But it is the government, not the central bank, that sets foreign exchange policy, and in that realm the export lobby is strong. So the best the central bank got was the gradual appreciation program launched in June 2010, and even that looked in doubt by the end of 2011, when market participants speculated that the global economic slowdown would lead the government to freeze or depreciate the yuan to sustain exports.

Faced with the inflation risk and a property bubble, the central bank gradually put a squeeze on credit. It jacked up the amount of reserves banks had to hold with the central bank, which reduced the funds available for lending. It also raised deposit and lending interest rates—though only incrementally—and imposed unofficial quotas on loans. By mid-2011, these measures were curtailing lending and they would claim a decline in inflation back to 4.1 percent at year-end. But this success in cooling the economy also exposed the challenges Chinese authorities face in taming the growth-hungry beast they have created. Stagnation and even some declines in home prices came as a welcome outcome within the red-hot real estate markets along the east coast, but the accompanying slowdown in the creation of construction jobs did not. In response, Beijing again doubled down its bets. The government announced a scheme to build 36 million subsidized dwellings by 2015, enough to house the combined population of California, Texas, New York, and Florida. This audacious program, which amounts to yet another acceleration in the same investment-construction treadmill, will need to be funded somehow. It will add to China's debt load, making it harder to bail out banks and municipal governments if and when the provincial debt bubble bursts.

And it wasn't just real estate developers who were squeezed by the credit tightening. Hardest hit were the many small and medium-sized businesses that proliferated during the boom, a sector accounting for 80 percent of China's jobs, according to some estimates. As they struggled with higher wages and stiffer competition for overseas markets, many became desperate for financing. So they turned to "shadow loans," partly because banks were financing them via new "wealth management" products that they marketed outside the purview of regulators. Facing onerously high rates on these loans, many of these borrowers started to go under in 2011, forcing the government to adopt "targeted easing" measures to subsidize struggling small businesses while cracking down on the shadow loan business. UBS estimated this shadow banking system to be worth a massive $1.9 trillion as of October 2011, or more than a fifth of total loans outstanding. Here lay the unintended consequences of contradictory government interventions in the marketplace. As state-sponsored infrastructure spending, artificially low interest rates, and a mercantilist currency policy fuel rapid industrial growth in favored sectors, others are constrained by the blunt measures to curtail economic activity. In such an environment, some financiers will find innovative ways to get around restrictions and arbitrage the discrepancies to their advantage. But those without access to this financial infrastructure, especially lower- and middle-income households, will lose.

Indeed, China's working- and middle-class households, the source of the nation's savings, have borne the burden of these distorting policies. Even as the central bank ordered a series of increases in its deposit rate ceiling as part of its monetary tightening in 2010 and 2011, this rate stayed at about three points below inflation for most of that time. That left household depositors constantly losing purchasing power. By contrast, businessmen could access bank loans at rates as low as 6.56 percent, the central bank's mandated minimum for lending. At just half a point over inflation as of mid-2011, these would be incredibly cheap commercial loans in any economy, let alone one that's growing at 10 percent. All this was made possible by China's giant pool of low-earning savings.

China's underpaid, underprotected workers are stuck in a vicious circle through which their undercompensated savings end up subsidizing the manufacturers for whom they work. Since these ordinary Chinese feel compelled to save and not spend, the manufacturers are left with an ever-expanding surplus of goods that must then be sold to the rest of the world. But as rising domestic costs eat into their profit margins, China must try other tricks to keep its exports competitive, primarily by holding down the value of its currency. Not only does that policy breed tensions with China's trading partners, it also further reduces households' purchasing power and leaves the country with an ever-growing portfolio of reserves. With this, it must keep making massive, internationally destabilizing loans to the United States and Europe. In this cycle we find the root cause of the economic and social imbalances that create problems both inside and outside China, and it arises directly from a system that fleeces Chinese households.

Balancing Act

The Chinese authorities are engaged in a delicate balancing act, one in which the whole world has a stake. They hope that the new five-year plan's shift toward higher-value-added and higher-paying jobs will bring them to the promised land of a consumer-led economy, but how they get there without disrupting the existing model and losing jobs is anyone's guess. If they are successful in gradually making this change, they will also comply with the "global rebalancing" demands of the United States, the European Union, the IMF, and others. But doing so will require giving up on their policy of manipulating China's currency and subjecting it to market forces. This would be a win-win for both China and the rest of the world. Why, then, is there such resistance to the idea in Beijing?

One explanation has to do with history and culture. Domestic nationalist sentiment makes Chinese leaders very sensitive to being seen as caving in to foreign pressure, and for the most part, revaluing the yuan has been portrayed as a foreign demand rather than a policy in China's own interests. This concern with saving face, many China watchers say, is founded on a sense of national injustice stemming from 150 years of subjugation by foreigners—first the concessions to Britain after the mid-nineteenth-century Opium Wars, then the Japanese occupation before and during World War II, and finally the imposition of a foreign ideology, Marxism. Now there's a sense that the Middle Kingdom's moment in history has finally arrived. Its people are determined to manage it on their own terms. Any efforts from outsiders to force them to do otherwise can backfire. Certainly that's one read of what happened when the U.S. Senate's approval of a China trade sanctions bill in October 2011 was followed a week later by an announcement by premier Wen Jiabao that, after fifteen months of slow appreciation, the exchange rate would now be kept "basically stable" to offset rising costs at home.

But Chinese intransigence on the exchange rate also reflects political and economic realities. Given the low profit margins with which a large number of export-focused manufacturers operate, many would go out of business if the yuan rose too quickly. And because of their entrenched position within the Chinese economy, this group's lobby is extremely influential, with strong allies inside the government who do their bidding with the ultimate power brokers, the leadership of the Communist Party. Throughout Hu Jintao's decade-long leadership, Chinese commerce minister Chen Deming was a vocal supporter of the weak yuan policy. And his rank within the Chinese cabinet was higher than that of current PBOC governor Zhou Xiaochuan. The technocrats who work for Zhou appear to favor a more flexible exchange rate, but political sensitivities compel them to move cautiously. Zhou has explained his approach with a medical metaphor, contrasting it to the impatience of his Western interlocutors. A Western doctor will prescribe pills for a quick fix, whereas traditional Chinese doctors rely on slower-working but healthier herbs, he said during a visit to Washington in 2010. "It solves the problem, not overnight, but in a month or two months," Zhou said.

Still, reformists in the central bank haven't been sitting on their hands. In 2010, the government accelerated changes that didn't so much alter the value of the yuan as set the stage for a more flexible trading regime in the future. Since Mao's time, it has not been easy to trade yuan for other currencies because of the strict capital controls. But the cracks opened wider in the second half of 2010. Foreigners were permitted for the first time to hold and trade yuan accounts overseas, with tens of thousands opening them in Hong Kong at the same time that the territory began hosting the issuance of yuan-denominated "dim sum bonds." The Chinese currency used in these transactions still can't be easily reinvested back into mainland China, but the measures nonetheless stoked speculation that China was looking to fully internationalize the yuan, to make it freely convertible for capital transactions.

The effect of such a move would be profound. For foreign investors to freely invest their money at will in Chinese shares, bank deposits, or other liquid assets, there must also be the freedom to take that money out. In other words, full convertibility implies allowing Chinese people to take their yuan and invest them overseas. That would really challenge the country's savings and investment model. It would also put to the test a thesis I heard from Andy Rothman, an economist with investment bank CLSA in Shanghai, who argued that the Chinese population's acceptance of negative interest rates was one side of an unspoken "compact" with the government, which promises growth, jobs, and steady improvements in prosperity in return. Would China's high-saving masses stick to their side of the bargain and continue accepting confiscatory interest rates if they could earn a healthier return in other currencies?

Fear of such a disruption will discourage China's leaders from rushing quickly toward full internationalization of the yuan, even as they make clear their aspirations for it to compete with the dollar on the world stage. The fact is that for all China's economic might, its legal and political system is far from what is needed for the yuan to be a serious store of long-term value for foreign investors. One of the many reasons the dollar remains the world's principal reserve currency and, despite a deteriorating fiscal outlook and a downgraded credit rating, U.S. Treasury bonds are still the main safe-haven investment in times of global stress is that investors have faith in America's capital markets. They know that property rights to their money will be protected. But in China there are no such guarantees. There are also serious doubts about the quality of its economic information, undermining the yuan's status as a trusted store of value. Whenever I ask senior bankers and economists based in Asia whether they think China's economic numbers can be believed, they just shrug. One case that sowed doubts occurred when the State Statistical Bureau reported on GDP and the consumer price index (CPI) in mid-January 2011. The 3.3 percent annualized growth in the CPI was glaringly lower than the 6.6 percent inflation rate that was used to estimate the real GDP growth. Either China's inflation-adjusted growth rate was even higher than the 10.3 percent it reported or prices were increasing at a rate twice that measured by the CPI. Such discrepancies are not looked upon favorably by those who move big sums of money around the world.

China is likely many years away from the right legal and information framework needed to turn its currency into a globally traded unit for capital investment, partly because it would require the ruling party to relinquish a great deal of control over the economy. What's more, it is likely that many within the party look at the prospect of big capital flows into and out of the country and can't help thinking of what happened to China's neighbors during the Asian crisis a decade ago. If Nixon didn't want to submit to the demands of foreign money speculators in 1971, why would China's ultraconservative leadership?

Pondering the idea of full convertibility for the yuan and that it might one day be liberally traded in vast quantities around the world is a way to think about how far China still has to go down the road of market reform. It demonstrates that for all the long-term fiscal and economic challenges confronting the United States, the Chinese government faces obstacles that are as big if not bigger. Whereas the government's initial decision to open its economy to trade with the rest of the globe has borne much fruit and has lifted hundreds of millions out of poverty, that phase of its development is now ending. The next steps that the Communist Party regime must take—those needed to build a consumer society—are critical. This daunting task faces Li Keqiang, who is widely expected to replace Wen Jiabao as premier in October 2012, and Xi Jinping, who is fingered as Hu Jintao's replacement as president. They and the rest of a political bureaucracy that's hell-bent on survival will be tested by the demands of this profound economic transition. Until China provides a host of new freedoms—free movement of capital, open and transparent information, equal rights for its citizens regardless of their birthplace, the freedom to choose the size of one's family—the savings and spending distortions that threaten to destabilize the economy and undermine the country's social and political stability will persist. The paradox is that those freedoms will themselves pose a threat to the regime. For China to keep developing, it will need to embrace a more complete form of free market capitalism. But is there a place for the Chinese Communist Party in such a China?

Global Fallout

China is now the second-largest economy in the world. How it deals with these problems will therefore have a profound impact around the globe. Much of what it has achieved so far has been of huge benefit to the world at large. In lifting the welfare of its 1.4 billion people, China has done far more in two decades to reduce world poverty than any international organization throughout the entire twentieth century. It is far and away the world's biggest consumer of a vast range of vital raw and processed materials, responsible both for surging global commodity inflation and for improving the livelihood of people involved in the production of those materials. Its purchases of motor vehicles have single-handedly kept U.S. and European carmakers from going bankrupt. Yet by establishing an overwhelming dominance in the manufacture of consumer goods, it has also driven millions of firms out of business in rich and poor countries alike. And with its gargantuan stockpile of foreign reserves, it now owns much of the industrialized world's government debt, most notably America's. That doesn't mean it *owns* the U.S. government, as pessimists suggest, but along with all the other impressive measures of its global economic clout, it does mean the world has an enormous interest in seeing China get this transition right.

So what will it be? Will China be as successful in its move into this new phase of liberalization as it was in the shift from communism to state-managed capitalism? Or will its leaders see their worst fears of economic slowdown and social turmoil realized?

Legions of China bulls are, for good reason, impressed with its progress over three decades of reforms and expect the same steady hand of gradual development, industrialization, and urbanization to continue through to the next decade. "China is just getting started," says Michael Klibaner, head of China research for property consulting firm Jones Lang Lasalle in Shanghai. For all the talk of a housing bubble, he says, 80 percent of the population is still without adequate housing, representing fifty years of pent-up demand. "They have a huge task ahead of them. But I think there is increasing credibility over where they are going."

The bears, on the other hand, focus on imbalances. Rather than seeing China's giant holdings of foreign assets as a strength, they view them as a weakness, the flip side of a misguided policy framework that leaves the country exposed to speculative investment, inflation, a weak consumer base, and the threat of retaliation from its critically important trading partners. They see the bulls' justifications for the excesses of China's business model as similar to the deep denial that economists and analysts were in over the U.S. crisis in 2007. Peking University's Pettis cites parallels between the problems created by China's investment-dependent growth and Japan's economic model before that country's asset bubble burst in the early 1990s and sent Japan into a deflationary funk from which it has not escaped. "In Japan and other Asian countries, this model has proved extraordinarily successful in the short term in generating eye-popping rates of growth—but it always eventually runs into the same fatal constraints: massive overinvestment and misallocated capital," Pettis wrote in an article for *Foreign Policy*. "And then a period of painful economic adjustment. In short: Beijing, beware."

Pettis points out that there are only two examples in history of countries accumulating foreign reserves on a pace akin to China's: Japan in the 1980s and the United States in the 1920s. Both periods ended very badly indeed. But whereas the Great Depression produced shock waves around the world, Japan's economic problems didn't. There's nothing to say China has to repeat history, and the fact that it still is at a much lower level of development compared with where the United States and Japan were at those relative periods stands in its and the world's favor. Yet there can be little doubt that China's current growth model *is* creating massive imbalances both inside and outside the country. Eventually, both market and political demands will seek to erase those imbalances and revert to equilibrium. China's investment levels will have to fall, its currency will need to rise, and its level of consumption as a proportion of its economy must increase. That process could be orderly—primarily via coordinated reforms with other countries, especially the United States—or it could manifest as a tumultuous, disruptive event, a crisis.

Whatever course these changes take, they won't happen in a vacuum. People and businesses in dozens of other countries will be affected, often significantly. Some will benefit from the diminished impact of competition from China; others will suffer a loss of demand for the items they produce that have fueled China's investment boom. As things stand now, these two groups represent the arbitrary divisions between winners and losers from China's two-decade ascent. We meet them in the next two chapters.

4

The Long Reach: China's Insatiable Appetite

Tango, Eva Perón, Diego Maradona, and beef. Those are the most prominent icons of Argentina. The first is kept alive by the bustling business of dance tourism in Buenos Aires; the second is long dead but still revered by fanatical members of the Peronist movement; the third is alive but frequently flirts with death and is no less fanatically adored by soccer-mad Argentines; and the fourth, well, that's the center around which Argentine life revolves. Without their beef, Argentines wouldn't have their weekend *asado* barbecues, where an array of different cuts and offal are laid out on the *parrilla* grill to be consumed with Malbec wine among friends. Without beef, there'd be no gaucho legend, that of the traditional, quasi-nomadic horseman of the pampas, garbed in beret and poncho, carrying a whip and brandishing an elaborate knife with which he feeds upon a slain beast. Without beef, the menus in Argentina's restaurants would have very slim pickings. Without its beef, would Argentina still be Argentina?

Until recently, the average Argentine consumed 155 pounds of red meat every year, or just under half a pound a day, almost twice as much as the 80-pound annual average for their neighbors in Uruguay, the world's next most prolific steak eaters. For Argentines beef is a staple, much as rice is to Chinese or pasta to Italians. But by 2010, they were weaning themselves off the meat. That year, average Argentine consumption was 124 pounds, marking a total decline of 600,000 tons nationwide, or 2.2 million cows. Why the precipitous plunge in beef eating? Two reasons: misguided government policies that grossly distorted the pricing equation for farmers and a change in dietary and living habits not of Argentines but of hundreds of millions of newly affluent, recently urbanized Chinese.

Barred since the mid-2000s from exporting beef or livestock and restricted by draconian price controls in the domestic market, Argentine farmers are giving up on an integral part of their country's agricultural tradition. They are ripping out their fences, slaughtering their herds, and turning the pampas' rich green pastures over to a crop that has virtually no place in the diets of meat-loving Argentines but sells fabulously in China: soy, a protein-rich plant that happens to grow extremely well in the region's famously fertile soil. And even with the 35 percent tax that the government levies on the export of soybeans and soy derivatives such as soy oil and soybean meal, the profits from selling these products to insatiable Chinese buyers far outweigh those available from raising cattle. The result is an agricultural transformation that threatens to destroy a uniquely Argentine way of life. The country's experience with this challenge illustrates the far-reaching, disruptive effect that China's expansion has had beyond its borders, and it offers lessons in how *not* to deal with it. The most important of those is that any attempt to confront these changes by manipulating prices will most likely backfire.

"Deep Down, We Are Cattlemen"

Argentine farmers first got on the soybean bandwagon in the mid-1990s after Monsanto Corp. introduced genetically modified seeds that could withstand the company's Roundup herbicide. Along with a new seed-sowing technique known as "no-till" farming, the use of these seeds allowed for a much faster turnover of crops and higher yield. But the real allure of the crop did not come until the 2000s, when prices for soy began to soar on world markets. The catalyst for that was the profound demographic and structural shift in China that accompanied its accession to the World Trade Organization in 2001. At that time, China's rural-to-city migration went into overdrive as coastal manufacturing centers ramped up operations to exploit the new market opportunities created by the trade deal. The newly arrived residents that filled up cities such as Zhu Hai, Shenzhen, and Shanghai saw their purchasing power rise from the meager amounts their families had received in the countryside. No longer subsisting just on rice and a few vegetables, they demanded pork and chicken with their noodles. And since they could not raise livestock as they had back in their villages, they depended on the industrialized food production model that had developed in the West. Rather than being free-range, animals were increasingly raised in factory-farming operations before they were professionally slaughtered, with their meat processed, packaged, and shipped to centralized retail outlets. What was needed was livestock feed—plenty of it, and with the capacity to cultivate enough meat for an additional 10 million mouths every year.

Up stepped the humble soybean, a perfect, turbocharged cultivator of chickens and pigs. With protein accounting for about 40 percent of their dry weight—compared with about 10 percent for corn kernels—soybeans are packed with growing power. What's more, soy oil, a by-product of which Argentina is now the world's largest producer, is increasingly becoming a mainstay of cooking oil, another grocery item that has seen an explosion in Chinese demand. For these reasons China was by 2010 importing 55 million tons of soybeans, six times the amount it had imported back in 2000. Argentine, Brazilian, and American farmers did their best to fill this gap, but the demand was so strong that prices still soared. In 2008, the Chicago soybean price peaked at $16.60 per bushel, almost four times its level eight years earlier. And although it dropped below $8.00 during the subsequent global recession, the price quickly recovered and by January 2011 was back above $14.00.

With the rising price enticing them, Argentine ranchers turned their pastureland over to the new wonder crop. In time, that had the effect of pushing up beef prices, which were also increasing in response to a general surge in demand for protein among the rising middle class of the developing world. There is a finite amount of land on the planet and it is capable of only so much agricultural output. Thus, as demand levels reached a critical mass in the most rapidly growing countries and competition for the world's land grew among different crops and livestock, the prices of foodstuffs started to rise, eventually in an exponential way. That struck a blow to household food budgets around the world, and in Argentina it meant that beef, the nation's staple, became out of reach for a large underclass of laborers and unemployed citizens, most of whom had seen their incomes slashed during the tumultuous financial crisis that their country underwent in 2001. Indignant at this slight to the people whom Eva Perón called her *"descamisados"* (shirtless ones), President Néstor Kirchner, a left-wing populist in the Peronist tradition, took dramatic action: he banned all beef exports except for a small portion dedicated to the European Union and put price controls on the local product.

Argentine farmers were left with a choice: keep rearing cattle and try to sell their beef into an oversupplied domestic market where prices were kept artificially low, or get on the China bandwagon and convert their fields to soy. Many opted for the latter, adding a further 4.6 million hectares to the total soy production capacity over the five years from 2006 to 2011. Meanwhile, the average weight of the beasts going through Argentine slaughterhouses started to drop and the number of females rose as farmers systemically liquidated their breeding stock to depart the beef business. The decline in the supply of domestic beef fell so sharply that retail prices tripled between 2007 and 2010—producing exactly the opposite of what Kirchner was trying to achieve. Gone are the days of the mid-2000s when dollar-carrying tourists to Buenos Aires would be pleasantly surprised by a meager restaurant bill after gorging on a delicious *bife de lomo* steak.

Beyond the prices, it's the death of a centuries-old farming tradition that is most striking. If the former cattle ranchers wanted to get back into the business now, the cost of restoring their herds and of reinvesting in the infrastructure needed to retain them, including fences, corrals, and upgraded windmills, would be great. And with a seven-year lead time before calves have been reared to an age where a natural reproduction cycle kicks in, it seems certain that Argentina's beef shortage will last a long time and will likely worsen. That will lead to higher prices and further declines in domestic consumption. In the meantime, with pastureland disappearing, Argentine cattle farming is going the way of American-style cattle rearing: toward corn feed in place of grass. The rich, gamy taste of pampas beef is disappearing.

Andrés Rosenberg, who runs two farms of 750 and 1,000 hectares with his father, is one of many farmers who lament what has happened. The Rosenbergs stuck it out for a number of years after the export ban was imposed, taking advantage of a small piece of the EU quota, but then an injury suffered by his father convinced them that the return on cattle rearing wasn't worth the effort. What pastures they have left at their farm in Buenos Aires province are now maintained purely for the family hobby of breeding show-jumping horses. Staff wearing the traditional gaucho beret, men who just a few years earlier would have been tending to herds of Aberdeen Angus cattle, now groom the horses and prepare them for dressage. And yet the fields of soybeans, their crops bound for China, are still surrounded by rickety fences to keep the cows in, and there are windmills around the property for irrigating pastures. "I don't want to give up the chance of going back," Rosenberg told me. "Deep down, we are cattlemen."

The Rosenbergs belong to what could be seen as a dying breed: farmers who tend to their own property. Increasingly, soybeans are cultivated by large agribusinesses on land rented from absentee owners. Giant multinationals such as Cargill and Archer Daniels Midland farm hundreds of thousands of acres across South America in this way, managing everything from seeding to harvest to the overland freight to company-owned ports, from which ships depart with regularity for China. This lost connection between owners and the land raises concerns among environmentalists. For his part, Rosenberg meticulously rotates crops, following each soy harvest with a planting of either wheat or corn to ensure that nutrients in the soil are retained and the land is preserved. But he pays a big cost for being responsible. That's because the government also imposes severe restrictions on wheat exports in addition to a 23 percent tax, while corn gets hit with a 20 percent export tax and fetches far less revenue per harvest than soy. He worries that his neighbors are just sticking to the most profitable crop and leasing out their land to the highest bidder each year. And if there is no crop rotation, not only his neighbors' land but also his own is at risk. Monoculture farming, which can have damaging effects on the quality of the soil, has become a real problem for Argentina's agricultural future, say critics of the country's headlong rush into soy cultivation.

Earning their revenue from soy brings other headaches to the Rosenbergs too. For one, that income is now at the mercy of Argentina's adversarial political system. President Cristina Kirchner, who succeeded her husband, Néstor, in a deal that saw him retain power in the wings until he died of a heart attack three years later, calls the soy plant a "weed." She has also stirred passions by describing farmers who've benefited from the soy boom as members of a landed elite bent on returning Argentina to the dictatorship of the 1970s. Yet her government is highly dependent on their soy output for revenue, courtesy of the 35 percent export tax. In protest of this tax, farmers have periodically staged shipment boycotts that have descended into violent clashes with union leaders aligned with the Kirchner government. Taxes on soybeans, soy oil, and soybean meal accounted for $6 billion in 2010, or about 6 percent of the government's revenue—more or less the value of its entire budget surplus. Without that inflow, the Argentine government—considered a pariah in world bond markets after the Kirchners spent almost an entire decade withholding more than $25 billion owed to foreign bondholders—would face serious challenges in financing itself and in running the Peronist political machine with which it dishes out patronage and hangs on to power. Indeed, no sooner had Ms. Kirchner won the election to another presidential term in October 2011 than concerns about a new global economic crisis and slowing Chinese demand exposed this vulnerability. Soybean prices went into an accelerating decline, dropping toward $11 a bushel in December. Not coincidentally, a rapid outflow of money from Argentina led the government to impose draconian controls on foreign exchange transactions. Pundits were even speculating about a rerun of the 2001 crisis.

In relying on soy tax revenues, the government's survival—and that of farmers such as the Rosenbergs—also hangs on how well Argentina manages its bilateral relationship with China, by now its most important trading partner. In April 2010, when China announced a boycott of Argentine soy in retaliation against Argentine tariffs on Chinese-made textiles, kitchen appliances, and other goods, it raised alarm in Buenos Aires. High-level delegations visited Beijing to resolve the dispute, but Ms. Kirchner refused to reduce the tariffs. Then, to the surprise of many, China relented and resumed its purchases of Argentine soybeans. With its need for soybean feed and soy oil continuing to rise, the Asian giant had no choice. Thanks to the impressive fertility of its soil, the efficiency of its farming techniques, and an artificially depressed peso that's managed almost as aggressively as the Chinese yuan, Argentina can offer soy at a price considerably cheaper than that of Brazil or the United States. China's surrender showed that "it is China that's dependent on soy, not Argentina," said Gustavo Grobocopatel, an Argentine whose giant soy-farming company produces 3 million tons of grains annually. The truth is that China's relationship with Argentina, much like its dealings with the United States, is really one of codependency. As a major buyer, China has the capacity to put Argentina in financial distress more than the other way around. And yet with food prices especially sensitive in China, Beijing cares deeply about how much it pays for soy. A sustained increase in a critical part of the supply chain could drive up the price of food in Chinese supermarkets, fueling social and political tensions. China has similar concerns about the prices of other raw materials and the threat they pose to inflation—and yet its own hunger for them is the root cause of those problems.

A Hunger for Raw Materials

As China strives to reach a self-mandated growth rate of more than 8 percent and employs its problematic export-and investment model to achieve that, it transfers large sums to other countries in return for the natural resources needed to feed that machine. On its own, China doesn't have enough food to feed its growing urban labor force, nor enough base metals to fill the steel girders or copper wire imbedded into modern buildings, nor energy to fuel its manufacturing plants. For those, China must go forth into the world, reluctantly acknowledging that the sheer size of its transactions will drive up prices.

Wherever China goes with this strategy, its spending power has a sweeping effect on local economies, no more so than in Africa. Trade with the continent grew by an average of 33 percent each year between 2000 and 2008, and in 2010 it was poised to reach $115 billion, or about 15 percent of Africa's total GDP. Most of China's spending goes toward the continent's natural resources, especially oil. But as China strives to win favor with governments and improve the economic infrastructure to make resource extraction and shipment easier, Chinese firms have also engaged in public works projects, importing tens of thousands of Chinese laborers to work on those sites. All around Africa, Chinese laborers can be found building airports, toll roads, gas pipelines, and housing projects.

Entering at such a low base, Chinese money goes a long way in Africa. Optimists argue that this newly wealthy and eager trading partner is offering the continent a sense of hope that Western aid has long failed to provide. Thanks in no small part to China, growth rates in sub-Saharan

Africa averaged about 6 percent throughout the 2000s—excepting a sharp drop experienced during the 2009 global recession. That has given rise to a new middle class in many African cities. But some accuse China of neocolonialism. According to *The Economist,* the China-Africa trade in crude oil has been cornered by a syndicate of Cantonese businessmen who have done little to improve the lot of people in the oil-rich states in which it does business. Meanwhile, Beijing's hands-off approach with African dictators has frustrated the West, most notably with regard to Sudan, where its investments flouted international sanctions. In Kenya, environmental organizations report an alarming pickup in the ivory trade, which they associate with the arrival of Chinese poachers. And in some places the influx of these very different-looking and differently speaking people has caused conflict, especially when there's a sense they are taking jobs from locals. Riots in Algiers against a large Chinese community led the government to build an independent Chinatown district for the migrants to live in. And as political unrest exploded across the Middle East in early 2011, Chinese firms and their workers came under attack in countries such as Libya.

These tensions reflect the prices paid on both sides of these relationships for the otherwise positive, wealth-generating effect of China's international investments. As we'll discover, this new wealth is not spread evenly. There are net losers and there are net winners. And those differences are massive. It's a binary situation: one is either on the right side of the Chinese juggernaut, as Argentina's soy farmers are, or on the wrong side, as America's makers of printed circuit boards are. And as popular as it is to describe China's rise as driving the decline of developed nations in the West and the advance of a developing East, this win-or-lose proposition pays no regard to that traditional divide. It simply depends on whether or not you have stuff that China needs. The next country we visit, one of the wealthiest developed nations on earth, is perceived as one of the biggest beneficiaries in this equation—and yet even there, a deep divide exists between those who own what China wants and those who don't.

The Magic Pudding

BHP Billiton's Mt. Whaleback mine on the outskirts of the dry, dusty town of Newman in Western Australia is the largest open-cut iron ore mine in the world. It stretches three miles lengthways, a mile across, and about a third of a mile deep. Viewed from a distant lookout, the twenty-foot-high Caterpillar trucks stacked with piles of ore look like a little boy's Tonka toys in a sandpit. This is one hell of a hole. And like the Magic Pudding, a children's classic from Australian literature, it keeps producing more goodies even as BHP keeps eating from it. A giant high-grade ore body descends deep into the rocky earth, so deep that the company believes the mine, already more than forty years old, has at least twenty-five years left in it. Indeed, recently BHP's biggest challenge—and that of other miners in Western Australia—has been the ability to dig up the ore fast enough to meet the demands of a giant customer to the north.

This massive pit, its walls staggered with ore-rich terraces of ochre, yellow, and black, stands as a monument to the economic shock waves that China has unleashed on the world and the global financial system. A circular line of cause and effect can be drawn from China's unbalanced trade relationship with the United States to the Asian giant's investment-driven rush to industrialize, then on to the feverish digging in places such as Mt. Whaleback before it heads back to China. In the preceding chapters we learned of the first part of this international cycle, where China's oversaving households defer their spending, ensuring that an excess of manufactured goods is sold at cheap prices to Americans who buy them with credit drawn in part from the same Chinese households' savings. We also learned how this absence of consumption means that China must fire its ravenous growth machine with constant investment in infrastructure projects, which in turn requires a relentless inflow of raw materials. Now, in the part we pursue here, that amped-up demand steers Chinese heavy industry toward Australia and other mineral-rich countries, where it drives up prices for those materials and delivers rising revenues to mining companies such as BHP. Yet the cycle also pushes up costs for Chinese producers, perpetuating a dependence on monetary and social policies that keep exports cheap, and it leaves the Chinese shipping to the rest of the world clothes, toys, and electronics that they can't consume themselves.

At least until late 2011, when a decline in metals prices raised inklings of doubt about the sustainability of the Aussie mining boom, the Australian leg of this cycle has generated ever-rising incomes to many in this thinly populated country. But in the same way that Chinese exports and cheap finance have benefited Wall Street bankers but clobbered both American manufacturers and Main Street homeowners, so too has China's top-price payments for imported Australian minerals forged stark divisions between the haves and have-nots here. How well Australia manages those divergent experiences could determine whether it continues calling itself the "Lucky Country."

In Mt. Whaleback, all is still rosy. In the three years ending in 2010, BHP added 400 people to the mine site's payroll, installed a host of new processing facilities, and inaugurated a beneficiation plant to enhance its product on-site, with many more additions to come under its latest expansion plan, dubbed Rapid Growth Project 5. It also expanded the capacity of a 264-mile railway line to its port in the northern coastal town of Port Hedland. Seen from the same observation platform, the end of that line is almost always occupied by a snaking 2.3-mile-long chain of 208 rail cars. After each rail car has been filled with a 125-metric-ton pyramid of rusty-looking dirt, six locomotives will drag the entire load on an eight-hour journey to the port while the next empty train comes in. Including the output from other nearby BHP mines feeding into the same rail line, eight trains make the trip every twenty-four hours, ferrying a total of 208,000 tons of iron ore. Based on a price of around $170 per metric ton in 2010, that's a total daily value of $35.4 million.

From Port Hedland, the iron ore will then make an eight-day sea voyage to Tianjin on the Hainhe River. From there it will be distributed to China's ore-hungry steel smelters. Through them, Australian iron ore ends up as the steel in the skyscrapers soaring above Guangzhou, Shenzhen, Shanghai, and other vertically growing cities, or in the bodies of the 18 million cars pouring out onto China's streets each year, or in the machines that migrant workers operate to make household appliances for Walmart. It also goes into Chinese-made railway and mining equipment, products that are sold back to BHP and other Pilbara-based mining companies such as Rio Tinto and the Fortescue Metal Group so that they can in turn increase their mineral production and ship it back to China at an even faster pace. As ore heads north to the coast along the company-owned rail lines, Chinese-made machines head south on Chinese-made rail cars on the opposite track. It's a symbiotic relationship, one that's making many people in the state of Western Australia very rich.

No Western Australian is richer than Andrew "Twiggy" Forrest, whose estimated $7 billion net worth made him Australia's richest man in 2010. Forrest's Fortescue Metals Group is the Aussie mining equivalent of a high-tech start-up—except that the capital required to start up is far greater. Whereas BHP and Rio Tinto, the two behemoths of the Australian mining industry, have been in the iron ore business for decades, Fortescue was formed in 2003, began digging for ore in 2005, and started shipments in 2007. In just two years, it built a fully functional mine, a 160-mile railway, and its own giant bulk-handling port. Forrest, who began by audaciously pegging out claims on hundreds of exploration tenements across the north of Western Australia while betting big on a radical new technique to extract iron ore from oddly shaped deposits, believed that this well-established industry had the potential for a giant second-generation expansion. He foresaw both the explosive growth in demand from China and the benefits of developing closer ties with that country. After a lengthy relationship with Chinese steel mills, BHP and Rio Tinto were by 2007 losing market share to companies such as Brazil's Vale and India's NMDC. In jumped Fortescue with attractive terms that earned an enthusiastic welcome from China's ore-starved smelters, winning a host of ten-year supply contracts from more than thirty of them. The Chinese mills were eager to bring competition into a market in which their own voracious demand was forcing prices toward a record $200 per metric ton. They saw the upstart Fortescue as a way to shake things up. (The Chinese government's discomfort with the pricing policies of the two older companies is suspected of being behind the 2009 arrest and subsequent jailing of four Rio Tinto executives on bribery charges in Shanghai.)

Fortescue gave China a big and beneficial stake in its expansion plans. It selected CSR, the local maker of the Guangzhou-to-Wuhan train, to supply it with 976 ore-carrying rail cars, a transaction that not only was cost-effective but also leapfrogged the transportation technology of rivals Rio Tinto and BHP, giving Fortescue the heaviest haulage capacity of any railway in the world. And in 2009, it sold a 16.5 percent stake in itself to state-owned Hunan Valin Iron and Steel Group, based in Changsha—the city of the waving Mao statue on that same bullet train route. The sale afforded the Chinese steelmaker security over vital supplies for the future, while Fortescue got the financial depth it needed to pay for its hectic expansion. By 2010, after an unprecedented increase in capacity, the company had leveraged its well-founded Chinese relationship to become the third-biggest iron ore producer in Australia. And after refinancing $2 billion in bonds in 2010, it set out to triple its output to 155 million metric tons per year by 2013 and to reach a whopping 355 million metric tons by 2017—a project on which it will eventually spend $8 billion.

Fortescue's meteoric expansion is accompanied by similarly aggressive plans in the Pilbara region from BHP and Rio Tinto. Rio Tinto will increase its annual productive capacity by a third to 333 million metric tons in 2015, while BHP says it will double its output to 264 million tons by 2013. This was being announced before Brazil's Vale, the biggest iron ore producer in the world, was due to add another 90 million metric tons of capacity in early 2011, and as miners in India were expanding their operations. Meanwhile, in China, where the iron ore industry is characterized by many smaller mines, the government is seeking to boost its domestic production from around 900 million metric tons in 2010 to as much as 1.3 billion metric tons by 2015. (Though those strikingly large domestic output numbers point to a possible reduction in China's dependence on foreign imports, most of its domestic ore is of very low iron content, which makes it expensive to use. Analysts typically reduce China's estimates by two-thirds so as to accurately represent its total contribution to world iron ore output.) Whether in China or abroad, what's driving all these growth plans is the expectation that surging demand from Chinese mills will continue, even after having risen in 2010 to account for almost half of the world's steel output.

Australian iron ore miners have three critical advantages over their competitors in India and Brazil: the proximity of their ports to China, the relative efficiency with which they can extract and ship the ore, and the high quality of their product. That brings cost benefits to smelters in China, but it also means Aussie producers run healthy margins, despite paying what are by far the highest wages in the industry. To a large extent, the pure chance of geography plays a huge role in Australian miners' success and explains why Aussie mine workers live better lives than do their counterparts elsewhere.

Mining isn't typically the realm of the rich—not for the laborers who actually do the mining. Anyone who watched one of the many television specials about the rescue of the thirty-three trapped Chilean miners in 2010 will know that these men came from a poor, working-class part of their country. Across the border in Bolivia, another big mining nation, there are even poorer people employed in the industry. In Potosí, home of the legendary Cerro Rico ("Rich Mountain") silver and nickel mine that made Spanish conquistadors wealthy, young boys work for self-contracted Bolivian miners to earn $3 a day. Inside the dark and dangerous shafts, noxious gases eat at their lungs, leaving them with a life expectancy of thirty-five years. In the Pilbara, the story couldn't be more different.

Superficially, you could say that the people who work in BHP's, Rio Tinto's, and Fortescue's mines, as well as those employed by the many contractors engaged in their expansion projects, are Australia's version of China's floating population. Most of these mine workers do not treat their place of work as their permanent residence. And like people from rural China who move to the coastal manufacturing hubs, they are drawn to these remote locations by the salaries on offer. But that's where the comparison ends.

These workers are called FIFO workers because they are on fly-in, fly-out contracts, deals that allow them to spend extended periods of R&R in places more hospitable than the hot, dry regions in which they work. According to varying schedules, which can sometimes run as tight as five days on and two days off or be as generous as two weeks on and two weeks off, the companies fly these staff in and out of the work site, to and from their place of residence. The ongoing cycle has been a boon to air carriers Qantas and Virgin. On site, the workers have their accommodations paid for, with food and other needs often provided or subsidized. While those working on remote sections of a railway line or an underdeveloped mine typically live in transportable units known as "dongas," others in more established places now enjoy comfortable housing and access to various recreation facilities. Inside the perimeter of Fortescue's Cloud Break mine site, the company has installed a swimming pool, a gymnasium, tennis courts, indoor cricket facilities, and a golf driving range.

FIFO workers will often put in long days, as much as ten hours, and many of them work night shifts. But although the heat in this desert region can rise to over 120 degrees Fahrenheit, the mine workers don't typically feel it. The work is done with excavators and giant Caterpillar 389 trucks. And at BHP's Mt. Whaleback mine, their operators sit in fully air-conditioned cabins fitted with high-tech sensors that watch eyelid movements to capture early signs of fatigue and send warning signals to the command center.

And then there's the pay. With contracts that go eight days on and six off, FIFO workers at Fortescue's sites start with annual salaries of A$80,000—which at the time of writing was more or less the equivalent in U.S. dollar terms. That's the entry-level job that a straight-out-of-school eighteen-year-old might take, with no higher education needed. If such workers earn their truck driver's license and start operating one of the giant Caterpillar vehicles, their salary can quickly go to around A$160,000 with the same schedule. And a lot more money than that can be made by FIFO workers in more-specialized positions—people such as Chris Harris, a twenty-six-year-old mechanical engineer who works for a contractor helping BHP with its rail expansion. He told me that by putting in as many hours as he could, he was on target to earn A$350,000 in 2010. He'd been working on the mines for about four years, since he left college, and already he owned three blocks of land and was building a house on one of them. On weekends he likes to tinker with his two cars.

Some FIFO workers fly back home to cities on the eastern coast of Australia, and a few even do their R&R in hometowns in Asia. But the biggest contingent comes from Perth, 750 miles southwest of Newman. Visitors often comment that Perth, with a pleasant Mediterranean climate, a long coastline of white, sandy beaches, and a wide, expansive river that lends itself to water sports of all kinds, feels more like a playground for grown-ups than a working city. And for the tens of thousands of residents who earn their living in the mines "up north," it's a pretty accurate description. The FIFO workers come home and spend their big incomes in Perth. In doing so, they have a tremendous, transformative impact on the city's economy.

Western Australia is four times the size of Texas. Yet it has a tenth of Texas's population, with three-quarters of its 2.3 million people huddled into this city way down in the southwest corner. The state as a whole commands more than half of Australia's mining and energy resources and in recent years has attracted more than two-thirds of the national investment in the sector. This has made Perth the nation's richest city on a per capita basis. And since unions have done a good job of strengthening labor's hand in these boom industries, the wealth gets spread—relative to the same sectors in developing countries, at least. Australians as a whole are ideally positioned to benefit as well. Compared with the other big iron-ore-producing countries—China, India, and Brazil, which jointly account for more than a third of the world's population—Australia's 22 million people make for a relatively small group with whom to share the bounty.

But this doesn't mean it is spread well and constructively. Most of the dividends and salaries generated by mining activity go to people who spend them far away from the rural regions in which that activity occurs. That means the tax base is small in those remote regions compared with the number of people who temporarily live there. Consequently, their infrastructure is underdeveloped—there aren't enough water, power, sewerage, or gas lines to sustain a large stock of permanent housing at reasonable prices. So, in a self-fulfilling response, the mining companies feel compelled to offer FIFO contracts to ensure that workers have a place they want to call home. And with the upstart Fortescue raising the bar with an eight-days-on-six-days-off schedule, the terms of these deals have become even more generous. That leaves even more workers with more time and more money to spend back in Perth, a city of millionaires that is becoming a magnet for immigrants from around Australia and the Asia-Pacific region.

I grew up in Perth but haven't lived there permanently for almost two decades. Over many trips home I've witnessed profound changes. The cars have become bigger, more expensive, and more numerous, creating traffic jams that were unheard-of in my youth. The quarter-acre lots on which my childhood friends and I played backyard cricket have all but disappeared as subdivision mania has doubled the number of houses in the more established suburbs. Yet prices for those newly shrunken lots have soared. I spent a Saturday afternoon on the rounds with real estate agent Jayson Renouf, a friend I'd gone to school with twenty years earlier. We stopped at open-home showings in the neighboring western suburbs of Swanbourne and Cottesloe, where we'd both grown up. The first home on Jayson's list was a run-down 2,000-square-foot cottage with a tiny, overgrown backyard on one-eighth of an acre in Cottesloe. It was going for A$1.7 million. I was shocked. I currently live in a middle-range town in Westchester, New York, and I knew that there, on the outskirts of the world's financial capital, $1.7 million would buy me a six-bedroom, 6,000-square-foot mansion. I also remembered that when I was considering buying property in my old hometown after the Asian crisis of 1998, when the U.S. dollar would buy two Australian dollars rather than the one-for-one level it reached in 2010, similar cottages in Cottesloe were going for A$250,000 ($125,000).

As in the United States after the bubble of the 2000s, home prices in Western Australia underwent a correction in 2008 and in the first half of 2009, especially in higher-end properties, as the global crisis drove resource companies' shares sharply lower and forced investors to sell their homes to meet their stockbrokers' margin calls. Jayson recalls one man telling him in distress that he had two days to sell his home. Houses in the well-to-do zone Jayson covers saw 20 percent declines that year, and his annual income shrank for the first time ever. And yet across Perth, the housing collapse was far less pronounced than in U.S. cities, and it was over and done with more quickly. By March 2010, the median price for a home sale in Perth was at a new record of A$518,000. Over the next five quarters, home prices in Perth dropped 4 percent, suggesting that a bubble had begun to deflate as concerns rose toward the end of 2011 about the sustainability of the Chinese-led rally in commodity prices. Yet a closely watched housing index still showed a 164 percent gain from nine years earlier and threefold gains in some suburbs.

The prior decade's boom changed Perth remarkably, redefining its economic power structure. No longer do white-collar professions dominate the ranks of the wealthy. Thanks to the constant demand for FIFO labor from the far-off mines, as well as from the massive Northwest Shelf Natural Gas project off the state's northern coast, Perth has become a city of well-to-do blue-collar workers. And they are not only led by itinerant miners; the construction workers and the laborers who live off the mining-fueled housing boom are also doing well. Whereas the city's wealth once lay among the lawyers, doctors, and merchant bankers who lived in older mansions in the leafy suburbs of the western reaches of the Swan River, the spending power is now found among blue-collar workers in other parts. Plumbers, electricians, roofers, cabinetmakers—these are the plum jobs to have in Perth now. Meanwhile, miners are the new elite: a magazine called *Mine Style* graces the lobbies of resource companies' city headquarters. It offers insights into wine, fashion, travel, and other aspects of the good life for miners. Try squaring that with the concept of what a "miner" is in Bolivia.

There is disdain among some of the educated white-collar professionals for the crass nouveau riche in their midst. Modifying a derogatory local slang word that loosely translates to "suburban redneck," they refer to this new moneyed crowd as "cashed-up bogans," or CUBs. Still, if we look beyond the neoclassical McMansions and the revved-up V-8 cars with $20,000 stereo systems, there is something appealing about the democratization of wealth that the China-led resources boom has delivered to my hometown. It's certainly different from how it has played out in China, where urban-dwelling professionals demand far higher incomes than *hukou*-deprived working-class laborers from the interior.

Yet there are some very real negative side effects, and Perth is at risk of being overwhelmed by them. Historically, there has been a higher degree of substance abuse among FIFO workers on- and off-site. Strict new drug and alcohol testing by employers means the mining camps themselves aren't the same wild, heavy-drinking places they once were, but the separation from families means indulgences are still taken to the extreme. Ironically, new rules requiring that workers take a day off to recuperate after ten straight work sessions mean that many can be found at the local pub on those days, where they do more damage to their health than if they'd stayed working. And when they're back in Perth with money in their pockets, these transient workers play hard. Qantas eventually stopped serving alcohol on FIFO flights in Western Australia, and flight attendants were given special rage alarms to deal with unruly drunken miners on board. Researchers at Queensland University of Technology found that the incidence of violence was higher among FIFO workers than among other members of the Australian population. The study was quickly refuted by people in the mining communities. But whether or not their workers can be cited for such sins, there are signs that violence is increasing in Perth generally. This rise is occurring at the same time that many young men are flying in with money to burn. Local media in Perth were running stories in 2010 and 2011 about an epidemic of "glassings" in city nightspots, which saw an average of nine people every month having their faces slashed by broken glass. There are indeed some uncomfortable elements to the city's boomtown transformation.

Two-Speed Economy

For the most part, though, Perth remains a pleasant, highly livable city. Its biggest problem is that the prices stoked by the mining-led economy are putting it out of reach for many. In what's called the two-speed economy, teachers and others who work in sectors detached from the mining boom—such as retail and hospitality—earn salaries half those of miners and are struggling to afford the ever-rising rents and property taxes. In Perth and elsewhere in Australia, social workers are now increasingly attending to what they call the "New Poor," families whose working heads of household earn too little to cover normal living expenses. Even in what were once comfortably middle-class households, people are locked into a vicious circle of rising costs.

Kelly and Anthony Curran, schoolteachers whose combined income runs to no more than A$114,000 a year, are among tens of thousands in Perth caught on the wrong side of the resources mania. They bought a tiny, two-bedroom cottage in the northwestern suburb of Scarborough for A$230,000 in 2003, always with the intent of knocking it down and building a larger place to accommodate their family of four. But as construction costs soared they could never afford the renovations. By 2011, their two boys were eleven and twelve and still sharing a tiny bedroom. By then their home was worth about A$600,000, almost three times the purchase price—and that was for a place made of fibrous asbestos cement, or "fibro," a cheap building material used in many working-class Australian homes until asbestos-related diseases came on the radar in the 1980s. Scarborough's rising home values were a golden handcuff for the Currans, however, because they could not afford the slightly larger home they needed—houses of that size in their neighborhood now ranged from

A$800,000 to A$900,000. Kelly, who specializes in music, is bitter about the stories she hears from people working "up north"—a friend who does temporary secretarial work and earns A$600 a day with accommodations, meals, and flights home thrown in; a cousin of Anthony's who talks of unskilled mine operators earning A$180 an hour. By contrast, she said, "I might get almost fifty dollars an hour teaching, and have studied for a total of eight years full-time. Yes, OK, four of those years were studying music composition, but because of limited money in the arts, it is extremely difficult to earn any money from this. Mining machinery operators would be unlikely to pay to see classical music concerts, so we 'musos' can't seem to get a positive knock-on effect."

The disparity in salaries creates distorting incentives in career preferences as workers are drawn to the resources sector. Throughout the 2000s, there was a chronic shortage of teachers in Western Australia that was resolved only after the 2008–9 financial crisis slowed the rate of resignations and after the government shipped in foreign graduates. But other sectors kept losing bodies. Western Australian manufacturers lost 17,300 jobs in the two and half years ending in August 2010, while the mining industry added 16,900. Perth's five universities are full, but that's partly due to a large number of Asian students who will take their acquired knowledge home with them. Meanwhile, local students are drawn to fields tied to the resources boom—mining engineering, geology, surveying—while other programs of study, including medicine and science, are less popular. At some point, there will be a glut of geologists in the city.

"There's something to be said for what people call the resource curse, the idea that if you have a huge amount of resources people's brains disappear," says Perth-based political scientist Peter McMahon, who has argued that Western Australia is risking its sustainability as a community because it has thrown all its eggs in the mining-for-export basket. He's especially worried that the state is not confronting the prospect of much higher energy prices, prompted by either global shortages or the imposition of a carbon tax on Australia's coal-fired power plants. That could hit the heavily energy-dependent mining industry hard and impose big burdens on a transportation network that must cover a giant landmass of vast, underpopulated spaces. It would also make costs soar for the fuel-guzzling desalination plants that have kept Perth hydrated ever since a spate of droughts and rapid population growth ran its reservoirs dry. There are some alternatives, but McMahon says the government is ignoring them. "It's ironic: we are probably the best place in the world for renewables—we've got solar, wind, wave, and geothermal. But it's not in the mind-set here," McMahon says. In fact, Western Australia has abundant supplies of natural gas in the Northwest Shelf gas project, which at $25 billion in investment is the biggest resource development in Australia's history. In theory, its gas could fuel the entire state for decades and help lower greenhouse gas emissions to boot. But it's not that easy. The Northwest Shelf's managing consortium has signed long-term supply contracts with foreign buyers in Asia—of which Chinese companies are among the biggest—that are willing to pay a high price to cover their growing energy needs. That locks up supply and raises issues about contractual obligations. But with Western Australians now paying the highest energy prices in Australia, tempers are flaring and both corporate and household energy users are lobbying heavily to force the mostly foreign companies behind the Northwest Shelf consortium to ship more gas south. The issue could breed pressure to break those export contracts. It could even raise delicate sovereignty issues, McMahon says, and the last thing Western Australia needs is a conflict of contractual rights with China, the resource sector's all-important customer.

By 2011, Australia as a whole was showing early signs of what economists call "Dutch disease," a phenomenon where high foreign demand leads to exploitation of natural resources, driving up a country's currency, which in turn undermines manufacturing and other sectors by making exports of those labor-generating industries less competitive. In July 2011, before renewed market turmoil in the United States and the euro zone made investors nervous about commodity-dependent currencies, the Australian dollar hit a high of $1.11. That was the Aussie dollar's strongest point since it was floated twenty-nine years earlier and more than double the lows it hit amid the 1997–98 Asian crisis. It was a key reason why Blue Scope Steel, Australia's largest steelmaker, closed plants and laid off 1,000 workers after reporting a A$1 billion loss in August 2011. For Blue Scope, the benefits of its relative proximity to Western Australia's rich iron ore mines were now outweighed by the lost exchange rate competitiveness that had been fueled by those same miners' sales to China.

Attempting to address mining's distorting impact on the wider economy, former prime minister Kevin Rudd proposed a 40 percent tax on extraordinary mining profits in 2010. But the idea was so vehemently opposed by a mining lobby led by Fortescue's Twiggy Forrest that Rudd's own Labor Party ousted him as the country's leader. The tax was later reintroduced in a less onerous form with a 30 percent levy after a new government led by Julia Gillard struck a truce-making deal with BHP and Rio Tinto. The idea, in theory, was to capture some of the wealth that miners generated when prices were high and to invest it in Australia's future through infrastructure investments as well as to cut corporate tax rates for nonmining companies. But the political opposition against Gillard, whose government's grip on power hinged on the support of four independent members of parliament, meant the measure took two years to introduce, and by then mineral prices were falling. In waiting so long, Australia had missed an opportunity to transfer wealth from booming commodity prices and was less prepared for the day when the gravy train of Chinese money halts. Other resource-rich countries such as oil producer Norway and copper miner Chile have created sovereign wealth funds that rise when international prices are high but can be drawn on when things turn sour. Some economists argue that these "countercyclical" strategies are better pursued by investing commodity windfalls into education and infrastructure—as the Labor government has sought to do—than by accumulating giant rainy-day funds that are invested in U.S. Treasuries or other foreign assets. But in Australia's case, the lack of a clear, politically accepted plan meant that the winnings from the good times could easily have been squandered.

Australia does have a well-regarded "Future Fund" into which the government deposits its budget surpluses, where they are lockboxed so that payments of future pensions and other long-term liabilities are guaranteed—an idea that the United States should consider. Meanwhile, Australia's debt-to-GDP ratio, just 15 percent in 2011 and on a downward path, was the envy of the advanced world; the United States and its European counterparts were pushing close to 100 percent. Australia also boasted a well-funded and highly effective universal health insurance scheme and a mandatory program of privately managed retirement savings that had amassed assets of $1.2 trillion, making it the best-funded social security system in the world. All of that has left Australia in extremely good shape to weather future financial storms. Still, there is a widespread sense among many Aussies that the country is not making the most of its mineral wealth and is wasting its good fortune. After all, throughout this period of prodigious wealth generation, the government continued to run budget deficits.

Miners are fiercely dismissive of the idea that their industry is purely driven by windfall profits. When Australians in the more populous eastern region disparagingly describe Western Australia as a "quarry," miners retort by pointing to the quality of their world-beating technology and know-how, all developed over a history that began with a turn-of-the-century gold rush in a town called Kalgoorlie. This technological proficiency, they say, is as important as the high quality of the ore and the state's proximity to Asia in ensuring that Australian minerals remain competitive in international markets and that the industry continues to develop skills and spread prosperity through other sectors of the economy. It is what allows mining companies to offer such generous terms to FIFO workers, they say, and to maintain high safety and environmental standards. And it is reflected in how Australian mining companies have taken their entrepreneurial verve to all corners of the globe. In part, it explains why BHP Billiton's market capitalization made it the fourth-largest company in the world at the end of 2010.

The industry is also highly diversified, thanks to the great variety of minerals embedded in Western Australia's mineral-rich earth. Although the big iron ore miners get all the press, hundreds of "junior" companies employ tens of thousands of people exploring and developing deposits of nickel, copper, manganese, silver, uranium, diamonds, and gold. The last of these functioned as a welcome stabilizer during the global financial crisis. While BHP, Rio Tinto, and other mega-miners were laying off staff and freezing projects as the price of their products plunged in 2009, many of the nimble, high-tech juniors simply shifted to gold, whose price held steady and later surged as nervous global investors sought a hedge against financial meltdown. (More on this in Chapter 9.) One could even argue that Western Australia's rich gold deposits offer it the equivalent of a sovereign wealth fund, as they provide a countercyclical buffer when demand and prices for its other minerals fall. "The history of Western Australia has been that we have survived every major financial downturn due to our gold industry," said Brian Innes, a Perth-based consultant to the resources sector.

Still, a big downturn in Chinese demand would have a profound impact on Australia's resource industry and on the economy as a whole. China went from accounting for 6 percent of Australia's exports in 2000 to 23 percent in 2010. That concentration leaves Australia's economy vulnerable if China's boom should end. And yet miners seem convinced there's little to worry about. Ian Ashby, the managing director of BHP Iron Ore, explains his company's bullish forecast in terms of China's "nation-building process." Assuming China's future steel needs are similar to those of other countries at the same stage of development in the past, BHP estimates that the consumption and infrastructure demanded by China's 1.4 billion people will require annual steel output to grow to 1 billion metric tons, up from 627 million in 2010; at that point it will start to plateau. That prediction is modeled on Japan's experience during its industrialization period, when installed steel capacity peaked at 120 million tons—that is, once it reached a 1:1 output-to-population ratio. (Japanese demand for steel will rise again in the years ahead on reconstruction needs stemming from the March 2011 earthquake, a tragedy from which Aussie miners stand again to benefit.) BHP assumes that China won't develop into as homogenous a society as Japan, which means steel demand won't be quite as concentrated and thus will fall short of the 1:1 ratio. Nonetheless, the projection amounts to a phenomenal increase over the next decade. And then for decades after that, Ashby said, it will need to keep sustaining its "capital stock of steel," all of which just drives demand for iron ore. Urban China will be a "vertical society," he said, living in high-rises that need a lot of steel. Based on this "bottom-up analysis," which is "stress-tested rigorously," Ashby said, "we from our perspective don't believe there is a bubble [in China]. We believe that from our industry perspective it is healthy and it's likely to be healthy throughout the next decade."

Meanwhile, Australian miners of other products are lining up to benefit from the next promised phase of China's development process: the consumer boom. "Growth in our industry is now all about what is going on with China, with 350 million people moving from the country having to be housed, the building of umpteen airports, and the creation, in a space of just fifteen years, of an underground system in Shanghai," said David Robb, managing director of Iluka, a Western Australia miner of mineral sands. Iluka's products include titanium oxide, whose highly refractive qualities make it a sought-after component for the white pigment that goes into paint, and zircon, which is used in ceramics. The greater the number of shiny-floored Chinese apartments and buildings such as the Guangzhou railway station that get built, the more Iluka's earnings improve. Robb says that when China's per capita GDP surpasses $5,000, it will do as other countries have done and trigger a rapid surge in demand for durable goods, which in turn leads to exponential increases in demand for pigment. Officially, China's per capita income was just below that threshold at $4,300 in 2010, but when adjusted for the effect of its artificially weak currency the figure is already above it, at $7,500, according to IMF estimates. "The Chinese consumption to date that has transformed the world has been for infrastructure, but the next phase is all about the Chinese consumer," Robb said. "I have every confidence that we are now entering that period."

Yet, as demonstrated by the U.S. housing crisis and countless burst bubbles before it, confident extrapolations about the future from current positive trends can prove dangerous. Various things could go wrong for the mining community. BHP and its rivals could find that the surging supply of iron ore from all their expansion plans could catch up with demand quicker than their projections suggest. China's own domestic mine sources could improve, for example. Or technological effects could kick in—improvements in steel smelting techniques or more efficient mechanisms for gathering, transporting, and recycling scrap metal. Or if prices suggest doing so, Chinese builders could shift toward greater amounts of reinforced concrete and less steel in their buildings.

And of course, as was discussed in the preceding chapter, China's overall growth rate could slow, with direct knock-on effects for Australia. By the second half of 2011, fears of precisely that were taking hold as Chinese manufacturing went into decline and the rising stockpile of steel led the country's mills to put their plants through periodic shutdowns. At first iron ore prices proved resilient, but after holding steady at around $177 a metric ton, they plunged in the last quarter of the year to below $120 in late November. Seemingly in anticipation of this correction, the Aussie dollar dropped sharply and temporarily fell back below parity to the U.S. dollar in late September. It later rebounded but remained volatile as hedge funds began selling it as a proxy bet against a downturn in China. The currency was becoming a key gauge of Australia's potentially dangerous dependence on its giant Asian customer.

In many ways Australia's relationship with China reflects the risks of a bubble mind-set: the blind faith in a new, compelling meta-theory that explains relentless price rises, much like the "New Economy" concept of the dot-com era. In this case the narrative is of China's unstoppable advance. But there is nothing guaranteed about that growth, and as we've seen, its continuation depends on the Chinese government successfully engineering an extremely difficult transition to a consumer society, without which it won't be able to pay for its expansion and thus for its future iron ore contracts. Meanwhile, the housing boom in Australia has gone on so long that it has seeped into the mind-set of the average Australian. Through its demand for resources, China may have created the same kind of "bubble thinking" that afflicted the U.S. economy before 2007, itself a result of China's contribution to its supply of cheap credit.

With many cashed-up mining workers borrowing heavily to finance their second and third homes, a downturn in demand for Australian minerals could spiral into systemic risks in home lending. Price-to-income ratios have risen in Perth and other cities to levels far higher than they were in the most bubble-prone regions of the United States before its crisis. Subprime lending is narrowly confined to the nonbank lending sector in Australia and mortgages typically require a 20 percent down payment, providing a buffer against the kind of negative equity dilemma seen in the United States and ensuring that delinquencies remained low as of 2011. But the Australian housing market does breed its own misplaced incentives. It has "negative gearing," for example—the right to a tax deduction based on the difference between interest paid on an investment home loan and lower rental income. Meanwhile, the approval process for foreigners investing in Australian real estate was eased throughout the 2000s, giving Asia's growing class of millionaires a much sought-after alternative destination for their excess savings. In 2010 new approval rules were introduced by the Foreign Investment Review Board, but it may have been a case of too little, too late. By then absentee proprietors were keeping livable home space off the market and driving up prices for those places still available.

This all has big implications for Australia's banks. Although better regulated than their U.S. counterparts and therefore able to weather the 2008 global financial crisis, they have their own risky imbalances. Until it responded to slowing global and domestic demand with two quarter-point rate cuts in the last two months of 2011, the Reserve Bank of Australia's benchmark interest rate carried a 4.75-percentage-point premium over the U.S. Federal Reserve's near-zero rate for a full twelve months. That gap encouraged a surge in cheap foreign currency borrowing by Australian banks and companies. But if a mining slump should drive the Australian dollar lower, those foreign loans could become a burden for Australian institutions. The banks have been frustrated by attempts to lend out that money to the resource companies, mostly because the boom is so strong that miners have enough cash to fund expansions without borrowing. So instead, the banks funnel the proceeds of their foreign borrowings to residential mortgagees, who are now up to their eyeballs in debt. By 2011, Australian household debt stood at 159 percent of disposable income, among the highest such ratios in the world, higher even than the 133 percent peak that the credit-dependent United States hit in 2007.

The biggest worry, therefore, is that a major external economic shock might shut off the jobs-generating export machine—primarily via a sharp downturn in China. Mass layoffs would ensue, leaving many Aussies unable to make their debt payments and giving rise to the specter of a U.S.-style housing crisis. To be sure, a fall in the Aussie dollar would again function as a convenient shock absorber, helping to offset the blow felt by exporters from falling world commodity prices. But a sharp fall in the currency could also provoke debt problems. Although the national government fiscal balance is currently in reasonable shape, the country as a whole runs a large current account deficit. Thus, the combination of currency collapse and job losses could put tremendous pressure on the mountain of private debt owned by the banks. And that could quickly change the fiscal picture for the government. In a worst-case scenario along the lines of what happened in Ireland and Spain, the sovereign might have to take over banks' debts to protect the system, thus transferring the burden to taxpayers and creating all the political and economic tensions seen in those countries. As of late 2011, most economists and credit rating agencies remained sanguine about such risks. They had very favorable views of Australia's well-capitalized banks, which had diversified their funding sources away from credit-crunch-prone international wholesale funding markets. But here again, cautionary lessons must be taken from the United States, where financial analysts and rating agencies also had a rose-colored view of America's financial system right before it was hit by the worst crisis in eighty years.

"All that needs to happen is for China to say, 'We don't need any more of your dirt,' and this whole thing goes away," said Paul Thompson, who was wearing yellow overalls sporting the logo of engineering firm Monadelphous, as he gestured toward dozens of equally colorfully dressed FIFO workers in a Perth Airport departure lounge. "And when that happens, it is going to be total anarchy." Since he knows "it won't last forever," Thompson was milking as much as he could out of China's demand for Australia's "dirt"—in his case, as a welder employed to upgrade Rio Tinto's iron ore handling port in the town of Dampier. The forty-four-year-old has been a FIFO worker for six months and is very much enamored with it. He spends five days a week either working in Dampier or making the 1,000-mile flight to and from Perth, followed by two days off in the city.

The main reason he took the job was the $120,000 annual salary, which he said he needed "to pay for an expensive lifestyle." But Thompson also gets to escape Perth's weekday traffic jams while enjoying the best it has to offer on weekends, which for him means yachting. He told me his ideal day involved racing his fourteen-foot skiff, *Lovebone,* on Perth's Swan River on a balmy afternoon, followed by an evening at his favorite nightspot near the river: an Italian eatery known as El Zucchero. Though I'm no sailor, as a Perth native who loves that river like any, I nodded in appreciation. The city's river, beaches, and wide-open green spaces, all combined with a highly accommodating warm climate, are what give Perth its playground-like appeal. It is a blessed city—and for now at least, the money China is paying for Western Australia's iron-rich dirt is giving people such as Paul Thompson the chance to revel in its blessings.

5

Race to the Bottom: Losers in the Global Economy

Saturday, January 8, 2011, was a classic summer day in Perth. The temperature got to 90 degrees Fahrenheit, and the sun shone from dawn to dusk. In the morning hordes of people took to the beaches, teed off on golf courses, or played tennis. Then, in the midafternoon, when the soothing "Fremantle Doctor" sea breeze swung in from the west as it does around the same time every day, it was time for yachting enthusiasts such as Paul Thompson, the FIFO welder of the previous chapter, to hoist sail and take to the river.

At that very moment, on the other side of the world, a group of employees at a shopping mall in Acapulco, Mexico, was leaving the premises at the end of their Friday night shift. The midnight darkness was broken by the sight of a white Nissan SUV ablaze. One of the group called the local police, who came to investigate. What they found can been seen as a symbol of the deep divide between the global economy's winners in places such as Perth and its losers in places such as Acapulco: a stack of fifteen bodies, each missing its head. The stark contrast between these scenes speaks to the highly uneven way in which China's advance has affected different parts of the world. It reflects the gap between those producing the commodities China needs and the manufacturers that compete with it.

Despite Acapulco's and other Mexican cities' reputations for wanton bloodshed, it is a city bordering El Paso, Texas, one that was once a thriving hub of factories and nightlife, that holds the undisputed title as Mexico's murder capital. In fact, in the three years prior to the Acapulco beheadings, Ciudad Juárez, a city with a population roughly the size of Perth's (1.5 million), had firmly established itself as the most violent place on earth. An accelerating war between rival drug gangs left 1,587 dead in 2008, 2,643 the following year, and 3,111 in 2010, with the killings increasingly carried out by youths of sixteen or younger. The city's murder rate was higher than anything Baghdad experienced during the Iraq war. And if we take into account the fact that some 250,000 former inhabitants are thought to have fled Juárez's violence over the past three years, the ratio of killed to living was likely even higher than official estimates suggest. This descent into madness might seem like a self-contained event, its circumstances explained by Juárez's unique form of dysfunction, but in fact it's intrinsically linked to the changes in the global economy that sucked the city's employment sources dry.

Cut-Price Murders

In seeking to assert dominance over one another within the highly lucrative border trade in cocaine and marijuana, the Juárez gangs set the benchmark for sickening brutality, the standard that the Johnny-come-lately criminals of Acapulco, Reynosa, and Nuevo Laredo have only recently tried to emulate. The national beheading craze began in Juárez, where the nation's attention was grabbed by the gruesome sight of a decapitated body left hanging from an overpass during the morning rush hour on November 7, 2008. The display, which looked down upon a Home Depot outlet, seemed to be a warning that Juárez's gangs were now operating with complete impunity and had decreed that a kind of collective madness would descend upon the city. Hundreds of such signature killings have since followed, many of them timed to optimize TV and press reporters' news-gathering needs, as if the gangs are putting on a ghoulish show for the public. Bereft of effective police who are not on the drug traffickers' payroll, the people of Juárez have been living out an apocalyptic nightmare.

Judging from the tally of dead on the second weekend of 2011, the one during which I visited Juárez, it did not look as if the city's drug-crazed hitmen were about to let up. Acapulco might have grabbed the international headlines that weekend, during which Mexico as a whole saw fifty-three gang-related murders, but it was Juárez that again claimed the highest number overall, with seventeen people slain over the two-day period. The first fifteen pages of the Saturday edition of *PM*, Juárez's daily afternoon tabloid, contained nothing but fully illustrated accounts of gang murders. The front page carried the image of a man's body slumped in the driver's seat of a red Dodge Neon, his severely lacerated body showing the impact of multiple rounds of armor-piercing ammunition. As in so many accounts of such events, the paper cited eyewitnesses noting that after raining bullets on their victims, the adolescent killers had easily fled the scene "without any elements of the various security forces appearing to confront them or try to detain them."

Juvéncio Vázquez López knows too much about this side of Juárez. He runs a private ambulance service and drives one of the vehicles in his fleet. His team is supposed to back up public emergency services at car accidents, but they find themselves increasingly called out to attend to victims of the daily shootouts. He has seen a one-month-old baby die in its mother's arms after being hit by a stray bullet; he has arrived at the scene of what he was told was a "simple accident" only to find that a massacre of eight people had taken place; and he once turned up at a real car accident in which young boys had been severely hurt, only to be ordered by federal police to abandon them and instead attend to two gang leaders injured in a gun battle. And, especially close to home, his brother, a former police officer, was "executed" by gang members, he says.

Vázquez López's current business is an accident of economic circumstance. He had initially set up operations as a security and medical officer for construction sites connected with the *maquiladora* industry. Not surprisingly, however, investors in many *maquila* factories have been scared off—the special tax advantages they earn for exporting their wares don't compensate for the risks of death or kidnapping faced by factory managers and the danger pay they demand in return. After a massive contraction in the industry in 2008 and 2009 due to the U.S. recession, the insecurity has hindered recovery. Instead, Vázquez López has gravitated toward attending victims of accidents and violence. Business is good, he said, "but it comes with big personal risks. This is not how I want to live."

I spoke to Vázquez López inside one of his ambulances. It was parked outside his home in a *colonia* on the outskirts of the city, one of the instant suburbs that state housing agency Infonavit financed in the mid-2000s to try to address the severe housing shortages for the swelling ranks of *maquiladora* workers who had migrated to Juárez from the south. Now, two years of violence had prompted a mass exodus, leaving the *colonias* dotted with abandoned homes that serve as hideouts for drug gangs. While we talked, young boys played war games in an empty lot across the street. They darted in and out of the abandoned homes as if on a search-and-destroy mission in a city under siege, occasionally firing bottle caps at each other with makeshift wooden stick rifles. It was like childhood play everywhere, but it was hard not to imagine they were mimicking the real-life experiences of their older brothers, cousins, and neighbors. "They often come to me and excitedly say, 'Did you see any *sicarios* today?'" said Vázquez López, using a local word for "hitmen." "The children are already sick. They are ill with all the violence they see."

Apart from people such as Vázqez López and my driver and guide, Miguel Macias—whose team of more than twenty trained security guards escorts *maquiladora* managers from their homes in El Paso to their jobs in Juárez—the economic outlook for small-business owners in the city is gloomy. According to the Juárez Restaurants Association, half of all dining establishments closed in the three years leading up to 2011, many shifting operations to El Paso. In a bitter irony, the neighboring Texas city boasts the lowest crime rate in the United States, a natural marketing advantage with which the newly relocated restaurants appeal to those Juárez residents who are free to travel to the United States and prepared to put up with a long wait at the border. Not so long ago, the flow went the other way. The Mexican city, where the margarita cocktail was invented in 1942, was an entertainment mecca, home to countless restaurants, nightclubs, casinos, bars, and hotels. In the mid-2000s, American teenagers would still wander across the International Bridge spanning the Rio Grande to visit watering holes on the Juárez side, where the drinking age was lower and where the scene was far more lively than in El Paso. But the bars on the street next to the bridge have all since closed, replaced by businesses catering to northbound travelers such as moneychangers and travel accessory stores. Meanwhile, those restaurants that still operate in other parts of Juárez now typically serve breakfast and lunch but rarely do dinner, because at night patrons are scared of being the target of a kidnapping or hit with a barrage of bullets.

As incomes from these legitimately derived means plunge amid persistent unemployment and underemployment, a vicious circle gets entrenched through which the gangs further insert themselves into the economy of the city. "Some 5,000 businesses have closed their doors in Ciudad Juárez in my industry," said Ricardo Ziga, president of the restaurants association. "Imagine the sheer quantity of work positions that have been lost. What happens with those people? Obviously, they are simple targets for the criminals to add to their ranks." According to Ziga, the whole process runs off a simple if brutal economic equation: whereas the price for ordering a hit on a rival used to cost drug traffickers more than $10,000, the swollen ranks of unemployed and uneducated teenagers fifteen to seventeen years old—whose status as minors protects them from long jail sentences—have since driven down the cost to $200 for a week's worth of multiple jobs.

Naturally, many level blame for Juárez's nightmare on the failed enforcement policies of both the United States and Mexico, with the former's lax gun control laws allowing a flood of assault weapons to cross the border and the latter unable to contain endemic corruption within its security forces. But this view misses half the story. The border region's problems and the lack of income-earning opportunities that make violence a comparatively appealing option for its young men cannot be viewed in isolation from how the area is situated within the global economy. By virtue of its unique relationship with El Paso, Juárez's well-being has always been dictated by the presence or absence of trade with the United States and the broader world. And from that angle, two dates are critical for understanding the city's decline: January 1, 1994, and December 11, 2001. The first is when the North American Free Trade Agreement, or NAFTA, went into effect. The second is when China became a full-fledged member of the World Trade Organization.

NAFTA prompted a massive migration of people and businesses to Mexican border towns as the *maquiladora* industry burgeoned. The border region had always been a powerhouse in global manufacturing, owing to its proximity to the United States, comparatively low wages, and the *maquiladora* model, which gives foreign investors special rights to engage in export activity. But it wasn't until tariffs came down in the United States after the 1994 pact that the *maquila* factories entered a new and explosive period of expansion. Juárez in particular became a magnet for NAFTA-inspired businesses, mostly on account of its deeply intertwined relationship with El Paso, which in 1981 was deemed a U.S. Foreign Trade Zone with special customs privileges, and because three-quarters of the Texas city's population speak Spanish at home. In 1995, Juárez proudly inaugurated a new technical plant for giant U.S. auto parts maker Delphi—which at that time was still a unit of General Motors—employing more than 2,000 people to test the performance of new car components. Swedish appliance maker Electrolux also boosted its presence in the region. But the biggest boom occurred among the small and medium-sized local- and foreign-owned factories making everything from clothes to toys to consumer electronics, all for shipment across the border. Initially, these businesses had an insatiable demand for labor, which meant the city added half a million residents through the second half of the 1990s as job seekers flooded in from the south. As the migrants kept coming, the ineffectual local government could not keep up, leaving the new arrivals squeezed into shantytowns with big shortfalls in schools, housing, and other infrastructure. At that time at least, unemployment was never a problem—the *maquiladora* industry soaked up all the incoming adults. It was their kids, left at home by their working parents, who became the problem.

"All this formed a highly productive broth for the narco-traffickers," says Rocio Gallegos, a journalist from the newspaper *El Diario* in Juárez. Having covered Juárez's mounting violence since 1996, Gallegos has learned all too intimately of its causes and its outcomes. Outside her office sits the empty cubicle of photographer Armando "El Choco" Rodríguez, with a dried rose and a sign bearing the words "El Choco Is Here" resting against his untouched computer. Rodríguez, one of two *El Diario* reporters to have lost their lives to reprisal killings by the cartels since 2008, was gunned down just as he was about to pull out of his driveway to take his eight-year-old daughter to school. Gallegos finds the roots of such tragedies in the early neglect that the children of *maquiladora* workers suffered. She estimates that 60,000 youths never studied and never worked, and that many of these became drug addicts. "They did not need incomes from their families so much, they needed drugs," she said. "And who was there to give it to them?"

When Gallegos began her job, Juárez was already gripped by violence. Shortly after the NAFTA-fueled wave of immigrants began, hundreds if not thousands of young *maquiladora* women were killed or never seen again in an epidemic that went unsolved. But even after that horrific beginning, things would get much worse. Juárez's descent into a new, even scarier version of hell began at the start of the new millennium. The catalyst was the twin events of a U.S. recession at the end of the dot-com boom and China's entrance into the WTO, which meant that U.S. tariffs were cut on that country's products. Not only did the overall volume of U.S. demand for Mexican products drop in the downturn, but Mexican exporters now found themselves losing their share of that shrinking market to an increasing influx of low-cost Chinese goods. Over the course of the next decade, their competitive edge steadily deteriorated. Mexican producers could not compete against the undervaluation of the yuan relative to the U.S. dollar, with which the peso tends to be closely correlated. On so many other counts as well—versus China's policy-induced high savings and low interest rates, for example, as well as its heavy investment in transportation and energy—Mexico's creaking bureaucracy and dysfunctional infrastructure were no match for China's efficiency. It still had its location and low wages as a strategic advantage, but even these were not enough to help it match the "China price."

As China doubled its share of the U.S. import market to replace Mexico as its biggest goods supplier over the course of the decade, it made especially significant headway in labor-intensive industries. In 2000, Mexico had dominated the U.S. clothing market, for example, accounting for 14.7 percent of America's textile and apparel imports, according to U.S. Census Bureau statistics. But by 2008, its share had dropped to 5.3 percent. Over the same period, China went from 11.3 percent of all textile and apparel sales to almost half of the entire U.S. market. This and other market share losses played out in a sharp boom-bust cycle within the *maquiladora* industry, which counts among its members many fleet-footed smaller firms that are willing and able to move quickly in and out of a region. In the first seven years after NAFTA went into effect, the sector added 1,545 firms and 730,000 employees, according to data from an industry council, but in the three years after the 2001 recession it lost 820 firms and 230,000 jobs. The U.S. economic recovery and a surge in outsourcing activity restored growth after 2004, but then the 2007 recession and subsequent financial crisis set in, which all but wiped out the gains. Jobs finally began growing again in 2009, as U.S. companies turned to low-paid Mexican labor to preserve their profit margins in an environment of weak demand. But even then there have been big setbacks, especially in violence-riddled Juárez, which lost out to Memphis, Tennessee, in the bidding for Electrolux's new 1,200-job kitchen appliance factory. Against such international challenges, the *maquiladoras* are compelled to compete on the one thing they can: low wages. In its way, it shows the workings of the "China price" and helps explain how a generation of young shantytown dwellers, the children of the migrants who'd moved there in the 1990s, lost their way. Not enough jobs were being created to absorb them, and what work there was earned a pitiful income. The drug cartels offered this unemployed, wayward youth an alternative.

To comprehend why, consider the financial price paid by those who have resisted the pressure to join the gangs, people such as twenty-nine-year-old Deissy Marquéz, who chatted with me along with other *maquiladora* workers in a shantytown strewn with waste and crumbling buildings. They live in a depressing, desolate place, where thousands of cast-off plastic bags flutter from the scraggly trees and barbed-wire fences to which they've become attached. Sitting around the well-worn Formica kitchen table of her neighbor Ruth Rodriguez, in a tiny house of rough brickwork and exposed concrete floors, Deissy said she earned 49 pesos, or $4, per day working in a factory making fire alarms. She had just received her annual raise of an additional one peso per day, the same nominal increase she'd received the two previous years. With annual inflation averaging more than 4 percent over that time, those three meager adjustments had left her employer with a 2 percent cost savings in real terms every year, while Marquéz was worse-off. As is the case with every other member of the world's poor, food takes up a disproportionately high share of her budget, and at the time we spoke there had been rapid inflation in that sector throughout the world. In December 2010, the agricultural produce component within the Mexican consumer price index registered an annual gain of 7 percent. The biggest contributor to that was corn, whose price on international commodity exchanges rose a massive 62 percent that year. Here too the impact from China's expansion was evident: the Chinese demand for wheat and soybeans that is transforming Argentina's rural landscape fueled competition for scarce farming land at the same time as much of the U.S. corn harvest was being diverted to ethanol production. This drove up the cost of the corn tortillas on Marquéz's weekly grocery bill, even though a government subsidy program had had some success in anchoring prices for the Mexican staple.

Of course, her rising food bill is not the only way in which Marquéz's standard of living has been undermined by Juárez's failure to compete in the global economy. Like everyone else's in the city, her life has undergone a serious qualitative decline as well: friends of hers who've gone missing are now counted as statistics among *las perdidas*—the lost women—and weeks before our meeting two teenage boys from around the corner had been shot dead at the entrance to their home. Marquéz says that with the values inculcated by her parents and mentors such as her neighbor Ruth Rodriguez, she knows that the world of drugs and gangs is a one-way path to ruin. But she is frustrated by the pitiful amount of money she makes and recognizes that the adolescent boys of her neighborhood, unsupervised by either schoolteachers or parents, could easily come to a different conclusion. To earn $200 to carry out a spate of killings for a gang leader, even with the risk of a five-year jail sentence, might to them be an attractive proposition in a city where a menial *maquiladora* job pays too little to cover the cost of tortillas.

The rise of the drug trade in northern Mexico over the past decade can be explained by applying the same kind of cost-benefit analysis at a higher level. As opportunities in cocaine trafficking opened up amid the setbacks suffered by Colombia's narco-guerrillas, the business offered distinct financial advantages over legitimate exporting activities. Its market, dominated by addicts, was far more resistant to recession than that of other products. And unlike the legitimate output of the *maquiladoras,* the drug business was not challenged by Chinese competition. What's more, virtually every part of the cocaine and marijuana supply chain used dollars, which left it immune to the competitive ups and downs caused by changes in the peso or the yuan. For all these reasons the payoff from drugs seemed higher than that of alternative income-generating activities and, to many at least, worth the risks associated with it. Thus drugs filled a vacuum that Chinese competition had left in other parts of the Mexican economy.

The total flows are massive. The cartels are estimated to bring in $40 billion a year from their various operations—from smuggling cocaine and marijuana to extortion and kidnappings. Sums of that magnitude leave plenty left over after the pittances paid to adolescent traffickers and hitmen, even after buying off cops and politicians. Amounting to a quarter of the total value of all officially recorded Mexican exports to the United States in 2010, the trade's revenues dwarf the $500 million annual contribution that the United States makes to the military-led campaign that President Felipe Calderón launched against the gangs in 2006. And whereas Mexico's legal commerce is spread across a wide array of large and small firms with countless shareholders, this illegal one is concentrated among only a handful of cartels, each of which covets the others' businesses. As in the legal business world, takeover battles tend to arise when sales are booming. It's just that instead of making plays for shareholders with financial enticements, the primary means of forcing a consolidation in this industry is through violence. The cheapest and easiest way to carry that out is to recruit lackeys from the shantytowns, where the ranks of unemployed and underemployed youths have risen sharply with the *maquiladoras*' loss of U.S. market share to their Chinese competitors.

Competitive Advantage

Going into 2011, the competition-with-China story was not all bad news for the Mexican economy, just as the Asian giant's boom was not all good news for Australia. Mexico should always have two distinct advantages: proximity to the United States and a flexible exchange rate, which means its costs automatically adjust lower in foreign currency terms when times get tough. Because of Mexican exporters' dependence on U.S. markets, the peso strongly correlates with the dollar. So while the greenback fell against most other currencies throughout 2010 and early 2011 as the Federal Reserve kept monetary policy at hyperloose levels, the peso weakened with it, including against the yuan, as China took incremental steps toward revaluing its currency. Mexico is in this sense a nonbelligerent participant in the much ballyhooed "currency wars," emerging as a kind of freeloading beneficiary from the fact that exporters in other developing countries tend to be more harshly hurt by a weaker dollar. Meanwhile, rising labor costs in China are now giving second thoughts to some foreign investors who previously moved operations there in preference over Mexico. Flextronics, yet another maker of integrated circuit boards as well as other electronic goods and components, beefed up its Mexican operations on account of this shift.

"There is convergence in the hourly wages of manufacturing across the world," Mexican finance minister Ernesto Cordero told me in an interview in early 2011. "The great advantage that China had in the past is vanishing. Now the gap between wages of China and Mexico is 13 percent, whereas eight years ago it was more than 200 percent." Cordero said his government's investment in infrastructure, worth about 5 percent of GDP annually, especially in transportation, has accentuated his country's advantages with regard to its proximity to the United States. This has boosted investment and exports in recent years. No longer the domain of "cheap manufacturers," as Cordero described the industries that first took advantage of NAFTA, the emphasis is now on value-added output. Half of the BlackBerrys produced for Canada's Research in Motion group are produced in Mexico, and there is also a vibrant aerospace industry. "We don't design planes, but you can be pretty sure that the plane you're flying in has components that were made in Mexico," the finance minister said.

Cordero was preparing for a presidential campaign at that time, so it's not surprising he would paint such a rosy picture of an economy he oversees. Unfortunately, the image that much of the world has of Mexico is that of a lawless, violence-ridden place, an image almost entirely shaped by the collapse of law and order and the mass killings in the border region. But whereas Juárez's murder rate in 2010 stood at 207 per 100,000 inhabitants—the highest for any city in the world—the figure for Mexico nationwide was 18.7, considerably less than that of Brazil, Venezuela, and a host of other Latin American countries. Indeed, Mexico's murder rate is about a third of the rate in New Orleans, and half of Detroit's and Baltimore's. It's perhaps not very fair then that some foreign policy wonks in think tanks such as STRATFOR, a geopolitical risk consultancy, have described Mexico as "failed state," a label that would put it on par with ungovernable African nations such as Somalia and Zimbabwe. The truth is that resource-rich Mexico is not only part of NAFTA but also a respected, democratic member of both the Group of 20 nations and the Organisation for Economic Co-operation and Development. Its finances and monetary balances are in sound shape, as evidenced by its investment-grade credit rating, which helped it sell two 100-year bonds worth $1 billion each in 2010 and 2011. It even boasts the world's richest man, Carlos Slim. And although that could speak to Mexico's failed anti-trust regulations and poor distribution of wealth more than anything else, it also reflects the benefits of free trade.

But although average incomes across Mexico are rising, an opposite reality confronts Deissy Marquéz and other marginalized residents of Juárez. For them, the damage has already been done by the competitive blow that the region's exporters took from Chinese competitors. The city's descent into chaos ensures that improving wage differentials won't help Juárez recover what was lost. The violence must stop before investors can return.

Juárez's new mayor, Héctor Murguía Lardizábal, liked to claim some success in the fact that "only" 1,428 killings were registered in the first eight months of 2011, a decline of 29 percent from the same period a year earlier. For this, Lardizábal credited Julián Leyzaola, the city's new hard-line police chief, whom the mayor nicknamed "Rambito" (Little Rambo). Meanwhile, a small number of large manufacturers in labor-intensive industries were testing the waters in Juárez as wages rose in China. Foxconn, the Taiwanese-Chinese behemoth that we met in earlier chapters, had expanded operations there, and a few other Taiwanese manufacturers were expressing interest, according to Manuel Ochoa, vice president of binational development at the El Paso Regional Economic Development Corporation. But there was no sign that the hundreds of small and medium-sized *maquiladoras* that once had fueled the city's jobs machine were coming back. After all, Juárez was still on target to top the world homicide rankings again in 2011.

It wasn't supposed to be like this. The city and others on the border were to be the vanguard of Mexico's advance into the global economy, the manufacturing hubs from which more and better jobs would be created. But although some big-name foreign companies such as Delphi and Electrolux have stayed in Juárez, in part because it's too costly to leave, it's unlikely that new entrants into high-tech, value-added industries will use this dangerous town as their base—not when improved transportation makes viable some of the safer options in the south. Meanwhile, the few smaller *maquiladoras* that stay do so because it's cheap, because they find people such as Marquéz whose only options are to accept their meager wages or work for the drug gangs.

These people, the poor of Juárez, are trapped in a race to the bottom. Even in the crime business, incomes per incident are dropping as armed youths have started freelancing their extortion jobs, acting independently of the cartels. Ransoms for kidnappings used to run to many thousands of dollars, but in 2010 demands of no more than $100 were sometimes reported. And whether the ransom was paid or not, the victim or the perpetrators often ended up dead anyway. On the flip side, the cheapening of crime, which in a supply-demand dynamic reflects how widespread it has become, makes doing business in Juárez more expensive, both in terms of the costs firms must incur for private security and in the mental anguish their managers endure for working there. The premium that companies demand in return for bearing such costs is that wages stay low. It's another market mechanism, one that drives the poor of the border region down the value chain rather than up. Juárez's nightmare demonstrates that the benefits of Mexico's trade-led growth have not been well spread and have left big parts of the country more vulnerable than others to changes in the global economic landscape, especially to the disruptive effects of China's ascent.

As Mexico's voters prepare for presidential elections in 2012, the left—led by firebrands such as Mexico City's former mayor Andrés Manuel López Obrador—will roll out their usual critiques of NAFTA and U.S. imperialism. But divisions within Obrador's Party of the Democratic Revolution (PRD) seem likely to ensure victory to candidates from either Calderón's National Action Party (PAN) or the Institutional Revolutionary Party (PRI), which ruled Mexico for eight decades until PAN's Vicente Fox came to power in 2000. Neither party has any interest in rocking the boat, and in the grand scheme of things that is a good thing. Mexico would do great damage to itself if it turned its back on free trade.

And yet Mexico's voters could do worse than to force a debate over *fair* trade and global economic reforms during the electoral period. The country's membership in global forums such as the G20 gives it a platform to do this, and its experience gives it both a right and a duty to be more vocal on that world stage. The stark contrasts and imbalances that define Mexico's economy and society stem directly from imbalances in the global economy, particularly those that favor Chinese manufacturers, such as China's exchange rate manipulation. Carlos Slim wins in that global system, whereas Deissy Marquéz loses. And as we'll see below in an examination of Indonesia's lopsided trade with China, free trade is no panacea for a country's ills if the playing field is sloping sharply in one team's favor. Developing countries need a bigger voice in reshaping the global financial system.

This is not merely a concern for developing nations. Integrating these countries into an international system of coordinated policies matters to everyone, including Americans such as my James Street neighbor, Scott. If we are to correct the problem of global imbalances and restore opportunities for U.S. producers and workers on the global stage, the rising cost of Chinese labor and five-year plans aimed at bolstering consumers won't go far enough. Low-paid Chinese jobs are already moving to places such as Indonesia and Mexico, or to poorer nations such as Bangladesh and

Vietnam, but it is not in the international community's economic interest for those places to stay trapped in a global system that prevents a broad underclass from ascending the value chain. By many measures, developing countries such as Mexico and Indonesia *are* playing by the rules in a way that China does not—they are more or less democratic, they practice free trade, and they don't use currency and banking policies as a mercantilist tool to help industry. These smaller countries' models need to be given a fair chance, or else the incomes—and spending power—of people such as Deissy Marquéz will continue to slide. And that only means these countries' markets will never provide the kind of sales opportunities that American and other developed-country producers of high-end goods and services are hankering for. Only when we jointly create a more equitable market system, a global level playing field on which competition is not only intense but also fair, will we unleash the innovative and productive energy needed to give people such as Marquéz a chance to improve their lot and join a giant global marketplace of consumers.

The Shoemakers

Indonesian garment manufacturers and shoemakers, who are among their country's biggest employers, know these challenges well and have seen them become more acute with the rise of China. As in other Southeast Asian nations, consumers in Indonesia have provided a convenient outlet for China's excess textile production ever since the Association of South East Asian Nations, of which Indonesia is a member, brought a free trade agreement (FTA) with the giant Asian nation into effect in 2010. That pact landed at an ideal time for China, because the United States and Europe had reduced their clothing imports in the wake of the global financial crisis, but it came at perhaps the worst time for Indonesia's textile industry, which was already grappling with competition from China for access to the clothing markets of the United States and other countries. Leaders of the industry believed that by opening up their own domestic market to Chinese products, their government risked signing the death warrant of the Indonesian garment trade. "Our main worry is not the exporter market," said Enorvian Ismy, secretary general of the Indonesian Textile Association, "because there everybody plays by the rules; in the U.S. we have the market for polyester and rayon blends while China has the cotton. The problem is the Indonesian market, where Indonesia's only rule is that anybody can compete. That's why we have had a deficit with China since 2004 and it's why I asked the trade minister, 'Why did you make an FTA with China? Why not make it with the United States? But not with China, not with our competitor.'"

Ismy and other producers complain that while their Chinese competitors enjoy artificially low interest rates and a pegged cheap exchange rate, their own government's adherence to international norms on free markets saddles them with the highest borrowing rates in Asia and a floating exchange rate that's making them less competitive. As with Australia's two-speed economy, Indonesia's commodities sector—led by products such as petroleum, coal, and palm oil—is enjoying a surge in foreign earnings due to Chinese demand for food and energy, while the manufacturing sector, in which most of its 220 million people work, struggles under rising energy costs and a burdensome exchange rate. Manufacturers also complain that the country's newly installed form of inclusive democracy, a 180-degree turn from the highly centralized system under the Suharto dictatorship that ended in 1998, is flawed. It makes it harder to achieve infrastructure improvements such as highway or port expansions because the projects require the signature of popularly elected regional leaders whose first instinct is to oppose them.

China, by contrast, with its state-sponsored transportation expansion, "is like a never-ending red carpet" for investors, says Hendrik Sasmito, chairman of the PT Panarub group of companies, which makes sports shoes for big brand names such as Adidas of Germany, Mizuno of Japan, and New Balance of the United States. "As you go inland, you always have the next town that is ready for development and ready for you to invest." Samito's plant is near Jakarta's chaotic, polluted Tanjang Priok port, which he says is the only viable place to build a factory, given transportation costs. "And that means the cost of land is much higher, because everybody comes here," he said. "Whereas in China, what happens? You move inland, they give you the factory. You just come in and turn the key. They have these old state factories and they don't want them empty, so you just move in. That makes a big difference to your working capital."

Despite these competitive imbalances, trade minister Mari Pangestu remains a strong supporter of the ASEAN free trade agreement that she signed. She acknowledges industry concerns but believes free trade will be a catalyst for reform within Indonesia to make its companies more productive, more innovative, and capable of achieving the holy grail of value-added production. She cites the case of the Kedaung Group, a forty-one-year-old Indonesian glassware and crockery maker that in recent years found it could no longer compete with the plain white ceramic cups and plates made by China. "So they adjusted. First, they imported the plain ones [from China], and they added value to them, with printing. Second, they went into medium and upper-end markets, working with creative industries. . . . They have a range with [Indonesian fashion designer] Ghea Panggabean. They even have a batik line."

Pangestu is under no illusions about the threat from China, however. Citing that country's new move into making prayer mats and the pilgrim outfits that Indonesian Muslims wear on the haj to Mecca, Pangestu describes its advance into all areas of production as "scary." She believes China needs to rebalance its economy and revalue its currency. "It is part of the [global] structural imbalances that have to be corrected. We agree that there is a fundamental problem there," she said over Javanese coffee at the Trade Ministry's headquarters in Jakarta. But she also believes Indonesia cannot use such complaints as an excuse to hide from free trade. "People might say Indonesians are not industrious. But I think we are creative. And that's what we are trying to tap into," she said, mentioning the country's rich cultural diversity, its democracy, and its comparatively open society as providing a competitive advantage.

Even before the free trade agreement opened the floodgates to cheap

Chinese imports, Indonesian clothing makers faced competition from the same producers overseas. After the international quota system governing textile trade was phased out in accordance with the global trade treaty that led to the WTO in 1994, a move that ended the distortions that had turned tiny countries such as Mauritius and Honduras into improbable clothing production hubs, Indonesia had a strong opportunity to boost its market share in the United States and Europe. But it couldn't keep up with China. The U.S. Office of Textiles and Apparel reports that while China's share of the American clothing market went from one-eighth in 1999 to just under one-half in 2010, Indonesia's share oscillated between 3 and 4 percent over the entire time. (This was while Mexico's plunged from 15 percent to 7 percent.)

In 1997, at the beginning of a financial crisis that would see longtime dictator Suharto deposed amid an orgy of ethnic conflict, Ina Indrawati and her mother, Wiwih Reksono, surveyed the international competitive environment for shoes. They decided that Wimo, the company Reksono had run for thirty-one years, could no longer succeed in the high-volume business of producing footwear on behalf of foreign companies. "There was no way we could compete with China," Indrawati said. "Once they joined the WTO, forget it. They stole everything." Instead she refocused the company on the local market, selling high-quality women's shoes on a niche marketing basis. "Now we've decided that we never want to go back to the export market again unless they buy our own brands." By running a boutique operation with key specializations—including offering custom-made shoes by mail order for people with odd-shaped feet and orthopedic needs—Indrawati has managed to survive the competitive threat from China. But the experience has left her aware of her country's limitations. "As a manufacturing country, it is impossible for Indonesia to compete," she said. "The resources are not there, the people are not there, the raw materials are not there, and the infrastructure is not there."

The sports shoe industry is perhaps the exception that proves the rule here, but this in part reflects the fact that Indonesian producers have strived to keep labor costs down, perpetuating the same race-to-the-bottom strategy that has condemned parts of Mexico to social decay and that works against the goal of value-added production. Indonesian sports shoe makers have become just one in a series of alternative production sites for the owners of big U.S. and European brand names, which tend to diversify their choices of outsourced suppliers across low-wage developing countries to minimize risks to supply associated with political disruptions or rising labor costs. After losing much of that business following the crisis of 1997–98, in the late 2000s Indonesian sports shoe makers began to win orders away from Thailand, which got a bad name from the clashes between soldiers and "Red Shirt" government activists in 2010, and saw some modest relocation from China as wages there rose. Still, Sasmito of Panarub warns that if the Indonesian government doesn't improve the business environment, this fleet-footed foreign business could again just up and leave. "We have the momentum now and we have to try and catch it, otherwise the opportunity goes. These fish don't stay around along," he said.

Rising to Sasmito's rallying call is easier said than done. The high interest rates, uncompetitive exchange rate, and poor infrastructure mean that even more pressure is brought to bear on keeping wages down. In addition, a delicate balance is required to manage the political sensitivities of Indonesia's poor and culturally diverse society. A visit to Panarub's 20-hectare compound offers a window into that challenge.

Whereas Sasmito and other senior staff members are ethnic Chinese, the bulk of his 11,000 employees are Muslim Javanese women, many of them conservatively dressed in *jilbab,* wraparound head scarves. They sit in well-organized assembly lines inside three 850-foot-long sheds, busily operating thousands of sewing machines that Sasmito recently imported from China. (At $1,000 each, their cost was a marked decline from the 5,500 Deutschmarks, or $3,600, that Panarub paid for their predecessors in the 1990s.) Amid the incessant whirring of needles, the workers focus on highly specialized tasks. Boards with numbers set the target time for each cycle—a goal of 27.7 seconds was posted above a stitching table, for example. Some of the staff operate machines that cut out nylon pieces for the shoes' upper portions, others stitch pieces of fabric together, some punch holes in them, and some simply thread shoelaces. At the end of the line, workers busily check that everything is in order in colorful shoeboxes marked with the logos of the giant foreign brands that will sell their contents for prices close to $100 a pair. At the end of the day, these employees will have jointly pumped out 20,000 pairs of shoes. For doing so, most earn a base salary that's not far above Jakarta's minimum wage, which was set at 1.5 million rupiah ($166) a month for 2012.

Panarub has a history of tense relations with its workers. In the years following the anti-Chinese riots that exploded in 1998, when angry mobs gathered outside its gates and threw Molotov cocktails into the compound, the company kept a tight lid on wages and worker activities, believing that would help it compete with the rising challenge from China and woo back foreign investors who'd been frightened off by the turmoil. But the strategy backfired after a twenty-eight-year-old union leader was jailed for organizing a strike at Panarub in 2001. The incident prompted Oxfam Australia to launch an investigation into the company and other Indonesian producers of foreign brands. The unwelcome international attention led Adidas, Panarub's primary client, to press the Indonesian firm's management to permit union membership. In retrospect, Sasmito sees the case as a catalyst for positive change. It "allowed us to change our paradigm quickly," he said. "Before, we saw unions differently; we never knew how to communicate with them. But that has changed."

Although labor rights groups acknowledge progress, Adidas and Panarub continue to come under fire for their treatment of workers. In October 2010, Oxfam again wrote to Adidas urging the German company to force Panarub to reinstate thirty-three union activists who were dismissed five years earlier for demanding higher pay. It also called on Adidas to support Muslim workers' demands for an increase in their annual Ramadan daily allowance from 5,000 rupiah to 12,000 to cover the rising cost of food ingredients for the evening ritual of breaking the fast. When I asked about the two cases, an Adidas spokesperson said the company had "responded to requests from Oxfam Australia to help the former union members find new employment through sharing information on open positions within our supply chain and . . . by engaging a local NGO to facilitate and support with job placements for those few workers who have yet to secure jobs." As for the Ramadan allowance, she said no such allowance existed and that it was an internal employer-employee matter in which Adidas would not interfere.

The food allowance case, which was spurred by worker angst over the rising price of palm oil, further highlights the tensions unleashed by a lopsided trade relationship with China. Even though palm oil is produced in great quantities in Indonesia, China's insatiable demand for it is driving up domestic prices—as with soy in Argentina, corn in Mexico, and foodstuffs of various kinds elsewhere. So at the same time that labor-intensive manufacturers such as Panarub are struggling to keep wages low in order to compete with China, Chinese demand for Indonesian commodities is creating inflation in the cost of living for those companies' workers. It's a recipe for industrial conflict.

The hope is that Indonesia's fledgling democracy makes the country better able to deal with such tensions than it was during the tightly controlled Suharto era, which left them bottled up for years until they exploded in fury. Removing that risk was a big plus for politically conscious foreign buyers such as Adidas. Sasmito even argues that because Indonesia has already been through that blowup, it has a more politically certain outlook than China. He also says that because China is more aggressively pushing education and technological advancement, Indonesia's similarly large pool of migrant laborers enjoys the blessing in disguise of being less educated, keeping a comparatively large low-skill population for employers to draw from. "In China, with its one-child policy, the last thing a parent would think is, 'I wish my son would work in a clothing factory,'" Sasmito said, punctuating the comment with a hearty laugh.

But it's not as if Indonesians don't have aspirations, or that these won't grow as they witness some of their countrymen get rich from palm oil plantations or coal mine concessions. That was clear even during a somewhat stage-managed interview with a Panarub seamstress who worked on an assembly line producing Adidas's Predator line of soccer boot—a premier product made famous by the endorsement of English star David Beckham. The twenty-two-year-old, who gave her name as Dinarni, told me she was intent on saving enough of her monthly salary of 2 million rupiah ($220) to put her two younger brothers through high school back in her hometown of Pemalang in central Java. After they'd graduated, she said, she would study communications. Dinarni misses her mother's cooking, especially a coconut milk dish known as *sayur lodeh,* but knows there's little hope of financial advancement back in Pemalang. The going rate for unhusked rice was 1,500 rupiah a kilogram, she said, which meant that her father's annual output of 6,000 kilos would bring home 9 million rupiah, or under $1,000 a year.

Dinarni's value proposition is thus very similar to that faced by a rural resident of China, someone like Wang Shen Ju, the assembly worker from Hubei province whom we met at Dingling Electric in Shanghai. The incentives to take the factory job in the city are high. What neither Dinarni nor her faraway Chinese counterparts would have fathomed when they took that option, though, is that their competition with each other might one day undermine their job security. In 2006, as producers in China and Vietnam ate into Indonesia's share of the global sports shoe market, two Korean-owned factories not far from Panarub's compound laid off some 10,500 workers who'd been producing Adidas shoes. According to Oxfam, only 1,500 were reabsorbed by other suppliers of the German sportswear giant. Such is the tenuous nature of employment in an industry whose buyers can easily shift outsourced production from one country to another if costs or political risks rise.

In the meantime, over a decade in which it expanded operations, partly by acquiring rival Reebok, Adidas has taken its brands to the pinnacle of world sport, with great financial payoffs to its shareholders. By shifting production to wherever it could lock in the lowest purchase price, Adidas achieved a juicy gross profit margin of almost 50 percent throughout most of those ten years. And at the same time, by aggressively promoting its brands in conjunction with three World Cup tournaments, for which it enlisted the endorsements of some very well-paid sports stars, Adidas grew its sales to $12 billion in 2010, a gain of 15.5 percent from the previous year, while its net profit more than doubled to $567 million. Throughout this time, David Beckham was taking in the fruits of a lifetime contract for associating his name with the same Predator shoe that Dinarni makes on a wage of about $10 a day. For that deal, signed in 2003, Beckham was paid £100 million. At the time, it was the biggest-ever deal for a commercial endorsement.

This offers another example of how the global economic system is fixed in favor of those commanding a monopoly on certain forms of production, in this case the business of advertising and brand management, while it throws up insurmountable barriers to others in their efforts to advance themselves. Contrary to popular wisdom, Adidas is not a shoemaker; it is a manufacturer of customer loyalty, loyalty to an idea, an image. There, in that ill-defined world of intangible assets and branding strategy, resides the true value-added power in the global manufacturing economy. Meanwhile, the real business of shoemaking, the industry that PT Panarub is in, has become commoditized. So long as the world supply of labor across developing countries is sufficiently large to keep it that way, Adidas can go anywhere to source the physical product to which it attaches its famous brand. Above all, the German company has the concept of the China price to thank for this profitable scenario. With the help of its targeted monetary, fiscal, industrial, and social policies, China has set the bar low for the costs that Adidas can now demand from all of its suppliers, playing them off against each other. And even if China becomes too expensive, the benchmark has now been set. That takes care of the cost side of the business and ensures that Adidas has plenty of working capital with which to engage David Beckham in the more uncertain enterprise of creating a branding hit.

Meanwhile, as assembly line workers in places such as Indonesia, China, Vietnam, and Mexico strive for a bigger portion of the global profit pie, their capacity to do so is hindered by the inequities in this unevenly balanced global economic system. They depend on their respective governments to enact policies that keep production costs low enough so that the other countries' producers don't siphon their jobs away. So long as middle-class consumers around the world keep forking over billions of dollars for sports shoes, and so long as Beckham and his cohorts help to maintain these shoppers' enthusiasm for Adidas's brands, there may be enough demand to keep most of the current Indonesian, Vietnamese, Chinese, and other nations' workers employed making its shoes. But as the crises of 1997–98 in Asia and 2008–9 in the United States showed, this global system is prone to bouts of turmoil. When the next one hits, it might deliver a portfolio loss to the likes of Beckham and Adidas's biggest shareholders, but ultimately they'll ride it out just fine. Dinarni and her colleagues, by contrast, will have to worry about how to feed themselves.

PART TWO

The Rise of Global Finance

6

Global Finance Between a Rock and a Hard Place: Too Big to Fail *and* Too Big to Succeed

From the Renaissance, when the House of Medici financed the extravagances of the Vatican and Europe's monarchies, to the Napoleonic Wars, when the Rothschilds bankrolled Britain's war effort, to the Wall Street panic of 1907, when J. Pierpont Morgan received anti-trust immunity so he could save the United States from financial collapse, banking and governance have long gone hand in hand. In greasing the wheels of economic development, and in funding imperial ventures, financiers have made and broken political dynasties for centuries. Good or bad, it is a fact of life that the most powerful economic nations have been those with powerful banks. Without banks there would have been no Industrial Revolution, Western nations would not have urbanized, and arts and culture would have taken a very different path. Equally, without political support, whether through central bank lending or government guarantees, banks' businesses would have been too unstable to deliver on such far-reaching economic projects.

But if government's cozy relationship with finance has been almost unavoidable, it has also sat uncomfortably with popular politics. Once democracies became more assertive, the concentration of power in the hands of financial elites and the privileges they received from political protection became a contentious issue. That was especially so in the vibrant democracy of the United States, where the tension between those who supported a role for government in backstopping the financial sector and those who wanted banks to sink or swim like the rest of society was manifest in the raging debates between Alexander Hamilton and Thomas Jefferson. Hamilton believed in the importance of a central bank to provide stability and promote economic development; Jefferson believed such an institution was unconstitutional and undemocratic.

Twentieth-century history mostly affirmed Hamilton's position. No doubt Texas congressman and perennial presidential candidate Ron Paul's strong following of anti-Fed supporters will read that history through a different lens, but few mainstream economists or financial historians will argue that the 1913 creation of the Federal Reserve System wasn't a constructive development for the U.S. economy. It reduced the frequency of financial crises and eased the market uncertainty that persisted between 1870 and 1913, a period in which a de facto gold standard prevailed without an official lender of last resort. The Fed wasn't perfect—as the debacle of the Great Depression proved—but after that tragedy, its crisis management improved, mostly because additional regulations curtailed the financial sector's capacity to take excessive risk. Those strict rules created a politically acceptable quid pro quo between a Hamiltonian government backstop and public restrictions on banks' power. The rest of the century saw relative financial security until its very end, when those regulations were dismantled and the political balance collapsed in banks' favor. This set the stage for the worst crisis since the Depression, which in turn breathed life back into the Jeffersonian mind-set.

With the repeal of the Glass-Steagall Act in 1999 and the carte blanche that gave for investment banks to merge with commercial banks, a period of widespread financial deregulation became the norm. We entered the age of "too big to fail," an epoch in which banks would hold taxpayers hostage to their expansive risk taking. Wall Street's giant new investment and commercial banking "supermarkets"—a product of the acquisitions upon acquisitions that gave rise to Citigroup Inc. and Bank of America Corp.—now had fewer restrictions on their use of customers' funds. And yet they still counted on the backstop of central bank lending, national deposit insurance schemes, and the implicit promise of a taxpayer bailout if these sprawling enterprises were ever to face bankruptcy. Comforted by those comforting guarantees, banks borrowed heavily and used financial engineering to ramp up their profitability, trading in underregulated and often highly risky derivatives, all at taxpayers' expense.

The other key development behind banks' expanded power was globalization. The rise of global capitalism was frequently cited by the financial sector lobby to justify deregulation, making the argument that bigger banks were needed to compete in the global marketplace. But in fact, the combination of deregulation and globalization was toxic for the interests of the general public. It subjected societies to greater instability and diminished their capacity to monitor and control these rapidly growing firms. We've already seen how globalization, and the insertion of an interventionist state-run Chinese economy into the world economic order, sent forth a deluge of both goods and excess savings, causing profound economic disruptions from the United States to Argentina to Indonesia. This process intrinsically fueled the expansion of a new, deregulated banking system in the West, where large banks ended up stoking credit bubbles. They recycled this flood of foreign money into loans that earned them fat profits for a decade, but when those loans went bad it brought disaster onto their home countries. In terms of their contribution to the crises of recent years, the globalization of capital and financial deregulation were two parts of the same team. They constitute a single, entirely dysfunctional and destabilizing system.

We see this in the way globalization diminished the regulatory clout that governments wield over these increasingly borderless banks. Financial institutions, which could now move billions of dollars across borders in seconds, operated across multiple jurisdictions and could raise funding from an international array of investors. That allowed them to engage in regulatory arbitrage, prioritizing investments in places with a softer legal touch or easier tax laws—as seen in the rapid rise in the number of hedge funds and other investment firms seeking refuge from taxes in havens such as the Bahamas. The sovereignty of a nation's electorate stretched only as far as its borders, but the power of global finance went much further.

The crisis that stemmed from this and the backlash it provoked have led us to a moment when "Jefferson's legacy again demands our attention," as economists Simon Johnson and James Kwak put it. The pendulum had swung too far in favor of concentrated financial power and it was time to swing it back some. Tighter regulations now under way in the United States and Europe could go some distance toward that goal, but the borderless nature of modern finance means these will work only if they are implemented uniformly across countries. Adapting a localized regulatory framework to one that's applicable to globalized finance must become a priority for the world's governments. Citizens everywhere, but especially in America, often fear ceding power to international treaties and multilateral institutions, believing they surrender sovereignty in doing so. But in truth, international governance offers the only way for individuals to restore control over their financial system and by extension over their economic destiny.

A Global Crisis

When Americans discuss the crisis of 2008, the protagonists they cite are typically those of their country's biggest names in finance, some of which were wiped from existence by it. The story, told in countless articles and books, revolves around firms such as Bank of America, Citigroup, JPMorgan Chase, Morgan Stanley, Goldman Sachs, Merrill Lynch, Bear Stearns, and, of course, Lehman Brothers. But even if the epicenter of the breakdown was in the United States, this was truly a *global* crisis. Not only did the U.S. subprime mortgage meltdown spread contagion to financial institutions overseas who'd invested in U.S. home loan assets, but some of its causes were also external—including, as we've discussed, the role played by liquidity from China's excess saving. What's more, many of the key players in the U.S. saga were themselves foreign-owned. For all the outrage in late 2010 when it was disclosed that foreign institutions were among the biggest recipients of the $3.3 trillion in emergency loans doled out by the Fed during the crisis, it would have been impossible for the central bank *not* to have included those banks in the program. In fact, it's debatable whether Wall Street should still be looked upon as an American capitalist institution. The traders and investment bankers who keep the Street's money machine turning over are just as likely to work for foreign-owned banks as for American ones—names such as Switzerland's UBS, the United Kingdom's Barclays, France's BNP Paribas, Germany's Deutsche Bank, or Japan's Nomura—and, on the flip side, many of the senior money earners at U.S.-owned banks are foreign citizens. As of December 2011, there were fourteen foreign-owned banks on the Federal Reserve's list of twenty-one "primary dealers," a group with which the New York Fed exclusively buys, sells, borrows, and lends securities to achieve the monetary policy goals set by the Fed's Open Market Committee. The primary dealers also play a vital market-making role in U.S. government bond trading, as they are compelled to bid in Treasury auctions. Yet all of these banks, even the nominally American-owned institutions, raise shareholder capital from a global marketplace. Many count on strategic, sovereign shareholders from China or the Middle East. Since the dollar is a global currency, the U.S. financial system is necessarily a global financial system.

In many respects, the Wall Street mega-banks of today were modeled on those that arose in the United Kingdom out of Margaret Thatcher's "Big Bang" reforms in 1986. Over time, banking in New York became seamlessly adjoined to banking in London, with the same kinds of excesses. And that's why when the crisis took hold, Britain's financial system unwound in tandem with America's. It's also why I've chosen here to focus on a U.K. bank rather than an American one to examine the dangers of government involvement in modern banking and the challenges that our societies face in unwinding that legacy. That bank, the Royal Bank of Scotland (RBS), lived a life very similar to that of fast-growing U.S. investment banks before the crisis. Were it not for a massive U.K. government bailout on October 13, 2008, RBS would have been the biggest failure in banking history. In fact, not only would a storied British firm have gone the way of Lehman Brothers, which had died just three weeks earlier, but the global financial system itself might have collapsed with it. And to the extent that RBS was able to limp back to health after the crisis, it did so because of indirect government support, not only from London but also from governments in other world capitals. Key to its revival were the earnings of its U.S. subsidiary, which were fueled by a bond trading bonanza that thrived off a mix of loose Fed monetary policy, interventionist exchange rate policies from foreign central banks such as China's, and massive U.S. government debt issuance.

Fittingly, RBS had its beginnings in one of the earliest moments in which a failed lending scheme threatened to bring down a country's financial system and brought banking and politics together. Its history starts with Scotland's ill-fated Darien Company, a joint-stock trading venture founded in 1695 with a legal trading monopoly on goods imported from Africa, India, and the Americas. Because it was conceived as a challenger to England's lucrative East India Company, the venture failed to win the backing of English investors, who were wary of a backlash from their own government. Still, the company's founders pressed on and established a 2,500-strong settlement in the tropical region of Darien in Panama. Five years later, with more settlers dead than alive after bouts of fever, alcoholism, and periodic attacks by the Spanish fleet, the project was disbanded. Its losses were so large that they wiped out a quarter of Scotland's liquid assets and undermined its independence from England. So when Scotland finally acceded to rule by London in 1707, the quid pro quo was a grant of bonds worth £398,085 and ten shillings from the newly formed British government to compensate Scottish investors for their Darien losses. When interest payments started flowing on those compensatory bonds years later, the society set up to administer them found itself with excess funds and so petitioned George I to allow it to form a bank. The king was supportive. He was eager for a rival to the Bank of Scotland, which had been founded alongside the Darien Company in 1695—a date that makes it the oldest surviving commercial bank in the United Kingdom—and which he suspected of having Jacobite sympathies. So in 1727, the Royal Bank of Scotland was formed by royal charter, setting up a rivalry with its crosstown counterpart that has lasted ever since.

Some 280 years later, this legacy of government-backed competitive banking had turned RBS into a colossus. Its December 2007 market capitalization, a measure that takes into account the stock market valuation of a firm's assets net of its liabilities, put the RBS Group as the seventeenth-biggest banking institution in the world. But when measured by the total dollar value of its gross assets, RBS was the biggest bank of them all. In fact, by those terms, it was the largest corporation on earth. After a decade-long acquisition spree that included the purchase of U.K. rival National Westminster and a controlling stake in Holland's ABN-Amro, RBS ended 2007 with $3.8 trillion on its books, a figure larger than the gross domestic product of every country except the United States, Japan, and China. To finance those assets, the bank had accumulated liabilities of $3.6 trillion, most of which were accounted for by deposits of $2 trillion and by some $1.4 trillion in bonds and other credits owed to other institutions. Problematically, many of the latter were falling due within the coming year, a period in which the British financial sector was to be hit by a cross-Atlantic tsunami.

Throughout 2008, as the scattering fallout from the U.S. subprime crisis began to drag down the recoverable value of RBS's mammoth portfolio of mortgage assets, the bank's capacity to make good on its debts fell into question. That caused other banks and lenders to cut their lines of credit or demand that RBS post increasingly larger collateral against their loans. An alarming scenario confronted U.K. chancellor of the exchequer Alistair Darling as well as the finance ministers of other countries whose banks had lent to RBS. If Darling didn't take the politically unpopular step of using taxpayer money to prop up this overextended institution, the millions who'd entrusted it with their savings would start a run on its deposits. Starved of funds, RBS would default on its obligations with other banks, many of which would then face the same risk of a bank run and difficulties repaying *their* creditors. This contagion of spiraling defaults would next put at risk the commercial paper market, where companies raise the short-term funds they need for important routine payments such as wages, and that of global trade finance, on which the world's exporters rely to pay for the shipment of goods around the world. (Both markets malfunctioned to some degree after the Lehman debacle, although they were later revived.) In short, when banks as big as RBS wobbled, an entire global economic system had the potential to break down, with calamitous effect. This is the essence of what financial regulators call "systemic risk." The bigger the bank, the more it embodies that risk. RBS, in this sense, was an archetypal too-big-to-fail bank.

Eventually, in the chaos of the post-Lehman financial meltdown, the U.K. government relented, injecting £20 billion into RBS in return for a stake that would ultimately grow to 80 percent. Ironically, the Bank of Scotland was also partially nationalized that day. RBS's rival of three centuries was at that time a separate unit within the struggling HBOS PLC group, which the government forced into a merger with the equally embattled Lloyds Banking Group, packaging the deal with a £17 billion capital injection and 43 percent stake for taxpayers in the merged entity. In the same way that many Americans reacted around that time to the $700 billion Troubled Asset Recovery Program (TARP) destined to save teetering Wall Street institutions, Britons were infuriated that their taxes had gone to rescue reckless bankers. But while the anger was understandable, their government had little choice. The outrage needs to be focused on the political-economic system that led taxpayers into these no-win situations in the first place.

Of all the flaws exposed by the crisis, none captures the financial system's dysfunction more than the too-big-to-fail dilemma. Making a mockery of the laissez-faire rhetoric that springs forth from Wall Street banks, this idea refers to the notion that a few financial institutions have become "systemically important" because of their size and breadth of relationships—so important that governments can't afford to let them collapse. That scenario means they enjoy an implicit guarantee of financial support, which only encourages the kind of reckless risk taking that will threaten the integrity of the system. The guarantee feeds into bankers' tendency to make asymmetric risk assessments. Knowing they will be saved from catastrophic losses on the downside, they are more likely to take bigger risks and shoot for knockout profits on the upside, especially when they have giant bonuses resting on such gains. It's another case in which a mispricing of risk creates misaligned incentives. Its distorting impact on the global economy is as significant as that of the mispricing of the Chinese exchange rate.

In 2010, two years after the crisis, policy makers introduced a barrage of legislation to overhaul the regulation of their financial systems. It will take another crisis to test whether the United States' Dodd-Frank Act, its equivalents in European Union countries, and a set of new international capital rules introduced by the Basel Committee of bank regulators will create a more stable financial system. Until then, "too big to fail" will remain the prevailing doctrine. Indeed, in various ways, governments have continued to aid big banks. The surviving institutions are now even bigger, thanks to government-encouraged mergers—those of Lloyds and HBOS, Bank of America and Merrill Lynch, and JPMorgan and Bear Stearns, to name a few—as well as the collapse of hundreds of smaller competitors in the United States. The six biggest banks in the United States now control assets worth a staggering 66 percent of GDP. Bank of America has 58 million U.S. banking customers; Citigroup has 21 million.

Even after the crisis had subsided, the world saw fresh direct bailouts. The Irish government spent €50 billion, or 30 percent of Ireland's GDP, to rescue its banks in 2010; a year later it was looking increasingly likely the governments of Germany, France, and Italy would conduct an even bigger round of "recapitalization." There were also indirect bailouts, as with the euro zone governments' financial aid programs for Greece, Ireland, and Portugal, and the purchases of Spanish and Italian bonds by the European Central Bank, which saved European banks from losses on their loans to those governments. Then there was the accommodative monetary policy, most aggressively introduced by the Fed—the de facto global central bank—which kept interest rates near zero and bought trillions of dollars' worth of bonds from banks. The Fed's actions created a highly supportive financial environment in which the wounded mega-banks could trade their way back to profits. Finally, as we'll discover in the case of RBS's U.S. capital markets unit, New York banks benefited from the People's Bank of China's and other emerging market central banks' continued expansion of their foreign currency reserves, which they invested into Wall Street–traded U.S. debt securities.

To be fair, the U.K. government, which took controlling stakes in the banks in which it intervened, undertook a more aggressive reregulation of the industry than its Washington counterpart. This had a significant impact on RBS's employees, whose numbers shrank from 233,600 in 2008 to 148,500 in 2011. By mid-2011, RBS had lost £750 billion in assets from its pre-crisis peak and had cut its dependence on short-term financing from other financial institutions to £148 billion from £297 billion. Its leverage ratio—a measure of how much bigger its assets are than its equity capital—had fallen from 28.7 to 17.8. And under the government's "Project Merlin" plan to reform compensation practices in the City, RBS shifted to a system of deferred year-end bonuses intended to align risk taking with long-term shareholder interests. In 2011, most RBS staffers had their 2010 bonuses paid out in shares they could not sell for three years, while the cash portion was limited to just £2,000 per person.

In this belt-tightening environment, it was a godsend for RBS that its U.S.-based operation was highly profitable. And that was mostly because of a specialization in trading U.S. Treasury bonds and its official status as one of the Fed's primary dealers, which put it in a real sweet spot at a time when government policies were favoring that market. The U.S. subsidiary's earnings aren't broken out separately, but mandatory balance sheet reports show that its assets rose by $37 billion from 2008 to mid-2011 even as the RBS global markets division as a whole shed about $133 billion in assets. And that's in a scenario where that investment banking division was a star within a wider, underperforming RBS Group. Whereas a painful restructuring and asset write-downs left the overall institution averaging annual operating losses of £2 billion in the two years ending in December 2010, the global markets division averaged a profit of £4.6 billion. It's clear that this had much to do with the success of the U.S. subsidiary, RBS Securities Inc.

From the moment it acquired Greenwich Capital in 2000, RBS Securities grew to be a giant market maker in the U.S. debt markets. And in the crisis period, the expansion went into overdrive. In mid-2008, while the head office in London was hemorrhaging money, the U.S. unit hired almost the entire mortgage-backed asset security team that New York brokerage Bear Stearns let go after it was forced to accept a takeover by JPMorgan Chase in March of that year. And in 2009, RBS moved its 3,000 U.S. employees into a brand-new high-tech building of glass and steel in Stamford, Connecticut. Now mostly owned by British taxpayers and partly financed with tax breaks from the city of Stamford, the $500 million eleven-story building contains 550,000 feet of floor space and boasts a massive trading floor the size of two football fields. There, almost 1,000 traders, analysts, and salesmen sit in front of flickering screens five days a week. The trading floor would have been the biggest in the world if not for the 1,400-position site that UBS operated directly across Stamford's Washington Boulevard from RBS.

The Circular Relationship

"I feel like a weatherman in California. Every day is sunny," said U.S. government bond strategist William O'Donnell when I visited RBS's Stamford trading floor on November 9, 2010, the day of the monthly auction for the Treasury's new ten-year notes, its benchmark issue. The Fed had begun its second round of "quantitative easing" bond purchases, and Brazilian finance minister Guido Mantega had just uttered his headline-grabbing "global currency war" remark. The global conditions reflected in these developments ensured that the U.S. government's $24 billion debt offering would do swimmingly well. The bid-to-cover ratio, which compares the dollar tally of orders received with the amount of debt the Treasury puts on offer, came in at a very healthy 2.80. And indirect bids—considered a proxy for foreign central banks—hit their highest level since records of that kind began being kept in 2003. O'Donnell, whose desk sported a postcard with a stylized picture of Ronald Reagan pointing outward in the manner of Uncle Sam and saying "I Need YOU to Stop Socialism," showed me on his Bloomberg terminal how traders from the primary dealers had done a "masterful job" in wooing investors into the market. They'd sold a small amount of the ten-year bonds just before the auction so that the yield—the interest return for investors at a given value, a number that always moves inversely to the bond price—would rise to enticing levels. Then, when the 1:00 p.m. auction came, the buying took off. It seemed like everybody had won.

Members of the RBS team were in a jocular mood after the auction. Their work area was arranged according to what Michael Lyublinsky, co-head of Global Bank and Markets for the Americas, described as an "egalitarian" model, where traders of differing rank, salesmen, analysts, and economists were intermingled and each assigned about four square feet of free desk space and three computer screens. They were mainly men of between twenty-five and forty-five, most dressed in open-neck or polo shirts coupled with khakis or other casual pants, with a sprinkling of women. A few traders tossed quarters back and forth, settling friendly wagers. There was a distinctly upbeat feel to the place.

O'Donnell explained how the Fed's second round of quantitative easing, or "QE2," had worked its wonders on the market. News of the seven-month, $600 billion program to buy Treasury bonds, a follow-up to a $1.75 billion initiative carried out in the year following the crisis, had not only supported the U.S. government bond market but driven down the value of the dollar. That's because quantitative easing, so called because the Fed's asset purchases increase the quantity of money in the economy, expands the supply of dollars relative to that of other currencies. But foreign central banks weren't happy with this trend, which undermined their exporters' competitiveness and generated large inflows of dangerously volatile "hot money" into their financial systems. So they moved to prevent their currencies from rising by buying greenbacks in their own markets, which they then recycled back into Treasuries.

The People's Bank of China led the pack, as always. Although the PBOC was by then letting the yuan appreciate gradually, it bought $199 billion in reserves during the fourth quarter of 2010 alone, much of which the PBOC plowed back into U.S. Treasury securities, albeit secretly via its U.K. money managers. And alongside the PBOC, QE2 also spurred the central banks of Japan, Korea, Taiwan, Brazil, and many other countries to buy dollars. Nearly all of these officially purchased greenbacks would be transferred to U.S. government securities—hence the strong foreign demand in the auction I witnessed. With central banks on both sides of the Pacific buying, prices could only rise for Treasury bonds, a market dominated by the U.S. subsidiaries of the world's too-big-to-fail banks. Whenever the average taxpaying Joe worries about the ballooning fiscal debt that his children will be burdened with, he should focus beyond the question of whether the government is spending too much or taxing too little and direct equal attention to the circular relationship between Wall Street and Asia's central banks that fuels that debt expansion.

If it weren't for all that central bank intervention, this would not have been a good time for bonds. After rolling out a $780 billion fiscal stimulus package in a period of plunging tax revenues, the federal government had run up a record-breaking budget deficit of $1.8 trillion in the fiscal year ended September 30, 2009. To finance the gap, it had to sell more or less the equivalent in notes and bonds. All things being equal, that would have driven down the price and created a riskier trading environment for the primary dealer banks. As part of their market-making obligation, the dealers agree to bid for Treasuries in the U.S. government's auctions, which they then aim to sell at a profit to pension funds, hedge funds, insurance companies, and other institutional clients. If the supply of bonds is too great and the underlying demand is weak, that juggling exercise can become harder to pull off. But in this case, the Fed was both buying bonds directly from the dealers *and* guaranteeing extremely cheap short-term finance for banks. The benchmark rate for loans in the so-called federal funds interbank market had been at between zero and 0.25 percent since December 2008, which translated into extremely cheap short-term funding for banks—especially the primary dealers that dominate the federal funds market—and meant they could lock in a healthy spread on any loans extended to clients. Even during the most panic-stricken moments in the post-crisis period, when ten-year Treasury bonds surged on "safe haven" buying and their yields dropped to record lows (below 2 percent), the gap of more than one point over the near-zero federal funds rate made for an easy profit. So as China and other emerging market central banks also aggressively bought into this market, the big primary dealer banks had the ideal combination of an increasing flow of bonds from a fiscally expansive U.S. government and virtually zero risk attached to this vast pool of securities.

As the Fed's QE2 program progressed through the first half of 2011—with limited economic success—and the dollar kept falling, concerns rose about inflation risks, which eventually knocked down ten- and thirty-year bond prices and drove up their yields. Meanwhile, although foreign central banks kept voraciously buying Treasuries, some diversified into other countries' bond markets and started buying directly from the U.S. government. These developments made life a little more complicated for the primary dealers, though the risks of trading losses were still very low. And in any case, in the third quarter of 2011 fears of a double-dip recession and capital flight from the euro zone's debt crisis pushed investors back into the safety of U.S. government debt. So as the ten-year Treasury yield dropped to a record low while the Fed toyed with other mechanisms for keeping it down there in a last-ditch bid to encourage household and business spending, the sun continued to shine on bond trading floors such as RBS's.

Killing the American Dream

Wall Street's chief executives will, on the other hand, tell you that the years after the 2008 crisis were the toughest of their lives. After having to lay off thousands of employees, they endured a public backlash that included a humiliating grilling in front of Congress, strict restraints on staff pay, and a host of new restrictive regulations under the 848-page Dodd-Frank Act. There was also a barrage of lawsuits: from individual homeowners and class action lawyers suing over predatory lending charges; from pension funds and insurance firms that claimed they had been lied to about the mortgage securities they'd bought; and from state attorneys general and the federal regulator of Fannie Mae and Freddie Mac, who took seventeen banks to court over the "robo-signing" scandal, in which faulty paperwork left millions of foreclosures in limbo. Bank of America was particularly hamstrung by legal action. Its shares slumped in 2011 on news of a settlement of up to $10 billion with American International Group that stemmed from the questionable practices of Countrywide, the giant home lender that the bank acquired in 2008.

The banking lobby argued that the regulatory demands and the uncertainty associated with their implementation, coupled with the increasing number of lawsuits, only hurt consumers and businesses by making credit more expensive. But the Fed's actions had driven thirty-year mortgage rates down to all-time lows in 2011. People were ignoring loan offers not because interest rates were too high but because they were still digging out from mountains of debt and, in a weak labor market made weaker by the crisis, their incomes were lagging. This in turn stemmed from a moribund housing market, where constantly falling prices had destroyed $7 trillion in homeowner equity to completely reverse the gains made during the boom. The "wealth effect" that once encouraged Americans to borrow and spend had turned negative and was destroying confidence. And banks played a central role in that destructive process.

Take the case of Bruno and Lisa Miglietti of Hartford, Connecticut, who in 2011 were still fighting a losing battle to recover what they claimed was $75,000 in overpayments to a mortgage broker and a Realtor in 2007. The Migliettis say they were misled into signing for a high-rate "negative amortization" loan whose outstanding value ballooned out of control because the payments were too small to cover even the interest. Although they eventually refinanced through Citigroup, their finances were destroyed by those early costs, which to make matters worse were followed by a reduction in Bruno's work hours as school janitor, a fate shared by millions of municipal workers across America as struggling townships introduced severe budget cuts. The Migliettis were reduced to depending on handouts from Lisa's parents to keep their family of three afloat. They made unsuccessful pleas for relief under the Obama administration's Home Affordable Modification Program, a scheme designed to reduce interest payments but which was roundly criticized for giving banks too much discretion and for doing nothing to fix the fundamental problem that one in five American mortgage borrowers owed more than their homes were worth. Citigroup repeatedly turned the Migliettis down and instead advised that they seek credit counseling. After numerous letters to state and federal legislators and other officials, and now locked into a situation from which there seemed no escape, Bruno Miglietti was in despair. He had arrived in the United States four decades earlier from Nardo, Italy, carrying a lasting memory of the generosity his dirt-poor family received from occupying American troops after the war. But now the struggling homeowner told me with tears welling up in his eyes that he felt like he'd been tricked. "They've killed the American dream," he said.

That bitter sentiment, recounted over and over by homeowners across the United States, is the source of the heat that bankers are feeling. Until these homeowners are free of the debt created by a reckless financial sector, the U.S. housing market will struggle to recover, which means the U.S. economy will also lag. As it stands now, the U.S. government owns nine out of ten new residential mortgages in a market that has $10.6 trillion outstanding—a result of the 100 percent takeover of mortgage firms

Freddie Mac and Fannie Mae in 2008 and the role played by other federal agencies that support housing. Private investors are too shell-shocked to return to this market. But its dysfunction stems from the hopelessness of those whose loans are underwater. Whether or not they should have known better than to get into this mess, we all have an economic interest in seeing such people back on their feet. It is only appropriate that the costs of achieving that are partly borne by those most responsible for knocking them over.

To be fair, Citigroup itself was not formally charged with predatory lending practices, perhaps having learned a lesson in 2002 when it paid what was then a record $215 million settlement over such charges. And although Bank of America's massive settlement over Countrywide's misdeeds dealt directly with such accusations, the sins were mostly committed at the local level by mortgage brokers and loan originators. Big banks also rightly argue that government policy helped encourage these practices, especially in ratcheting up the purchases of low-quality mortgages by the massive quasi-official lenders Fannie Mae and Freddie Mac, which enjoyed a distorting government guarantee as part of a congressional mandate to promote home ownership. But the fact is that the Wall Street mega-banks and their aggressive bundling of mortgage-backed derivatives engineered the economy-wide lending mania that fostered the predators' bad behavior. And they are the ones, after trillions of dollars in bailouts and cheap credit, that have been left with available cash. While Fannie's and Freddie's management and shareholders were wiped out by their 2008 government takeovers and are now subjected to strict new bureaucratic constraints, the top Wall Street bankers got to live another day and kept paying what many Americans regard as obscenely high salaries to themselves and their senior staffers. It's a no-brainer for lawyers and regulators to come after them.

In any case, the reregulation of the American financial sector has to happen. There's not much doubt about the failings of the previous, deregulated system. Banks cannot forever hide behind the argument that this is a bad time to regulate. When is the right time? For too long the

U.S. economy was dominated by a financial sector that crowded out the "real economy," the part that creates most of the jobs, and subjected it to financial volatility. It's time to rebalance, to get away from finance and back toward jobs.

The Gap

An instructive way to view the systemic nature of the U.S. crisis is through the prism of income differences. The ninefold difference between the average $361,000 in annual salary and bonuses paid to employees of Wall Street's top three investment banks in 2009 and 2010 and the average American wage of $41,000—which happened to be Bruno Miglietti's exact income—speaks to a fundamental distortion in the U.S. economy that arose from the excessive public support that is indirectly afforded to the finance sector. The problem is not the gap in incomes per se, for if it were a function of a working market economy, it could be explained by skills and productivity. Rather, the issue arises because of the *anti*-free-market framework in which an overcompensated finance sector is given special advantages denied to the rest of us. The bulk of the income that millionaire hedge fund managers earn, for example, is taxed at a tiny 15 percent because it is deemed to be "carried interest," a form of capital gain. Bankers, meanwhile, get an indirect but massive subsidy from other taxpayers because their institutions are seen as too big to fail and, as we'll discuss below, are insufficiently capitalized.

This era makes a mockery of the high-rolling late 1980s with their "greed is good" ethos. The $200,000 bonuses and hard-nosed negotiating that a twenty-four-year-old Michael Lewis chronicled in *Liar's Poker,* his tell-all book about his days at Salomon Brothers, now seem "quaint," he says. At the height of the credit bubble, bonuses of $2 million and up had become commonplace, while the top traders took in $50 million or more. For the Street as a whole, the crisis shrank the bonus pool to $20 billion in 2009 from $33 billion in 2007, according to the New York comptroller's office. But for the three biggest investment banks—Goldman Sachs, JPMorgan, and Morgan Stanley—life only got better. Along with Citigroup and Bank of America Merrill Lynch, they'd shared in a total of $135 billion in bailout money under the Troubled Asset Relief Program. But unlike Citigroup and Bank of America, their operations were concentrated on investment banking rather than commercial services and so were less weighed down by heavily indebted consumers and businesses. They could more easily exploit the Fed's near-zero interest rates to quickly trade back to profitability. This way they repaid their TARP debts before the end of 2009, got out from under that program's strict pay constraints, and lured talent away from banks that were harder done by. As the trio quadrupled their aggregate profits in 2009, topped by a further 16 percent in 2010, they paid out employee compensation totaling a record $81 billion over the two years. At the top of the heap was Goldman Sachs, paying bonuses that *averaged* $700,000 across its entire 24,000-person payroll in December 2009. (It's worth noting that almost exactly a year earlier Goldman controversially received a $12.9 billion payout under credit default swap insurance contracts that would have been uncollectible if the Fed had not made an initial $80 billion injection into insolvent insurer AIG and if Timothy Geithner, then New York Fed president and later Treasury secretary, hadn't instructed AIG to honor its deals with the investment bank and others.) The year 2009 wasn't exactly hell for many Citigroup and Bank of America employees either. Citi was contracted to pay a bonus of $100 million to star commodities trader Andrew J. Hall but was blocked from doing so by TARP compensation tsar Kenneth Feinberg. So it sold the entire division Hall worked for to Occidental Petroleum, which was able to honor its traders' lucrative contracts. As for the bosses at the top, public scrutiny meant they paid themselves a bit less after the crisis, but they were hardly suffering. Whereas JPMorgan Chase CEO Jamie Dimon and Goldman Sachs chief Lloyd Blankfein had claimed packages of $20.7 million and $68 million, respectively, in 2007, the same year in which the subprime crisis took root, in 2010 they took home pay of $17.4 million and $12.6 million, respectively. And of course in this era, hedge fund managers continued to take home even bigger incomes, with many of the top earners enjoying $100-million-plus years.

The massive financial payouts came as America's income inequality reached its widest level in eight decades. Income disparity had doubled between 1980 and 2005. Together, the top-earning 300,000 Americans now took home as much as the bottom 150 million, with the former's average income 440 times higher than the latter's. It wasn't just the finance sector that was behind this either. Compensation for CEOs at non-financial public companies rose exponentially into the multimillion-dollar range while real average wages stagnated or fell. And yet this too stemmed from globalization and from what Johnson and Kwak describe as the "financialization" of the U.S. economy. As jobs were outsourced to China or replaced with new technologies, and as ever greater efficiencies were extracted from workers whose bargaining power had diminished, corporate profits continued to rise, which automatically meant that the compensation of upper management did too. Together, a global and financial paradigm shift in the U.S. economy helped drive the income gap to almost unprecedented levels.

To be fair, throughout most of the post-war period in the United States, wide wealth and income differentials did not hinder overall growth, whereas in poor countries similar gaps coincided with economic failure. This perhaps reflects America's unique entrepreneurial ethos and the relatively high mobility that allowed many to dream that if they couldn't be rich, at least their children might be. To aggressively redistribute U.S. income would not serve much if it drove a stake into that aspirational aspect of American capitalism, which breeds innovation and creativity. But there comes a point where the top tier of wealth becomes too sticky and the mobility declines. That occurred during this era, and especially in the financial sector. Electronic trading and the thinner price margins it imposed on Wall Street meant that the big money was no longer to be made in commissions-based brokerage and trading, which had previously attracted modestly educated if street-smart men; rather, the opportunities lay in investment banking and the quasi-scientific field of structured finance. Those jobs required Ivy League MBAs and math PhDs. With college tuition and student loans spiraling upward in the same way that housing and mortgages worked together, steep barriers to entry arose in the highest-paying industry in the country. This model then filtered into other parts of the broader economy, which meant that the upper class became more entrenched, the middle class shrank, and the working class expanded and saw its incomes stagnate. Eventually, the sheer concentration of power and wealth at the top messed with the functioning of the economy and helped bring about a financial and political crisis.

In 2005, economists from the University of California, Berkeley, and the Paris School of Economics prophetically noted that the last time American society was so economically divided was in 1928, just before the 1929 crash and the Great Depression. Sure enough, three years later, in 2008, we had the worst financial episode since the Depression. This evidence of the dangerous, destabilizing effect of income disparity on sustainable economic growth needs to be part of any debate over taxation or other policy response to the United States' inequitable wealth distribution. It offers a technocratic view of the problem that permits an argument for reform that businessmen, workers, and the unemployed can unite around. It's quite separate from the moral case that's angrily presented by the Occupy Wall Street movement on behalf of the "bottom 99 percent."

The widening U.S. wealth gap came as finance increasingly dominated the American economy and crowded out the nonfinancial sector, the "real economy" where most of the jobs are created. Between 1978 and 2007, the finance sector expanded its share of gross domestic product from 3.5 percent to 5.9 percent while the ratio of private credit to GDP went from 90 percent in 1981 to 210 percent in 2007. Meanwhile, financialization meant that the proportion of borrowing by banks and other financial institutions increased fourfold. The finance sector went from borrowing $13 for every $100 borrowed by the real economy in 1978 to $51 in 2007—there, within the finance sector's mass of intertwined debts to itself, lay the time bomb that would become the crisis.

This explosive growth in what Wall Street calls "leverage" facilitated an equally explosive growth in profits for bankers. In a period of rising assets prices, the more that investments could be financed by borrowing rather than with equity, the greater the measured return on equity, the key metric by which share prices rose and bankers claimed bigger compensation. Between 1978 and 2005, inflation-adjusted profits in the financial sector rose by 800 percent, while those in the nonfinancial sector increased 250 percent. That meant that by 2006, the financial sector accounted for 30 percent of the earnings reported by companies on the S&P 500 index, whereas its contribution had historically been around 15 percent. This overdependence on credit-driven profits fed through to other sectors of the economy, especially real estate and construction, which similarly took on disproportionate roles as generators of income and wealth before the crisis. But it carried huge risks for them. The sudden tightening in lending standards after the bubble burst meant that demand for new and existing homes dried up almost overnight, leaving a massive inventory of unsold homes that depressed prices and real estate activity. Thus these large credit-sensitive sectors of employment went from being creators of jobs to creators of joblessness.

The enticing salaries in the financial sector fostered a brain drain from productive industries. In the 2000s, PhDs in mathematics who might otherwise have become, say, civil engineers were drawn in by promises of seven-figure pay at investment banks and hedge funds to build mortgage CDOs and other derivative products that offered no discernible technological benefit to society. Nor did the huge profits being generated result in greater numbers of jobs: although the financial sector's share of GDP exploded, its contribution to overall jobs stagnated at 2 percent. Yet arguably the biggest distorting effect of the sector's pre-crisis boom lay in the illusion of real prosperity that it planted into the minds of Americans. It did this by inflating financial returns, primarily in the value of their homes but also in stock portfolios. Again, this distorting "wealth effect" arose from the overly easy access to credit that an increasingly risk-hungry finance sector was delivering while global money flows from Asia fueled the debt-creating factories of Wall Street.

In 1988, U.S. consumer debt owed on credit cards, car loans, and other such short- and medium-term liabilities ran to $9,061 per household. By 1998, that figure was at $14,000, up 50 percent, and by September 2008, right before a flood of credit card defaults, it had swollen by a further 65 percent to $23,000 per household. This access to credit helped disguise or at least modestly ameliorate the widening differences in income between the haves of Wall Street and the have-nots of Main Street. Before the crisis, "credit was the great equalizer," says Raghuram Rajan, another former IMF chief economist and now professor at the University of Chicago's Booth School of Business. By making it available to subprime borrowers and low-income credit card holders, banks allowed average income earners to stock up on consumer goods and forget for a moment that a small subsector of society was making 440 times more than they were for reasons that had little or nothing to do with their productive contribution. In this way, credit helped sustain social cohesion but fostered political complacency across classes.

Don't get me wrong—we need strong, stable financial institutions to generate credit and facilitate development. Banks and investment managers play a vital role in allocating capital and as agents of the monetary policy through which central banks manage the health of the economy. But at the end of the day, they are merely financial intermediaries. They gather the excess funds of savers and deliver them as loans to those short of funds. For this, they are rewarded with commissions, mostly via the difference in the interest they pay on deposits or other sources of finance and the interest they charge for loans. But it is nonetheless just a middleman's job. From a social perspective it is of secondary importance to the production of actual goods and services in the real economy. Thanks to a series of gravely misguided ideas, we have elevated these middlemen to powerful positions as kingmakers and locked ourselves into an economic and political model that weakens people's control over how their tax money is used.

When Reform Goes Bad

Among the most misguided of those ideas was the notion that if we broke down the wall between the highly regulated commercial banking industry and the freewheeling world of investment banking and securities brokerage, we'd be better-off. In fact, the 1999 repeal of the Depression-era Glass-Steagall Act, which ended sixty-six years of a legal separation between these two models, left us worse-off. By letting deposit-taking banks run casinos, as some described it, we subjected our economy to unsustainable risks and left taxpayers to pick up the pieces when they fell.

The reforms shifted our financial system away from a traditional model where public deposits provided the finance with which banks lent for lengthy periods to household and business clients in accordance with prudential regulations. That old model, under which people such as the Boissoneaus of circuit-board maker Electropac developed long-standing personal relationships with local bankers who knew them and their businesses intimately, was overwhelmed by a much larger, delocalized, and impersonal global system. As banks and asset management firms grew bigger and explored opportunities offshore, both became more reliant on the rapidly expanding, globalized wholesale money market. There, financial institutions could lend to and borrow from each other on a short-term basis without relying on the high-overhead business of attracting deposits. These giant money markets, dominated in the United States by the "repo" market, in which institutions lend out securities in return for cash, were a cheap, liquid source of finance. Rates stayed close to the Fed's benchmark, and unlike with their deposit holdings, banks borrowing in this market were not subject to rules requiring that they put aside at the central bank a portion of what they owe—which meant they could put more of that money to work in loans that generate income.

For the institutions that lent into these deep money pools, however, the market came with a risk: unlike depositors, who were then insured up to $100,000 in the United States by the Federal Deposit Insurance Corporation, they received no third-party guarantees to protect their loans.

What they got instead was a pledge of collateral. In these repo transactions, borrowing institutions "lend" securities to other institutions for short periods, receiving cash loans in return. As the demand for such funding grew, so too did the need for collateral, which is one reason mortgage securitization went into overdrive creating collateralized debt obligations, whose top-tier tranches were given AAA ratings. Since these were regarded as high-quality collateral, finance-needing banks had an incentive to create as many as possible, which in turn meant that more home loans had to be generated. Rather than sell all the CDOs to institutional investors, they kept a portion on their books for repo transactions. In this way, the Wall Street–led "shadow banking system" grew ever larger as it fed off the mortgage mania under way on Main Street and the flow of money into the American financial system from Asia.

As the securitization process trumped traditional banking, the loan originators who'd done the initial face time with homeowners were left with no skin in the game. They quickly sold the debts to investment banks, which bundled them into securities and in turn sold them on to institutional investors such as pension funds and insurance firms, now three steps removed from the borrower. Few knew it then, but this cycle of origination, securitization, collateralization, and ever-expanding short-term borrowing was turning the shadow banking system into a ticking time bomb. The all-important "tri-party" repo market, in which the Fed also participates to keep interest rates at its target level, had grown to a peak of $2.8 trillion in trades every day. Two giant banks—JPMorgan Chase and Bank of New York Mellon—were the central custodians in that market, creating a dangerously centralized risk: if one failed, the whole global financial system could seize up. After the crisis, the New York Fed tried to pressure the participating banks into making their own reforms to mitigate such risks. But by late 2011, with the euro crisis reviving concerns about systemic problems in short-term lending markets, very few substantive changes had been made.

In 2008, this system was gripped by a reinforcing panic, producing a viral-like run on the financial system that was much harder to control than the bank runs of old. As Standard & Poor's, Moody's, and Fitch began downgrading subprime CDOs and the institutions holding them, banks became wary of one another's capacity to repay and demanded ever-larger "haircuts," meaning they required more collateral for a loan of a given size. Although many had taken out insurance against a default by their peers, they'd done so in the credit default swap (CDS) market, where the same peers were, in essence, their counterparties. Since everyone was trapped in the same vicious spiral of declining credit quality and confidence, the CDS market failed. All this struck a blow to the confidence of depositors too, who withdrew money from savings and money market accounts, squeezing even this traditional source of bank funding. The run on the system was halted only with the staggering intervention of the U.S. government, which drew on the Fed's printing presses and on federal tax revenues to strengthen deposit guarantees, extend trillions of dollars in emergency loans to banks, and eventually buy shares in them.

The far-reaching impact of this risk-prone system was most disturbingly evident in the paralysis that its collapse provoked in the global market for trade finance, something that economists had wrongly assumed could never happen because loans for goods shipments were securitized against physical goods. From there it was a short step to the complete breakdown in global trade that occurred in the winter of 2008–9, which suddenly left Chinese exporters without income and forced the authorities in Beijing into their desperate measures to keep their job machine running. Such was the pervasive, global reach of this giant shadow banking system. No one knew how much the world depended on it until it was taken away.

The shadow banking system's capacity to self-destruct has since led economists to identify a pernicious "leverage cycle" in which "procyclical" behavior creates excessively easy lending standards during bubbles and excessively tight conditions during busts. These self-perpetuating problems reappeared in the euro zone crisis three years later. There, falling bond prices prompted lenders and clearing agents to increase margin requirements, thereby demanding more money to compensate for the declining value of the collateral. This encouraged banks to further sell down their exposures to European sovereign bonds to placate nervous shareholders, which only put even more upward pressure on those governments' borrowing costs. This hyper-sensitive market-based system has taken the problem of Keynes's "paradox of thrift" to a new, more dangerous level: when one entity acts prudently to save its skin, it does harm to the whole community and, by extension, to itself.

Still, even within this dysfunctional system, the threat to the economy wouldn't be so dire if the main players weren't so big and interconnected. The largest banks have become too big to fail; if one was to go bankrupt, the cascading defaults would reverberate throughout an ad hoc network of liabilities and securities contracts, bringing countless others down with it. Lehman Brothers was the test case that proved this. And the giant banks weren't the only ones that had earned this less-than-honorable status. The massive insurer AIG had written so many credit default swap contracts against other financial institutions that it was also too big to fail. AIG eventually had to take in a total of $182 billion in official assistance, making it the biggest recipient of government aid.

Here's the catch: if the banks had had enough share capital, taxpayers would not have been on the hook. In a free market system, shareholders bear the risk of losses. It's the price they pay in return for a claim on potentially unlimited profits. If shareholders in any industry but banking haven't put up enough capital, the firm goes bankrupt and there is a conclusive reconciliation with creditors. But because banks are so heavily leveraged, the biggest among them can't easily be unwound without threatening others. The best way to avoid this systemic result, then, is to demand a high enough capital buffer—in other words, reduce the leverage—so that shareholders bear losses. If that's in place, it's less likely banks will default on their loans, which means *their* creditors won't in turn default on *their* loans. In this way, capital functions as a vaccine against systemic meltdown. In 2008, banks were woefully undercapitalized. Their leverage ratios—the value of assets relative to share capital—had risen as high as 30 for many investment banks, double the 15 ratio typical at the start of the decade. That strategy translated into outsized shareholder profits in the boom times, but it amplified losses in a downturn. It meant creditors bore a big part of the enterprise's risk.

These distortions matter greatly to the average Joe. When banks are systemically important, any capital shortfall is by definition borne by taxpayers. Since society can't stomach the chaos that their collapse would bring, both creditors and shareholders in these too-big-to-fail banks carry an implicit government guarantee. That in turn gives them the confidence to aim for the sky in profits and take bigger risks. Precisely because bank capital ratios were too small, we taxpayers subsidized Wall Street's excess. Through the idea of "carried interest" we also mollycoddled rich hedge fund managers and encouraged them to swing for the fences with their own risk taking. The U.S. tax system lets such money managers treat the income they earn from their clients' investment winnings as capital gains, thus incurring the low 15 percent rates established by the Bush tax reforms of 2001. And yet they bear no personal liability if their clients suffer a capital loss—it's another case of taking all the upside benefits but bearing none of the downside risks. To make matters worse, the tax code, which treats interest payments as a deductible expense but taxes dividends twice, leads firms to build up risky liabilities rather than raise new share capital, which all adds up to more business for financial firms. These asymmetric risk-reward structures and the incentives for reckless behavior that they create represent indirect subsidies to the financial sector from ordinary taxpayers like you and me. It is a gross distortion of free market principles.

Getting the Regulators Together

The bailouts, unpalatable though they were, were unavoidable. It is critical to acknowledge that. Without them an unfathomable economic meltdown would have gripped the world. The focus of the public anger over Wall Street malfeasance therefore needs to be directed at the system that makes such taxpayer-funded action necessary rather than at the decisions to enact the bailouts per se. A key focal point should be the straightforward demand that banks hold higher capital. Regulators do now at least recognize that imperative, but they are doing so in an ad hoc manner, without the international coordination that's needed.

In September 2010, after more than a year of wrangling, the twenty-seven-member Basel Committee of international bank regulators unveiled its so-called Basel III agreement on minimum capital standards for banks. This was a revision of the dismally failed Basel II accord, which among its various flaws allowed banks to use their internal "value at risk" (VaR) models to gauge how much capital to set aside against different categories of loans. Since the future is ultimately unknowable, these models could not contemplate the outlying "tail risk" of a systemic crisis, when multiple variables were thrust into a chaotic and destructive interrelationship. Thus Basel II–regulated banks entered 2008 blissfully ignorant of the atomic bombs lurking in their balance sheets and were woefully undercapitalized to withstand the explosions when they came. Although it leaves the base requirement for total capital unchanged at 8 percent of a special risk-weighted measure of their assets, Basel III more than doubles the proportion to be held in common shareholder equity, the most basic and effective form of loss-absorbing capital. It adds to that a 2.5 percent "conservation buffer" and recommends that national regulators place an additional "countercyclical buffer" of up to 2.5 percent during periods of strong credit growth, each of those also consisting of common equity. Critically, Basel III additionally imposes a common equity capital surcharge of up to another 2.5 percent for the twenty-eight big banks that the committee has deemed to be "globally systemically important."

These changes will strengthen the system. They will also reduce banks' leverage, diminish existing shareholders' claims on assets, and constrain profitability. Banks will simply be unable to meet the high return on equity they've been promising shareholders until now. It is the necessary price to be paid for making the system safely self-sustaining. And yet, given the size of the mess created under the previous rules and the nervousness that continues to plague markets about default risks, critics argue that the new rules are still too weak. Banks will have until 2019 to phase them in, by which time another crisis could easily be upon us. Accounting rules remain inconsistent, which means capital requirements vary enormously depending on the mix of assets, while the principles of risk-weighting are still fraught with flawed assumptions. Glaringly, the initial Basel III accord continued to accept a zero weighting for sovereign debt, perpetuating the absurd notion that lending to Greece, Portugal, or Ireland carried no risk and needed no capital held against it.

The sharp declines in bank shares that occurred during the euro zone crisis demonstrated that investors still felt the global regulatory framework was insufficient. So officials in different countries took matters into their own hands and began pushing for tougher rules than Basel III. This forcefulness was welcome in principle, but in acting independently of one another they raised the risk that regulations could become *too* stringent or create opportunities for "regulatory arbitrage." They might succeed only in curtailing lending but fail to enhance the security of an inherently global system. Switzerland's bank supervisors demanded that the two giants of its banking sector, UBS and Credit Suisse, accumulate total capital worth 19 percent by 2019, almost twice the new Basel requirements. The United Kingdom considered a different but similarly tough path: a government-commissioned report recommended forcing banks to "ring-fence" their investment bank divisions from operations that draw funds from the depositing public. And as the euro zone's crisis reached a climax in the fourth quarter of 2011, the European Commission pushed for all EU banks to immediately adopt a minimum 9 percent common equity capital ratio, a dramatic move that would swiftly force a heavy recapitalization of the sector or subject banks to government takeovers. Meanwhile, Daniel Tarullo, the Fed Board of Governors' resident expert on bank supervision, raised the ante by suggesting in a speech that systemically important U.S. banks should carry a minimum of 14 percent capital.

Not surprisingly, such developments prompted a backlash from Wall

Street, where bankers complained that governments were simultaneously telling them to boost lending while denying them a profit incentive. "Do you have a fear, like I do, that when we look back and look at them all [financial rules], that they will be a reason it took so long that our banks, our credit, our businesses and most importantly job creation started going again?" JPMorgan Chase CEO Jamie Dimon provocatively asked Fed chief Ben Bernanke during a panel discussion shortly after Tarullo's speech. It was standard Wall Street stuff: the counterargument to higher capital requirements is that they curtail growth. Three months later, Dimon took it further, suggesting it would be "anti-American" for the United States to ratify the Basel surcharge for big institutions, on the grounds that it discriminated against U.S. banks. With good justification, he was roundly criticized for this jingoistic rebellion against the international coordination that bankers such as he had until then publicly professed to believe in.

To be fair to Dimon, U.S. banks had raised much more capital than their European counterparts after the 2008 crisis and so were in a healthier state. They also followed stricter mark-to-market rules for asset valuation, which means that their balance sheets better reflect the risks they face. Dimon also had a point in noting that Basel rules place higher capital risk weightings on the kind of mortgage-backed assets that U.S. banks hold than they do on the European equivalent, known as "covered bonds." But this sounder capital buffer should be seen as a strength of the U.S. banking sector, not a weakness. It leaves U.S. banks better placed to withstand shocks than banks in the crisis-racked euro zone. Instead, Dimon equates strength with size and higher profit margins, and he argues that American citizens should share those objectives for their banks. We taxpayers have no business caring about such things. Our interest lies in the soundness of the global banking system as a whole, not in having the biggest, most adventurous banks in the world. And that means that every country must recognize, ratify, and implement the same standards.

By the second half of 2011, banks were seeing their financial performance slide. Market volatility spurred by the euro zone crisis was undermining the trading profits they'd earlier enjoyed in securities markets. So too was an associated freeze in bond and share offerings, which ate into their underwriting business, while demand for residential and business loans remained low. Small U.S. banks were especially hard hit, with 2,500 of them laying off more than 20,000 staff in total during the third quarter. But the pain was also felt by the big ones. In that same period, Goldman Sachs returned its second-ever quarterly loss and in the next one Citigroup announced it would let 4,500 staff go, bringing its total worldwide workforce to just below 210,000.

In this climate, the regulatory reforms added to investors' nervousness and contributed to month-long declines in bank share prices. Investment banks would pay bonuses of about a third less than those of the two prior bumper years. But the truth is that Wall Street paid an astoundingly low price for a decade of excess that did profound economic damage. The new restrictions were less onerous than what many had predicted amid the 2008 meltdown, and they only started dribbling into effect after the banks had enjoyed a two-and-a-half-year post-crisis boom financed by cheap Fed money and public bailouts. And even the provisions in the Dodd-Frank Act that did survive will be difficult to enforce unless Congress vastly expands regulators' resources.

One flash point was the act's "Volcker Rule," named after former Fed chairman and then Obama advisor Paul Volcker. The rule mimics the Glass-Steagall division between commercial and investment banking by barring deposit-taking banks from using any more than a small portion of those funds for trading on their own account. But banks successfully fought for exemptions, which left the exceedingly complex regulatory documents running to 298 pages and fraught with ambiguous distinctions between banned "proprietary trading" and legitimate "market making." Different problems arose with a separate requirement to standardize derivative contracts—the instruments that Warren Buffett described as "financial weapons of mass destruction"—and trade them transparently through regulated central clearinghouses. That rule change was intended to avoid an AIG-like scenario in which billions of dollars of over-the-counter liabilities were hidden from view and, because they lacked a central clearing system such as those that exist at stock exchanges, were vulnerable to default risks that could in turn mushroom throughout the financial system. But the Commodity Futures Trading Commission (CFTC) had to delay implementation of the rule by a year as it reviewed thousands of comment letters from lobbyists and, despite a much wider remit that required an increase in resources, faced an antagonistic House of Representatives. The House sought to cut the Commission's 2012 budget by 15 percent, which amounted to little more than half the $308 million President Obama had requested. An amount of $205 million was eventually agreed to in a compromise with the Senate, but that still left the agency woefully short of resources, a vacuum that was exposed a month later when CFTC supervisors failed to prevent bankrupt investment bank MF Global from losing $1 billion of customer money. In putting the squeeze on the CFTC, House Republicans regurgitated Wall Street bankers' spurious arguments that some end business users of derivatives, such as farmers, would be penalized by higher costs under the Commission's plans for a centralized clearing system. Even if nominally correct, this argument ignores the far greater cost that those end-users would suffer if the financial system went through another crisis.

Then there's the act's boldest reform: the "resolution authority" with which the Fed, under the guidance of a Financial Stability Oversight Council headed by the Treasury secretary, can take charge of systemically important banks if they are judged to be on the verge of collapse. This provision has already made the Fed more interventionist in determining whether big banks can pay dividends or large bonuses. But while the provision might be well intentioned, many financial experts worry that by formally pre-identifying such banks as too big to fail, the government will reinforce its implicit guarantee. Creditors, they argue, will be more willing to lend to such banks, providing them with comparatively cheaper finance with which to grow even bigger than their small-enough-to-fail competitors. What's more, the system depends on the discretion of regulators who are vulnerable to political pressure. "If you have a bunch of people with hundreds of billions of dollars of debts who call you every day and say, 'Don't let us down, we're systemic, if we all go down, the economy goes down,' it's very hard to ignore them," says John H. Cochrane, another professor of economics at the University of Chicago's Booth School of Business. All this has led various commentators and officials from both sides of the ideological divide to argue that the only real way to fix the problem of banks being too big to fail is to physically break up the biggest of them. "Given the danger these institutions pose to spreading debilitating viruses throughout the financial world, my preference is for a more prophylactic approach: an international accord to break up these institutions into ones of more manageable size," says Dallas Fed president Richard Fisher.

A breakup would be a truly desirable result and could have been achieved immediately after the 2008 crisis when governments had control over the banks they'd rescued. We saw the benefits of having institutions that are small enough to fail in November 2011, when the collapse of the relatively small but high-profile MF Global under former New Jersey governor Jon Corzine resulted in headlines and some severely bruised egos but did not provoke a systemic event in the financial system. However, when it comes to giant global banks such as Citigroup, a forced breakup might now carry risks. Untangling the sweeping, crosscutting interests could itself trigger systemic events. The best we can hope for is that the world's regulators produce uniform, targeted, and tough but balanced minimum capital rules that steadily ratchet up the equity safety net. That way we put enough pressure on the mega-banks such that they act on their own accord and split their more conservative commercial units from their freewheeling investment banking divisions. Of course, these higher capital needs *will* constrain the lending capacity of the banking system in its current form, which *will* curtail credit-led economic growth. But globally coordinated fiscal and monetary policies could soften the blow for those in society who are hardest hit. We must embrace reform with our eyes open: a period of slower growth is inevitable. But it is the price we must pay to overhaul the current, destructive system. Western countries' currencies will weaken in this environment, but that will boost their economies, spur exports, and steer investment toward high-value, job-creating production and away from a toxic financial sector that still dictates how our societies are run.

"Heads They Win, Tails We Lose"

However much JPMorgan Chase and the other mega-banks might complain of regulatory overreach, the Obama administration's approach to the crisis was accommodating to their interests. Even after the government handed over the TARP money while the Fed dished out its emergency lending, the authorities kept the management of the biggest banks intact. Rather than assuming ultimate control, as it did with Freddie Mac and Fannie Mae or as the U.K. government did with RBS, the government purchased interest-bearing preferred shares and simply placed restrictions on executive pay and other practices for the duration of the TARP loans. With the help of near-zero interest rates, the return of Asian savings flows, and a post-crisis bout of speculation in stocks and commodities, the big investment banks had little trouble repaying their loans and shaking off these pesky restrictions. The U.S. government did not place a single director on the board of any bank receiving TARP monies. In the end, we were left with the same shadow banking system dominated by an even narrower clique of even bigger banks.

What's more, with the rapid expansion in high-speed trading, which allows computer-driven investment vehicles to enter and exit trades within milliseconds, the investment banks and wealthy hedge funds that own them have seized control of the last great area of competitive advantage they can grab over pension funds and the average Joe investor: time. Proponents of these controversial systems say that by placing thousands of automated orders that humans cannot physically place, they add vital "liquidity" and make the market more efficient. But that argument must be weighed against the unprecedented day-to-day volatility of this high-speed era. The "flash crash" of May 6, 2010, in which the Dow Jones Industrials lost and gained 1,000 points in the space of just fifteen minutes, was exacerbated by these trading systems in conjunction with other herd-mentality-encouraging innovations such as index-based exchange-traded funds. These events suggest that markets have become dependent on the high-speed machines for liquidity, but when their operators turn them off—as they are wont to do in times of extreme volatility—the sudden disappearance of their orders leaves a dangerous vacuum that translates into wild price swings. Despite this recent record, the machines have deepened their hold on trading as a technological arms race has unfolded among financial institutions. In one example of its distorting effect, there has been a property boom in Jersey City, across the Hudson River from lower Manhattan, where investment firms compete to place their servers closest to those that the stock exchanges Nasdaq and NYSE Euronext house in their back offices, all so that their trading systems can gain millisecond advantages over their competitors. It offers an Orwellian image of a world run by rich bankers' machines. Add in the mergers, bailouts, and trillions in government support, and it seems to me that we not only failed to build a new financial system out of the crisis but also let the existing flawed one morph into something even more powerful and dangerous.

The Obama administration's inability to enact a wholesale shakeup of the financial industry when it had the chance in 2008–9 shows that it was trapped by a "presumption that it would be easy or even possible to go back to the previous world, the idea that there was some normal functioning of the economy that would return once they got over the crisis," says University of Texas professor James K. Galbraith. The worst manifestation of that mistake, Galbraith contends, was that "they didn't fire the lobbyists." By letting the banks live, the government preserved the political power at their core: the senior executives who run them, a group incentivized to protect their vast personal wealth at all costs.

Where does this immense political clout come from? The answer can be found at the Center for Responsive Politics' Opensecrets.org website. A search of "heavy hitter" donors reveals the big names of Wall Street.

Goldman Sachs and its employees accumulated the fifth-biggest tally of spending on political donations between 1989 and 2010 out of a list of institutions that includes industry associations, lobby groups, and giant multinationals with up to thirty times more staff than there are on Goldman's payroll. Over those twenty-one years, the investment bank accounted for $33.4 million in political donations, with the bulk coming from individuals employed by the bank but with large amounts also channeled via its political action committee. What's also striking is the spread of that money among parties and congressmen. Although a slim majority of Goldman employees' donations favored Democrats—including grants totaling almost $1 million to Barack Obama's 2008 presidential campaign—plenty of dough went the Republicans' way. In the 2010 interim elections, when Republicans enjoyed a big swing to seize control of the House, Goldman staff gave them $1.5 million, $500,000 more than they gave to Democrats. That year, they gave to 154 members of the House and 42 senators. In investment strategy terms, they diversified their investments.

Goldman is far from alone among big campaign contributors in the finance sectors. Employees and in-house PACs from other investment banks also figure prominently on donor rolls. And then there's the mega-money controlled by successful hedge fund managers, who tend to fly further beneath the radar than top bankers do. This group includes players such as John Paulson of Paulson & Co. (estimated net worth: $12 billion, via *Forbes*) and Louis Bacon of Moore Capital (estimated net worth: $1.4 billion, according to *Forbes*). As of November 2011, their political contributions for the 2012 electoral cycle were already running at $1,046,600 and $563,500, respectively, according to CampaignMoney.com, which takes its data from the Federal Election Commission. Of those totals, Restore Our Future Inc., a political action committee whose website describes it as being opposed to Obama administration policies that leave "businesses tied in red tape and shackled by the federal government," received $1 million from Paulson and $500,000 from Bacon. Numerous other hedge fund managers donate similarly, clearly in an attempt to ensure that their interests are protected in the current reform agenda. In this context, it's worth noting that proposals to end the 15 percent capital gains taxation treatment of "carried interest" for hedge fund managers have died in Congress.

In total, campaign contributions from individuals and political action committees within the financial services, real estate, and insurance sector grew from $61 million in the 1992 presidential election year to $500 million for the elections of 2008, making it far and away the biggest contributing sector in America. Compare these sums to the 2008 handouts from industries more commonly associated with lobbying, such as health care ($174 million) and defense ($24 million), and you get a sense of the newly found political clout of our financial institutions. The biggest individual congressional recipient of donations from the financial services sector in the 2009–10 election cycle was Spencer Bachus (R-Ala.), who took in $874,000 from banks and other financial institutions and was rewarded with the chairmanship of none other than the House Financial Services Committee. Bachus, who in late 2011 was the subject of investigations into alleged insider trading, has been quoted as saying he thinks Washington should "serve the banks" rather than regulate them, a comment that led Democrats to charge that Republicans had put the fox in charge of the henhouse. Yet Democratic politicians are no strangers to Wall Street's moneyed influence. New York senators Charles Schumer, whose lifetime donations from the financial services and real estate sector ran to $18.7 million as of late 2011, and Kirsten Gillibrand, who had received $5.4 million by then, both signed a letter in May 2011 urging regulators to go soft on a derivatives rule lest it "hurt American competitiveness." Former senator Chris Dodd (D-Conn.) took in a career total of $15 million in campaign contributions from the financial services, insurance, and real estate sector, much of it coming from hedge funds in his state of Connecticut. Could that have influenced his work on the Dodd-Frank Act?

It is impossible to separate this trough of money from either the too-big-to-fail dilemma or the constant resistance to regulation. It's also tied to the "revolving door" problem, whereby politicians, government officials, and their staff move seamlessly in and out of both lobbyist and banking jobs when they enter or leave public service. Hank Paulson's memoirs and various accounts of the crisis paint him as a man who may have made a few mistakes but who honestly tried to do what was right during those desperate moments. Yet it's simplistic to think that Paulson's former employment at Goldman Sachs had no bearing on his decision making. When it became impossible to handle the desperate deal making of 2008 without negotiating with Goldman, Paulson sought a presidential waiver from his previous recusal from associating with the firm. After that, Goldman walked away with some of the plummest goodies from the Treasury and Fed. The same sorts of relationships exist across Wall Street with the Treasury and the Federal Reserve, organizations for which countless bankers and Street economists have worked and through which they form strong personal ties to existing staffers.

In the post-crisis wrangling over regulatory reform, Wall Street demonstrated the impact that its lobbying firepower affords. In addition to gumming up the CFTC's rule governing derivatives trading, it killed President Obama's appointment of Elizabeth Warren, a tireless defender of consumer rights, to the new Consumer Financial Protection Bureau she had championed. Thanks to the close ties between Wall Street, the regulatory bodies, and the politicians, we've ended up with a scenario in which banks enjoy *deregulation* to bolster their high-tech information monopolies, but bank-friendly *regulation* in the form of promises of taxpayer bailouts if they get into trouble. We've denied them the "discipline of failure" on which a market system depends, says Robert Johnson, a former managing director of Soros Fund Management and now director of the Global Finance Project at the Roosevelt Institute. Too-big-to-fail banks have missed out on the equalizing power of bankruptcy, which throughout American capitalist history has ensured that firms fail when their ideas fall short and so learn from their costly mistakes. Big banks have no such costs to worry about. Wall Street has become the antithesis of the free market capitalist model with which it is rhetorically associated.

"We produced the dumbest socialism ever invented by man: socialized risk and privatized benefit, a kind of heads-they-win, tails-we-lose structure, an insanely stupid way to run a financial system," says Lawrence Lessig, Stanford law professor and public accountability activist. Lessig, whose pet crusade is campaign finance reform, knows that grassroots action is the only way to fix this situation. Power must come from Main Street, where the foreclosures are happening, where the jobs have disappeared, and where local and state government services have been slashed to cover for lost tax revenue. And it must be directed against the money flow that Wall Street sends to Washington.

When will ordinary Americans—and by that I mean those who earn around 0.5 percent of Jamie Dimon's income but who don't typically join the protest groups occupying city parks—push to end that system and so improve their lives? Sad to say, it may have to wait for another crisis. The last one appears not to have been extreme enough. Fully destructive financial episodes, those that turn societies upside down, have a history of galvanizing action—much as the Depression did to spur bank reform eighty years ago. The same may need to happen again. Indeed, for a contemporary example of this happening we'll now take a trip to the tiny island nation of Iceland, which in 2008 went through hell.

7

The Little Nation That Could: Cutting Bankers Down to Size

The approach into Keflavik International Airport evokes a moon landing. The countryside surrounding the airport, which was built on a former U.S. military base thirty-one miles from Reykjavik, Iceland's capital, is entirely covered with an ancient lava flow that left an undulating terrain of deep rusty browns and metallic grays. It is a barren, wild, and oddly extraterrestrial place. As with the giant ash cloud visible from my window at the time of my visit—the Eyjafjallajokull volcano's output, whose southeastward drift was holding air travelers hostage across Europe—the landscape speaks profoundly of the fragility of human civilization against the raw power of the earth's core. Nothing grows in the hard basalt rubble of Keflavik. It is land that can never be tamed. Just like Europe's grounded airplanes, it offers one of those humbling reminders that for all our sophisticated, high-tech means of harnessing it, we cannot control nature, and that we are limited in our capacity to shape life to our desires.

Iceland is an ideal place to reflect on these human limitations. For a brief period of collective blindness, the 320,000 people who inhabit this rugged island fell for the fallacy that they could conjure up material wealth out of nothing. In the decade before the 2008 financial crisis, a proud nation of hardy people turned its back on a storied past of Arctic fishing and farming and, in a metaphor offered by Michael Lewis, converted itself into a giant hedge fund. By the end of the decade the entire venture had collapsed under its own hubris.

Iceland's story since then has been one of painful adjustment mixed with rebuilding and renewal. As of 2011, it was on the path to recovery, and unlike other debt-burdened nations in Europe, it had more or less put its banking crisis behind it. It wasn't an easy process. Tensions ran high as the old political and economic order was overturned. And the psychological scars of the crisis still run deep. But in the end, the drastic reforms and a sharp devaluation in the krona allowed Icelanders to find a base of stability upon which to fix their battered economy. They reduced their once globalized banks to a size more befitting their small island economy, they forced foreign bank creditors to share losses with them, and they refocused their country's economic policies toward its underlying strengths in natural and human resources.

Iceland's experience is thus both a cautionary tale and a source of hope. It speaks to the instability that's aroused when global finance is an economy's central driver—exposing it as a threat both to the country in question and to others with which it has financial ties—and it shows how that instability is exacerbated when national regulations are out of touch with international money flows. But this story also demonstrates that renewal is possible when citizens, angered by how they were exploited, seize control of their destiny and stand up to those powerful financial forces. Iceland might seem like a tiny, irrelevant nation; to be sure, the country's small size means that it is harder to translate its experience to bigger countries. Nonetheless, its self-contained economy also functions as a laboratory for understanding the critical interplay between politics and finance. Americans and Europeans have much to learn from the recent Icelandic experience.

Starting in 2000, Iceland's three main commercial banks—Glitnir, Kaupthing, and Landsbanki—began to search for business beyond their meager domestic market. As they ramped up their operations, they found cashed-up foreign investors eager to help them. The international bond market was flush at that time with savings flows from China and other emerging markets, while the sixteen countries of the recently formed euro zone were swimming in money unleashed by a borderless new capital market that stretched from Portugal to Germany. Borrowing heavily from this deep pool of foreign currency financing, the Icelandic banks went on a prodigious overseas spending and lending spree. By the time of their collapse in 2008, they had generated a combined balance sheet worth more than eleven times the country's GDP. The story of these banks offers financial scholars a prime example of how uncontrollable, bubble-like expansions occur when an underregulated, overleveraged national banking model is placed in the context of a powerful international credit boom.

The three banks' foreign growth unleashed a financial and construction boom back home in Iceland, one that their countrymen joined in droves. People gave up traditional jobs in the fishing industry and farming to join banks or get into property speculation. Meanwhile, tens of thousands of Icelanders obtained what seemed like cheap loans, with bank officers often convincing them to double the size of their requests, assuring them of affordable interest rates on debts that were denominated in low-yielding yen or Swiss francs. This translated into higher incomes for the increasing number of locals who were feeding at the banks' trough and, for a time, into a sharp increase in the exchange rate of the local currency, the krona. Icelanders found a new taste for imported goods; many went on frequent foreign holidays. These weren't just good years; they were spectacular years.

Nobody, however, lived them as decadently as the brash young bankers who fueled the bubble. Dubbed the new "Vikings" of European finance, they maintained an increasingly exorbitant lifestyle as they took the U.K., Scandinavian, and mainland European banking markets by storm. Armann Thorvaldsson, the son of teachers from a working-class neighborhood of Reykjavik who joined Kaupthing at the age of twenty-six and launched its U.K. operations nine years later, recounted the experience in a memoir published after the 2008 collapse. One passage about an early 2007 lunch party at the famous La Voile Rouge beach restaurant in St. Tropez summed up the era:

> Perhaps it was the Russian billionaire sitting in an actual throne with a crown on his head drinking Château Lafite from the bottle. It could have been the waiter dressed up as Spider-Man, holding a 20-liter Melchizedek champagne bottle, which he sprayed over the guests. Or it could have been the sight of my Icelandic friends, many in their youth known as the neighborhood bullies, taking tequila shots with the former chairman of one of the UK's largest banks. Whatever the reason, the thought crossed my mind that this was like the last days of Rome.

Sure enough, Iceland's banking orgy ended in a splitting, long-lasting hangover in the last quarter of 2008. And as is too often the case, the steepest costs for the excessive indulgence were paid by members of the general public, those who indulged the least. Unemployment, virtually unheard-of in Iceland before the crisis, surged to 9 percent, an alarming figure for a small country in which a work ethic is prized. Meanwhile, as the banks collapsed and the local currency lost two-thirds of its value against the dollar—and even more against the so-called safe-haven currencies of high-saving economies such as Japan and Switzerland—krona-earning Icelanders were left with impossible debts in yen and Swiss francs while their assets shrank in the face of falling local demand. (After the collapse, there was an unusual spike in freak accidents in which cars caught fire as their owners tried to liquidate their assets through insurance claims.)

For now, most of the BMWs and Range Rovers acquired during the boom still travel the country's roads. But they are a reminder of what is already a bygone era, with some pessimists even suggesting that in decades hence they will still be there, as much a symbol of a country frozen in time as Cuba's rusty 1950s Chevys are now. Having built their centuries-old society on hard work and primary production, Icelanders had briefly believed they could perpetually create ever more wealth out of pure financial speculation. They are now part of a long, sorry history of deluded investors who've fallen victim to the folly of that idea. Icelanders have paid a heavy price for wrongly believing they could master the universe.

The metrics of the price they paid are striking: a 10 percent contraction in Iceland's economy over two years, a crash that destroyed 90 percent of the stock market's value in a matter of months, and a nationalized banking system that left the government with a total external debt of $110 billion. That's $350,000 for every citizen. (The government rightly insisted that the figure was much smaller when netted against the foreign assets of the banks it forced into receivership, but it will continue to be difficult to put a fair recovery value on those claims until they come due many years into the future.) The crisis also left Iceland embroiled in a bitter, drawn-out dispute with the United Kingdom and the Netherlands over unpaid deposit insurance to British and Dutch citizens who'd entrusted their savings with Icesave, an underfunded Internet-only bank owned by Landsbanki. That international brouhaha, in which Internet forums became a battleground for sparring countrymen from both sides, left Iceland's taxpayers with a debt that will take almost four decades to repay.

Yet Iceland's experience merely differed in degree from the social and economic breakdowns that happened at the same time around the world and disrupted hundreds of millions of lives. Although Iceland's homegrown excesses were destined for a reversal at some point, the country's catastrophe was precipitated by the same September 2008 trigger behind the global meltdown: the Lehman Brothers collapse. What's more, Iceland's failures—to constrain risk taking before it was too late, to limit the damage when the collapse came, to restore its economy so that it would be stronger and more stable in the future—would have not occurred if not for shortfalls in our ill-defined international economic system. In this way, Iceland offers another humbling reminder of the realities of life on this little rock orbiting the sun: we humans are all in this together.

Making Bankers Do the "Perp Walk"

Much to his joy, Reykjavik-based designer Thor Hallur got approval in August 2008 for a long-standing bid to adopt a baby boy from India. Hallur, a diminutive and soft-spoken man of forty-five, had been required to accumulate significant savings to show his good standing as a parent. He and his wife had scrimped and saved for five years after the adoption of their first child, a daughter, also from India. On top of that they had to come up with the cost of the trip and the hefty fees owed to the various bureaucrats who have turned international adoptions into a logistical nightmare for prospective parents. And yet to Hallur it was all worth it. It was all for the good of his soon-to-expand family. Unfortunately, his timing could not have been worse.

"I was very happy at that moment," he told me. "I was also doing well at work. I was overseeing two people and earning good money." Hallur had studied fashion design but had ended up working for a company making granite kitchen countertops, a big business during the pre-crisis construction boom in Reykjavik. For the rest of August, although work was showing early signs of slowing, life progressed calmly and happily. He was not to know that banking problems brewing on the other side of the Atlantic would turn this moment of bliss into a nightmare.

A month later, global credit markets seized up in panic after Lehman Brothers announced its historic decision to file for bankruptcy on Sunday, September 15. Iceland's three big, overextended banks were among the first to be cut off from financing and hit with collateral demands. They had relied heavily on foreign money markets to fund their meteoric growth, but once this generous flow was halted, they were suddenly unable to roll over their debts. The three main ratings agencies—Standard & Poor's, Moody's, and Fitch—sharply downgraded both the banks' and the country's credit ratings. Previously, those same agencies had given the country's banks stamps of approval, something for which they were now being heavily criticized. The agencies had viewed the banks' comparatively elevated levels of capital as sufficiently high to force shareholders—rather than creditors and depositors—to bear the cost of potential asset write-downs but had downplayed the structural weaknesses in the Icelandic banking system as a whole, especially the underresourced state of the country's central bank. These flaws would eventually drag down the krona, the currency in which the banks' capital was denominated. The ratings agencies had also failed to see the Ponzi-scheme-like risks in the banks' practice of lending to their top managers and owners against the security of those executives' own shares in the same banks. Of course, all this is said with the benefit of hindsight. But the crucial point is that in the post-Lehman environment of mid-September 2008, those overly positive assessments were subjected to a sharp reversal in valuations that stoked widespread panic among the Icelandic banks' creditors. In short succession, these fears extended to depositors and a run on the banks' local and international branches ensued. Over the following two weeks, as global financial conditions rapidly deteriorated, the trio hung on for dear life until the Icelandic Financial Supervisory Authority took drastic action. On September 30, it nationalized Glitnir, which by then had run out of funds. That move merely shed doubt on the health of the other two, Landsbanki and Kaupthing, and within nine days they too were in government-mandated administration.

By then, Iceland's predicament was sowing alarm overseas. As a bitter dispute over deposit insurance liabilities brewed with the U.K. and Dutch governments, the krona came under full-blown attack, a trend that was worsened when the United Kingdom invoked anti-terrorism laws to freeze Icelandic assets in Britain. By mid-October the Icelandic currency had lost almost two-thirds of its value from the previous month, even as the Icelandic Central Bank spent $280 million of its reserves trying to support it and jacked up interest rates to 12 percent to entice money back into the country. Those measures had the perverse effect of hurting the more prudent local borrowers who'd opted for krona-based loans, and in any case they ultimately proved futile. The foreign debts of Iceland's now bankrupt financial system dwarfed the central bank's resources; there was no way it could withstand the swarm of hedge funds dumping the krona. So in mid-October Central Bank chairman David Oddsson imposed the first set of draconian restrictions on foreign exchange transactions and raised interest rates to 18 percent. But even that didn't help. Despite an initial $2.1 billion emergency rescue from the International Monetary Fund and a government breakup of the three banks intended to ring-fence their local operations from their foreign affiliates, the hemorrhaging of krona deposits continued. So in November, Oddsson shut down the foreign exchange market altogether. Iceland was cut off from the world.

This was devastating for Thor Hallur. "Iceland suddenly didn't have any foreign currency anymore. So I became very worried that I mightn't be able to go to India as I had planned. I was mixed up, fearful," he said. "Eventually I managed to find someone to give me some dollars, but at 145 kronur per one dollar [compared with around 75 kronur to the dollar days beforehand], so instead of costing 1.5 million kronur, the trip cost me 3 million."

Making matters worse, the owners' cooperative at Hallur's apartment building had voted just two days before the October 8 meltdown to start a 34-million-krona renovation, to which he would contribute half a million kronur, or what was then $3,500. Since he still owed a foreign currency loan to Kaupthing bank, the combined effect of the krona's collapse, the building work, and the overseas trip meant that in just a few days, Hallur's financial position went from comfortable to de facto bankruptcy. Yet the worst was to come: a few months later, as the Icelandic home-building industry ground to a halt, he lost his job. When I met him in mid-2010, his six months of unemployment benefits had ended twelve months earlier and Thor was still looking for work. Having had net assets of 7 million kronur before the collapse, he was now 28 million kronur in the red (then around $212,000), with the ownership and occupation of his apartment in a state of suspended animation. His bank, now known as Arion following a post-collapse restructuring and brand makeover, was refusing to modify his repayment schedule and threatening to seize his home.

"I say to them, 'Sorry, but it is your bank that created this situation. I have been preparing my case for five years of adopting my child, and I had to have all the money to show for that, so everything was OK before the collapse that you created.' But they don't want to help me," Hallur said. "I am getting very angry, but of course I just take each day as it comes. At least I went to India and got my little boy. Only that has kept me positive."

I met Hallur at a Reykjavik community center for unemployed Icelanders set up by Elin Asmundsdottir, a local social worker and psychologist. Asmundsdottir, who goes by the name Ebba, introduced me to eight locals who'd organized a support group at the center to help one another overcome the trauma of losing their jobs. Among them were an unemployed engineer, an architect, the owner of a bankrupt publishing company, the former head of a hardware store, a former transport manager for a shipping firm, and two trained fashion designers, each of them well educated, articulate, and fluent in English. All between their mid-forties and late fifties, they were far from retirement age and young enough to have mortgages and dependents but too old to easily retrain themselves or do as younger Icelanders were increasingly doing and emigrate (although many agreed they would take a foreign job in a heartbeat). They'd all been out of work for the better part of eighteen months, an abrupt and traumatic change for people who'd never known anything other than gainful employment.

"At thirteen years old, every kid in Iceland gets the opportunity to work," explained Ebba. "Because we had long summer vacations, the kids had to help the farmers and the fishing industry in the summertime. Everybody was working, and nobody looked at this as child labor. I think it gave a structure to your life and you got a little bit of money. This is why work is Icelanders' identity."

This industrious spirit helps explain some of Iceland's past success, including the achievements, however transitory, of its high-flying bankers. Regardless of their failure to see their limits—or perhaps because of it—the three institutions expanded at a remarkable rate, conquering the sophisticated investment banking markets in London and Luxembourg as they went. Their rapid expansion surely also owes something to Icelanders' dogged determination—on display every time a fishing trawler takes to the freezing seas to the country's north—as well as to their refusal to admit the inherent constraints of their country's small size and isolated location.

Stigmatized by the prospect of long-lasting unemployment, many of these hardworking Icelanders dealt with their joblessness alone. Confronted with thousands of hungry people too ashamed to ask for handouts, the Red Cross eschewed its usual soup kitchen approach and instead organized "volunteer" campaigns and church functions where food was provided. Meanwhile, its anonymous twenty-four-hour hotline was flooded with calls. "The other night, I was there for three hours and couldn't get up for a cup of water. People of all ages kept calling in," said Gunar Jonsson, a volunteer at the hotline service. "I am very scared about this. . . . There are many thousands out there without jobs. And among them are many people who are not feeling well." Jonsson, who himself had lost a job as a shipping manager and had since joined Ebba's group, said he often got callers who threatened suicide. Once the long, cold sunlight-deprived winter sets in, "it could be catastrophic," he said, "because the banks have been freezing their loans, not helping these people at all."

Capturing a defining humanist objective of Ebba's group, Sigurbjorg Alda Gudmundsdottir, an elegant woman of fifty-four years, handed me a piece of paper on which she had written, "Remember: behind all those facts and figures there are people with feelings!" Gudmundsdottir was trained as a fashion designer, but like many Icelanders, she had been lured into a finance company during the boom. After one year on the job, she was laid off. That had been twelve months earlier, and she had been looking for work ever since. "The feeling I have is one of betrayal, this idea that we are not important at all, not as we thought we were," she said.

There it was: that same sentiment I had heard from people in many crisis-affected places, a feeling that society had defrauded them. The institutions they trusted to protect their interests—banks, government, employers—had instead pursued self-interest at the expense of the common good. For many Icelanders, the breach of trust unleashed a raw anger that allowed them some symbolic ownership of their predicament. This seething national mood was expressed evocatively in a handwritten placard seen at one of Reykjavik's many rowdy protests during the winter of 2008–9. It read simply, "Helvitis Fokking Fokk"—"Bloody Fucking Fuck." A similar message was conveyed by a customer of Islandsbanki, formerly Glitner, who was caught carrying a coffee machine out the bank's head office. "I can't get my savings back, but at least I can take this," he matter-of-factly told the staffer who confronted him. The security guards just let him go.

Meanwhile, people took to throwing red paint at bankers' homes, an act of vandalism that insurance policies wouldn't cover. In a town as small as Reykjavik, the red stains were a way to publicly shame executives. Not surprisingly, many who'd been in senior management during the boom fled to places such as London, among them Bjorgolfur Thor Bjorgolfsson, the former owner of Landsbanki, who had become his country's first billionaire. Yet the attackers also indiscriminately targeted less culpable players—including the squeaky-clean new managers who'd taken over from the former discredited ones. This new management was charged with the daunting but vital task of reconciling the interests of tens of thousands of essentially bankrupt Icelandic retail customers with those of the old banks' foreign creditors (who'd taken control of the equity in two of the three big banks' local operations). Having to confront the red paint brigades made those managers' jobs even harder.

Even Ebba, the thoughtful social worker, had no reservations about sticking it to the finance guys. As we walked through the downtown area she pointed to a soulless glass tower built during the boom that was now empty and casting a long shadow over the traditional corrugated-iron Reykjavik houses. "I think they should turn that tower into a prison and all those bankers should be forced to walk around in front of the glass naked," she said, "because I'm sure they all have small penises."

All the World Loves a Clown

The disgust for bankers was directed to only a slightly lesser degree at Iceland's political establishment. As early as January 2009, the public outcry forced Prime Minister Geir Haarde to resign. That ended the long reign of his center-right Independence Party and brought the Social Democrat Alliance into power in coalition with the Left-Green Movement. Led by Johanna Sigurdardottir, a former flight attendant who became the world's first openly lesbian head of government, the new administration cut a sharp change from the conservatives who'd overseen the financial transformation of Iceland in years prior.

Despite starting out with a 73 percent approval rating, Sigurdardottir saw her popularity quickly wane. A year later, she was pelted with eggs in a protest against economic hardship. Anger was by then directed at all politicians, as a far-reaching government inquiry into official ties to the now vilified banking elite put members of parliament from both sides of the aisle in a bad light. But it also reflected people's frustration as a bad economic situation was made steadily worse by the global recession. Angry Icelanders, daunted by the giant external liabilities confronting their country and hounded by banks seeking payment for unpaid mortgages and car loans, turned in droves against politicians.

Ultimately, this rebellion would prove cathartic and constructive for the country. But the process took some bizarre turns, including the victory in Reykjavik's May 2010 mayoral elections of Jon Gnarr, a well-known Icelandic comedian whose nascent Best Party ran an entirely satirical campaign. Under the slogan "Whatever Works!" and with a platform that included promises of a polar bear for the city zoo, palm trees for its icy waterfront, free towels at swimming pools, and a commitment to "sustainable transparency," Gnarr's win delivered a profound message from Iceland's voters, a giant raspberry blown at the country's political class. "I just like the idea of giving traditional politics the middle finger," said Kristjan Arngrimsson, a junior college philosophy teacher, explaining why he had voted for the Best Party. Arngrimsson wasn't sure where it would all lead, but he hoped Gnarr's win would be a wake-up call for the country and allow "a transition period" within which to "figure out a new way to do politics."

Gnarr, whose rhetoric shifts almost indiscernibly from that of the simpleton character he played in his campaign to the analysis of a political activist practicing what he calls "anarcho-surrealism," told me he was seeking to expose the old, worthless political system for being a "ridiculous joke." By doing this with theater, he was forcing Icelanders to reinvent their relationship with politics. In his official campaign speeches, Gnarr never broke character, and that, ironically, is what filled his victory with meaning. There are no foreign equivalents to this message of voter discontent—former professional wrestler Jesse Ventura's election as Minnesota's governor might come close, but like other politically successful celebrities such as Arnold Schwarzenegger and Al Franken, Ventura ran an ostensibly serious campaign. The only true parallels I can think of would be if comedian Stephen Colbert's bids to run in Democratic and Republican primaries in South Carolina had been accepted and he had gone on to be the state's candidate at either party's convention, or if Britain's Conservative Party had been forced into a coalition with the Monster Raving Loony Party instead of the Liberal Democrats.

Although a similar backlash against traditional politics was seen in elections across the Western world that year, Iceland's voter rebellion was unique for the severe economic context in which it occurred and the extremes to which it went. Facing decades of humiliating debt repayments, the bankrupt country was at that moment stuck in a deep ravine with no clear way out. That only made supporters of the traditional parties more alarmed by Gnarr's victory in Reykjavik. With the country in the midst of do-or-die negotiations with its foreign creditors, many were horrified that its capital city was now, quite literally, in the hands of clowns. True to form, the Best Party responded to these people's concerns with a whimsical statement that I doubt would have calmed their nerves: "Nobody needs to be frightened of the Best Party because it's the best. And we only want what is best—if we didn't, we'd be called the Worst Party or the Bad Party."

Little England

The anger and cynicism unleashed by this crisis were not isolated to Iceland. The country's financial expansion had been a distinctly international phenomenon, so it caught many flatfooted when it went into reverse. Iceland's turmoil did not really trigger widespread economic contagion, but in certain places it did enormous damage to people's trust in local financial regulators.

One such place was Guernsey, the autonomous British territory in the English Channel, just thirty miles from France's Normandy coast. There, residents who'd put their savings in a local subsidiary of Iceland's Landsbanki bank and their trust in Guernsey's vaunted financial services authorities were let down by both. Their case demonstrates that the popular narrative of Landsbanki's failure in the United Kingdom, which paints it as a battle between one of the world's smallest economies and one of the world's biggest, is skewed. It would be more accurately described as a struggle by ordinary citizens in both places against public and private institutions that failed in their duty to protect their interests.

From the air, Guernsey appears the polar opposite of Iceland's molten rock landscape. A patchwork quilt of different shades of green, it's a scene that says England. Over many centuries the French have left their mark on Guernsey—the occasional name in the phone book, a few elderly residents who still speak in Guernsey French, and, most important, a Napoleonic civil code that makes legal affairs such as the bankruptcy of a foreign-owned bank complicated. But it is the English who've made it their home. The narrow roads and stone walls that define farmers' property lines recall the bucolic countryside of southern England; it could just as well be Kent or Dorset.

The easygoing lifestyle of this gentle, homely place of 60,000 people appealed to Eric Graham when he decided in 1982 to move his young family to Guernsey from his native Yorkshire. It also helped that the autonomous government of the Bailiwick of Guernsey States had reproduced the stability associated with the British rule of law. Economic and financial security had delivered close to zero unemployment and relatively high standards of living for the island's residents. Graham, who'd worked as an aide for people with learning disabilities, and his wife, a mental health nurse, took up similar jobs on the island and set out to raise their three children, all under five, as Channel Islanders. They also transferred their modest life savings into the island's banking system, which was then starting to aggressively internationalize. A quarter of a century later Graham would come to regret this decision. When the Icelandic collapse came, he found his interests and those of hundreds of other savers were subordinate to those of some other recently arrived Guernsey residents, a group who'd brought with them a lot more money than he had.

Many of these deep-pocketed migrants have taken up residence in the business district of St. Peter Port, identifying themselves with bronze plaques and logos on the low-key buildings that line the town's winding streets. Theirs are among the biggest names of European finance: BNP Paribas, Barclays, HSBC, Credit Suisse, and Deutsche Bank. Intermingled with these banking giants are a host of asset management firms looking after the savings of wealthy individuals, trust funds, insurance companies, and pension funds. As of October 13, 2011, the Guernsey Investment Fund Association listed 125 members, a group with £274.5 billion under management. As a low-tax jurisdiction with what had been a reputation for efficiency, stability, and regulatory consistency, Guernsey has long been an appealing domicile for owners and managers of wealth.

The money under these people's control filled the deposits of the island's thirty-nine licensed banks and allowed them to amass assets worth £139.2 billion by mid-2011. In dollar terms, that ran to almost $3.6 million per Guernsey resident, dwarfing even the $280,000 in per capita banking assets that Iceland boasted at its peak. Yet the risks are very different in each case. Guernsey has no currency of its own and thus no national central bank. It also has no "indigenous" banks backed by local capital. Its banks are all subsidiaries or branches of foreign institutions. That makes them less vulnerable to a systemic breakdown within the island itself, but it also means the Guernsey Financial Services Commission (GFSC)—recognized under international agreements as a "host regulator"—must keep a close eye on the health of its banks' foreign parents and on the financial relationships the local banks maintain with them. It also must rely to a significant extent upon the work of the foreign parent companies' "home regulators." The challenges that the GFSC faced in doing so were to be Landsbanki Guernsey's undoing.

In September 2006, Landsbanki of Iceland purchased U.K.-based Cheshire Building Society's Guernsey subsidiary. Landsbanki, keen to secure a stable foreign source of deposit finances, had its eye on the international depositor base that Cheshire had attracted, but it also assumed responsibility for the deposits of local people. Few suspected any risks at the time. Cheshire sent a letter to depositors lauding Landsbanki's 120 years of experience and declaring that their "business and your savings are in good hands." And Landsbanki offered a parental guarantee to that effect. In any case, it was to be regulated by the highly regarded GFSC.

But just two years later, Landsbanki Guernsey went into bankruptcy, stranding 1,600 depositors with £120 million in frozen savings. To their dismay, those individuals learned that their deposits weren't protected in the way that deposits in failed banks on the mainland were. Whereas the U.K. government stepped in when Landsbanki's online Icesave bank went under, depositors in Landsbanki Guernsey had no deposit insurance scheme to fall back on and so were simply thrown into the broader Landsbanki bankruptcy proceedings. Eventually Deloitte and Touche LLP, the administrator of the estate, predicted a return of between 85 and 91 percent of what depositors were owed, including unpaid interest. But to get to that point it would take more than two years, during which time all funds were frozen. And for much of that period there was no money, no information, and a shroud of uncertainty.

Some of the injustice these people felt stems from Landsbanki Guernsey's practice of "upstreaming" loans to Heritable Bank on the mainland, another Landsbanki-owned U.K. subsidiary that collapsed on October 8 along with Icesave and all the other Icelandic subsidiaries. In this way, the Landsbanki group exploited the Guernsey unit's access to cheap, insurance-free deposits to finance its risky lending in U.K. mortgages. Eventually the GFSC put a stop to this unsecured upstreaming and required the island bank to take a direct stake in the portfolios of the mainland property loans that Heritable was managing. But by the time of the collapse, there was still an unexplained £36 million loan from Landsbanki Guernsey on the bankrupt Heritable's books. That, along with £52.5 million in property and commercial loans, should have been available to pay the Guernsey depositors. But whereas depositors in Heritable itself received up to £50,000 in compensation from the U.K. government, the Landsbanki Guernsey depositors had no immediate recourse to the money their bank had lent to Heritable, which remained unsecured by any other assets. The way it seemed to people such as Eric Graham, their trapped savings were subsidizing mainland depositors and taxpayers.

Graham had retired only a year earlier and had deposited a payout check of around £30,000 into the bank. When he learned his money was frozen and was led to believe he would eventually receive only 30 percent of it, he was incredulous. "You are just numb at that stage. You find it very, very difficult to believe," he said. Graham thought he'd been cautious. He hadn't invested in the stock market or taken undue risks. He had deposited his modest savings in a well-regulated bank. It was the final responsible act in a life of careful, prudent savings.

"It isn't about the money. It's what that money represents," he said, describing the anger he still feels about the way depositors were treated. "It represents my life work. It represents what I and my wife might wish to do in the future, to go on holidays. It represents anything that my own children or my grandchildren have rights to." Now he's questioning the wisdom not only of banking with Landsbanki but also of bothering to save his money at all. "Somewhere along the line in all that, I'd love to have gone to Australia and seen all those [cricket] test matches and had a ball of a time with me and the boys. Well, you can't do that—well, you can but you don't, because it is a very selfish thing to do. So at times like this you think, 'Why is it that because I've been responsible, because I've done this and saved, because I've acted in a normal way, this is the result? What a fool I am. I should have blown the bloody lot.'"

In a classic case of shutting the stable door after the horses have bolted, the GFSC introduced a deposit insurance scheme a month after Landsbanki Guernsey's collapse. Following the U.K. model, it would in the future guarantee deposits of up to £50,000, although unlike the unlimited programs in most countries it placed a £100 million cap on the total that could be paid out in any five-year period. Seven months later, Guernsey's Channel Islands sister territory, Jersey, introduced a similar plan. Even with these limitations, this was an about-face for the Channel Islands, which had long resisted official recommendations that they introduce U.K.-style deposit insurance. (Notably, the Isle of Man, another low-tax U.K. territory, had for some time a plan guaranteeing up to £15,000 per deposit, which was later increased to £50,000 with retroactivity after yet another failed Icelandic-owned subsidiary bank, Kaupthing Singer, went under.)

In Guernsey, "the reason we didn't have one is because the overall majority of our deposits are institutional and corporate in nature—some 93 or 94 percent," explained chief minister Lyndon Trott, who holds the highest government position in the Guernsey States. "So a very tiny part of our deposit base is retail. There simply wasn't the demand for it." In essence, the banks' big clients didn't want to pay the costs that would accrue to them for creating a small, retail-oriented scheme from which they would derive no benefit. With the collapse of Landsbanki Guernsey and the reputational risk generated by the bad PR, however, they were ultimately persuaded.

None of this was any comfort to the depositors, who formed the Landsbanki Guernsey Depositors Action Group to fight for their money. The group lobbied unsuccessfully for the Guernsey government to cover their unguaranteed losses as the U.K. government had done with Icesave. The way they saw it, Guernsey regulators had not fulfilled their duty to supervise and regulate banks in the territory. But other taxpayers on the island saw it differently. In the comments sections in local Guernsey press articles about the affair, many island residents said the depositors had been greedy, that they'd been drawn to the high interest rates offered by Landsbanki Guernsey without considering the risks. It's a notion that infuriates Action Group members. "We are depositors, not investors," said Eric Graham, outlining what he called "a very important distinction" that captures the trust with which individuals put their savings in a bank.

"When I put money into a bank or open a bank account, they don't give me a piece of paper that says, 'Your savings may be at risk, your money could go up or down,'" said Janson Bewey, another Action Group member. Bewey, who had £90,000 trapped in Landsbanki Guernsey and who says he's had "stand-up blazing rows that have nearly become physical" with other Guernsey residents, likes to point out the logical inconsistencies of his critics' position. He reminds them that most of them had money in Guernsey subsidiaries of British banks, which similarly had no deposit guarantees and which survived only because British taxpayers bailed out the U.K. banking system and so indirectly saved the Guernsey subsidiaries.

Oliver Day, a forty-one-year-old project manager at a local building company who put aside money in Landsbanki Guernsey to save for a holiday home for his family, speaks matter-of-factly about the basic values of trust that he saw being violated. "We are not greedy people," he said. "The [interest] rates were average, they weren't brilliant. . . . And you know, we all rely on professionals in their fields of experience every day of the week—doctors, dentists, everything. I put my trust in the financial system and its regulation. It is ironic, really, that as a taxpayer, I've been paying for the Guernsey Financial Services Commission. . . . I've been paying for my own downfall, really, haven't I?" He says he is now embarrassed for Guernsey, whereas he was once proud of it. "I'm no longer an ambassador wherever I go."

Most of the Landsbanki Guernsey depositors were residents of the islands, but it is the nature of international banking that its customers were also recruited from thirty-five different countries, including many from the mainland United Kingdom. The depositor list included figures within the Guernsey government and so-called tax exiles who have made the island their home to lower their tax bill. Such people did not make their names public, though the Action Group members say they know who they are. By contrast, lower-income savers on and off the island came forward with indignant anger. Among them was Sailesh Carlyle Patel, a young West Londoner whose parents died during his childhood. Patel, aka "Icy Chill," makes low-budget hip-hop videos in his spare time. In "Give Me Back My 100%," he raps about losing his inheritance money:

Devastating news for people's lives at risk
Back to my last pennies, I crunch my fist
This is the sort of thing that will leave the dead
Landsbanki Guernsey, give me back my 100 percent.

The Landsbanki Guernsey depositors represented a small minority, but the local government was concerned about the image of the island's regulatory system and so went into damage control mode after the bank's collapse. From both GFSC director Phillip Marr and members of the Guernsey government, I heard the same response to the depositors' allegations of wrongdoing: local authorities had been exonerated in an investigation led by Michael Foot, chairman of the Promontory Financial Group U.K. and a former senior official of the Bank of England. On three occasions during our chat, Trott used the words "no regulatory failure" in referring to the report's conclusions. And sure enough, Foot had declared that "the GFSC measured up to good practice and met its obligations under the Basel Core Principles" of international banking regulations. The Guernsey regulator, said the report, "understood the parent's strategy and the subsidiary's role; it maintained adequate oversight of activity, staff and systems; it monitored the parent bank and relevant countries/

areas of lending; it volunteered information to other supervisors and it formulated and kept current its own strategy."

The central problem, however—one that was also integral to the Icesave affair and relevant to many other case studies explored in this book—was that those international standards had become inadequate for the world we live in. The subsequent overhaul of the Basel rules to which the Promontory report referred is recognition of this. One key inadequacy lies in the policy mismatches that arise when a single banking group is owned, operated, and regulated in different places, especially when they are as distinct as Iceland's "home country" system and the "host country" model of Guernsey.

Guernsey and other island crown dependencies such as the Isle of Man and Jersey claim they attract international finance because of their high standards of financial management and prudential regulation. But although Chief Minister Trott insisted that Guernsey be referred to as a "low-tax jurisdiction" and not a "tax haven," no one would deny that large amounts of money are deposited there precisely because of the tax advantages. To be sure, the low-tax regime does also promote investment in various innovative services, but for the most part it really just provides a domicile for the managers of funds destined to be invested elsewhere. Any amendment to those tax laws, and the territories could be vulnerable to a swift outflow of this money. And in the wake of the financial crisis, there is pressure for reform both in the United Kingdom and in the European Union, where critics argue that the islands' tax regimes amount to a massive subsidy from U.K. taxpayers to a now much-maligned financial sector and an unfair competitive disadvantage for other financial centers in Europe.

Guernsey has capitulated to a degree, bringing in a flat 10 percent rate for anyone doing business there. So far the impact has been limited. The territory is still flush with cash, but there have been periodic deposit outflows—a decline of 11 percent in 2009, mostly reflecting the loss of wealth during the crisis, and a 4 percent drop in 2010 as investors moved cash into equities. But a bigger tax hike could drive more money away. More generally, the Channel Islands' limited fiscal and monetary powers create a different kind of vulnerability during a crisis, as the Landsbanki Guernsey case showed. Financial institutions in the City of London can reduce their tax burden in good times by shifting operations to the territories without facing exchange rate risks. But they can just as easily remove those funds to meet liquidity shortfalls elsewhere during a crunch. Meanwhile, the lack of a local central bank leaves the islands with only limited control over their financial systems. They are beholden to an outsider's management of the monetary base—in this case the Bank of England—and to the work of the "home country" bank supervisors and the mainland United Kingdom's Financial Services Authority. Although they maintain separate lines of communication with the International Monetary Fund and other multilateral bodies, Guernsey's financial authorities are subordinate to their mainland counterparts in all such international settings, not only vis-à-vis other countries such as Iceland but also in settings such as the Basel Committee negotiations. That's an awkward, disempowered position to be in when your economy is wholly dependent upon international financial inflows.

The Guernsey Financial Services Commission is no more superhuman than are the Bank of England, the European Central Bank (ECB), or the U.S. Federal Reserve. None of those central banks proved capable of keeping up with the complex, fast-footed world of global finance in the early twenty-first century. But in the Guernsey case, there was a unique mismatch between its regulatory and constitutional structures and those of other international jurisdictions. Its problems with Landsbanki Guernsey speak again to the need for global consistency in policies and legislation, as well as to the challenges that are posed by the limits of domestic regulation when global financial flows are managed by giant, stateless institutions. The Landsbanki Guernsey depositors were too small in number to pose a threat to the island's full financial system, but what's important is that they represent the aspirations of middle-class savers everywhere, people who feel they've been betrayed by this system. These people—the vast majority of us, in other words—need to feel reempowered and to regain a sense of political control over this system. What's at stake is the all-important intangible quality of public confidence.

Inevitably, members of the Landsbanki Guernsey Depositors Action Group see conspiracy in what happened to them. They are bitterly dismissive of the Promontory report, which they point out was commissioned by the GFSC itself. Speak to them and they'll share their painful realization that the little guy has lost. Guernsey "has become a complete puppet for the finance industry," said Oliver Day. "It wanted to introduce a compensation scheme, but it was told by the big powers—the big banks and the big finance houses—'Look, we don't want it. If you introduce it, we're going somewhere else.'" To Janson Bewey, known in the group for his strong opinions, the threefold failure of the Icelandic authorities, the Financial Services Authority in the United Kingdom, and the GFSC in Guernsey reflected the intermingling of politics and big finance. "They are all closing ranks because of the contagion of the mire that they've allowed," he said. "And they've all had their noses in the trough. It has been the old big mates' arrangement—you help me and I'll help you."

Bewey's cynicism and mistrust are by no means unique. Such opinions are a defining feature of the post-crisis global political landscape. This widespread loss of confidence will be a major challenge for Western societies going forward, especially if the economic recovery doesn't last. We need entrepreneurial types such as Bewey, who made his money developing a small but successful business on Guernsey doing paint jobs and other car and motorbike repair. We need them to maintain their confidence in the economic system. When they entrust their savings to the financial system, it has the virtuous effect of feeding capital investments. As a retiree, Bewey also belongs to a demographic upon which philanthropic causes depend. So it's especially disturbing to find him gripped with indecision over what to do with his money, fretting over the crippling debts of sovereign governments and pondering what he sees as the biggest threat: hyperinflation.

"That's what will wipe out everyone's savings—you know, like Weimar Germany," Bewey said. "So, do we buy gold? I've always said, in a nuclear situation, you can't eat gold. But the trouble is that with the pound in our pocket under hyperinflation it is going to be cheaper to use it to wipe your backside than to go buy toilet paper, because toilet paper will cost you 20 quid. . . . In Weimar Germany people who had property were not allowed to put the rents up. So they were wiped out. How do retirees like me live when that happens? With the sympathy we've got from Guernsey because we've lost our savings, it's clear that if we are seen to have something, there is going to be no sympathy. So I've got to be self-sufficient for the rest of my life. . . . So, do I give to charity now? No, because I don't know what costs are coming up. . . . And I know I'm not going to put the money back into the economy, because I'm worried."

"Send Cash, Not Ash"

In comparison to Bewey and the other Landsbanki Guernsey depositors, the 400,000 British and Dutch citizens who put their money in high-interest-paying accounts with Icesave, Landsbanki's Internet-based bank, were lucky. Their governments bailed them out. But their case also demonstrates the inadequacies of international banking regulation.

When Landsbanki went into receivership on October 7, 2008, the Icelandic Depositors' and Investors' Guarantee Fund had just €68 million in its coffers, an amount woefully insufficient to satisfy Icesave's giant roll of depositors. This left Iceland in breach of obligations to a treaty of the European Economic Area—a body that incorporates the EU and two other non-EU states in addition to Iceland—under which depositors were entitled to up to €21,000 each in the event of a bank collapse. Faced with the risk that panic among such a large body of savers would spread to other banks, the British and Dutch governments picked up the tab on behalf of the Icelandic deposit scheme, eventually paying £2.35 billion and €1.2 billion, respectively, to the Icesave depositors—a total of about $5.2 billion at December 2011 exchange rates. The two governments then insisted that the Icelandic government repay the amount.

As alarming as this was, Iceland's new Social Democratic Alliance government was inclined to reach a deal. It had always run on a platform of seeking full membership of the European Union, for which it would formally apply in July 2009, an objective with no chance of success if Iceland broke its contractual obligations on EU deposit insurance rules. Iceland's 320,000 taxpayers were far less keen, however. Many believed their tiny country was being bullied into covering the debts of private citizens—a clique of greedy, corrupt, and imprudent Icelandic bankers on one hand and some irresponsible foreign depositors on the other who were lured by improbably high interest rates. The full claim from Britain and the Netherlands was equal to almost half of Iceland's GDP, or around $50,000 for each Icelandic household. It seemed like an impossible obligation to take on. By contrast, the U.K. claim represented around $50 for each British household.

As public resistance grew in Iceland, bad blood and mistrust festered on both sides. Britons relished putting the Vikings of finance back in their place as U.K. message boards carried vicious attacks on Icelanders and calls to boycott Iceland's products. Likewise, Icelanders barraged U.K. websites with complaints about their treatment. A year and a half later, when the relationship was tested again by the disruption to air travel caused by the volcanic eruption, the mood was lightened only slightly by humor. A tweet from some wag's Twitter account read, "Iceland, we said send cash, not ash!"

Despite this hostile environment, Sigurdardottir's Social Democratic Alliance–led coalition eventually agreed to a deal: Iceland would honor the full amount of what was then about $5 billion in debt, with payments occurring over the fifteen-year stretch during which the Landsbanki estate's assets were expected to mature. It included a seven-year grace period before payments would start, but the debt would accumulate interest at 5.5 percent over that time.

When he heard the terms, David Blondal was horrified. "This is 50 percent of GDP, so it scared me a lot," said Blondal, a member of InDefence, a loosely organized group of ten or so activists who organized popular resistance to the Icesave deal. "I felt that some people were just signing this due to guilt, saying we need to sign this, without seeing that this could bankrupt Iceland." After forming InDefence in mid-2009, he and his colleagues gathered a whopping 56,089 signatures—a full fifth of the electorate—and delivered them to Iceland's president, Olafur Ragnar Grimsson. They did so in cinematic style, gathering with hundreds of supporters at the snow-covered grounds of the presidential palace in January 2010, many of them holding orange flares. Against the twilight haze that counts for daytime sunlight at that time of year, the photogenic sight was captured as a powerful and evocative image in the world's press. What's more, it was successful: Grimsson announced that he would not sign the bill implementing the Icesave deal and instead called a referendum on March 2010. That vote returned a 93 percent rejection of the deal.

"The one thing that people were saying with this referendum was that we are not ready to pay the debt of a private bank with our welfare," said Eirikur S. Svavarsson, another member of InDefence. A lawyer, Svavarsson had joined me, Blondal, and a third InDefence member, social psychologist Ragnar Olafsson, in a Reykjavik café that fronted the country's most important but now most maligned institution: the Althing, its 1,000-year-old parliament. Blondal had just laid out what he believed was at stake: decades of high taxes and strict restrictions on imports, all aimed at giving the government access to the foreign currency needed to repay the United Kingdom and the Netherlands. That kind of blow to one's livelihood was not a price Icelanders were willing to pay, Svavarsson said. "That does not mean that we won't do something or that we don't have some responsibility [for the Icesave losses]. But we do not pay private bank debt with our welfare."

The referendum forced the government to plead with the United Kingdom and the Netherlands for more favorable terms. It couldn't just walk away from the debt, as many Icelanders wanted. Already, disbursements from a $10 billion international emergency loan were being withheld from Iceland as the British and Dutch governments exerted their voting powers inside the IMF. A downgrading of Iceland's credit rating also loomed.

The government feared international isolation would make a basket case out of its affluent country—until then one of the ten richest in the world on a per capita basis. But negotiations would now be even harder. Not only had the U.K. and Dutch governments believed they already had a deal, but they now had the uncomfortable sensation of negotiating with a government that did not have the electoral mandate to do so.

Nonetheless, in December 2010 a new deal was reached with a longer, thirty-year time frame and a lower interest rate of 3 percent. Yet even then the plan failed its political test in Iceland. Although in January 2011 the Althing passed a bill implementing the terms, President Grimsson again refused to sign it, declaring the matter too important not to be put before the people. Another referendum was called, and the deal was rejected, albeit by a narrower majority of 58 percent. The governments that had signed the agreement expressed their great disappointment. It meant that the next chapter of the Icesave saga would be resolved in an international court administered by the European Free Trade Association, where Iceland's arguments were not expected to prevail.

The Money Flows

These torturous negotiations were not merely a function of Icelandic stubbornness or British and Dutch belligerence, as popular narratives on opposite sides would have it. They also reflect the failings of international policy making in an age of globalized finance. The EU treaty's deposit guarantees were insufficiently defined to deal with an ambiguously domiciled Internet bank. Nor were there provisions for what happens when the home country's entire banking system goes bankrupt. "Insurance is the idea that the many insure the few," said InDefence's Blondal. "If everyone crashes their cars on one day, a car insurance firm cannot guarantee payment to all owners." Does that mean the state should step in? It's not clear. Either way, the EU directive never explicitly required state guarantees. And that was for good reason: a fully mandated state bailout promise would exacerbate moral hazard, encouraging risk-hungry bankers to be even more cavalier with people's deposits.

There is a fundamental disconnect between regulatory systems controlled at the national level and the international nature of twenty-first-century finance. Glitnir, Landsbanki, and Kauputhing were operating with 90 percent of their loans and assets in foreign currencies and foreign locations, but the central bank, their "lender of last resort," was backed by only a small pool of krona-based reserves consistent with a tiny domestic financial system. To monitor this international colossus, Iceland's Financial Supervisory Authority employed just forty staff, mostly clerical. Meanwhile, the country's deposit insurance scheme was denominated in kronur, which left Iceland prone to exchange rate fluctuations that would misalign its locally invested assets with its potential liabilities on foreign currency deposits. "The big flaw is that the financial authorities are local while the banks are international," said Blondal. "This by definition means that different authorities have to work together, especially when you have banks growing as fast as the Icelandic banks."

When the crisis came, there was no common safety net for the citizens of Iceland, the United Kingdom, and the Netherlands, as each government went into look-after-number-one mode. Confronted with extraordinary circumstances, they reached for that special sovereign license that countries reserve for such times and put their national interests first. But in the midst of a crisis, that's the last thing the international system needs. If survival instincts start trumping everything else, they automatically provoke counterproductive responses. If governments abide by international covenants most of the time but abandon them during a crisis, then safeguard agreements are useless.

The stakes are high. As with trade protectionism, tit-for-tat financial sanctions can have dangerous consequences for the global financial system. Banks shut off from financial inflows in one place will deny credit to others in another place. Luckily for the rest of the world, the Britain-Netherlands-Iceland dispute did not expand into a global beggar-thy-neighbor policy cycle like that seen during the Great Depression. That was partly because attention was focused on bigger financial problems on the western side of the Atlantic. But it was also because Iceland was too small to matter and too small to fight back. The rest of the world had problems of its own, but for the most part Iceland's did not spread far from its shores, excepting the pain inflicted upon Landsbanki's and Icesave's foreign creditors. The country's dysfunction became a spectacle for a while, but mostly it just drifted quietly into a solitary meltdown while Europe moved on to its own, bigger problems.

Yet precisely because it was an isolated incident—one that can be looked at relatively cleanly, free of the confusing, interrelated factors that defined the wider global crisis—the Icesave dispute is an instructive case study in the failings of international financial regulation. After the crisis, various reforms were made to the European Union agreements on deposit guarantee schemes, including increasing the mandatory insurance to €100,000 per depositor, boosting the schemes' long-term funding structures, and clearing up ambiguities so that host countries make the first payout and then seek reimbursement from the home country's fund. But it's not clear that these changes would have helped the Icesave situation. Truly supranational guarantees and safeguards are needed—perhaps a deposit insurance scheme that's administered centrally by a single European bank regulator.

The creation in January 2011 of the European Banking Authority, which can overrule national regulators within the EU, is a positive step toward more integration. But in a mark of how contentious this idea is, the United Kingdom refused later that year to agree to a treaty amendment that would have enhanced fiscal coordination within the EU and helped resolve the euro zone debt crisis, all because its EU counterparts (quite reasonably) refused to accept Britain's singular demands for a unique veto over financial regulatory developments. The British government described its rebellion as an act of protecting its sovereignty but it was also clearly done in the interests of London's powerful banks and money managers.

There will always be political resistance to such reforms. Financial institutions, the source of this resistance—at least against anything that adds to their cost of funds—are gatekeepers for the stuff that greases the wheels of politics. In Iceland's case, as the national commission's investigation into the crisis revealed, the improper relationships between politicians and bankers were egregious. But it is hardly the only case where money from big financial firms has flowed into candidates' campaign coffers. (Notably, a *Financial Times* article published one day before Britain's veto of the EU treaty reform showed that hedge fund managers had become the biggest donors to Prime Minister David Cameron's Conservative Party.) Therein lies one of the most valuable lessons from Iceland's crisis and from the national soul-searching the country underwent afterward: for the sake of the global financial stability we all crave, we must break the poisonous connection between big finance and politicians. We can be thankful that by the time 2011 rolled around, Iceland's experience offered a few tips on how to do that too. And that's what brings us to the hopeful part of its story.

Fighting Back

To tell that story we must compare Iceland to Ireland, the fallen Celtic tiger whose banking crisis took it from its brief ranking as the richest country in Western Europe back to its traditional place among the poorest. Amid the global crisis, both island nations saw a giant banking bubble burst with devastating consequences. Initially, as Iceland plunged into chaos, many observers thought Ireland had gotten it right, as it intervened quickly to guarantee its banks' debts and institute tough austerity measures to pay for the fiscal cost—including steep pension and pay cuts for public servants. But as time went on and the true depth of its banks' problems became known, Ireland needed to come up with more and more money to cover them. In September 2010, it announced that its total bank capitalization costs could run to €50 billion, accounting for a staggering 30 percent of GDP or $11,200 for every Irishman. The equivalent for the United States would run to $4.4 trillion. Eventually the government called for financial assistance via a new fund that the European Union and the International Monetary Fund had set up in the wake of an earlier sovereign crisis in Greece. Under the tough rules applied in that program, Ireland took on ever sharper cost-cutting measures and got embroiled in a dispute with the euro zone's power brokers—Germany and France—over its low 12.5 percent corporate tax rate.

As the Irish economy shrank and then stagnated, unemployment rose from 4.6 percent in 2007 to 14.3 percent in October 2011. Meanwhile, consumer prices were driven by post-crisis cutbacks into a pernicious spiral of decline, dropping 5.4 percent from 2008 to the end of 2010. In the first half of 2011, hopes were raised that Ireland's contraction had bottomed out as exports of pharmaceuticals and farm products fueled a recovery, and for that it won the applause of euro zone leaders, who cited Ireland as an example of a country that had taken the tough steps needed to resolve its debt crisis. Even so, flight from Irish bonds drove their yields up to a worrying peak of 14 percent in July 2011, and while they plunged back to 8 percent during the following three months, those levels would still have forced the country to default on its debts were it not for a special EU bailout program that expires in 2014. And in any case, hopes for recovery were given another setback when third quarter data were released showing that Irish economic growth returned to negative territory for the three-month period to post a 1.9 percent contraction in GDP.

Though its results have been erratic, Iceland's economic performance has been much healthier than Ireland's. It posted quarterly growth rates in excess of 2 percent in three of the five quarters leading to September 30, 2011, with an impressive 4.7 percent gain in GDP in the last of those. By then the government was confidently forecasting average growth of 3 percent until 2016. Icelandic unemployment was still high at 7.1 percent in November 2011, but it was half that of Ireland and was comfortably down from its own 9.1 percent post-crisis peak. The government expected the jobless rate to ease to 4.3 percent by 2016. Unlike Ireland, Iceland experienced no painful deflation, but neither did inflation get totally out of control: Icelandic consumer prices rose by an average annualized rate of 12 percent in both 2008 and 2009 but after that moved in a range of 1.3 percent to 5 percent.

Then there are the diverging debt profiles. The IMF projected that Ireland's gross public debt would hit 114 percent of GDP in 2011 and then break and hold above an unwieldy 120 percent for the following five years. The same IMF forecasts had Iceland's debt ratio peaking at 103 percent in 2011 before steadily falling to 73.8 percent by 2016. (To put that into context, U.S. public debt, which was at 91.6 percent in 2010, is expected to keep growing to 111 percent over the same period.) And when adjusted for foreign reserve holdings—which sit as an asset on the central bank's books and are currently inflated by the foreign assets of the Icesave estate and those of the other two failed banks—Iceland's debt ratios fall well below half of Ireland's throughout the five-year period. That lesser debt burden will free up Iceland's growth prospects, while Ireland's—as well as those of the United States and other indebted euro zone nations—will be constrained.

Why the different outlooks? One reason is that Iceland has its own currency. There are two ways to revive the competitiveness of an economy whose assets and incomes were previously overvalued. One is to devalue the currency, which reduces the cost in foreign currency terms of the goods produced; the other is to undergo a deflationary "internal devaluation" via a decline in incomes and wages. One or the other must eventually happen. But the first option is inherently more desirable, as it externalizes some of the costs and is applied uniformly to all sectors of the economy. Deflation, on the other hand, is borne internally and, because of the inherent stickiness of wages, is carried out in a discriminatory way, mostly via layoffs and general unemployment. It is unevenly distributed and politically complicated, and it tends to take longer to finish.

Devaluation isn't an option for Ireland. For various reasons that will be discussed in the next chapter, it would be extremely difficult for Ireland or any other euro zone country to unilaterally dump the euro without virtually killing its financial system. So it was stuck with the euro, which to make matters worse strengthened versus the dollar and yuan after the global financial crisis, creating an even bigger competitive burden for Ireland and other debt-crisis-racked euro zone countries such as Spain, Portugal, and Greece.

Even so, why did Ireland's debts grow while Iceland's declined? A weaker krona should in theory have made the latter's predominantly foreign currency debts higher. The answer is that whereas Ireland was wary of scaring off the foreign investors upon which its open economy depended, and so immediately put up taxpayer money to protect the banks and their creditors, Iceland forced them to take losses. Shortly after nationalizing Glitner, Kaupthing, and Landsbanki, the Icelandic government restructured them by separating their asset and debt books into three "new banks"—primarily incorporating the domestic retail and commercial banking operations of the trio's local branch networks—and three "old banks," into which were lumped the far bigger pool of foreign assets and institutional loans from foreign creditors. These three old banks would cease to operate and would become recovery vehicles of the bankrupt banks' estates. The bankers and their shareholders were wiped out entirely, and there was no guarantee for their creditors. Instead, the various mutual funds, hedge funds, and foreign banks left in possession of the Icelandic banks' defaulted bonds were offered equity stakes in the much smaller new, domestically focused banks. In the case of Glitner and Kaupthing, the creditors accepted. Not only did this differ greatly from Ireland's approach, but it also diverged from the bailout approach used in the United States, where both the banks' shareholders and creditors were protected from losses.

To be sure, the Icelandic banks' balance sheets were not as systemically risky as Ireland's. As outsized as the Icelandic banks had become, they were coming from a much smaller base; Ireland's economy was fifteen times the size of Iceland's. That made regulators in the European Union more nervous about widespread contagion from any default—especially the risk that U.K., German, and French banks would respond to losses on their Irish loans by dumping assets in other parts of Europe. That Irish banks' assets were mostly onshore in the politically sensitive housing sector and not offshore like those of Iceland's three expansionist institutions also made it harder to fence off the worst parts of their balance sheets in "bad bank" structures. Still, it's not clear that the Irish economy was doomed to perform any more poorly than it did if the banks and their creditors hadn't gotten bailouts. What is clear is that a pure free market system, where good investments are rewarded and bad investments punished, was not allowed to function in Ireland. We also know that, by comparison, Iceland's reformed and pared-down banking system proved resilient. It was able to absorb the losses and reorient itself toward domestic clients. In this way it became a contributor to domestic economic recovery, not a hindrance to it.

Whereas Ireland went out of its way to save banks and their creditors, shifting the burden onto taxpayers, Iceland let the former suffer losses, precisely in order to protect its taxpayers. And whereas Ireland resorted to a deflationary contraction in its real economy so that the banks might live, Iceland shrank its banks so that its real economy might grow again. Columbia University economist and Nobel laureate Joseph Stiglitz says that cutting banks down to size meant they were no longer driving up the costs of credit, labor, and other resources, which in turn created opportunities for firms in the nonfinancial sector—"the biotech firms, the software companies, the geothermal [energy producers], the fisheries." Indeed, when I met with the directors of the online gaming company CCP, creator of the popular futuristic virtual world of Eve, they were thrilled about the access to local talent that bank layoffs afforded them. And with the devaluation in the krona, foreign-sales-dependent companies such as Iceland Air and the fisheries company Iceland Group were finding innovative ways to reach new customers.

Meanwhile, radical change was occurring within the new domestic banks created out of the shells of Iceland's failed international banks. Under creditor ownership, Glitner became Islandsbanki and Kaupthing became Arion. They got new names, new missions, new value systems, new risk profiles. "This was about getting back to basics," said Birna Einarsdottir, the down-to-earth new CEO of Islandsbanki, whose shock of blond hair is a feature she shares with many Icelanders. "After what had happened it was a major challenge to get going with this new bank. Imagine, in 2008 we had 1,000 very scared and devastated staff members. We had 100,000 very angry customers. And we didn't have a balance sheet. And a balance sheet for a bank is very important."

Winning over the staff was the first hurdle. During the boom, Icelandic bank employees had been encouraged to put their savings in the banks' soon-to-be-worthless stock. In fact, their employers offered them loans in foreign currency to buy those shares, setting them up for the double whammy later of a depleted asset and an inflated loan. These lower- and middle-ranking bank employees were arguably the Icelanders most hurt by the banking crisis. "I have a forty-year-old staff member who had all of her savings in the bank's stock because she believed in the company," said Einarsdottir. "She doesn't understand what happened to it. She comes to me from time to time and asks, 'Will my stock be OK again?' and I have to answer, 'Phew, no, I'm afraid not.'"

To create a new bank from scratch, Einarsdottir knew she had to engage her demoralized staff in the rebuilding effort. So one Saturday she called an all-in, all-day brainstorming session, putting groups of seventy or so people into huddles to fulfill different tasks: design a new logo, craft the bank's mission statement and values, decide upon core strategies. From this unique approach to problem solving, these bruised but determined staff members came back with a blueprint for a traditional bank, one that would focus on loans in Iceland, not overseas, and in areas in which the country's true comparative advantages lay: fishing, tourism, and, most important, the rich-with-potential geothermal energy sector.

Meanwhile, after two years of wrangling between bankers and struggling mortgagees such as Thor Hallur, the government produced a law at the end of 2010 that automatically wrote down the value of people's home loans to levels that could not exceed the assessed value of their properties. This drew objections from the foreign creditors that now owned the new banks, but without a local constituency behind them, their protests went nowhere. The move did away with the problem of negative equity, the same one that dogged the U.S. housing market in the years following the subprime crisis that began in 2007 and left homeowners with an incentive to "mail in the key." In removing much of this overhanging foreclosure risk, it helped stabilize home prices at a level from which they can recover. Additionally, the government decreed that banks had to charge the lower rates mandated by the central bank for the outstanding foreign currency personal loans on their books. It could afford to force such changes on the banks because by the end of 2010 they were in much better shape. Despite the new costs and the loan write-offs, the trio posted net profits of a combined $165 million in the first quarter of 2011.

More important, the loan modifications helped rebuild consumer and voter confidence, which in turn produced a positive political feedback loop—a critical ingredient in long-term economic recovery. (There are lessons here for U.S. banks, which began the post-crisis period stiffly resisting any concessions to debtors.) Happier Icelandic homeowners and consumers meant a much larger number of them were now willing to vote in favor of the Icesave deal and put the affair behind them. That the yes vote still failed in the April 2011 referendum reflected how deeply the scars of the crisis run. But we can also view the affirmative's advance from a 7 percent tally in the first poll to 42 percent as a measure of improved public confidence in their country's progress. While the unresolved Icesave issue will add uncertainty to Iceland's outlook, it's worth noting that the referenda have helped its people regain a sense of ownership of their future, having previously lost it to a small clique of arrogant bankers and politicians. That's gold.

It helped as well that there was a sweeping political housecleaning. Iceland wasn't alone in experiencing political fallout from the crisis—incumbents in different parts of the Western world were also thrown out of office—but very few places saw the same degree of wholesale, disruptive change. Elsewhere, political overhaul was merely a changing of the guard. The Tea Party in the United States, for all its attention-grabbing influence on the national discourse, mostly just brings a more aggressive tone to the Republican Party. In Washington, there has been no common post-crisis consensual effort to reform the political process as a whole. If anything, its politics have become more partisan and interest-driven than before the crisis. Iceland's change, by contrast, was the real deal.

It's not just that Icelanders voted for a satirist as mayor of their capital and replaced a long-running ruling party of conservative men with a new group of progressives headed by a lesbian. It's that they demanded and received a sweeping inquiry into what had happened. What they got was an eye-popping account of corruption and the abuse of power. The bankers, the people learned, had taken depositors' money and invested it in multibillion-dollar speculative foreign ventures and in the wasteful activities of their friends and families, a group that accounted for an inordinate amount of their investments. The banks had done so right under the noses of national regulators, who effectively gave them their blessing.

With its release, the report triggered a far-reaching international criminal investigation. Just before I arrived in Reykjavik, two senior executives from Kaupthing Bank—Hreidar Mar Sigurdsson and Magnus Gudmundsson—were placed in police custody while prosecutors prepared a case against them. They were later released, but the investigations against them and others who had fled to different parts of Europe continued. In March 2011, Britain's Serious Fraud Office cooperated with the Icelandic prosecutor's office to arrest nine men in London in connection with the failure of Kaupthing. The arrestees included well-known London property entrepreneurs Robert and Vincent Tchenguiz.

But beyond the prosecutors' actions, the media trials, and the public shaming of extravagant financiers, the inquiry's most powerful effect lay in its disparaging treatment of the pre-crisis political culture. Unlike President Obama's commissioned inquiry into the U.S. financial crisis, which identified all the bits and pieces of a failed regulatory system but studiously avoided dealing with the elephant in the room—the influence of bankers' money in campaign finance—Iceland's inquiry was focused squarely on the rotten politics at the center. Above all, it was the transparency of the exercise that was striking. At first it fostered even more disdain for politicians, as representatives from all parties, including those of the new Social Democratic Alliance–led coalition, were implicated in various improprieties. But over time, the inquiry's most valuable contribution was to give legitimacy to the difficult policy decisions the new government had to make. The report was in this sense an expression of good faith. With so much wrongdoing now exposed, there was less to be suspicious of. In the end, it helped heal Iceland's wounded society.

"It showed our sincerity, that we are determined to investigate, to find out the truth, that we are not going to sweep this under the carpet, and that Iceland is going to deal with this in a fair and honest way, even if the evidence we get from this research is painful," finance minister Steingrimur Sigfusson told me. "Shouldn't other nations do the same? Isn't there a need for a broad, independent investigation [into their experience with the global financial crisis] which is not part of a criminal investigation but which is more general and takes ethics into account?" The finance minister himself embodied some of this sentiment. A committed man of the left and a principled internationalist, Sigfusson did not always leave his countrymen feeling confident in his knack for deal making, as he yielded to what many saw as the extortion of the U.K. and Dutch governments. Nonetheless, he was widely respected for the simple fact that, unlike so many before him, no one could say that Steingrimur Sigfusson was corrupt. With his stubbly gray beard, understated attire, and a snuff-snorting habit, Sigfusson displayed the slightly eccentric quirks of a career left-wing intellectual. That might not have worked in a "normal" country, where PR managers mold their politician clients into slick, polished caricatures. But in crisis-weary Iceland, a place that had had its fill of bankers in pinstripes, this was perhaps the kind of finance minister the country needed.

8

PIIGS and the Systemic Crisis: When Bond Vigilantes Get Their Dander Up

Throughout 2010 and 2011, as governments of the seventeen-country euro zone struggled to devise a coherent, common strategy to prevent the mounting debts of its weaker members from dragging them all into financial disaster, Europe seemed ensconced in a cultural war. With the people of a relatively financially sound northern Europe resisting helping out their neighbors in the heavily indebted southern and northwestern periphery of the continent, the dispute was frequently portrayed as a clash between different national characters. Depending on one's point of view, the bankrupt Greeks were either lazy spendthrifts or victims of the unduly harsh rules imposed by their creditors in the north. The purse-string-holding Germans, on the other hand, were either industrious and frugal or tightfisted and heartless.

In a series of *Vanity Fair* articles that formed the basis of his book *Boomerang,* Michael Lewis introduced new stereotypes and updated some old ones: Iceland's hardy fishermen were conned by the myth of easy financial wealth; Ireland's once-rebellious masses had become pliant patsies; Greece's irony-blind anarchists were fighting for the right to sponge off the state; and Germans, Lewis argued, fed their scatological obsessions by simultaneously indulging the "dirty" excesses of their undisciplined European neighbors and chastising them for having no self-control. And then there was the religious theory I heard from a marketing executive friend. As voters in Germany, the Netherlands, and the Scandinavian nations rejected both bailouts and defaults for the disparagingly nicknamed "PIIGS" (Portugal, Ireland, Italy, Greece, and Spain), he saw a Lutheran north, with its focus on personal responsibility, clashing with a Catholic and Orthodox south, with its ingrained belief in absolution for one's sins.

There's some truth to all this. Cultural differences across euro zone nations clearly hindered a unified response to the crisis, if only by reinforcing people's expectations. Those cultural differences had spawned a great variety of political systems in which each country's citizens had different expectations for their social compact with government, which in turn dictated their leaders' divergent policy stances before and after the crisis. Europeans identify more readily with their compatriots than with a pan-European identity, so these entrenched domestic political norms bred resistance to the kind of institutionalized burden sharing that's taken for granted within nations. This was evident even though the alternative to sharing the costs—disintegration of the euro—was a surefire route to continent-wide calamity. So, yes, culture and national differences did matter.

But this intra-European squabbling is a distraction from the root causes of the crisis, which were inherently structural and systemic. Here, in the simplest terms, is what happened: The advent of the euro allowed the giant banks of the wealthier, more productive north to provide cheap loans to the poorer and less competitive "peripheral" nations of the south, which they did with gusto for a decade. But as Greeks, Portuguese, and Spaniards took out their first-ever mortgages, drew down generous pensions from their increasingly indebted governments, and splurged on German cars, Finnish electronic goods, and French fashion accessories, their spending power was overstated by a currency that was too strong for their comparatively uncompetitive economies. In a mirror image of what happened with Chinese savings flows to the United States, the flow of cheap bank credit from the north subsidized the exports of northern producers and inflated asset bubbles in the south. It lasted until 2008, when the U.S. debt crisis provided the catalyst for a collapse. And even then, the northern banks spent the next three years minimizing the losses on their by now underwater investments while their countries' taxpayers reluctantly funneled new loans to the southerners to keep them current on their bank debts. This constant deferral of bank losses, the failure to clear debts, and the insidiously destructive fiscal austerity that the northerners demanded in return for rescue loans merely extended the euro zone's problems. The absence of a central political mechanism through which the euro zone countries could devise a coherent strategy, share fiscal resources, and enact uniform banking policies meant that the crisis lacked a sweeping master plan to clear out bad loans and apportion losses. Without that, recovery could not begin. Eventually the banks were asked to accept and write down losses on their Greek loans, but by then the problem had spread and the costs to all—including to the banks, for whom the market value of their assets kept plummeting—were becoming astronomical. Why weren't banks made to accept and write down losses as soon as it became obvious that Greece or Ireland couldn't repay their debts on their own? Because politicians feared that too much red ink at just one major financial institution could trigger widespread economic destruction. The problem was no different from that of the Lehman crisis: banks were still too big to fail.

From here let's briefly regress into cultural reductionism and observe that the mega-banks of Germany, France, the United Kingdom, and the United States came to this powerful position by way of an international financial system that was a distinctly Anglo-Saxon creation. This system, in which global capital markets rather than local banking relationships determine the price of credit, emerged out of Britain's "Big Bang" reforms of the mid-1980s and was entrenched by the deregulatory fervor with which the U.S. financial sector was overhauled after that. Much to the annoyance of euro zone leaders, the "demands of the market," which constantly set the parameters for policy making in Berlin, Paris, Madrid, Rome, and Athens, are not conveyed by representatives of the common currency area so much as via the investment banks and hedge funds of London and New York.

Their interests are defended by the U.S. and U.K. governments, which consistently advocate a less interventionist approach to financial markets than the Social and Christian Democratic governments of continental Europe. The conflict between those two models was ratcheted up to dangerous heights in December 2011 when British Prime Minister David Cameron, backed by the euroskeptics in his Conservative Party, refused to agree to an amendment to the twenty-seven-member European Union's treaty that would have helped soften the crisis experienced by the seventeen members of the EU that use the euro. Cameron insisted on British autonomy over certain financial regulatory matters, a move that appeared to put the interests of London's bankers and fund managers over those of the euro zone citizens whose debts they trade. After all, in London and New York, traders earn salaries and bonuses denominated in pounds or dollars, which means they lack skin in the game of the euro crisis. Among them are the latest recipients of a label that first arose during the Clinton era: the "bond vigilantes." Their decisions to buy or sell debt securities can alter governments' borrowing costs and so force them to cut spending and forswear default. Continental Europeans are naturally frustrated by having to kowtow to these brash outsiders and to witness their fates seemingly controlled by a bunch of unelected, overpaid, pinstripe-wearing twentysomethings in Canary Wharf.

European patience for the United Kingdom's self-interested defense of the laissez-faire financial model is now wearing thin. In the aftermath of the first crisis in 2008, Germany and France put their weight behind a "Robin Hood" tax on financial transactions to discourage excessive risk taking and build up an insurance fund against future financial bailouts. But Britain, whose London-based firms would lose the most from such a tax, refused to go along. On other occasions, continental European governments slapped temporary bans on short-selling of financial stocks, hoping to block a strategy by which speculators profited from falling share prices, but that simply meant that these players took their business to London. Now, after Cameron's dramatic veto of the fiscal pact, there is even speculation that the U.K. will eventually split from the European Union and that the seventeen members of the common currency area will enact measures to force financial business away from London and into continental banking centers such as Paris and Frankfurt. One can imagine both the euro zone's Lutheran northerners and its Catholic southerners wanting to escape the grip of opportunistic Anglicans, who appear to them to treat self-interest as the only dogma worth following.

But it's pointless to blame one nation or culture for Europe's problems. Indeed, the French and German governments were as guilty as the British of mollycoddling their powerful banks. And they did so because a pan-European banking system let these institutions develop gargantuan debt exposures to the troubled sovereign governments of Europe. For that flawed aspect of financial policy, all EU members share blame. According to the Bank of International Settlements, between March 1999—after the first quarter of the euro era—and March 2011, French banks' loans outstanding to the five most troubled nations—Italy, Spain, Ireland, Portugal, and Greece—grew from $109 billion to $671 billion. Over that same period, German banks' exposure to the five nations went from $118 billion to $533 billion and U.K. banks grew their positions from just $38 billion in 1999 to $374 billion in early 2011. During the first decade of the euro's existence, this big credit growth was seen as a sign of the single currency's success, proof it had fostered a giant, continent-wide capital market that was efficiently unleashing a flood of investment to the benefit of the poorer regions. It represented welcome convergence between the center and the periphery. But by 2008, German and French officials saw their banks' large exposures as an indicator of systemic risk. Money flows were now heading back into the safe havens of German bonds, and as convergence became divergence, the risk of default in the peripheral countries grew. In this environment, governments feared that if a few banks were to book a big a loss on, say, their Greek bond holdings, they would cover their losses by selling their positions in Spanish or Italian debt. And this could in turn pressure those countries' finances, provoking risky contagion selling in those bigger economies.

Yet, as with Wall Street's 2008 crisis, this risk could have been avoided if banks had carried enough equity capital so that shareholders could absorb the losses. Flawed regulations not only left banks undercapitalized but also encouraged their binge on sovereign debt. Once London's bond vigilantes began bashing the peripheral countries' debt markets, the too-big-to-fail European banks, which were sitting on giant holdings of these flimsy securities, became vulnerable to a system-threatening collapse. But euro zone leaders acted differently from what governments had done to avoid systemic meltdown in 2008. Rather than inject capital into banks and impose restrictions on what their managers can do with taxpayer funds, they funneled money to the banks' debtors—in this case, the governments of the euro zone periphery—and imposed strict rules on *them.* It still amounted to a backdoor bailout of the banks, one that was supplemented by the European Central Bank (ECB), which gave them billions of euros in emergency loans. But in this case the price charged for these transactions took the form of the spending cuts and other austerity measures that were demanded of the governments receiving the bailouts. This was not even an indirect or deferred cost to taxpayers; in this case, the European public bore the direct and immediate burden of their governments' decision to let shaky banks survive.

Of course, the borrowers in those peripheral countries do share the blame. In Greece and Italy, public servants were overpaid and underproductive, countless inefficient industries enjoyed government protection, and tax evasion was a way of life, all of which left their governments deep in debt. In Spain and Ireland, it was the individual households that borrowed beyond their means, and to such an extent that when the mismatch between income and debt payments was exposed by the 2008 financial crisis, their failed mortgages left local lenders in need of large capital injections from their ill-prepared governments. But just as the mismatch between Chinese savings and U.S. spending is best explained by the low price of credit and the globally misaligned policies that keep it that way, the euro zone's problems are a function of the various policies around which a flawed intra-Europe financial system is built. These have bred glaring economic imbalances between different euro zone countries. The causes of this crisis are thus systemic and structural in nature; there was little that individuals in the debtor countries could do about it—whatever their cultural predisposition.

As it is now, the costs to those populations are mounting, and diminishing their general well-being. In Italy and Greece, where elected governments were forced out of power so that unelected technocrats could take charge of reforms demanded by the powers-that-be in Berlin, Paris, and Brussels, angry citizens protest that they've given up their democracy and national sovereignty. In this poisonous environment, mistrust in the entire project of European integration is growing. The future of the European Union, whose impressive success in breeding peace and prosperity has made it a global symbol of what's possible in international cooperation, is at stake. To preserve it, governments must avoid foisting all the costs of mending the financial system onto ordinary citizens and instead impose sweeping, internationally coordinated reforms on their financial institutions to make them more accountable for those costs.

A Spectacular Fall from Grace

Much of the attention during the first two years of the euro crisis was directed toward the basket case of Greece, whose use of false data to measure its deficits triggered the first market panic in late 2009. Later the focus turned to Italy, the third-biggest borrower in the world, where scandal-ridden Prime Minister Silvio Berlusconi played and lost a dangerous game of brinkmanship with the ECB, which reluctantly agreed to buy his government's bonds. But Spain is arguably a better place from which to comprehend the complex, far-reaching, and systemic realities of the euro problem. Lauded by economists for making orthodox reforms to its labor market and economy, Spain attracted a veritable flood of foreign investment between 1995 and 2007. Throughout this period, the advent of the euro had the almost magical (though unsustainable) effect of reducing credit prices and fostering a boom in borrowing.

After having been one of Europe's poor backwaters for most of the twentieth century, Spain used this opportunity to expand its footprint in the world. As its economy grew to become the eighth largest in the world, Spain's banks, telecommunications, and technology companies gained prominence in Latin America and elsewhere. But if Spain's meteoric rise was eye-catching, its fall from grace after 2008 was spectacular, with much at stake for the rest of Europe—and, by extension, the rest of the world. Spain's government wasn't as spendthrift or dishonest with its data as Greece's was, and its banks weren't quite as excessive in their mania for property loans as Ireland's were. But because of its relative size and rapid economic growth, and because of the breadth of investment it received from European firms and individuals, Spain's fate was vital to the survival of the euro itself. As with Italy, it was never clear that the EU and IMF could come up with enough funds to bail out Spain were it to need them, and yet a default by its government would be so much more devastating to the euro project. This put enormous pressure on the government in Madrid and, ultimately, on the Spanish people.

Spain's case is also especially instructive for our study of the global financial system. The roller coaster it rode shows how illusory financial gains can obscure the unsustainable imbalances that build up when there is insufficient policy coordination across countries. And because its real estate boom was in part stoked by individual, middle-class investors from the United Kingdom and Germany, it is also a reminder that the ups and downs of globalization are caused not only by giant multinational banks and corporations but also by the countless savings and spending decisions of ordinary individuals.

Expats in Crisis

If Spain was at the center of the euro zone's transition from financial miracle to crisis, then its ground zero was the Costa del Sol in Andalusia, long one of the poorest of Spain's seventeen autonomous regions. The sunny climate from which it takes its name and the lower cost of living meant that the Costa del Sol became one of the most sought-after places to buy holiday or retirement properties in Europe. Encompassing beach towns such as Málaga, Torremolinos, and Marbella, as well as dozens of traditional "white villages" in the surrounding hillsides, this strip of land just inside the Strait of Gibraltar's gateway to the Mediterranean was transformed into something unrecognizable by a phenomenal construction boom.

One clear manifestation of that transformation is the "Little England" community, to which a half million Britons now belong. Drawn to the region in increasing droves from the late 1990s onward, these English transplants constructed a self-contained subeconomy that functions almost as if the Andalusian Spaniards aren't there. A flick through the ads in *The Sentinella,* a monthly English-language magazine, provides a snapshot. Dr. Michael Mannish, a University of London–educated "English Dentist," gives "Peace of Mind @ Local Prices"; Don Brown touts his "Dream of Eden Gardening Services"; and Terry McCormick from "Investments Direct UK" offers a "no obligation friendly chat." The magazine is full of ads for plumbers, dog minders, beauticians, restaurants, and, most prominent, real estate agents—virtually all citing owners with distinctly English names. Other examples of the subeconomy at work: the Tuesday farmers' market that a group of Brits runs in the town of Vélez-Málaga to sell their own produce; the English signs everywhere; the commercial districts of seaside towns such as Torremolinos and Marbella, where it's easy to believe there are more English pubs per square mile than in a typical English village.

When I visited in May 2010, this subeconomy was in a state of trauma.

A three-year plunge in the British pound and the sharp losses sustained by U.K. financial markets had halved the pensions and U.K.-based interest and dividend earnings that served as the main source of income for many British expats. These relocated Englishmen were carrying out a decade-long role as agents of a sharp boom-and-bust cycle in southern Spain. Initially they were the conduit through which the United Kingdom exported the spoils of the City's financial expansion. But when the expansion turned into a contraction, they then helped to export Britain's crisis. It's an example of the subtle ways in which the too-big-to-fail banks of London exert their far-reaching influence on the world.

Few of these expats would have had work experience in the U.K. as bond traders or stock brokers, but the amount of extra money they had to spend in the south of Spain was nonetheless determined by the London financial district's fortunes. For many years, their retirement and investment incomes consistently rose as their financial and property investments back home steadily climbed on the back of the City's highly leveraged investment bets. Meanwhile, the expansion produced a super-strong British pound—which bought at least 1.50 euros for most of the European currency's first eight years of existence—and ensured that their money went a long way. Tens of thousands of British citizens joined a buying frenzy, snapping up farmhouses, condominiums, villas, restaurants, hotels, and bars. There was a parallel influx of expatriates from Germany, the beneficiaries of an industrial boom in their home country that was similarly fueled by the credit boom in the euro zone and the global community. The financial impact from big-spending foreigners on the Costa del Sol was then magnified by the speculative excesses of Spanish property developers who had access to increasingly easy credit. And from there, it rippled outward into a nationwide real estate bubble that exceeded even that of the United States. Eventually, after housing prices had trebled in twelve years, a combination of overdevelopment, excessive debt, and regulatory failure pushed the Spanish property market to a tipping point. In Andalusia, all it took was a sharp correction in the overvalued, mispriced British pound to send that market over the edge.

Official estimates of the price collapse for the entire Spanish market talk of a 10 percent decline from its 2007 peak to its 2010 trough, but those are considered unreliable. An index produced by real estate evaluation group Tinsa puts the drop at just under 24 percent and shows it continuing well into 2011, with a decline of 30 percent for the coastal regions. The illiquid nature of the property market, where many homes are subject to fractional ownership due to complicated inheritance laws, means that market-wide price readings are hard to gauge and could well entail bigger falls than these readings. At the time of my visit, some 1.2 million defaulted properties were controlled by Spain's dysfunctional *caja* savings banks; many of these properties were empty condominiums for which the heavily indebted developers were unable to find buyers. Anecdotal evidence suggests this overhang drove prices sharply lower than official figures suggested, especially in Andalusia. Lorenzo Bernaldo de Quirós, a Madrid-based economist, told me in May 2010 that he'd been eyeing a particular property in southern Spain since 2007, over which time the offering price had gone from €900,000 to €190,000. (*"Fantastico"* is how he described the price change—surely not a word the seller would use.)

This financial squeeze hit the Costa del Sol's Little England hard. Many retirees and prospective retirees were forced to dust off their skills and ply the trades they'd left behind—presumably to the benefit of *The Sentinella*'s advertising revenues. This area is not exactly a French Riviera–like place of jet-setting expatriate elites. It's a working- and middle-class community of modest means that found a way to make its money stretch further. Now many of its members were in dire financial straits. In addition to their exchange rate losses, they were sitting on giant investment losses.

Mark Bellamy moved with his wife, Stephanie, to the region in the early days of the boom and bought a house in a village called Iznate, setting himself up as a taxi driver. He also purchased a van and carved out a lucrative niche carrying other new arrivals' belongings from the Málaga airport to their new homes. When we met he was having a tougher time. A few years prior he'd bought a seaside pad in Benalmadena for €100,000. It was now worth €60,000, he estimated. And there was little demand for his regular taxi service, which was why he was grateful to have the van. It was now doing a decent trade shipping people's stuff back to the airport. By 2010, thousands of returnees had headed back to Britain, their dream of a comfortable life in the sun destroyed by a falling pound and a dysfunctional real estate market.

Others who'd invested in properties for profit were frustrated not only by the fall in demand and prices but by a regulatory backlash from local authorities. Some British homeowners were told that the homes into which they'd sunk their life savings were not properly licensed and were to be demolished. "They have cotton wool in their ears. There's no logic," said Toni Waterman, my host at Escuela la Crujía, a bed-and-breakfast in Vélez-Málaga, who moved to Spain from London in 2002 with her Basque husband and two sons to set up a small real estate firm geared toward British investors. "We just don't understand what the Andalusian government has been doing," Waterman went on. "Up until now, there has been a steady supply of northern Europeans attracted to this beautiful area and wonderful climate. And they were bringing in money, not only to buy properties but also to do up houses and do them up beautifully. . . . They employ local people. Everybody benefits from it, right down to the guy who sells the gas bottle."

There is likely *some* logic to the local authorities' decision making, although it would not make English property owners any happier. Overdevelopment left the region with a giant oversupply of unoccupied condos and villas—"poxy little flats" in "multiunit monstrosities," Waterman called them—many built by people with close connections to local politicians. So one way to deal with the oversupply's negative impact on prices was to restrict development by less politically connected people. And small, powerless foreign investors were the perfect target. It is a familiar story: construction is dependent on the blessing of local government authorities, but too often the licensing process is unfairly shaped by politics and corruption in ways that contradict sustainability and economic objectives. When the market is hot and the sums get larger, the incentive to bend the rules is even greater. It is a frequently occurring element in the cycle of greed that feeds into every property bubble.

The results of this unbalanced policy making were visible in a drive I took along the Costa del Sol: row after row of bland, pro forma condo buildings lined the shores of seaside towns, nearly all of them sporting signs that read "Se Alquila" (For Rent) or "Se Vende" (For Sale). There were pockets of foreign tourists, but German and British homebuyers were no longer coming. Most hard hit: the local construction industry, which had ground to a halt.

"Before the crisis, we had too much work. I couldn't keep up," said a contractor who provided only his first name, Miguel. He owned a cement mixer that once had been constantly in service laying foundations for new homes. When I met him, he'd hardly had a job for six months. "And what there is, isn't good work," he said. "You do the job, but it is difficult to collect what the guy owes me." Miguel was especially upset with the way the banks treated him. When he'd sought a home equity loan during the boom years, he'd asked for 6,000 euros and the loan officer had said, "Why don't you take 10,000?" So he did. But now, he said, "even though I can't get people to pay what I'm owed, the bank is telling me they will take my house if I don't pay them." He grabbed his crotch to indicate how the bank had him trapped.

Everyone was corrupted by the boom, Miguel said: the construction workers who took on excessive debt, the bankers who irresponsibly ramped up credit lines, the real estate agents who took advantage of fresh-off-the-boat Englishmen to demand extra commissions, and the local officials who saw construction licenses as a route to power and wealth. And then all the speculation blew up in their faces. "In this region, what you would normally construct in thirty years, they built in ten," he said.

The economic impact of such a rapid rise and fall in work was profound. Adela Díaz Pardo, who ran the bar at the Alaska 2 restaurant in Torre del Mar, a now dead-quiet seaside town, said the biggest blow to business was the absence of construction workers during the breakfast *tapas* shift. "They used to stop by around 6:30 a.m. and have some squid, or potatoes, or a pastry," she said. "These days, there's nobody. Not a soul." Outside the bar, the cars in an adjacent taxi rank did not move for the entire hour I was there. A driver who also gave only his first name, Federico, said he'd been driving for fifteen years and had never seen things as bad. He seemed bewildered. "We don't really have any explanation for how this has happened, exactly. Some professors might have some ideas, but I don't have any," he said.

When Everyone Loved the Euro

Sure enough, plenty of professors of economics do have explanations. Most revolve around the effect that the euro's arrival had on the price of credit. With the disappearance of the legacy currencies from the economies of the first eleven states to adopt the euro on January 1, 1999—the Deutschmark, the French franc, the Italian lira, the Spanish peseta, and seven others—people investing in those countries' bonds no longer worried about the risk of depreciation when transferring their earnings back into their home currencies. Without this exchange rate threat, the risk premium that was priced into different bonds' interest rates no longer seemed relevant. So in the second half of the 1990s, as the committed member states got their monetary policies into line in preparation for currency union, bond markets underwent a rapid convergence in rates. They all converged downward toward those of Germany's "risk-free" benchmark bonds rather than gathering in the middle. In 1995, ten-year Spanish government bonds commanded a five-percentage-point risk premium over German bonds. But by the time the euro came about, this gap had narrowed to a spread of just one percentage point. These declining rates for governments naturally dragged down the rates paid by private creditors due to the benchmarking intrinsic to all bond markets.

Then in 2004, new capital adequacy rules under the now much-criticized Basel II accord on bank supervision deemed government bonds to be assets of sufficiently low risk that banks did not need to hold any capital at all against them. This ruling's egregiously flawed logic was exposed six years later by Greece's fiscal collapse, but for a number of years it sharply lowered the cost of holding such bonds, which boosted demand for them, further adding to price gains and declines in yields. Interest rates paid by governments became very low, while banks' exposure to these sovereign borrowers grew rapidly.

This twelve-year period also saw a sharp fall in real interest rates—the amount investors earn once the nominal rate on an investment is adjusted for the diminished purchasing power caused by inflation. The market put greater trust in the new European Central Bank's inflation-fighting credentials, which it inherited from the famously hawkish German Bundesbank, than in those of the previous national central banks, so it accepted a lower interest rate in compensation. Meanwhile, the euro instantaneously created a continent-wide pool of available investment funds, which made capital markets deeper and more efficient. The investment opportunities in corporate bonds, mortgage-backed securities, and other private debt instruments grew rapidly for banks, insurance companies, and pension funds, which now had markets with the depth and liquidity they needed. In all, these trends meant that the cost of credit plunged. And, of course, all this happened while the savings of China and other emerging market surplus countries were flowing into world financial markets. It was a boom time from Shanghai to New York to Dublin, and places such as the Costa del Sol were in the thick of it.

In Spain, the cheaper credit came with an easing of mortgage lending standards. Before the boom, virtually all borrowers, regardless of their employment or income status, were limited to mortgages of ten years, had to put down 30 percent of the value of the purchase in cash, and still needed a third-party guarantee, typically from a parent. Interest rates then were around 18 percent, or 6 points above inflation. Come the 2000s, home loans looked much more like the U.S. model: thirty-year terms and down payments as low as zero with rates only 1.5 percentage points over a markedly lower inflation rate. This was a paradigm shift, and it created all sorts of new opportunities for businesses and consumers. As analysts at the political risk consultancy STRATFOR noted, the reduction in interest rates in Spain and other southern European beneficiaries of this new structure was so big that it equated to a saving on monthly payments of more than 60 percent for a standard thirty-year mortgage. No wonder Spaniards acted as if all their Christmases had come at once. With no frame of reference and a dearth of productive industries in which to invest this cheap capital, they plowed it into real estate, as housing developers tapped a network of underregulated *caja* savings banks to build vast new residential complexes.

For a long time, this credit and property boom worked wonders. Spanish unemployment dropped from 20 percent in 1995 to below 8 percent in 2007. And GDP growth averaged around 4 percent, about two points more than the EU average. With the inflow of cheap credit, Spaniards started buying expensive cars and other quality goods produced by their northern neighbors. But the dominance of housing in the economic equation should have raised concern. Investment in the residential sector rose by 150 percent over the same period, far outstripping growth in the economy itself, such that it more than doubled its contribution to GDP to almost 10 percent. In the Costa del Sol, housing's role in the economic expansion was even greater. Meanwhile, there was some sleight of hand in the improved employment picture. Reforms in the 1990s permitted firms to hire new workers under temporary contracts without adjusting the notoriously steep worker protection costs for existing employees, who were eligible for forty-five days' severance for every year they had worked. To gain more flexibility, employers created millions of new temporary jobs, many of them in the booming residential construction industry. But when that sector went into its precipitous decline, these workers were summarily laid off. Unemployment spiked back to the early 1990s level of 20 percent, while youth unemployment surged to 43 percent, the young primarily being the recent job seekers who'd received temporary contracts without severance penalties.

The post-euro credit boom also produced an elephantine bubble in Ireland's housing sector. Home prices in Dublin increased fivefold and rent yields dropped as low as 1 percent in some parts of the city, meaning that it would cost you $1 million to buy a house that you could rent for just $800 a month. Overzealous lending left that country's six biggest banks exposed to massive losses on their mortgage portfolios, blowing out a giant hole that the government would try to plug with guarantees, only to see its finances dragged into the mire with them. In Greece, the flow of cheap money went into short-term government debt, which the financial authorities refinanced on a persistent basis to prop up one of the most generous welfare states in Europe. The typical male Greek worker retired at fifty-five, while women did so at fifty, both with a pension that averaged 94 percent of their pre-retirement income. Germans, by comparison, retired at sixty-five on a pension worth 40 percent of their earnings—a key bone of contention when German voters were asked to support rescue funds for Greece. Similarly, Portugal and Italy used this new flow of euro funds to stoke their economies, patching over waning productivity and sagging exports. Iain Begg, an economist at the London School of Economics, points out that the narrower interest rates provided Italy's government with a windfall of reduced public debt payments worth 5.5 percent of GDP. "It's quite easy in such circumstances to defer structural reforms," Begg said.

Sitting at the economic core of the euro zone, Germany and France had very different experiences with monetary union. Largely because of wage and cost freezes implemented to pay for post–Cold War reunification, Germany entered the euro in 1999 with a lean, highly efficient industrial base. Its productive manufacturers then got a giant financial fillip as the creation of a single Europe-wide capital market combined with a global liquidity glut filled with surging Asian currency reserves to give Germans access to cheap credit. With that they expanded their operations and broke into markets in the peripheral countries of the newly formed euro zone, where tens of millions of customers now had access to cheap credit for the first time, much of it indirectly provided by German banks. Gains accrued to French producers too. They weren't as efficient as their German counterparts, but they counted on three of the largest and most internationally adventurous banks in the world—Société Générale, BNP Paribas, and Credit Agricole—to flood newly discounted loans into the now integrated southern European markets. Both money and goods began to rapidly flow from Europe's wealthy core to its wannabes at the outer, with countries from the former now growing their current account surpluses while those from the latter ran ever-larger deficits. Disguised in this was the fact that the recipients of those flows weren't keeping up in the productivity or industrialization game. It was similar to the way that excessive debt enabled lower-income U.S. households to believe they were keeping up with the wealthier Joneses, only here the disguised gap in true earning capacity was a nation-versus-nation problem.

When the international credit binge was brought to a halt in 2007 by the subprime mortgage crisis in the United States and the banking problems in the United Kingdom, these structural inefficiencies and cross-border imbalances were glaringly exposed. As the global recession took hold, governments embarked on stimulus programs. They also moved with varying urgency to backstop their failing banks. Suddenly all the risk was transferred to the government. Bond investors, now more discerning, started dumping the sovereign debt of the peripheral countries. After converging to near-zero with the rise of the euro, risk premiums once again blew out in a differentiated way across the euro zone. Charts comparing the trajectory of interest rates for Greece, Ireland, Portugal, and Spain to those of Germany now present a bowtie image: starting out wide and differentiated in 1995, narrowing to a single line from 1999 to 2008, and then fanning out again in 2009. The dispersal continued through 2010 and 2011, with those countries that were forced to accept a bailout under a new EU-IMF facility seeing their rates rise the most. Ireland's ten-year bond rate ballooned out to 14 percent, eleven and a half points higher than Germany's. And in a sure sign that investors were betting on an imminent default, yields on Greek one-year bonds were in early December 2011 showing an eye-popping 300 percent. By contrast,

Germany's one-year bond yields traded below 0.5 percent. That gap is a compelling descriptor of the currency union's failure.

Europe's stewards of the financial system seemed oblivious to the risks during the pre-crisis era. In the first half of 2008, even with the United States grappling with recession and a mounting subprime crisis, the ECB routinely declared after its monthly interest-rate-setting meetings that "the euro area economy has sound fundamentals and does not suffer from major imbalances." Each month, the repeated statement—much of it cut and pasted from the previous month's—would talk of "resilient" growth, "ongoing" investment expansion, "sustained" profitability, an absence of "significant signs of supply constraints on bank loans," and "labor force participation [that has] increased significantly . . . to levels not seen for 25 years."

As had happened in the United States, this optimistic mind-set was fed by a cocktail of capital inflows, easy monetary policy, soft regulations, and a major structural change in the financial marketplace (in Europe with the introduction of the euro, in the United States in Wall Street's structured finance industry). As investors raced to match their peers' high rates of return, the cheap money created an illusion that risk had been neutralized on both sides of the Atlantic. The result was a drop in lending standards and a deep, systemic state of collective denial. In Europe's case, it stemmed from a fundamental failure in the system of continental governance, a flaw that can be traced to the beginnings of what was intended as a new, more integrated Europe.

The Disconnect

On a wintry February day in 1992, foreign and finance ministers from twelve countries gathered in the southern Dutch city of Maastricht on the banks of the tranquil Meuse River. Two thousand years after Romans had settled in the same place, this polyglot gathering was to make its own history. The ministers representing Germany, France, the United Kingdom, the Netherlands, Belgium, Italy, Spain, Portugal, Ireland, Denmark, Greece, and Luxembourg signed what became known as the Maastricht Treaty, giving birth to the European Union. They turned the European Economic Community, which had centered on a common market trading area, into a more cohesive political and economic institution. It was a proud moment for Europe, one that signified how far the continent had traveled from a recent violent past toward a legally recognized common identity and purpose. The treaty also laid the groundwork for the boldest international integration project in history: the creation of the European Monetary Union, which was to take the euro as its common currency seven years later.

To get there, the signatories in Maastricht agreed on "convergence criteria," which along with goals for low inflation and currency fluctuation established two critical rules on government financing: no candidate country could enter the euro zone unless it kept its fiscal deficit below 3 percent of GDP and its total public debt below 60 percent of GDP in the year prior to entry. Those same limits would then apply in perpetuity after entry. In 1997, ten of the original twelve signatories to the treaty joined with two new candidates—Austria and Finland, which replaced the opting-out states of Denmark and the United Kingdom—to enshrine these same rules into the monetary union's Growth and Stability Pact.

So much for good intentions. In late 2009, when the EU statistics agency Eurostat announced that Greece had missed its fiscal deficit target by almost 10 percentage points, a decade's worth of data massaging and excuses was laid bare. It was no secret that Greece had frequently understated its debt statistics and fudged its way through the Growth and Stability Pact rules, but minimal attention had been paid to it. Now, with the euro zone's banks hobbled by the preceding financial crisis, the folly of the pact signatories' mutual lenience was clear. Throughout the prior decade, the European Economic and Financial Affairs Council, or Ecofin, was empowered under the so-called excessive deficit procedures to sanction Greece. It could have forced it to place funds worth 0.4 percent of GDP in a non-interest-bearing account, for example. But it never acted because that would have invited charges of a double standard. Within the first four years of the euro zone's existence, Germany and France, the two power brokers at the center, had themselves surpassed the limits and no one had stopped them. And Italy, the third-biggest country, showed nothing but contempt for the rules, maintaining a debt-to-GDP ratio over 100 percent from 1992 onward. Ironically, it was Spain, which was to suffer so badly during the 2008 crisis, that proved one of the most disciplined and upstanding adherents to the Maastricht criteria.

The failure of the rules-setting process highlights what influential Harvard economist and longtime euroskeptic Martin Feldstein identified in the early days of monetary union as "the inherent conflict between the simultaneous existence of a single currency and the independent fiscal policies of the member countries." In the absence of a central treasury with its own fiscal agenda, the euro zone instead relied on treaties—something for which fully integrated federal unions such as the United States have no need. If California gets into trouble, its creditors will punish it, but unemployed Californians will receive federally subsidized unemployment insurance and other benefits from Washington with (almost) no questions asked. In this way, the presence of a common revenue-raising entity brings to the United States a stability that is nonexistent in the euro zone. Europeans had to fall back on agreed-upon but seemingly unenforceable rules.

Making matters worse, as Feldstein also accurately predicted, bond investors' deference to a single implied benchmark interest rate for all euro-denominated bonds meant they initially treated the otherwise fiscally varied euro zone member countries as equivalent, leaving "no market feedback to discipline large budget deficits." This weak political structure, established during a period of abundant and cheap global credit, induced yield-hungry creditors to lend excessively to both private and public sector borrowers across the euro zone. But because the money flowed so easily, it obscured the risks of bad behavior among the various governments, such that when it dried up these same creditors began to worry about the fiscal risks they'd previously ignored. As their selling drove down bond prices in the peripheral countries, their heavily indebted governments' borrowing costs soared, trapping them in a vicious, self-perpetuating cycle of eroding market confidence and rising difficulties in refinancing themselves.

The euro zone's disparity in fiscal and economic policies clashed with a unified, one-size-fits-all model for monetary policy. At first, while all the zone's economies were growing together, it didn't matter that the ECB was applying a single benchmark interest rate for all of them. But that setup became extremely complicated after 2008. The peripheral countries went into a nosedive, while Germany's giant economy got an additional boost of cheap credit from safe-haven-seeking inflows into its bond market and from growing Chinese demand for German manufacturers' sought-after industrial machines. With commodity prices rising and concerns growing about inflation risks in the booming German economy, the ECB differentiated itself starkly from the Fed in 2011 when it began hiking rates. This was the last thing that embattled countries such as Greece and Spain needed. For them, deflation was a far bigger concern than inflation. Credit Suisse analysts concluded in April 2011 that the optimal average interest rate should be 4.5 percent for Germany, which accounts for almost a third of euro zone GDP, and –4.6 percent for Spain, Portugal, Ireland, and Greece, representing about 17 percent of euro zone GDP. That month, the ECB raised its refinance rate by a quarter point to 1.25 percent and it followed that with a hike of similar magnitude in July—excessive moves that it then had to undo in November and December when data started pointing to a recession in the euro zone.

These contradictions and structural flaws in the euro zone were what brought it to the verge of collapse and left its leaders bereft of solutions to the crisis. The Maastricht Treaty and subsequent pacts barred one government from directly bailing out another, so the group instead created a special "off balance sheet" bailout fund known as the European Financial Stability Facility, or EFSF, and granted it €440 billion in loan guarantees. The idea was that if ever a struggling government ran out of cash it could turn to the EFSF, which because of the supposedly sound credit of core countries such as Germany and France could cheaply raise money in bond markets and finance a bailout loan with the proceeds. In theory, the mere presence of the EFSF was supposed to placate nervous markets and avoid any actual transfers of money. But it would prove impossible to marry theory with practice.

Greece, which started with a €110 billion loan in mid-2010, soon entered a second wave of fiscal problems. A vicious circle of shrinking economic demand, rising debts, and soaring interest rates arose, exacerbated by the deep cuts in spending that then–Prime Minister George Papandreou agreed to implement. Athens's Syntagma Square became the focal point of a Greek populace angered by the cutbacks, a place where anarchists did battle with riot police. In one especially wild outburst, banks were torched and three people died, scenes of which were piped straight into television sets on London trading floors, which only worsened investor sentiment about the prospects of Greece "sticking with the program." The self-evident failure of the Greek rescue plan planted the idea in bond investors' minds of an eventual Greek default, which then got them worried about how investors might react toward the debts of other peripheral countries. Thus those countries' bonds also fell and a self-defeating process of "contagion" set in. Half a year after Greece requested its bailout, heavily indebted Ireland, by then unable to pay the high interest rates demanded by bond markets, turned to the EFSF for funds. Six months later it was Portugal's turn. By the second half of 2011, the disease had spread to Spain and Italy, which saw their ten-year bond yields trade above or near 7 percent in November—a rate that, if it continued, would leave their giant debt loads growing faster than their economic output and beyond their capacity to repay without outside help.

The problem now was that the EFSF's emergency lending capacity, as defined by the guarantees behind it, was too small to rescue these two mega-economies. (Italy's hulking mass of outstanding liabilities alone ran to €1.9 trillion, making it the third-largest public debt tally in the world, and it needed to refinance more than €200 billion of that in 2012.) But by now, voters in the wealthier core countries had had enough. The euro zone, they insisted, was intended as a union of "stability" where governments kept their own finances on firm footing, not a "transfer union" where money flowed from the most fiscally sound to the weakest. Never mind that it was by then patently clear that without a political center in which taxation and spending powers were coordinated by a supranational authority, the monetary union's internal imbalances could not be resolved. Faced with a political impasse, markets went into panic mode.

The tortured debates involved all seventeen euro members, but in reality Germany held all the cards, such was its economic weight in the monetary union. Chancellor Angela Merkel faced a stark choice: presiding over a messy, chaotic breakup of the euro zone or supporting steps to create a proper political and fiscal union with a centralized authority managing taxation and spending. The creation of a United States of Europe was as unthinkable to German voters as the destruction of the euro was to German political elites. The same went for other "core" countries, where people increasingly felt that their sovereignty was under threat. So Merkel and her sixteen fellow heads of government took the middle path, trying to muddle through with stopgap solutions. Amid a constant cacophony of competing headlines, officials from seventeen different countries, the ECB, and the IMF sought to assert their different demands and interests. Thus the euro bloc bickered, postured, and haggled its way to a series of gimmicks, each intended to boost the lending power of the EFSF without putting more taxpayer money at risk. Every step seemed too little, too late, and too complicated. Ultimately, the world was left with an alarming picture of political dysfunction.

All of this just fired up the bond vigilantes, those well-paid agents of a globalized financial sector's knack for self-advancement and self-preservation, and made them even more inclined to dump the debts of struggling euro zone countries. With the banks that employ them sitting on mountains of poorly documented credit default swaps (CDS), which left governments permanently terrified of a systemic meltdown, these guys were more or less out of the reach of a poorly integrated global regulatory system. (It's not unlike the way that the United States and other countries fear being unable to sanction North Korea if it gets full nuclear capacity.) Bond traders, rather than governments, were setting the agenda. They were even dumping France's bonds, putting at risk the borrowing power of the EFSF, which depended upon the good credit of the guarantor core countries. Most troubling, European banks faced their own worsening funding crisis as they were turned away by U.S. money market lenders who feared that these banks' holdings of plummeting sovereign bonds made them risky credits.

Amid fears of a Lehman-like run on the financial system, European Union authorities decided to get tough. Belatedly recognizing that the region's over-leveraged banks were a key part of the problem, they estimated that they were short more than €100 billion in buffer capital and so ordered them to increase their ratio of capital to risk-weighted assets to a minimum of 9 percent by mid-2012 from their current 6 percent. It was a move that would have been eminently sensible during the boom but, because of the way it was handled, now merely raised the stress level in the financial system and shifted it to the global arena.

To understand how it could backfire, consider that after regulators have defined what constitutes both "capital" and "risk-weighted assets," a bank's capital adequacy ratio, which merely divides the former by the latter, is an easy metric to understand. It can be increased by either making the nominator bigger (increasing capital) or the denominator smaller (reducing assets). But at a time when eager investors in European banks were few and far between, acquiring fresh capital was an extremely expensive undertaking for the banks' owners. With the price for their shares so low, the banks had to sell many more of them to raise the amount of capital required to cover their asset base. The more they sold, the more it would dilute existing shareholders' stakes in the enterprise. So banks instead tried to improve their ratios by working to reduce the denominator and so sought to sell assets. They dumped whatever they could, both inside and outside the euro zone. This process of accelerated "deleveraging" merely perpetuated and exacerbated the death spiral in peripheral countries' bond markets. Falling prices and rising yields pushed their governments' borrowing costs ever higher.

In fact, euro zone regulators were too timid. In this desperate situation, they could have forced banks to meet their 9 percent target by raising capital rather than through asset sales. Those that couldn't attract enough demand for their shares would be taken over by the state. Shareholders and top management would be wiped out and the government would restructure the banks, preferably by splitting them into smaller units before reselling them to the private sector once the crisis had passed and risk appetite had returned. They should have done what the Obama administration didn't do with U.S. banks in 2008, in other words. A key problem was that for all their efforts to coordinate and centralize their management of the financial crisis and despite the formation of the European Banking Authority, the euro zone's bank regulators were still tied to national governments. That inevitably left them under political pressure to go easy on their own, powerful national banks. This was seen in the region's "stress tests," which were supposed to subject banks to worst-case-scenario tests of their ability to withstand major market shocks but which were repeatedly criticized for being too soft. Although banks operated freely across a globalized, international marketplace, their regulators were constrained by domestic political prerogatives.

Meanwhile, the domestic political resistance in the northern countries toward providing more aid to the struggling "PIIGS" left the euro zone reaching for financial engineering solutions that were reminiscent of those that fueled the U.S. subprime crisis. The entire EFSF, whose borrowings were guaranteed by member governments but were not formally recognized as existing liabilities, was an off-balance-sheet vehicle akin to those that U.S. banks used to purchase mortgages for bundling into CDOs. The structure became even more dubious once it was clear that the €440 billion in guarantees weren't enough to backstop Italy or Spain. Then the euro zone leaders drew up a plan to entice outside investors—with sovereign wealth funds such as China Investment Corp.

(CIC) being a prime target—into a fund in which the EFSF's contributing governments would bear the first 20 percent of losses if the borrowing governments defaulted. It was, many observers noted, a sovereign version of the hierarchical tranche structure used in CDOs. No wonder CIC and others said "thanks, but no thanks."

Against this failure of the government-led bailout plan and the flawed handling of the banks' undercapitalization, the European financial system fell into a cycle of self-perpetuating fear. The problem wasn't that the banks couldn't withstand taking a loss on, say, their Greek loans—a result that euro zone leaders came to see as inevitable—but rather that there was uncertainty over how all other actors in the market would react to such a "haircut." Banks faced a prisoner's dilemma: not knowing whether their peers would cover their Greek losses by selling Spanish or Italian bonds, they were guided by self-preservation and got ahead of that risk by selling their own holdings of the same debt. This of course only expedited the crisis they sought to avoid.

A key risk lay in credit default swaps, the same gigantic, opaque derivatives market that contributed to the 2008 disaster. Trillions of dollars' worth of default insurance had been written against the bonds of euro zone sovereign borrowers. If Greece were deemed by the derivatives industry's International Swaps and Derivatives Association (ISDA) to have defaulted on its bonds, all those contracts would be triggered. That left officials terrified of a systemic meltdown akin to the one that AIG's failure threatened to trigger in 2008. The fear was that banks that had written the CDS insurance would be compelled en masse to honor claims when there was no assurance that their balance sheets were strong enough to make the payments. This all-pervasive fear of "counterparty risk" underlay everything. For that reason, officials from the EU, the IMF, and the ECB—the so-called troika—worked in consultation with the ISDA to devise a Greek debt restructuring plan that would be deemed "voluntary" for creditors even though most big banks would be pressured to participate. Expediently, ISDA complied, indicating that under those terms it would not likely declare a CDS trigger. But that meant that investors who held these contracts as insurance now regarded their investment hedges as effectively worthless. So they opted for a more basic form of default risk hedging: they sold the bonds outright. And to make matters worse for the battered government debt markets, the loss of trust in CDS hedges meant investors would now charge a higher interest rate premium whenever they bought new bonds. The wrangling to avoid systemic contagion had backfired.

Yet the root cause of this particular problem was not the officials' ham-fisted effort to contain the systemic risk but the underlying structure of the CDS market. For all the post-Lehman efforts to make trading in those over-the-counter securities more transparent, this giant insurance market was still only as reliable as the banks that underwrite the contracts. And since there was still insufficient information about the interwoven global web of counterparty relationships, the risk that a mega-institution's collapse could trigger systemic losses in a mushrooming of CDS claims was an unquantifiable but very real risk. This huge problem had not been fixed since the last crisis. And that meant that when funding stress arose, investors facing the unknown had to assume the worst. So they adhered to an old adage: "sell first, ask questions later."

It wasn't just in Europe that this self-reinforcing, *procyclical* spiral took root. Banks everywhere, including big U.S. firms, were under pressure from shareholders to show that they were paring back exposure to euro zone debt lest the region collapse in a full-scale crisis. The failure of Jon Corzine's MF Global, which had bet big on Italian bonds, emphasized the need for conservatism. But as Keynes observed in the paradox of thrift, what is prudent for one institution can be disastrous for the group if each one acts to save its own skin. Meanwhile, European banks' rapid exit from their overseas interests and the crunch in short-term dollar credit made banks less willing to provide trade finance. That threatened to derail the wheels of international commerce. So, amid fears of the same paralysis in world trade that occurred in late 2008 and early 2009, the Fed made dollars cheaper to borrow overseas by cutting the fees it charges for currency swap lines provided to its central bank counterparts overseas. This came as a relief to the market but it did nothing to resolve the underlying structural problem that entwined the euro zone's overburdened governments and its undercapitalized banks.

The once unthinkable idea of countries leaving the euro zone now rose to the forefront of people's minds. If countries were insolvent and emergency aid from others was not forthcoming, the combination of default and devaluation—a tactic that was effective in reviving growth in emerging markets hit by the crises of the 1990s—offered a way out of the nightmarish cycle of austerity and growing debt burdens. Greek resort owners looked enviously across the Aegean Sea at Turkey's booming tourism business and its 8 percent growth rates, both helped by a relatively weak Turkish lira. Italy's fashion industry longed for a new competitive edge in export markets and Spanish property owners pined for the return of English homebuyers with strong pounds in their pockets. But while dumping the euro would ultimately have a cathartic effect, Argentina's example from 2002, when it broke a strict one-for-one currency system that resembled a currency union with the U.S. dollar, suggests these countries would first experience financial devastation. A euro exit would produce mass bankruptcies and legal chaos as commercial contracts would be broken en masse. And then there was the logistical conundrum: how to introduce an entire stock of new notes and coins without signaling the change in advance and triggering a mass exodus of savings to the banks of other euro zone countries. Any such bank runs would utterly destroy their financial systems. And if one country were to leave the euro, wouldn't others do the same? If that included Italy, the competitive blow to French exporters from a weak lira would force the reintroduction of the franc as well. And if France fell, the euro would be over. Indeed, it is easy to imagine a euro domino effect provoking a true, 1930s-style global currency war.

Unfathomable as such events were, Europeans began openly talking about and even preparing for an end to the euro. Banks, brokers, and clearinghouses that managed the back-office systems through which currencies are traded began testing contingency arrangements so that their systems could transact in the currencies of the pre-euro era. Lawyers devised complicated plans to reconcile the billions of euros' worth of myriad competing claims that would need arbitration if euro-based contracts were converted to those legacy currencies. Yet no matter what preparations they made, there was no getting around the fact that a euro breakup, encompassing a region that accounts for an entire fifth of world GDP, would likely do unprecedented damage to the international system of trade and payments. It took sixty-four years from the last time the global economy saw a contraction in aggregate output for there to be a worldwide recession in 2009. And yet here we were facing the risk of another one just three years later.

So with the governments of the euro zone failing to deliver the sweeping reforms needed to save the euro zone, many politicians and economists were by the last quarter of 2011 virtually screaming at the European Central Bank to take action. They wanted it to make large-scale purchases of the peripheral nations' sovereign bonds with freshly minted euros—in effect, to print money. But the ECB, abiding by a strict charter of independence, resisted going beyond a small program of ad hoc purchases to which it reluctantly agreed in mid-2010. Instead, it lent hundreds of billions of euros in cut-rate emergency loans to the region's stressed-out banks. This revealed the contorting efforts to which the central bank would go to keep the European financial system afloat without bending its own rules. In late December, the ECB launched the first of two long-term refinancing operations (LTROs), providing a record €489 billion in three-year loans to 523 liquidity-starved banks at the newly reduced rate of 1 percent. The hope was that the banks would use that money to do what the ECB could not bring itself to do and buy the Spanish and Italian governments' bonds. The logic was that with ten-year yields between 6 percent and 8 percent, the ability to borrow from the ECB for three years at 1 percent made this an attractive "yield spread." But in a free market system, financial authorities can't compel banks to lend where they don't want to lend. And since they were terrified of owning bonds that might easily go into default, many banks simply gave the money back to the ECB. (Some €500 billion was kept on twenty-four-hour deposit at the central bank.) To be sure, some banks steered their newly obtained cash into sovereign bonds under the urging of national authorities. And in time, the massive liquidity injection also allowed U.S. lenders to get over their fear of European banks while fund managers such as George Soros took bold bets on the peripheral nations' bonds. But although yields eased from their alarming late-2011 levels, not enough money went into long-term bonds, whose borrowing rates were still unsustainably high. Instead, banks mostly plowed the super-cheap long-term financing into comparatively safe six- , twelve- , or twenty-four-month notes. Italy and Spain would have to keep rolling over their debt at short intervals, raising fears of auction failures each time. The can, to use the most overwrought cliché ofthe crisis, was being kicked down the road.

To many it appeared that the ECB was bending over backward to help distressed banks but doing nothing to aid distressed taxpayers. That approach was not only inequitable, the central bank's critics said, it was also suicidal. Unlike the quantitative-easing-happy Federal Reserve and Bank of England, the ECB refused to take on the vote of "lender of last resort" during a market meltdown. Holders of Italian and Spanish bonds had no reason *not* to panic, in other words. This reluctance to print massive amounts of money was founded on some real concerns. For one, the ECB was steeped in the strong-money traditions of the Deutsche Bundesbank on which it was modeled, an institution whose DNA was shaped by long-held memories of the hyperinflation nightmare of the Weimar Republic. Second, there was the issue of moral hazard: the idea that if the ECB bought their bonds in large amounts, peripheral nations would have no incentive to enact the reforms needed to get their fiscal and economic houses in order.

The ECB was not supposed to play politics. Its own independence rules, upon which its credibility as an inflation fighter is founded, required that it leave fiscal policy making to governments. And that made intervention in the high-risk Italian and Spanish cases extremely complicated.

But if the ECB was worried about retaining credibility, it was even more worried about a euro breakup, which would take the central bank out of existence altogether. It's on that basis that the wonky central bankers in Frankfurt were dragged against their will into the political maelstrom, where their actions had subtle but powerful effects. Amid a standoff between Italian prime minister Berlusconi and his euro zone counterparts over his wavering commitment to cut pensions and make key reforms, the ECB halted its incremental purchases of Italian bonds, which meant their yields rose above the alarming 7 percent threshold. With his country's financial system gripped by turmoil, Berlusconi was forced to resign within a week, and Mario Monti, a technocrat-minded economist and former EU commissioner, was appointed to head an unelected interim government. After that, the ECB began purchasing bonds again. That this happened in the month in which another Italian, Mario Draghi, took the helm of the central bank from the outgoing Frenchman Jean-Claude Trichet only encouraged speculation that it was playing politics.

Democracy Under Threat?

Draghi wasn't the only official arousing suspicions that outsiders were meddling in euro zone countries' political affairs. A *Wall Street Journal* exposé published in late December revealed that when Italy's bond market started to spiral out of control, German Chancellor Angela Merkel made a phone call to Italy's eighty-six-year-old President Giorgio Napolitano and discussed her view that Berlusconi was perhaps not politically strong enough to push through the austerity measures. According to the report, Merkel thanked Napolitano in advance for doing what was "within your powers" to promote reform. Days later, the octogenarian was sounding out leaders of Italy's fractured political parties over the prospects of appointing a new prime minister to replace Berlusconi.

There weren't many tears shed among the Italian left for the erratic, loose-lipped playboy and media mogul. Berlusconi's antics had made him the laughing stock of Europe while his Machiavellian politics had taken Italy to the brink of economic collapse. Nonetheless, this episode highlighted a growing concern among the throngs of "Occupy Rome" protesters: a perceived threat to national sovereignty. Greece had also seen an elected prime minister, George Papandreou, replaced by an unelected "eurocrat," former ECB vice president Lucas Papademos. It was hard not to note that these machinations had taken place in Athens and Rome, the cradles of modern democracy. Nor could many avoid the uncomfortable optics of Germany's role in these matters. The institutional memory of a painful past left many Europeans fearing that the industrial powerhouse at the continent's core was again picking and choosing the region's leaders. It was hardly a Nazi occupation, but the symbolism was powerful. Of course, the interim governments in Greece and Italy were only caretakers, put in place until elections could be held. But given the timing of their appointment, it was unavoidable that these unelected officials, in office at the will of external powers, would be charged with making monumental decisions about their countries' economic futures.

Yet the peripheral countries had already seen their sovereignty compromised—first by the bond vigilantes, who held policies hostage to their financial demands, then by the EU-IMF-ECB troika, which ordered austerity in return for financial aid. As such, they offered little resistance when yet another crisis-tackling plan was hatched toward the end of 2011. This one aimed to change the EU treaty so that euro zone governments would be subject to strict enforcement actions by EU authorities if they let their budgets stray from the Maastricht Treaty's limits on deficits and debts. This ceding of power to Brussels was unimaginable only months earlier and showed how desperate things had become. Many hoped that signing this pact would give the ECB sufficient confidence in Italy's and Spain's fiscal programs for it to commit to "unlimited" bond purchases and in doing so help those two countries roll over some €400 billion in bonds falling due in 2012. In reality, the planned treaty amendment was a fairly small step toward fiscal union and was pursued because it was more palatable to Germany than an alternative French plan for member countries to collectively issue "euro bonds" to be serviced out of a pool of shared tax revenues. Nonetheless, the planned treaty change showed that euro zone governments were increasingly, if reluctantly, ceding some control over their financial policy making to a more centralized structure. If this painful, piecemeal integration process undermined national sovereignty, it was still more favorable than the financial chaos that lay down the path of disintegration.

It was therefore a great frustration to euro zone governments that they could not convince one of the ten non-euro-using EU member countries to agree to a treaty change. The United Kingdom's veto meant that the seventeen euro-users had to instead craft an intergovernmental pact between twenty-six of the EU's twenty-seven members. This would not have the same legal weight as an EU treaty amendment and so left doubts over how well it could be enforced—including at the ECB, whose approval, and money, were badly needed. From the outset of the euro, the EU had proven incapable of enforcing the Maastricht Treaty provisions of fiscal rectitude. How would this flimsy pact be any different? It was becoming clear that a misalignment between the interests of the wider EU group and those of the monetary union subgroup was hindering efforts to stanch the hemorrhaging in debt markets. This was clearly evident in credit rating downgrades. The more that the euro zone's shift toward fiscal centralization stalled, the more ratings agencies raised doubts about member governments' capacity to service debts whose interest rates were spiraling. Eventually, in mid-January 2012, Standard & Poor's downgraded the debt of a host of euro zone sovereigns, including France, which lost its AAA rating, and it seemed only a matter of time before the other two big agencies, Moody's and Fitch, would do the same. As a natural consequence, the EFSF, whose credit was only as good as that of its guarantor governments, lost its AAA rating, a qualification that had previously been depicted as a vital pillar in its ability to cost-effectively lend to struggling peripheral nations. All of this only further rattled investors, who sold bonds and pushed euro zone member nations' borrowing costs even higher, thus elevating their default risk and demanding even tougher spending cuts and tax hikes as an offset. Europe seemed left with the worst of both worlds: an integration plan that was too weak to stem the turmoil in its debt markets and an increased level of interference in domestic affairs by outside powers. Meanwhile, social unrest was brewing as austerity measures took root just in time for winter.

Euroskeptics, particularly those in the U.K., will say that these governments have been forced into this unholy compromise because of the fundamental flaw of the euro project mismatch between monetary unity and fiscal disparity. And that is so. However, it does not necessarily follow that integration per se is a bad idea. In fact, the most constructive way to think about Europe's failure is to see it as a compelling example of the damage done when domestically determined national policy making is placed in the context of an increasingly integrated and globalized financial system. It speaks to the need for more, not less, integration—this time at the political level. After the euro's launch, Europe's financial system quickly evolved into a single, giant pool of credit with money freely flowing across the region's national borders. Its financial institutions now also gained access to even larger pools of money in the United States and elsewhere, much of it emanating from China and other developing-world high-savings countries. Yet governments stuck to national structures. They fell far, far behind the global capabilities of Big Finance.

The "marketization" of finance also played a destabilizing role. There was broad consensus that Greece could not repay debts worth more than 160 percent of GDP, but authorities still struggled to engineer a sought-after "orderly default" because they couldn't control how the market would react to a debt restructuring. It wasn't that large banks and pension funds didn't recognize the benefit of helping Greece clean its slate and of reducing the contagion risk to the rest of Europe. But even as these institutions complied with a troika diktat that Greece's private creditors accept a "voluntary" debt write-down before getting anymore bailout money, there was no guarantee that hedge funds and other strategic investors would tender their bonds into a loss-making swap. Greece needed near-full participation to make the debt restructuring worth it, yet if it amended contracts to coerce these potential "holdouts" into a deal, ratings firms would deem its terms "involuntary," likely triggering credit default swaps. That would pose a risk to the euro zone financial system that the EU and IMF could not tolerate. Confined in this way, the negotiations repeatedly broke down. Meanwhile, the troika refused to finance a planned cash enticement for bondholders until the three Greek political parties signed off on yet another round of unpopular pension and wage cuts. Amid furious rioting by opponents of this latest austerity law, the Greek parliament reluctantly agreed to it in mid-February 2012, which kept the restructuring and the bailout agreement intact for the time being. But the social chaos left serious doubts about the capacity to sustain the austerity program after Papademos's interim administration was to be succeeded by a new government following elections in the spring. And that would leave doubts over future debt payments.

This scenario could not have arisen twenty years earlier, when international credit mostly took the form of direct loans by banks, which held them on their books from start to finish. It was much easier then for a country facing default to sit down with its creditors and organize a mutually beneficial debt restructuring. I remember covering the negotiations over crisis-wracked South Korea's debt in the winter of 1997–98 in New York. We waited outside in the cold while a group of bankers led by Citibank's William Rhodes engaged in all-night haggling with Korean officials around a table. It was tough, but in a matter of a few days a deal was done. Greece does not have that option. Its bond-holding creditors are too multitudinous to fit around a negotiating table and they range from banks to pension funds to individuals to hedge funds, each with a different agenda and a profit profile. Authorities have no control over how these investors might react to a debt restructuring. They also have no control over the highly sensitive feedback loop that transmits those reactions via lower bond prices back into the borrowing costs of the debt-laden government. And yet even in this volatile situation, euro zone defaults and bond restructurings would have been manageable were it not for the too-big-to-fail problem. In this sense, the euro crisis demonstrates how a highly globalized and marketized financial system that's dominated by institutions big enough to trigger systemic events leaves governments—and us, the general public—disempowered in our management of financial crises.

The broader issue of global imbalances, which as we've seen are themselves a result of uncoordinated policies and of a failure to integrate, also played a key destabilizing role in the euro zone crisis. Here, China bears much blame yet again. Because of the sheer size of its reserve accumulation, China was compelled to purchase euro assets as it diversified its portfolio away from dollars. But although it made much fanfare about buying Spanish and Portuguese bonds early on, its purchases were concentrated in safer French and German bonds once the crisis got really serious, traders say. As such, China was doing more harm than good. Its buying, along with that of Japan and other reserve-holding countries, widened the interest rate spread between the bonds of the core and those of the periphery and simply drove up the value of the euro, preventing a depreciation that would have brought relief to the peripheral countries. What's more, China placed conditions on its promises of help, relishing a dramatic shift in which emerging market nations that had been in hock to the European- and U.S.-controlled IMF a decade earlier were now calling the shots with the advanced world. At one point Premier Wen said that as a precondition for aid the EU had to recognize China as a "market economy," a technical label that would benefit Chinese companies in trade disputes. Other officials said they would demand European support for greater Chinese influence at the IMF. Yet all along China's subsidized exporters were taking over European producers' markets. The flip side of the Asian giant's reserve accumulation was a yuan that remained undervalued, especially against the euro, and that only further undermined the debt-laden peripheral countries' competitiveness.

As with the U.S. crisis before it, the contribution played by these imbalances in our global financial system got limited attention in media coverage of the euro crisis. That's perhaps because stories about intra-European conflict and cultural and political differences were easier to tell and comprehend. But if we ignore these broad structural problems and deal only with the divisions that exist within Europe, the region's exit from the crisis will be longer and more painful, not only for Europeans but for the rest of the world too.

Leaving Town

At the time of writing it was a legitimate question as to whether the euro zone would survive. The integration effort that was needed faced enormous resistance. Many of the region's citizens now perceived the whole European project as the source of their problems. This sentiment was accompanied by a profound sense that people had lost control of their destiny, that their future was now at the mercy of bond traders in London, bureaucrats in Brussels, and unelected central bankers in Frankfurt.

Spain's experience is again emblematic. Even without a formal EU bailout program, Spain had to commit to sweeping reforms and sharp fiscal cutbacks to win the trust of nervous bond investors. But in doing so, it also lost the trust of its own citizens, who only four years earlier were reveling in what seemed to be a grand new future opened up by the creation of the euro.

During my visit in May 2010, Prime Minister José Luís Rodríguez Zapatero announced plans to slash €15 billion from the budget in two years, all part of his government's commitment to the EU to reach a Maastricht Treaty–compliant deficit of under 3 percent of GDP by 2013. Public servants' salaries were to be cut by 5 percent and pensions frozen until 2012. It was a desperate about-face by a socialist prime minister who previously had vowed to expand the welfare state. Resisting vehement opposition from the unions with whom he was allied, he even acceded to a long-standing demand by business to reduce penalties for laying off workers, cutting their severance entitlement to thirty-three days of pay for every year of employment from the previous forty-five.

But to push through the legislation, Zapatero had to broker concessions from Spain's various political parties, whose interests ranged from the ideological demands of hard-leftists to the narrow nationalist claims of regional parties from the Spanish kingdom's seventeen autonomous regions. The horse trading threatened to bring about the worst of both worlds: fiscal austerity coupled with special-interest pork-barrel entitlements. The ugly process dragged Spaniards' confidence in their country's future to new lows. Masses of people calling themselves *"los indignados"* (the indignant ones) took to the streets to stage repeated protests. By now, Zapatero was deeply unpopular. Eventually he bowed out of the 2011 electoral race so that his struggling Socialist Party could find a more palatable candidate, but that didn't prevent it from losing the November election. Zapatero's conservative successor, Mariano Rajoy, will face fewer challenges within his own party, but his own stated commitment to austerity at all costs could clash with the intransigence of Spanish trade unions and other bastions of resistance. By the New Year, Rajoy was already warning of even harsher cutbacks as his government revealed that Spain would miss its 2011 deficit target by a full two percentage points.

Zapatero's government made major reforms, but the magnitude of the financial mess meant that Spain still teetered on the edge of a severe financial crisis. The government cleaned up many of the country's politically connected *caja* savings banks, whose unchecked lending had helped foment the housing crisis, forcing them to merge with stronger banks and to write down troubled loans. But as of early 2011, the *cajas* still had a combined €217 billion in mortgage assets on their books, accounting for about half of the total in the banking system, and the Bank of Spain was estimating that almost €100 billion of that, equal to 10 percent of Spanish GDP, would be difficult to collect. Such a giant overhang was bound to weigh on economic growth for years.

No group faced a bleaker future than Spain's young people. Due to the legacy of the worker redundancy scheme, which favored older workers, youth unemployment rose to 46 percent, double the national average. Confronting a dearth of job opportunities, Spain's most able and well-educated young workers were going abroad, feeding a brain drain. A country that had been a magnet for immigrants in the prior two decades, attracting Latin Americans in droves and a constant flow of North Africans, was now turning the tide the other way.

Ernesto García, twenty-three, was a sociology student from Madrid whom I found drinking cheap beer with friends in the city's Plaza Dos de Mayo, the center of a street-drinking subculture known as *botellón*. He said his job prospects had gone from bad to terrible since he began studying five years ago. "Then you could expect temporary contract jobs paying 800 euros a month, and better ones only if you put in many more years of study. What has changed is that for now not even those poor-paying jobs are available. There's nothing. . . . So of course, I'm thinking of [leaving Spain]. Many of my friends have already left, to London, to Berlin, to places in northern Europe." Nearby, twenty-eight-year-old PhD candidate Jesús Fernández said many of the engineering students he taught during the academic year had left when they finished their undergraduate studies. There were no more jobs in the construction industry that had once absorbed them, he said, and government cutbacks meant less funding for post-graduate studies. "I can think of two [ex–students] in New York, one in London, two in Germany, and others in South America," Fernández said. His friend Sandra Rueda, a twenty-four-year-old geological engineering student with long dreadlocks, was despondent. She reflected on the contrast between the unbridled optimism of the generation that came of age around the time of Franco's death in 1976 and the pessimism that pervades hers. "In 1976, the poor had absolutely nothing, but at the same time, they had everything. They had hope. They had the future ahead of them," she said. "Now we have everything, but we don't have a reason to believe in the future. I hope my children can get work in the future. I hope so. But I don't know."

Not only are jobs for people such as Sandra Rueda now at risk, but so too is a renaissance in Spanish culture that began with the end of the dictatorship and succeeded in making impressive inroads into the art and business worlds. It was a period in which Spain's painters, filmmakers, writers, and musicians formed a distinctly Iberian avant-garde, while companies such as Banco Santander and Telefónica were dubbed the "new conquistadors" as they revived a Spanish presence in Latin America and other parts of the global economy. Spain's impressive economic growth from 1980 to mid-2008, during which it rose to be the world's eighth-largest economy, had earned it a voice in world institutions such as the World Bank and the United Nations. It had sponsored generous foreign aid and development programs. Now it was reduced to a state of virtual bankruptcy.

"Spain is in the worst crisis of its economic history and the biggest political crisis since the civil war," said Madrid-based economist Lorenzo Bernaldo de Quirós. "We are not simply in a recession, but in a recession that is going to evolve into a period of stagnation for many years with very weak growth rates." The only solution, he said, was a harsh downward adjustment in Spain's standard of living and an economy-wide debt restructuring. This process would continue to put pressure on the wider euro zone, he said, for which Spain posed a serious dilemma. "Spain is too big to fail and yet too big to rescue," he said.

Banana Economics

Spain's problems are a more acute version of a mismatch in income and liabilities that has swept up much of the industrialized world. Whether it's the United States, the U.K., Japan, or the euro zone countries, excessive sovereign debt has become the defining problem of our age and it threatens to be so for many more years to come. We know the cause of this problem: a mispricing of credit that fueled a bubble in consumer and commercial lending and a banking crisis that forced governments to absorb much of the bad debt. But as a global society we are divided over what to do about it—whether to cut back on spending and raise taxes or to borrow even more to stimulate demand in the hope that tax revenue growth will make it easier to repay those gargantuan debts.

Of the two, Europe has adopted the take-your-lumps-now approach. In addition to the specific goals laid out for the most severely affected nations, all twenty-seven countries of the EU agreed on common fiscal austerity goals to halve their fiscal-deficit-to-GDP ratios by 2013, with their leaders describing them as essential to win back the confidence of markets. Critics worried that they were acting in haste and as proof they offered the massive economic contractions felt by Greece and before that Ireland. Governments outside the euro zone also worried that their economies would have to absorb more of the world's goods if Europe's cutbacks weakened demand there. The United States, which did not want to again become the "consumer of last resort," argued unsuccessfully during a G20 summit in Toronto for a postponement in the European cuts.

But the EU commitment to austerity was unanimous, even for Britain. There, the new Conservative–Liberal Democrat government unveiled £40 billion in service cuts and tax hikes in its first annual budget in 2010, prompting a backlash from the labor movement. "The scale they are talking about is far more money than Thatcher ever cut," Hugh Lanning, director general of Public and Commercial Services, a 300,000-strong union, told me. "This can't happen without there being deep inroads into the welfare state." Noting that 17,500 temporary staff at the Department of Work and Pensions would likely lose their jobs right when more unemployment benefit claims would need to be administered, Lanning said, "Those workers will go straight from one side of the counter to the other. We think that's bananas economics."

Bananas or not, EU governments said they had no choice. The bond vigilantes were demanding that the bill be paid for the bailout and stimulus costs run up after the Lehman crisis. And that amounted to a long-awaited reduction in cradle-to-grave entitlements. By committing to such tough reforms, Britain successfully avoided the fate that had befallen the United States, which was stripped of its coveted AAA credit rating by Standard & Poor's. But it was hardly a recipe for social cohesion, which, as the wild London riots of the summer of 2011 demonstrated, was a serious priority for Britain. Workers who bore the brunt of the cutbacks understandably felt they'd been sacrificed for the well-heeled bankers who'd caused the crisis. "Our people were not getting huge pay increases, they were going along doing their job without brilliant pay, and now suddenly they are being told they have to pay the price for something they were not involved in," Lanning said. "They are really, really pissed off, because it just isn't fair."

It might be tempting to dismiss this notion of what's "fair" as a fuzzy-headed liberal idea with no place in a market economy. But in this case it's critical to Europe's capacity to break free of this crisis. From the start, the EU was a project of elites. The treaties on which it was founded were forged with minimal input from electorates or national parliaments. Now, many voters in both the EU and the euro zone believe they've been duped by finance executives and politicians who forced them into an economic arrangement that's working against their interest. If European governments cannot win these people's support, the vicious cycle of financial deterioration will drive the region toward disaster. We should all hope that European voters understand that breaking up the monetary union would ignite financial chaos and could roll back the wider European community's successes as a builder of peace and common prosperity. Though Europeans would be the biggest losers, the whole world has a stake in avoiding that outcome. And yet European voters have the right to demand that the cost of fixing this mess is shared by those responsible for creating it. Meeting those demands means finding a mechanism for making banks and private creditors take appropriate losses on the ill-conceived loans from which they profited handsomely during the boom. In this sense, what's fair is consistent with the free market concept of investor accountability. It's about aligning democracy with markets.

9

The Global Liquidity Machine

Roni Rubinov runs two firms: New York Liberty Pawn Shop, which lends money against security deposits of jewels and other precious keepsakes, and New York Estate Buyers, which buys and sells the same kinds of things outright. Their offices sit side by side up a flight of stairs from the chaotic, multiethnic sidewalk of Manhattan's 47th Street between Fifth and Sixth Avenues. There, in the city's diamond district, stores owned by Orthodox Jews display rows of watches, necklaces, and diamond rings. The trade has thrived here since the 1940s, when the Nazi invasion of the Netherlands and Belgium forced the Jewish diamond dealers of Amsterdam and Antwerp to flee to New York. Since the financial crisis, however, their specialized art of appraising and dealing in diamonds has been overtaken by a more commoditized business, one represented by a proliferation of hired scouts, most of whom are either Hispanic or ethnic Chinese and who, when they catch the eyes of passersby, will ask, "Are you selling?" Some of these street hawkers hand out pamphlets, all of which deliver the same message as those displayed on neon signs affixed to store windows: "We Buy Gold."

While I waited half an hour to talk to the "esteemed Roni Rubinov," as he is described on the company website—he is also known as "the charming Roni" on a connected site for his wife's hairdressing business—his two street scouts kept escorting prospective clients up the stairs. Six were introduced in total, all of them African American. Rubinov would apologize and tell me to wait as these bag-toting customers walked into one of the two offices to show him their wares. Depending on whether they were there to borrow or sell, Rubinov would exit one office and enter the other to ensure they were received in the appropriate setting. His tall blond secretary would dutifully get up and swap places at each room's desk to accommodate the shift.

When I visited him, both the pawnshop and the buying business were doing a busy trade. The sidewalk was bustling with street touts and prospective customers, while at a construction site nearby, workers were laying the foundations for the thirty-four-story International Gem Tower, a shimmering monument to the diamond district's boom times. It was mid-2010, and the 47th Street jewelry dealers were in the sweetest of spots: they occupied the nexus between a deflationary reality in the United States and an inflationary trend in global financial markets. This unique situation meant that cash-hungry people kept entering the dealers' premises to pawn or sell gold, while gold-hungry investors drove up the price at which the dealers would resell it. The dealers might not have known it, but they were beneficiaries of the global imbalances we've explored throughout this book.

The inflation-deflation contradiction arose because of the distortions introduced into the global economy by a mixture of Chinese policies that incentivized savings and kept the yuan exchange rate undervalued and American policies that rewarded financial speculation and encouraged credit-fueled consumerism. Because China repressed consumption and produced a surplus of savings and unsold goods, it exported deflation to the West by establishing the "China price" benchmark that sapped firms of their pricing power. There was nothing in the U.S. government's domestic toolkit to battle this global juggernaut, not while its economy was still geared toward consumers who were trapped in a vicious spiral of declining real incomes and wealth. That meant the government had to fall back on a last resort: the Federal Reserve's printing presses. But with many Americans' finances in disarray and subject to stricter lending standards, banks were reluctant to lend out those fresh dollars to U.S. businesses. Instead, hedge funds steered them toward speculative investments of little benefit to the U.S. economy: oil, copper, agricultural commodities, Asian real estate, and other markets boosted by the euphoria surrounding China's construction boom. By mid-2010, this flood of Fed-fueled speculative money had driven the dollar to new lows and pushed energy and food prices to new heights. But it did virtually nothing to create jobs for the millions of unemployed or to arrest the persistent declines in real wages and home prices. So while Wall Street stoked commodity inflation, Main Street continued to be crushed by deflation in the labor and housing markets. The first phenomenon encouraged cautious investors to buy gold; the second led cash-strapped households to sell it.

In this brutal environment, income-deprived people scrambled to pay bills and avoid having their homes repossessed. But because banks were now denying loans to anyone with poor credit, shutting off the refinancing options that were abundantly available before the crisis, they turned to pawnbrokers such as Rubinov. The ever-growing flow of clients was a "gradual process," he said. It was "not a sudden assault as if someone robbed them . . . It's that the well is slowly drying up." He described the economic conditions as "the worst I have seen in thirty years of business." But while most Americans' well-being either went slowly backward or stagnated, the prices of gold, silver, and diamonds soared to new heights on world markets as cautious investors—those with excess cash—sought insurance against a perceived inflation threat that they feared would deplete the future purchasing power of paper currencies such as the dollar. That sent a different type of client to Rubinov's buying business: people who believed that the price of gold was now high enough to warrant selling their family heirlooms. "It's usually one or the other that drives this business. Either the economy has come down and people need money, or the gold value has gone up. But in this case it's both," he said.

Since most of his pawnshop clients could not stay current on their loans, Rubinov was by default accumulating jewels. In past times, this might have been a problem because he would bear the risk of having to sell secondhand goods to retail customers. But at that moment, with world gold prices on a tear, he could easily sell any gold jewelry to refiners who would melt it down and convert it into bullion. A year later, the price rally had gone to even greater extremes, as investors who fretted about worsening U.S. and euro zone debt crises and a deteriorating global economic outlook poured into the gold "safe haven." In just three years after the collapse of Lehman Brothers, the price of gold had tripled to an all-time high, above $1,900 per ounce in early September 2011. Mounting fears over a global economic slowdown and the euro zone crisis sent cash-needy investors to dump gold later that month. The true believers were at that point reminded of the hard truth about the precious metal: when you need to spend money, you still have to get back to the fiat currencies you've been avoiding. Gold is not cash. Before September was over, gold had dropped as low as $1,600 an ounce. It spent the rest of the year trying but failing to get back above $1,800 and eventually succumbed to year-end selling. But the gold price still remained well above its 2011 opening of $1,422, allowing it to mark its fourth consecutive year of gains. That relentless rally meant that gold refiners had become a bigger and more reliable source of revenue for Rubinov and other 47th Street dealers than the shoppers for necklaces, brooches, and engagement rings upon whom their businesses used to depend.

Gold's advance was fed by a veritable investor mania. Although the biggest buyers were invariably deep-pocketed funds and central banks, the price rally had a popular, Main Street feel to it. Americans were barraged with TV commercials and website ads touting retail investments in gold coins, gold bars, and gold-only investment funds, while others offered new ways for people to sell their gold jewelry for cash. Many were backed by celebrity spokespeople and had direct endorsements by conservative talk show hosts, who parlayed the theme into critiques of President Obama's and the Fed's easy-money policies. Bullion marketer Goldline

International put former senator, presidential candidate, and actor Fred Thompson in its camp. Rosland Capital, which also sells gold coins and bars, hired convicted Watergate operative and loose-tongued conservative radio host G. Gordon Liddy for a series of ads. Glenn Beck's and Bill O'Reilly's shows on Fox were heavily sponsored by gold sellers. Cash-4gold.com, an outfit controlled by Green Bullion Financial Services of Florida, ran a Super Bowl spot in February 2009 featuring hip-hop star MC Hammer and TV legend Ed McMahon riffing about mailing in their gold sledgehammers, gold toilets, and gold microphones. Mr. T, star of the *A-Team* television series, became the spokesman for pawnbroker Cash America's gold mail-in service, telling a Bloomberg TV interviewer he believed in it because gold was one of the gifts given to the Baby Jesus. Meanwhile, friends and neighbors started hosting gold-selling parties. As the blurb on one promoter's website put it, "Think Tupperware party, [but] instead of spending, everyone leaves with large sums of CASH!" And German company Ex Oriente Lux installed vending machines dispensing small gold bars in Germany, in the Arab Emirates, and eventually in a strip mall in Boca Raton, Florida. There was a pre-2007 housing bubble feel to it all.

The illiquid state of physical gold markets, which had been constrained by the problems of transportation and the low overall supply of the metal, was eased by the introduction of exchange-traded funds (ETFs), which gave small investors a chance to own tradable shares that tracked the price of the underlying asset. By mid-August 2011, SPDR Gold Shares, an ETF known by its ticker symbol GLD, had grown to be the biggest such fund in existence, with its $77.5 billion in assets surpassing even the giant SPDR S&P 500 ETF, which tracks the benchmark stock index of the same name. By following the price of gold—although not always replicating its gains—the GLD fund more than doubled in price in the three years after the Lehman collapse.

At the other end of the spectrum were the world's governments. In 2010, emerging market countries as diverse as India, Iran, Russia, Thailand, and Bangladesh upped their reserve holdings of gold. Ten national central banks in the European monetary system more or less suspended sales under a decade-long pact with the IMF to sell up to 400 metric tons of gold each year in order to finance cheap loans for poor countries. For the first time in twenty-one years, central banks became net buyers of gold, according to the World Gold Council.

A modern-day gold rush was under way, one stoked by the popular notion that governments had run out of solutions. Policy makers' apparent failure to resolve the world's various crises led disheartened investors to instead put their faith in the age-old security of an alluring precious metal. And yet this frenzy occurred at the same time that cash-needy Americans remained hungry for gold's intrinsic counterpoint, greenbacks. In the middle of those divergent forces sat diamond district dealers such as Roni Rubinov, who raked in profits as they sent a trail of precious antiques to refineries, where they would be melted out of existence forever. Their success was in many respects a measure of the mammoth problems confronting the global economy.

Structural Distortions

Throughout the three-year period following the financial crisis, most of the debate about gold, the dollar, and inflation paid little attention to the global structural distortions that fostered the instability in prices. Instead, it focused, sometimes hysterically, on the Federal Reserve. The Fed had done something extraordinary, something that its critics—with some justification—saw as highly risky. In addition to slashing interest rates to zero, it had pumped an unprecedented $2.35 trillion in fresh dollar bills into the global economy via its "quantitative easing" bond-buying programs, the second of which ended in July 2011. (At the time of writing, speculation continued that it would resort to a third program.) Until the second round ended, that additional money supply naturally had a depressing effect on the value of the dollar, which meant the price of everything the greenback could buy had to rise or at least cease falling.

People who believed in strong money at all costs feared this would create inflation, and possibly hyperinflation. And while there were no clear signs of that in U.S. consumer price data—whose moderately positive readouts instead stood as a measure of the Fed's success in avoiding a Japan-like trap of perpetual domestic deflation—inflation did take hold in certain sectors. Prices for energy, grains, stocks, Asian real estate, and emerging market currencies all soared higher.

The Fed was generally applauded for its first $1.75 trillion bout of quantitative easing, which took place during 2009 in concert with a reduction in the benchmark federal funds rate to near zero. At that time, those moves were credited with saving the world from financial disaster. But the global mood was very different in September 2010 when the central bank started the second, $600 billion round of Treasury bond purchases, or "QE2," as this phase of quantitative easing became known. By then, emerging market economies were growing strongly, led by the amped-up recovery in China. So the flood of extra dollars headed into these countries' financial markets in search of growth opportunities and higher interest rates. There it drove up their currencies, which angered their exporters and stirred up international relations. Foreign governments accused the Fed of deliberately weakening the dollar to aid the American export sector. Amid what Brazilian finance minister Guido Mantega called a "currency war," various central banks began intervening to weaken their exchange rates to offset the declining greenback, which fell 17 percent on a trade-weighted basis from March 2009 to August 2011. But in many cases, these actions only made it cheaper for speculators to shift their cheaply obtained dollars into those countries' markets. The influx of money constantly pushed up the cost of housing and other assets in these countries' local markets.

Chairman Ben Bernanke and other members of the Fed's Open Market Committee refused to concede they had a role in this. They described the dollar's descent as a by-product but not a goal of Fed policy, which they insisted was focused on driving down yields on "long-end" Treasury bonds to make it cheaper for people and companies to borrow and invest for longer periods of time. Bernanke and his cohorts leveled blame for inflation back at interventionist foreign central banks, arguing that by holding down their currencies they imported inflation into their economies. But to outsiders, the link between the Fed's actions and the rise in prices and currencies elsewhere seemed irrefutable. As the world's reserve currency, the dollar is the principal unit of exchange for international commercial transactions. Whenever the Fed prints dollars, their holders do not merely circulate them within the U.S. economy but also take a good chunk of them offshore. One popular strategy in this period was to deposit them in high-yielding bank accounts in fast-growing emerging markets, where central banks had cautiously kept their interest rates much higher than the Fed's. That gave investors a "carry trade" opportunity: they could borrow in dollars at near zero percent and invest the proceeds in, say, a short-term deposit in Brazilian reais earning more than 12 percent.

As the greenback nosedived in 2010–11, prices for world commodities, which are mostly traded and quoted in dollars, naturally did the opposite. This coincided with shortages caused by natural disasters (Russian droughts, Australian floods, Japanese earthquakes), market-distorting policies (such as the U.S. subsidy for corn-based ethanol), and the relentless demand for more food, energy, and building materials in China and other emerging markets. Prices for oil, copper, corn, and other resources soared, which fed into inflation and even acted as a catalyst for the Middle East uprisings. Developing countries could have let their currencies rise and reduced imported inflation, but a dependence on exports led many to instinctively intervene to lower the exchange rate. That perpetuated a cycle in which the Fed printed new dollars and foreign central banks bought them, together breeding the risk of a bubble and of global financial instability. Sure enough, in September, a mini-collapse ensued, leaving the benchmark Western Texas Intermediate oil contact below $80 a barrel, down from $113 in April. That month silver almost halved its value and gold lost $300 in a week. In an indication of the instability caused by the dollar's reserve currency status, suddenly everyone was scrambling to get greenbacks. A shortage of commodities became a shortage of dollars. This caused funding stress for Europe's beleaguered banks and refocused attention on the Fed, which started hinting at "QE3." This signal then pushed commodity prices higher again in October, only for them to be hit with declines again going into the end of the year as fears of a euro-centered global crisis took root alongside an economic slowdown in China, which softened demand for things like corn and copper. Yet even this late-year decline was effectively endorsed by the Fed, because it pulled back from providing more stimulus in response to some surprising, if still modest, improvements in U.S. economic data.

The Fed's activism was subjecting markets to wild gyrations, especially the stock market, where hopes ebbed and flowed over how much more money printing was to come. Never had the Dow Jones Industrial Average experienced as many daily moves of 400 points or more as it did in the summer of 2011. And for that we can at least partly blame the Fed. As with commodity prices, the infusion of cheap money and the opportunity cost of holding it in bank accounts earning zero interest encouraged buying sprees in the equity market, artificially boosting prices through the first half of 2011. But after the crutch of QE2 was removed in the summer, investors took stock of the underlying weakness of the U.S. economy, which was being hurt by the rising price of gasoline, a debt crisis in Europe, and the threat of a slowdown in China. That spurred talk of QE3, the hopes for which kept stocks relatively bouyant despite the pall of pessimism that was by then pervading the world's financial press.

These repeated stimulus programs—or expectations of them—functioned as temporary palliatives for an ailing stock market; whenever their effect wore off and prices nosedived, investors would demand a second dose. But if the Fed complied, it would exacerbate the moral hazard problem and reinforce what became known as the "Bernanke Put." This update to the "Greenspan Put," which was said to exist during the previous Fed chairman's controversial tenure, referred to the notion that investors are persuaded to take excessive risks when history tells them to expect a Fed bailout if they fail. (A "put," which is an option to sell a security at a fixed price in the future, provides insurance against losses if the market falls too far.) It is yet another example of official policy creating distorting incentives for market decision makers.

To be fair to Bernanke and company, the dysfunctional global financial system had left them with few choices but to give the market its tonic. With the U.S. financial sector now structured around a shadow banking system whose proper functioning depended on there being a steady appetite for risk-bearing securities, the Fed needed to see it propped up. Lax regulations exacerbated the dilemma because the world's banks were still not holding sufficiently high levels of buffer capital and continued to pose a systemic risk. With the sword of Damocles hanging over the market, the Fed had a strong motive to try to calm investors' nerves whenever they began to fray. "What you want is a regulatory system that's robust enough that you don't have to fall back on such backstops," says MIT Sloan School of Business economist Simon Johnson. The failure to create such a system in prior years was, in his view, "what the Greenspan Put was all about . . . and now the Bernanke Put is the Greenspan Put with a cherry on top."

Although it kept the financial system afloat in the short run—and by the Fed's own estimates shaved 0.2 percentage point off long-term rates, providing a benefit to corporate borrowers and mortgagors—quantitative easing had many flaws. It appeared to have little success in creating jobs, yet at the same time encouraged the distorted stock market decision making outlined above. It fomented the kind of periodic volatility that the Fed sought to avoid, which in turn added to economic uncertainty and made banks reluctant to lend to consumers and small businesses. In all, it exacerbated the unease that firms already felt over a shifting regulatory environment and poor economic backdrop. The massive monetary expansion left banks with more than $1 trillion in "excess reserves"—a measure of the inactive cash held in reserve at the Fed above the 10 percent of customer deposits that's required. To be sure, the low rates perpetuated by QE allowed the federal government to double the average maturity profile of its liabilities, which will make its explosive debt problem somewhat easier to manage in the future, and it allowed large companies to raise money cheaply in the bond market. But for the most part the newly borrowed money was simply hoarded rather than invested in the risk-laden business of expanding plants and hiring workers.

Advocates of "hard money" became vociferous in their attacks against the Fed. Republican presidential candidates Rick Perry and Ron Paul made the Fed their whipping boy. The latter authored a bestseller titled *End the Fed* and sponsored legislation requiring a congressional audit of the Fed's policies, a move that economists said would undermine its coveted independence. Meanwhile, long-standing conspiracy theories about the Fed gained favor. Some took to labeling Bernanke a "Bilderberger," a reference to what they claim was his attendance at two Bilderberg Conferences, an annual invitation-only gathering of elite decision makers whose publicity-shy ways inevitably feed beliefs that there's some kind of secret cabal of financial elites running the world. There's no denying that Fed policy has of late favored a small group of bankers, but the imbalances in the global system almost make that unavoidable. Most Fed decisions are made with reasonable transparency and clear economic justification. The problem is not that the Fed answers to the wrong masters but that the only policy tools that are left to it bring greater benefits to market traders than to the general public. While this problem demands reform, its root causes are systemic, not part of some shadowy conspiracy. And any reading of the history of crises and market panics in the late eighteenth and early nineteenth centuries, when America did not yet have a central bank, makes a strong case against the extremists who want to do away with the lender of last resort.

Still, this was the most difficult and divisive period for the Fed since the Depression. Even within the policy-setting Open Market Committee, divisions were strong. Inflation hawks such as Thomas Hoenig, Charles Plosser, and Richard Fisher—the presidents, respectively, of the Federal Reserve Banks of Kansas City, Philadelphia, and Dallas—worried that by buying Treasuries the Fed was undermining its independence from the government and that when the dormant cash stockpiles it had created made their way into the economy, domestic prices would rise uncontrollably. They made their differences public by dissenting against policy decisions at the Fed's Open Market Committee meetings. However, the committee was dominated by Bernanke, vice chair Janet Yellen, and the influential president of the New York Fed, Bill Dudley, who tended to favor the monetary activism arguments of the doves, a group that would trot out reams of data to back their case. For three years after the crisis, the core consumer price index (CPI), which excludes volatile food and energy prices, remained at or below the Fed's 2 percent target. And when the hawks retorted that American households still had to consume food and gasoline and that when those prices were added back in, overall CPI inflation got as high as 3.9 percent in September 2011, the doves just pointed to unemployment, which was for a long time stuck above 9 percent, far from the 5 percent number that's loosely assumed to signify full employment. Thus they could argue that the Fed was falling short of its dual mandate, which required it to promote not only price stability but also full employment. And in any case, by year-end declining commodity prices had led the headline CPI back down toward the core number. This all fed into the Fed chairman's view of what was happening, a view informed by his own PhD dissertation, which centered on how the Fed had prematurely tightened monetary conditions during the Depression. Bernanke was mindful of repeating those mistakes.

Regardless of who was right, the Fed entered the second half of 2011 with no real bullets in the chamber. Meanwhile, the housing market was still depressed, with 4.1 million mortgage loans either in foreclosure or delinquent for more than 90 days, which in turn meant that consumers weren't spending and that businesses were either deferring hiring or reorienting their investments toward foreign markets and operations. The sluggish economy weighed on tax receipts, so the unresolved problem of the federal government's $14 trillion in liabilities was still that: unresolved. With budget deficits at record highs and Congress bitterly divided over how to reduce them, the Obama administration was politically hamstrung. The tense impasse over the debt ceiling in July 2011 and the hurried compromise that ended it simply further undermined business and consumer confidence and crimped growth. Standard & Poor's decision to strip the United States of its coveted AAA rating a week later provided a disturbing coda to the whole episode. One solution lay in providing *more* immediate fiscal stimulus, preferably geared toward infrastructure, while committing to longer-term cutbacks in Social Security and Medicare. But although that would have been a cheap option—record-low Treasury yields ensured that the government could borrow for ten years at less than 2 percent, a rate below current inflation—the ultraconservative Tea Party's hold on a Republican-dominated Congress made any talk of stimulus politically poisonous.

So the Fed remained the last line of defense against economic decline, although the more it tried and failed to revive the U.S. economy the more ineffectual it looked. Many saw evidence of what Keynes called a "liquidity trap," a state in which looser monetary policy can no longer stimulate demand; this was the same dilemma the Bank of Japan had faced for two decades. In a last-ditch effort, the Fed tried tinkering with the maturity profile of the assets it had bought to try to push down thirty-year bond and mortgage rates to get people to invest and buy houses. It also made it explicitly clear that it planned to hold rates steady for two years. And yet, notwithstanding a surprise drop in the unemployment rate in November, December, and January, the rate of hiring remained abysmal and housing prices wallowed. Ben Bernanke had inherited one of the most thankless jobs in the world.

The mismatches in the global economy were a key cause of central bankers' headaches. The excess of manufacturing output from China continued to flow out into the world and breed deflationary pressures, especially in the debt-laden advanced economies of Europe and the United States. In this unbalanced state, the dollar's reserve currency status worked like a toxic drug in the latter stages of two junkies' shared addiction. The United States, which could borrow cheaply because of the global demand for dollar reserves, and China, which needed the greenback's deep, liquid capital markets as a home for its excess savings, were locked into a self-perpetuating, destructive relationship. Up until the summer of 2011, many of the dollars that the Fed printed to fight stalling growth just escaped offshore, but because Beijing kept a tight grip on the yuan, they spilled over into other countries' currencies, which undermined *their* exporters' competitiveness and prompted *their* central banks to intervene to weaken their currencies. That sent the dollars flowing back into U.S. Treasury bonds but did little to boost the U.S. economy.

Since neither China nor the United States was willing or able to end its part in their codependent addiction, they both fell back into patterns that sustained the status quo. In China the government ramped up construction to a breakneck pace, while in the United States the Fed printed money at a rate no other central bank had ever done. China thus upped its demand for the energy and metals it needed to keep its investment treadmill going, while the United States provided the dollars for speculators to purchase futures contracts in those commodities and funnel them into the currencies of higher-yielding emerging market countries. Later, as fears over global growth and financial crises returned, the money flowed out of those currencies into the "safe havens" of the Japanese yen and Swiss francs, whose governments then took their own measures to try to stem their currencies' ascent. The world had trapped itself in self-reinforcing cycles of monetary expansion and tit-for-tat exchange rate interventions.

The Price People Pay

Although blame for this perpetual liquidity flow lies mostly with the financial policies of the United States and China, the price paid for its distortions are borne by individuals everywhere. With China applying capital controls and absorbing tens of billions of incoming dollars through daily currency market interventions, the flood of money unleashed by the Fed was deflected elsewhere, disrupting people's livelihoods and creating rifts in societies.

Residents of Hong Kong were caught right in the middle. Uniquely, their territory functions as a gateway for investment and trade flows in and out of the booming Chinese economy but has a currency, the Hong

Kong dollar, that's rigidly tied to the U.S. dollar under a strict "currency board" arrangement. That awkward mismatch fueled an unstoppable property bubble as liquidity flooded into the territory and fueled inflation. As in Australia, soaring home prices created a two-class society split between those who owned and those who rented.

In effect, Hong Kong's strict currency board system subjected it to the same monetary policy that was designed for the U.S. economy. Thus a hyperaccommodative, low-rate policy designed to attack chronic labor and housing problems in the sagging U.S. economy became the standard for an economy that was locked into the gangbusters expansion of its giant neighbor. In the diametric opposite of what was needed in a boom, Hong Kong bank accounts paid virtually zero interest and the Hong Kong dollar depreciated in lockstep with the U.S. dollar. That gave local residents and mainlanders no incentive to save their money. Instead they went on a shopping binge. Annual inflation leaped to 7.9 percent in August 2011, having been just 1.9 percent a year earlier. Meanwhile, prices in the territory's notoriously land-starved property market went through the roof. In many districts, prices doubled or even tripled from their levels half a decade earlier. It became commonplace to find three-bedroom apartments offered at more than US$20 million. By March 2011, one street in Hong Kong's exclusive Peak district was fetching US$8,689 per square foot, the highest price in the world.

Although Hong Kong rents didn't keep up with property prices, by September 2011 they had gained 50 percent from two and a half years earlier. This meant that retailers who rented from Hong Kong landlords faced sharply rising costs at the same time as their customers saw their Hong Kong dollar earnings lose purchasing power. Bo Bulai, the owner of Squeeze Ltd., a small smoothie shop on the waterfront of the tourist district of Stanley, told me that just one year after she started operations, the owner of the building housing her small storefront jacked up the rent from HK$50,000 a month to HK$60,000—about US$7,690 for a space no bigger than 400 square feet. "I can't raise smoothie prices, so that's money I've lost," she told me forlornly. This kind of pricing uncertainty is ultimately unsustainable. And sure enough, by the second half of 2011, Hong Kong's economy was showing signs of a slowdown.

The bubble-like spillover from the fertile combination of China's boom and America's monetary expansion was not limited to this "special administrative region" of China. Cities in countries that produced the commodities sought by QE2-charged speculators and by Chinese importers became costly places to live and work, including in many emerging market countries. By early 2011, office space in Rio de Janeiro—a city surrounded by *favelas,* or shantytowns—was more expensive to rent than in New York City. And in Singapore's Sentosa Cove, a new canal-based housing development built on reclaimed land, average prices tripled between 2006 and 2010. When I visited, the place was abuzz with news that a single "bungalow" had sold to an undisclosed mainland Chinese buyer for S$36 million (US$30 million in 2011 exchange rates). Many of the Cove's properties were left unoccupied by their well-heeled foreign owners, who took advantage of the fact that this was the only place in Singapore where nonresidents could legally own land. But that only created more of a bubble in prices, as it left less space available. In what sounded like a dangerous case of bubble thinking, local real estate agent Markus Tay explained that most of the big-spending homebuyers in the cove were investing not to live there, nor to earn rental income, but "for capital appreciation." This abiding belief—that an asset's price will rise not because of its earning power but because it is *destined* to do so—is one of the most dangerous an investor can have. It's what fueled the U.S. housing bubble, and here it was appearing three years later on the other side of the world, spurred once again by excess liquidity in the international financial system.

The Fix Is In

Understanding the economic impact of this bubble-inducing mentality would not be complete without a deeper look at the gold market. As with buying a Sentosa Cove house that you'll never occupy or never rent out, investing in gold does not yield any income per se—unlike bonds, which earn interest, and shares, which receive dividends or at least have a claim on corporate profits. And whereas oil, wheat, copper, and other such commodities are intended for a defined end purpose, gold has few practical applications beyond its aesthetic appeal. Some of it is purchased for the kind of items carried into Roni Rubinov's pawn shop. A large amount is used for dowries in India, for example, a country that accounts for more than 20 percent of the world's consumer demand for gold. But much of it remains in the same form it takes after it leaves the refiners to whom Rubinor sells his pawned jewelry. It is melted down into 24-karat gold bars, each of uniform "good delivery" size and weight, serialized, and stored away in the vaults of large banks. There, the gold changes ownership frequently but rarely sees daylight. It serves no useful purpose for either the owner or society as a whole, other than to simply exist and act as a store of value in the collective imagination of the global marketplace. Unless a gold investor is convinced we are returning to the gold standard or that all paper currencies will literally become worthless and unwanted, and is willing to wait for that outcome, he or she will need to convert the gold back into a fiat currency before buying something with the proceeds of that investment. Gold has little intrinsic value beyond what investors assign to it under the circular argument that it has always held value throughout history. There's nothing wrong with that view—all markets are an abstraction from the underlying reality in which the traded item actually exists—but when the rising price of gold becomes the most high-profile indicator of investors' mistrust in global economic policy making, it's worth remembering that a bet on the precious metal is founded on the same logic applied by buyers of high-end Singaporean real estate: it will go up because it will go up. Such a mind-set is a fundamentally flawed way to approach investment.

Gold's appeal as a de facto "currency" lies in its exchangeability as a pure commodity. In this way, investing in it is actually very different from buying property in Sentosa Cove, where the variability of architectural design, structural details, and location add valuation risks. There's just one universally recognized daily price for 24-karat gold. Unlike crude oil, which has more than one benchmark depending on which futures market you're trading in, the price of gold is always anchored to what is agreed on at 10:30 a.m. and 3:00 p.m. every trading day in London by the five banks that belong to the London Gold Market Fixing Ltd. At those times, officers from Barclays Capital, Deutsche Bank, HSBC, Société Générale, and the Bank of Nova Scotia confer to decide upon a price based on how intraday demand and supply factors have functioned until then. Though the banks charged with this role have changed, this routine has existed since the first gold price fix at 10:00 a.m. on September 12, 1919. The ritual would be a quaint anachronism in an era of electronic trading, where prices are kept up-to-date in milliseconds, except for the fact that the whole world still pays attention to it. Although gold prices change throughout the day, the London fix is the one against which all physical transactions are referenced. Whether it's the price of a necklace sold in New York's diamond district, the cost of a truckload of ore in South Africa, or the daily valuation of the International Monetary Fund's 2,800-metric-ton holdings of bullion, the gold price set by those five bankers in London is the basis for the calculation.

The simplicity of the London fix fosters a sense of order and confidence in the market. Although the system could in theory fall into oligopolistic control, checks and balances from the intraday trading records minimize the prospect of a pricing conspiracy. Instead, what people pick up on is the tradition. Having a single, universally recognized benchmark helps breed confidence in gold's status as a pure commodity, which in turn makes it an almost perfect substitute for money were it not for the fact that it isn't legal tender in most countries. At a time when there is so little confidence in the global economic system, that brings a sense of comfort for many.

But if the traditions of the gold market offer some investors a soothing sense of order in these uncertain times, it also has far-reaching and often unsettling implications for people elsewhere. Lust for gold can turn lives upside down, just as it did during the European conquest of the New World. And if surging gold prices prove to be the "ultimate bubble," as George Soros called it, the end of that euphoria and the unwind in prices could also have a destructive impact on people's lives. To examine that idea, our last side trip to investigate the human consequences of global economic dysfunction will unite New York with Peru, the former center of the Spanish Empire and now once again a flash point in the West-meets-East battle over this ancient and most precious of metals.

Andean Gold Rush

On the first day of 2010, New York–based hedge fund manager John Paulson used $250 million of his own seed money to launch a fund dedicated solely to investing in gold. Over the course of the next few months, he would attract new investors to the fund. Putting most of it in gold ETFs, Paulson then leveraged up his bets by structuring separate investments in equities and other assets around his gold position. In 2010, as the price of gold soared, his personal income from the fund ran to $5 billion, beating his own record of a $4 billion profit during the housing crisis. Paulson had a much poorer year in 2011, clocking up losses as high as 51 percent in some of his funds due to bad bets on banks and U.S.-listed Chinese companies. But his gold investments stayed positive throughout the years. He laid out his rationale for them to the French newspaper *Les Echoes*: "Given the risks of inflation in three to five years and the volatility of the euro, gold offers good protection against the paper currencies' devaluation," Paulson said. "Over time, the price of gold will rise in proportion to the creation of paper dollars."

Paulson was articulating the dollar-bearish views of many individual investors. And it seemed many agreed with him. Within a week the London gold fix was $25 higher and had broken through the psychological barrier of $1,500 an ounce, a new record high. Four months later, it popped above $1,900. Throughout, other hedge funds piled on—George

Soros's Quantum Fund bought gold mining companies, for example, and Eric Mindich's Eton Park Capital Management bought gold ETFs—and smaller investors flocked into gold investments throughout 2011.

Jorge Pérez was far, far removed from the Paulson-Soros-Mindich milieu. Yet he too was caught up in the same wave that these hedge fund managers were riding. For much of 2010, as Paulson and others were ramping up their gold bets, Pérez (not his real surname) was struggling to support two kids and a wife on the 20 Peruvian soles ($7) a day that he earned at a grocery store in Las Lomas, a dusty town of 10,000 people in the northwest of Peru. Then some of his pals started disappearing during the week and returning on weekends with money in their pockets. They would tell him that, like them, he could earn 35 soles a day digging for gold, an amount almost double his daily wage. So in August he quit his job, left his family in the care of relatives, and set off for a mine site close to the Ecuadorian border.

The rising price of minerals has turned Peru into a magnet for mining companies, converting the country into one of the world's biggest exporters of gold, copper, and zinc and—after China—the world's second-fastest-growing economy during the last four years of the 2000s. But the new wealth was not shared widely, a situation that helped leftist Ollanta Humala seize victory in the mid-2011 presidential elections. Around the northwestern Piura region where Jorge Pérez lives, it's common to see houses built of sticks. Roadsides are strewn with plastic bags and puddled with dirty water. The most common form of transport is the *motokar* (a motorbike converted to a passenger vehicle by adding a two-wheeled rickshaw cabin). Goats and donkeys wander across country roads. It is a long way from John Paulson's 28,000-foot mansion on Manhattan's Upper East Side.

This perpetual poverty has driven Peruvians into mining. A few lucky ones have found jobs in the large-scale operations of companies such as U.S.-owned Freeport-McMoran, Australia's BHP Billiton, and Peru's own Compañía de Minas Buenaventura, but many more, such as Pérez, work for *minas informales* (informal mines). Often digging in areas where ore deposits are less concentrated than those exploited by big companies, the low-capitalized informal sector is traditionally categorized as "artisanal mining," a label that associates them with the jewelry and handicrafts of indigenous people dating back to the Inca period and that comes with minimal government oversight. Once the London gold price got above $600 per ounce in 2007, however, small-scale industrial miners began also calling themselves "artisanal" even though their intentions were entirely commercial. Thus they claimed exemptions from environmental approvals, safety standards, worker contracts, and other bureaucratic demands under dubious pretenses. As prices rose even faster, these small-scale mines proliferated. In 2010 alone, the number of people engaged in informal mining jumped from 7,000 to 12,000 in the districts of Las Lomas, Suyo, and Sapillica, according to a local news report citing sources at Peru's Mining and Energy Ministry. The region was undergoing a twenty-first-century version of the California gold rush—all because a dysfunctional global economic system had led investors elsewhere in the world to scramble for a centuries-old source of perceived financial security.

There's a reason why the Las Lomas mines weren't overrun with people such as Jorge Pérez until the gold price soared: this type of mining is extremely dangerous, uncomfortable, tiring, and unhealthy. A high return was needed in compensation. Deaths and injuries were common, I was told, and a visit to one site made it clear why. The mineshaft started with a forty-meter vertical drop to the first seam and then in separate stages of fifteen meters it eventually got down to a hundred meters underground, where at the time of my visit five men were working on the latest productive seam of gold. To get there, the miners descended a bamboo ladder into a hole that was crudely cut into the red clay and secured with recycled wooden boards. They wore no helmets or other safety gear and had flip-flops on their feet. Twenty meters away sat their source of oxygen: a generator-powered compressor that pumped air down a long tube.

At the entrance to the shaft, one worker waited under a canopy, *cumbia* music playing from a portable CD player nearby. When a cable attached to a winch powered by the same generator began to move, he gestured to us to step back as he took delivery of two hessian bags full of rocks with a combined weight of about 100 kilograms. After swinging the bucket onto the surface, he picked up one of the bags and waddled with it between his legs to a pile of rocks before returning to do the same with the second bag. (Having suffered a herniated disk three years earlier, I winced at the thought of the extreme pressure on his lower spine.) There was half an ounce of gold per metric ton in the current seam, I was told, which meant that the 500 kilograms of rocks that had been dug out that morning were worth $350 at prevailing international prices.

But while the London fix price was the starting point for their calculatory earnings, the mine's cut from the payout would be much smaller once a processor based in Nazca, a town south of Lima, deducted its charge for extracting the ore and for transportation by a truck that comes by for pickup once a week. To reduce these middleman costs, other miners did their own extraction locally, using archaic methods. One nearby facility consisted of two sections—a first phase where two people would jump up and down on wooden boards attached to a concrete ball to crush the ore and a second in which the broken-up particles were placed in a pool of mercury to undergo a process known as mercury amalgamation. A more effective procedure is that of cyanide leaching, in which one of the most toxic chemicals in the world is applied to the ore to break down the unwanted matter. It was used in various poorly maintained plants in Las Lomas. Both methods exposed the workers and the environment to noxious chemicals.

I asked Pérez what it was like underground in the dark, narrow mineshaft in which he spends twelve hours a day with only two breaks, all in return for 35 soles. *"Bonito,"* the taciturn miner replied—"beautiful." He said it with a blank face that made it impossible to tell whether he was being sarcastic. After just six months on the job, Pérez's body already showed the effects. Short but muscular, with leathery skin, he had scars across his arms and legs and looked a lot older than his twenty-seven years. I couldn't help but think of the Western Australian FIFO workers and the $160,000 salaries they earned driving air-conditioned trucks with safety sensors trained on their eyes. By comparison, this part of Peru was two centuries in the past.

If there's one thing that explains the stark gap between the lives of miners in those two countries, it is how well their societies have entrenched the rule of law and, in particular, property rights. Despite their faithful adherence to the institutions of the London fix and the international gold market, most other aspects of Peru's informal mining operations shunned the use of officially institutionalized rules. Ownership seemed ambiguous. In Las Lomas, the mines were on land controlled by an indigenous group, so a cut was typically negotiated for a *comunitario,* a community representative, who would take a passive partnership stake. Beyond that, settling the question of who would have first mining rights tended to follow might-is-right rules. Violence and power imbalances are ingrained in the system. The mine I visited was owned by the mayor of Las Lomas, the staff told me. Yet it was, like all the mines, essentially illegal. There is no way these industrial activities should qualify for the "artisanal" exemption, but they operate without environmental protections nonetheless. They also exploit workers and pay no taxes. The whole lawless enterprise is fundamentally dangerous and destructive. What's more, other vices flourish around informal mining. Prostitution and drug trafficking have surged, locals said. When we visited mines on a Sunday many weren't operating because, as one miner said, laughing, it was the *día de la chupa,* using a slang word for oral sex.

The problem the government faces is that if it dismantled the informal mining business, it would break up the vast subeconomy attached to it, impacting everything from the hostels for itinerant miners to the truck drivers who ferry equipment and ore. Bureaucrats face fierce opposition to their efforts to regulate the industry. While I was in Las Lomas, a clash between police and miners near Madre de Dios in Peru's Amazonian region left two dead and thirty-seven injured after miners rose up in response to the government's efforts to "formalize" their industry.

There is also rising antipathy toward the miners among other land users. Around Las Lomas, farmers see the environmentally suspect mining operations as a threat to the fruit orchards for which the Piura region is known. People and towns are either "pro-*agro*" or "pro-*minero,*" with no gray area in between, perpetuating a conflict that dates back to a violent episode in 2001 when agricultural workers in the nearby town of Tambogrande torched the exploration camp of Canadian mining company Manhattan Minerals. The company's plans for a giant open-pit gold and copper mine would have required relocating almost half of the town's 16,000 inhabitants into new housing. But after the attack and a subsequent referendum in which a majority of voters said they did not want the mine to proceed, Manhattan abandoned the project.

I arranged to meet Tambogrande's current mayor at the very place where he had personally led the attack on the mining campsite. It was the tenth anniversary of that event, so he was to speak at a function organized by a group of residents now living in a public housing complex on that very site. After arriving in a *motokar,* Mayor Francisco Riofrío spoke rousingly of "*la lucha*" (the struggle) over the past ten years and about the lawsuits he and others had battled over charges of vandalism during the 2001 uprising. "If there was violence and arson, it was not the fault of the Tambograndinos, because they were the ones who had invaded us," Riofrío said of the mining company.

The popular narrative, played out in international accounts such as the award-winning German documentary *Tambogrande,* holds that the mine would have threatened the town's mango and citrus industry, the bedrock of its economy. Ever since, politicians in the town's immediate surroundings have routinely declared themselves "100 percent *agro*" and "anti-miner." When I visited, houses in the town were painted with ads and slogans for the upcoming congressional and presidential elections, and the most prominent ones were those of the Poder Agricola (Agriculture Power), which bore the symbol of a lemon so that illiterate voters could identify it.

Yet for all the political mileage that Mayor Riofrío and others derive from their struggle against mining, his town is dirt poor. The poverty rate in the province of Piura, to which both Tambogrande and Las Lomas belong, was 45 percent in 2009, and as high as 95 percent in the poorest rural areas. Like so many such places, the town is strewn with trash, most of its roads are of rocky gravel, and the houses are basic huts. Riofrío has erected a giant welcoming monument with the words "Smile, This Is Tambogrande" at the entrance, but there is still no footbridge for crossing the adjacent river. People must pay one sol—about 33 cents—to boys who drag them across it on inflated tractor tire tubes. At the municipal offices, old men with typewriters sit outside on the steps, where they help write petitions for illiterate residents seeking financial aid from the local government. If they took them to the mayor's office, however, they would find a note on the door saying, "We won't accept any solicitations for economic assistance because of all the debts accumulated by the previous administration." When I asked him why the town has not progressed even as export prices for mangoes and lemons have risen, Riofrío blamed the national government. "They have not given us any help," he said.

Yet critics such as Piura journalist Jorge Arévalo Acha put the blame squarely back on Riofrío and other firebrand leaders of the anti-mining movement. During the campaign against Manhattan, Arévalo Acha says, "the political discourse from [these] 'defenders of the people' was a crude justification to satisfy their yearning for power and money." He estimates that the mine would have brought in $405 million in investment, boosted regional economic output by 20 percent, and generated $200 million in annual exports. Whether that could have occurred while preserving the region's agricultural base can't be known, but what is clear is that in Manhattan's absence, the more dangerous, unregulated, and lower-return business of informal gold mining has been allowed to flourish. And that, says renowned Peruvian economist and anti-poverty campaigner Hernando de Soto, speaks to the broader problem of a lack of formal property rights.

Without proper title to their property, De Soto says, local landowners in places such as Piura are at a disadvantage when they negotiate with big Western companies. So they instead gravitate toward deals with informal miners. "The informal miner makes a deal with them according to informal law—which means local customs—and they know that under informal law they do not lose control," he says. The real solution for Tambogrande and countless other impoverished places, De Soto argues, is to formalize the ownership of their residents' homes into property deeds. That way they gain a stronger bargaining position when a company such as Manhattan arrives brandishing a legally enforceable mining concession from the national government. As it stands now, there is no meeting of equals, not when that piece of paper allows such companies to raise hundreds of millions of dollars in international capital markets while local landowners have nothing with which to prove the ownership of *their* property. Since this leaves them in a weak bargaining position, they eschew any dealings with these legally established entities and instead favor the kind of informal relationships that reinforce and perpetuate the fragile extralegal structure of the local economy.

De Soto and researchers from his Lima-based Institute for Liberty and Democracy (ILD) have taken his ideas to slums in Cairo, Mexico City, Port-au-Prince, and other cities. They have advised dozens of governments on how to create formal property titles for the poor so as to unlock what De Soto calls the "mystery of capital"—the key, according to his vision, to why capitalism has succeeded in developed countries such as Australia but failed in underdeveloped places such as rural Peru. Not only do property rights generate capital via mortgages and other forms of collateral, but they also collectively and organically form a vast legal framework that strengthens societies, facilitating taxation, regulation, and an efficient and accountable state. The poor in the developing world, by contrast, are sitting on what De Soto has provocatively estimated to be a whopping $9.3 trillion in "dead capital," assets they own but can't tap to generate extra wealth or finance new enterprises. (That late 1990s estimate, if accurate, would surely be far higher now.)

Despite some progress with ILD's land-titling programs, the gap between those operating within the bounds of legalistic Western economic structures and those in extralegal economies in the developing world remains wide and growing. Worse, De Soto says, the latter group's "alienation" from the wealth generated in the West and by titled urban elites within those developing countries is growing because central banks—led by the Fed—are pumping money into a dysfunctional global financial system. That flood of cash is obtained by financial institutions in return for titled pledged property—in this case, financial securities—before they channel it into food, energy, and minerals markets, where it inflates prices. This then foments what De Soto calls a "worldwide land grab" as investors seek out new sources for those commodities in resource-rich countries inhabited by poor people without land titles. "Whether it's the Chinese or big agro-industrial companies, they are all buying up land in Africa, in Latin America. Those poor farmers, and those hunter and gatherer tribes, they always happen to be right where you find things. But if it's all untitled property . . . we are heading into another huge class cleavage situation," De Soto says.

De Soto's work, which Bill Clinton has called "the most promising anti-poverty initiative in the world," is in essence aimed at avoiding these clashes and delivering to poor countries a Western system that has done a better job at democratizing wealth and creating stable economic growth. But here we run into a bigger problem: his project coincides with a moment in history when that superior system itself is under threat. Western capitalism, with its emphasis on executable property rights, has succeeded in advancing prosperity, and its march into the global sphere has extended some of that success to other parts of the world. But beyond property rights, its continued success also depends on sustained public confidence in the legal and financial system within which those rights are priced and valued. That trust is now in serious jeopardy, precisely because many who thought they had secure rights to valuable property—such as U.S. real estate or Wall Street–issued CDOs—later learned that they were worth a lot less than they'd been told. The rally in gold prices reflects that loss of confidence. To safeguard the democratic ideal of Western capitalism in which Hernando de Soto's dream for the world's poor resides, we must restore that lost trust.

10

What Is to Be Done? Toward a Less Tumultuous World

We are just one decade into the new millennium and already the world is undergoing wrenching change, its political and economic order being redefined before our eyes. American consumers, once the envy of the world, face an uncertain, debt-laden future, while 30 to 70 million Chinese leap into the ranks of the middle class every year. Meanwhile, world markets are beset with exaggerated volatility and are heading in contrasting directions, which in turn introduces new fissures into and between societies. We live in a two-speed, bifurcated global economy that's increasingly prone to instability while it simultaneously undergoes its greatest period of economic expansion ever. In this contradictory world, a lasting *structural* shift in relative wealth standings—from developed nations, toward developing countries—coexists with an intensified *cyclical* pattern in markets, where booms and busts are bigger, shorter, and more frequent. Too many people overly fear the first trend and complacently ignore the second.

The structural shift is leading companies and fund managers to gradually but consistently reallocate capital away from mature, developed economies, where giant debt burdens will restrain growth for years to come, and toward the rapidly expanding markets of the developing world, where the ratio of debt to income is much lower. Societies such as China are going through a once-in-history process of industrialization and urbanization, the same societal transformation that Europe underwent in the late eighteenth and early nineteenth centuries and the United States after that, only faster and in the context of a much bigger, interdependent global economy. These wealth adjustments mean that American economic and geopolitical clout is waning. The financially constrained United States cannot as easily impose its will on other countries. The carrot of its giant market is less enticing and the stick of its military might less threatening. That makes for a less predictable, multipolar world in which various countries or groups of countries vie for influence. Notwithstanding Americans' fear of lost dominance, this structural change need not be threatening if developing nations keep growing at a rapid rate. A world where prosperity is advancing and spreading more widely should in theory be a safer, happier one. The incidence of violent deaths across all societies fell sharply after World War II and has plummeted since the end of the Cold War. Such results are inseparable from the positive, peaceful effect of global economic integration.

There are huge challenges to that rosy outlook, however. In addition to the stress that accelerated industrialization places on the world's resources and natural environment, there's the ever-present risk of financial instability. Faster-moving markets are producing trading profits for those best placed to exploit them, the same groups we've observed enjoying political advantages and de facto government subsidies. But they are also encouraging dangerous collective behavior. Commodities, emerging market currencies, and stocks are at any moment capable of surging in closely correlated "risk-on" moves, only to be swept aside by sharp "risk-off" sell-offs when the entire world dumps them and heads for the safety of dollars, Treasury bonds, or Japanese yen.

This disorientating, herd-driven volatility is increasingly blamed on innovations such as exchange-traded funds and high-speed trading. Others cite the practice of "benchmarking," where money managers are judged not by the absolute returns they deliver to their investors but by how well they perform relative to their peers. The arguments are strong in both cases, but these are really institutional manifestations of the broader failings of our financial system. And when we look for the root problems, we find they are global and structural in nature. These were outlined in the preceding chapters—China's savings-biased policies and distorted exchange rate, the Federal Reserve's ultraloose monetary policy, the American dependence on credit-led consumption growth, and Europe's failure to properly integrate around its common currency—all facilitated by a powerful, speculative and taxpayer-guaranteed financial sector that is now detached from the ordinary people whose funds and debts it manages.

Add it all up and you get the eerie sense that we could soon return to some kind of financial chaos like that which followed the Lehman collapse—or worse. Before this book went to print, a two-year run of post-Lehman global market euphoria was looking vulnerable as indicators flashed warning signs of a meltdown in Europe's financial system. Price charts for commodities—oil, corn, iron ore, and most energy, mineral, or agricultural products—were showing an ominous twin peak pattern. After reaching lofty heights during the pre-crisis bubble period in 2008 and then plunging by as much as 75 percent in the recession of the following six months, most rebounded with almost the exact same steepness over the following two years to get above or within range of new record highs. In the middle of 2011, with anger running hot over worldwide food and energy inflation and the squeeze it put on household budgets, there was a sense that something had to give. Sure enough, in September through December 2011, steep price declines in oil, gold, copper, and other commodities signaled a downturn in global demand, even though the U.S. economy enjoyed a modest pickup in that quarter.

The next crisis will differ from that of 2008–9. It won't revolve around U.S. middle-income households, whose overvalued assets have already been cut down to size. Risks now focus on the debts of governments—the United States, for one, with its $14 trillion in liabilities, its deficits worth almost 10 percent of GDP, and its aging population demanding more social services—and their currencies. It is, in a sense, the moment at which the ultimate cost for past excesses is being paid by our societies. In that equation, governments must somehow balance a need for fiscal rectitude with the risk that by cutting back on spending too fast they might tip a fragile global economy back into recession. It is an undertaking of frightening proportions, not least because their debt loads and the growing mistrust of their populations mean that governments do not this time have the same financial or political resources with which to stimulate demand.

As for the actual trigger of a new crisis, it could be another "black swan" event, to use Nassim Taleb's term for something that investors are incapable of imagining. Even so, I'm going to take a shot at naming four possible sources, not to make forecasts per se but to identify the dangerous shoals ahead. We might escape all of these, or we could be hit by a nasty combination of all four. By mid-2011, Nouriel Roubini, dubbed "Dr. Doom" for his accurate predictions of the previous financial calamity, was warning of such a "perfect storm" producing another global recession.

A Euro Crisis

A breakup in the European monetary union, an event that remained entirely feasible at the time of writing, could spell global financial disaster. There would be a flood of defaults and bankruptcies, giant losses for the world's banks, and quite possibly a breakdown in the global trade and payment systems, a prospect made more likely because of the disproportionate role that European banks play in financing the world's exporters and importers. European banks are three times more invested in emerging markets than are U.S. banks, for example. (With the pullback seen in late 2011, those countries were starting to hurt.) A complete crisis would reverberate around the world even more than Lehman's collapse did. The extent of the damage would depend on whether there is a partial or full breakup in the euro zone, but even if only Greece were to leave, the ramifications would be profoundly painful and far-reaching.

That said, deciding to actually exit the euro zone will throw up a logistical and political nightmare for the government in question. Chad Wasilenkoff, the CEO of Fortress Paper, which produces the security paper used in around 10 percent of all euro banknotes and in a dozen other currencies, says it typically takes up to four years to design, manufacture, print, distribute, and circulate a new currency. Governments need that time to come up with banknotes that can't be easily counterfeited by the high-tech organized crime syndicates that are by now well ahead of the technology that was used for the euro zone's previous national currencies before 1999. In a frantic rush, they could perhaps achieve the rollout in a year. But even that is 365 days too long. Since it is impossible to instantaneously replace all the euros in circulation with reissued Greek drachma, Spanish pesetas, or Italian lira, governments would have to take the extreme step of freezing bank accounts to prevent people from spiriting their saved euros away to Germany. The country would likely have to rely on barter, as many Argentines did when their government froze their banking system in 2001. Meanwhile, all individual contracts would be redenominated into the new (or rather, old) currency, leaving millions of disgruntled creditors holding the blunt end of the stick and unable to pay their own debts. The financial and political chaos that Argentina experienced when it abandoned its quasi-dollarized currency in 2001 would be tame in comparison to that which Greece or Italy would suffer by getting rid of an overvalued currency that's completely imbedded in the economy. And because of the vast network of cross-border debt that has built up, the rest of the euro zone would be dragged into this mess.

Ironically, this alarming scenario of mutually assured destruction provides a vestige of hope that a euro solution will be reached. Government leaders and the ECB know that a breakup would be suicidal. Hence the widely held view that they will "muddle through" with two steps forward, one and a half back, a shuffle that will eventually deliver the euro zone to the safe port of a more or less unbreakable fiscal union. But there's no guarantee that the pressures created by the region's internal imbalances won't reach the same breaking point that Argentina's reached. Public trust is the wild card in all this. Already, citizens' confidence in the euro financial system is at an all-time low and to a large extent that's because they perceive that the costs of saving the euro are not being shared fairly by those who profited before the crisis, including by bankers. The lifestyle cutbacks that these people are enduring will only become deeper as their economies shrink, driving up their governments' debt loads and their interest rates. Many will be angered by the strings attached to the external financing that keeps their governments operating—the policy overhauls demanded by the EU and the IMF, for example, or the trade concessions demanded by China and Japan in return for investing their reserves in euro zone bonds. Any government anywhere that has to ask its people to give up sovereignty will inevitably face a grave test of its legitimacy. The social unrest could become unbearable. Ultimately, that's how the euro could collapse, not as part of a calculated strategy but as a dramatic rupture, the endpoint of a revolution.

At the time of writing, I was still hopeful that the euro could survive. But here's the rub: no matter what, Europe is destined for a lengthy, painful adjustment to a period of much slower growth, high unemployment, and ongoing asset deflation. It is the price it must pay for failing to restructure its banking system when it had a chance to and for procrastinating over the foundation of a more workable economic and political union. Even if it succeeds in muddling through, Europe will lose its geopolitical clout, especially relative to the Asian creditor countries on which it will have to rely. Six centuries of European domination of the globe are coming to an end.

A China Crisis

But if the euro zone's crisis offers a way for China to claim more influence in the world, that idea comes with a caveat: that the Asian giant does not itself succumb to one. And by the last quarter of 2011, that risk was growing. By then the question was not whether China's gangbusters economic growth would slow but by how much. Would it suffer a "hard landing" or a "soft landing"? This was the crunch moment for the knotty dilemma China's government faced over the rising prices of goods, wages, and housing. One risk was that if it moved too slowly to restrict credit and let inflation gain too much, people's cost of living would rise and Chinese firms would rapidly lose competitiveness. The other was that if the central bank tightened monetary conditions too fast, jobs growth would slow. This came amid warnings of a crisis for the country's banks, which had lent heavily on the presumption of continued growth. Fitch Ratings sovereign analyst Richard Fox put the odds of such a crisis within two years at 60 percent. All these scenarios raised the prospect of civil unrest, about which authorities were downright paranoid, as was evident in their 2011 crackdown on dissidents that included the arrest of high-profile artist Ai Weiwei. In the end, the government erred in putting a big brake on credit conditions but it did little to alter the construction-led model on which its growth depended. By December, the policy tightening was showing effect, but with terrible timing. A deteriorating global environment was now weighing on China's export outlook, manufacturing was shrinking, home prices in many cities were falling, private housing construction was paralyzed (prompting Beijing to expedite a massive public housing program), and daily outflows of speculative investment were evident in foreign exchange trading. Right ahead of a once-in-a-decade transfer of power, China's leaders faced a vexing choice: whether to revitalize the growth machine by reopening the credit spigots or to stay the course with restrictive conditions that would squeeze the economy but prevent the kind of debt and asset bubble that had debilitated the United States. China's unorthodox growth model had finally delivered its government to a crossroads.

The severity of a Chinese downturn is no idle concern. China accounts for between 40 and 60 percent of global demand for copper, aluminum, steel, iron ore, and coal, the prices for which could plunge if its economy slowed too much. Such declines would strike a blow at resource-rich countries such as Australia, Brazil, South Africa, Indonesia, and Canada and hurt manufacturing economies that are closely integrated with China's such as South Korea and Taiwan. The endgame for China's battle with inflation could thus be global deflation. Most mainstream economists remain optimistic that China will continue growing at a healthy clip, that price gains will ease, and that the Chinese government, with a giant pool of public savings behind it, has resources to stave off a debt or property crisis. Even so, huge challenges lie ahead. There is much staked on the ability of a nondemocratic, rigid political system to finesse China's transition to a new, globally integrated economy.

A Dollar Crisis

The way some commentators describe it, this would be the mother of all crises: a day in which the rest of the world decides it will no longer finance the government, businesses, and households of the United States. The dollar would plummet, inflation would surge, and U.S. interest rates would soar in a disruption that would hit the world's dollar-dependent capital markets like a tidal wave. Yet in a mini–"stress test" of this prospective crisis—S&P's shock move to cut the U.S. credit rating from AAA to AA+ following the 2011 debt ceiling dispute in Congress—the counterintuitive result was that panicked global investors poured into the "safety" of U.S. Treasury bonds rather than fleeing them. Clearly, investors were more worried about tumultuous global financial markets than about the United States failing to pay its debts. The lesson here is that the dollar's privileged reserve currency status will continue to mitigate the risk of a U.S. debt crisis in the short and medium term. But that's not necessarily a good thing. As we've discussed elsewhere and will address below, this special currency status creates dangerous distortions and misplaced incentives in U.S. credit markets. It enables America to carry a current debt load that cannot be sustained indefinitely.

The United States' long-term fiscal challenges are indeed daunting. Future obligations of Medicare, Social Security, and other retirement programs showed total unfunded liabilities of $62 trillion as of 2009, according to the Peter G. Peterson Foundation, or $540,000 in claims per household. With baby boomers now leaving the workforce, these liabilities will inevitably precipitate a crisis if they aren't reduced, an exercise that will weigh on growth for years, probably decades. Such is the price to be paid for the credit binge of the previous decade and for the transition the country must make from a financial economy to a productive one in which exports play a more fundamental role. The challenge is how to share the cost of that adjustment so that it is both fair and the least damaging to productivity. My view: convince retirees, those with the most distorting electoral clout, of the counterintuitive but truthful notion that their long-term interests lie in having their entitlements reduced. If the burden of paying for them is instead borne by the young, the productive generation on which our future depends and the group hardest hit by the 2008 crisis, all will be held back.

Investors' fears over America's fiscal burden are far from fostering a solvency problem à la Greece. Nor have they created an Italy-style liquidity problem, not with short-term U.S. T-bills earning near zero-percent interest rates. Rather, this is a political issue—it resolves around the doubt that lawmakers can find the will to compromise on their constituents' narrow self-interests and work out a solution acceptable to a cross-section of American society. Sadly, the ugly partisanship which characterized Democrat and Republican negotiations over the mid-2011 debt ceiling debate and the subsequent failure four months later of the joint "supercommittee" on deficit reduction merely added to these concerns. The notion that this committee would be forced into an agreement by the threat of triggering $2.4 trillion in mutually undesirable automatic cuts proved flawed as both sides made the bet that this legislation could later be unwound in their favor by a new government. That means that these important questions, dealing with matters of fundamental importance to the future of the republic, will in effect be put to the voting public on November 6, 2012. But even then, following what will be one of the most important U.S. elections in decades, the odds are that we again end up with a divided Washington. If so, it will be up to Americans, and especially those of us with a voice in the public domain, to urge Congress and the White House not to squander this crucial opportunity to set the country on a more sustainable growth path.

This style of brinkmanship and ultimatum-heavy negotiations does not lend itself to a carefully thought-out, strategic realignment of priorities. It raises the risk that nuances about balancing the U.S. economy's short-term and long-term needs are overlooked. On one hand, the United States needs to be assured of long-term fiscal consolidation that reduces the burden on future generations. On the other, the sputtering economy cannot afford immediate cuts in government spending or big new taxation programs. Proper public investment in future growth is also desperately needed, but is being stalled by political myopia. As of late 2011, the Treasury could borrow money for ten years at less than 2 percent, an unprecedented bargain. It should be tapping those markets and investing in job-producing infrastructure projects, education, and other initiatives to boost productivity and growth. The United States' unique borrowing privileges mean it does not need to follow the path of Greece or Ireland, where austerity has hindered growth, reduced tax revenues, and only worsened the long-term debt metrics. The whole world—not least the United States' biggest creditor, China—has an enormous vested interest in the United States not following those countries' experiences.

A Trade Crisis

In the early stages of the 2012 presidential campaign there was one issue that seemed to draw bipartisan support: the idea that China posed a risk to American economic well-being. Depending on their political persuasion, candidates in U.S. elections will now routinely attack incumbents for allowing U.S. jobs to be outsourced to China or for mortgaging the country's future to Chinese creditors. This ebb and flow of rhetoric mostly reflects the electoral rhythms of American political theater, but the voter anger it taps is real.

If either country were to go a step further and impose stiff protectionist measures against the other—perhaps triggered by the United States formally labeling China a "currency manipulator" and curtailing Chinese access to its markets, as a Senate bill that passed in October 2011 with a 79–19 majority would have it—we would run the risk of tit-for-tat sanctions. That could do enormous damage, not only to bilateral relations but to world trade in general. It's conceivable, even, that China would embark on a form of financial warfare and instruct its central bank to use its massive reserves as a weapon by dumping U.S. Treasury bonds en masse.

Eventually, domestic inflation will eat into China's trade advantage and resolve these tensions. China's current account surplus shrank quietly but considerably in 2011, a result Beijing used to argue that the yuan was nearing fair value and that it was doing its part in "global rebalancing." Yet the gross imbalances in its trade relationship with the United States remained near record levels, and by various other measures the yuan was still heavily undervalued. Inevitably, the slow cycle of economic adjustment is not fast enough to meet the demands of a short political cycle. Meanwhile, dangerous swings against globalization and toward xenophobia are occurring everywhere. In Europe, Greeks and Germans are resorting to cultural stereotypes in their attacks against each other, right-wing nationalist parties are growing, and there's talk of ending the EU's common labor market policy. In China, virulent protests against Japan erupted over a minor shipping incident. And in the United States, the anti-immigration lobby has shepherded through an extensive upgrade in border security at the Mexican border and some contentious new ethnic profiling laws in certain states. Already there are eerie similarities to the Depression in the twin financial crises of the United States and Europe; the world does not need them to be complemented by the same beggar-thy-neighbor policies that rammed a nail into the global economy's coffin in the 1930s and hastened the rush to war.

We can be thankful that there now exist international safeguards that weren't in place in the 1930s, and which have functioned quite well since the 2008 crisis. One natural barrier to a trade war lies in the integration of the world's highly globalized supply chains. Producers in one country now often have operations in many others, while the inputs that go into their finished products come from a variety of countries. This complexity creates disincentives for national producers to lobby for trade actions. That system is reinforced by the World Trade Organization, whose two-decade reign has coincided with a quintupling in global trade. In a virtuous circle, respect for the WTO and its arbitration panels makes countries less willing to break the rules, which in turn reinforces them. Although a global trade war remains a scary prospect and one that world leaders must avoid at all costs, it is increasingly less likely to occur within this constructive arrangement.

The success of coordination by the WTO has not been matched by the same in multilateral financial policy. Yet it's clear that a mechanism for enforcing common financial policy standards is desperately needed. Attempts to address such matters got off to a well-intended start in the 2008 crisis, when the Group of 7 nations—the United States, Japan, Germany, Britain, France, Italy, and Canada—ceded leadership of international financial policy making to the wider Group of 20. That brought ten developing nations into the tent, including the four rapidly growing BRIC countries—Brazil, Russia, India, and China—at a time when they were increasing their stake in the world economy. But apart from agreeing to simultaneously launch fiscal and monetary stimulus programs at the Washington summit amid the market chaos of November 2008—a move that successfully halted the global recession—the group's goal of achieving lasting, stabilizing change in the global financial architecture proved elusive. That failure made it harder for the United States and Europe to properly recover and elevated the risks of another crisis.

Yet there is a reasonable consensus among experts inside and outside the G20 on what an ideal global financial system would look like. The problem is that world leaders can't agree how to achieve it. The central objective is a global economy in which prices best reflect competition for goods and resources and are distorted neither by private monopolies nor by government intervention. In this ideal world, market forces would encourage private investors and companies to pursue wealth through investment and innovation but would also force them to take full losses whenever their bets failed. Governments would act as fair and firm regulators, promoting competition and protecting the financial system from excessive risk and panics, all while using targeted policies to optimize infrastructure development in education, energy, transport, health, and environmental protection. The end result would be sustainable and balanced global growth.

In line with these principles, I lay out below some of the themes that I believe should shape a reform agenda for the international financial system. With the United States and France both facing elections in 2012, and with China preparing for a leadership transition in the same year, now is the time for citizens to put these matters front and center on the political stage. My suggestions are mostly derived from the problems I've perceived in researching this book. They are summarized into subtopics, but they are intertwined such that success in each is mutually reinforcing. They reflect a long-term process; none of these changes will be achieved overnight.

A common approach to financial regulation. There remains a disturbing lack of coherence in the world's post-crisis financial rulemaking, despite efforts to coordinate reform by the G20's Financial Stability Board. The United States and the United Kingdom have been at loggerheads with the European Union over a financial services tax. A rush to introduce stricter capital requirements is occurring in a haphazard, ad hoc manner, with different minimum thresholds, different timetables, and different notions of what constitutes capital. And accounting standards, though converging, remain split between those of the Europe-dominant

International Accounting Standards Board and the United States–based Financial Accounting Standards Board, especially over the critical question of how to measure banks' loan portfolios. This lack of international consistency makes it harder for regulators to monitor and control global financial activity and easier for big financial institutions to shift capital around, thwart the rules, and take bigger risks.

Transparency. The global financial system is both market-based and opaque. That combination creates what Donald Rumsfeld might have called a series of potentially dangerous "known unknowns." Rather than enter into financial deals in a transparent way—via, say, the various exchanges on which investors trade stocks and futures contracts—mega-institutions engage with one another through over-the-counter contracts hidden from common view. In the derivatives markets, including that of credit default swaps, which are ostensibly used to insure against a bond issuer's default but have evolved into the main benchmark for gauging investor sentiment on bearing risk, it is still very difficult to know the nature, size, and settlement risks associated with countless bilateral contracts that are hidden from public scrutiny. The fear is that if we get a credit event such as major euro zone sovereign default, contracts will be triggered en masse, unleashing a wave of defaults that lead to systemic contagion. Because of this, governments go to great lengths to prevent the contracts from being triggered, but that only means that the holders of CDS insurance lose faith in their ability to hedge their investments and so unwind their bond holdings instead. Fear of a CDS meltdown is also used as another excuse to maintain the too-big-to-fail doctrine. The market is dysfunctional.

Transparency is the way out of this trap. Financial institutions that exploit the opaque nature of the market will see their profits decline, but that's of no concern to society. All swaps, options, and other contracts should trade on exchanges, and if they can't be standardized to do so, they should be banned. That would make prices and information widely available. This is indeed the principle behind aspects of the Dodd-Frank

Act, but congressional obfuscation has stymied their implementation and left a host of loopholes and exemptions in place.

Yet it's not just the private sector that needs greater financial transparency. All governments should be compelled to give clear and timely information on their reserve holdings and on the investment activities of their sovereign wealth funds. Global imbalances have turned these investors into the biggest movers of capital in the world. So it is extremely counterproductive to financial stability that countries such as China can hide their foreign securities purchases by channeling their activities through complicit money managers. Bodies such as the G20 and the IMF should be doing their utmost to force nations to submit far-ranging information on their external asset holdings and on internal asset markets such as housing. That would give both policy makers and investors a much clearer outlook and help defuse the threat of future crises.

Cutting banks down to size. There's widespread acknowledgment of the need to end the systemic risks that arise when banks are so big that they can't be allowed to fail. But the preferred solution is wrongheaded, in my view. Governments are adopting Dodd-Frank-style "resolution authority" regimes that allow regulators to wind down the assets of such banks when their failure to meet liabilities threatens market contagion. Yet in addition to the problem posed by human discretion in what is inevitably a politically fraught exercise, huge questions remain over how to wind down institutions that operate across borders. If a U.S.-owned bank's foreign operations must be taken over, whose taxpayers would foot the bill: those in the United States or those in the foreign country? "Citibank is a $1.8 trillion company, in 171 countries with 550 clearance and settlement systems," one regulator at the Fed told the *National Journal*. "We think we're going to effectively resolve that using Dodd-Frank? Good luck!'" Ideally, the world would create a multilateral global resolution authority, but that would require a giant pooling of tax revenues. Good luck with that too! A simpler solution is for all countries to agree on an equivalent capital surcharge for banks that are universally recognized as systemically important financial institutions. The goal would be to squeeze their return on equity so that they are incentivized to break themselves up, preferably along the lines of the old Glass-Steagall division between investment and commercial banking. Luckily for us, the Basel III agreement already encapsulates such an approach. Governments should now embrace these rules, urge their parliaments to quickly ratify them, and agree to review them periodically with the prospect of tightening them if "too big to fail" remains a problem.

Equal income opportunity. This is not a socialist goal. Quite the opposite. It's a plea to make the concept of a level playing field the central objective of government. Only when policies don't unduly benefit one class of citizen over another can the free market be allowed to efficiently allocate capital to the most productive members of society. A fairer, more evenly based set of rules will also reduce the frequency of credit-fueled bubbles and busts, as price gains will be founded on fair valuations rather than policy-induced market distortions.

In the West that means doing away with a range of unfair subsidies and tax benefits, most of all in the financial sector. Ending the implicit guarantee for too-big-to-fail banks will bring payouts to bankers down to more reasonable levels, as it will mean they face a risk of losses when striving for excessive commissions. Such gains could be undone in the United States, however, if proposals for a flat tax and/or a sharp reduction in the top income tax rates are enacted, as they would reward those who've benefited from the distorting policies of the past. That said, there are very good reasons to simplify the tax code and rid it of loopholes. In particular, there needs to be a reasonable distinction between "income" and "capital gains" so that hedge fund managers and other millionaires who make a daily living investing in securities markets aren't limited to an outrageously low 15 percent tax on their "carried interest" earnings. Alternatively we could make sure that anyone in that tax category who earns income managing other people's money is held personally liable for losses. That would be the more drastic option but it would be consistent with the principles of the capital gains tax, whose low rate reflects the fact that investors take a risk when they put their capital to work in the economy and should not be overly discouraged from doing so.

Another worthy playing-field-leveling proposal comes from Paul Woolley, the director of the London School of Economics' Center for the Study of Capital Market Dysfunctionality. He wants pension funds and other custodians of ordinary people's savings to impose limits on the frequency with which their brokers and external asset managers buy and sell securities on their behalf. Woolley has figured out how the constant churning of positions creates bubble-like momentum in asset prices, as fund managers who pay too much attention to a benchmark index and not enough to preserving capital engage in herd-like behavior. Rather than basing their decisions on fundamental valuations, these external money managers buy securities when prices are rising and sell when they are falling, all of which creates exaggerated market movements and delivers a river of unnecessary fees to brokers and traders. If Woolley's manifesto was widely adopted, it would drastically reduce the financial sector while saving pension funds and their working- and middle-class contributors billions of dollars.

All around the world, there is also a need for a more comprehensive approach to competition and anti-trust policy aimed at ending the dominance of crony capitalists and monopolists. And everyone needs fair access to education, universal health care, and other forms of social welfare. This is of utmost importance in China, which must do away with inequities such as the *hukou* residency system so that migrant workers have the same rights to public services and that their savings aren't trapped in a banking system that pays them confiscatory rates. Only then can China become the consumer society that the world needs it to be.

Floating exchange rates. Many of the lopsided patterns in international trade laid out in the preceding chapters stem from uneven exchange rates and the misaligned incentives imbedded into the array of currency regimes that replaced the Bretton Woods system. Unfortunately, in the age of "currency wars," these distortions are now proliferating. We would all be better served if all central banks agreed to truly float their currencies (a goal that's asserted in every G20 communiqué even though it's far from reflecting reality) and backed it with WTO-like enforcement. No more "crawling pegs" such as China's managed appreciation or "dirty floats" such as Brazil's ad hoc currency purchases. Signatories would agree to let capital flow freely into and out of each currency, guarantee full convertibility, and forswear market intervention. (Gold standard advocates will insist that their alternative—one of fixed nominal exchange rates—is a better solution, but I see their model as impractical and politically unfeasible in a world of fast-moving global capital and liberal democracies.) A floating exchange rate pact would contain some exceptions to give a few central banks, including China's, time to adjust to the shock of capital flows, but only according to an agreed-upon process and time frame overseen by a multilateral body such as the International Monetary Fund.

A new reserve currency. It's not fair to ask emerging markets to forgo control of exchange rates without the United States giving up its own exorbitant privilege: the world's dominant reserve currency. Relinquishing that role will pose big challenges to the U.S. economy, as lenders will demand higher interest rates from Americans. But in the long run, the United States will be better served by losing its reserve currency role and by ending what Peterson Institute for International Economics director Fred Bergsten calls its "addiction to cheap capital." With Americans' debt too high and their savings too low, the strength of the dollar is no longer a measure of the health of the U.S. economy. Such a change would also prevent savings-surplus countries from having to entrust their assets to a fiscally challenged and divisive U.S. political system. The dollar, whose value would now be determined by the business cycle rather than by unpredictable swings in financial market sentiment, would enter a lengthy decline consistent with a drawn-out period of spending restraint to reduce debt. That would in turn steer investors away from consumption- and finance-dependent businesses and toward exports and high-end manufacturing. Igniting the jobs recovery that the United States desperately needs, this would relieve the Fed of the excessive burden of having to prop up the economy. No longer acting as the world's de facto lender of last resort, the U.S. central bank would regain its independent power to promote growth and price stability with limited international fallout from its monetary actions.

What replaces the dollar? Rather than a single nation's currency knocking it off its perch, as the greenback did to the British pound, University of California at Berkeley economist Barry Eichengreen believes a multiple-currency reserve system will develop in which the euro and yuan compete with the dollar for reserves. But before then, the euro zone needs much deeper fiscal integration so that it can put its currency's existential crisis behind it, while the yuan must become free-floating, fully convertible, and backed by the rule of law and property rights—changes that will provide enormous challenges for the existing political regimes in both regions. Alternatively, the international community could agree to synthesize a multinational system into a single, centrally managed quasi-currency that's used solely by central banks for lending and borrowing reserves. This could take the form of an expansion of the IMF's existing Special Drawing Rights (SDRs), a currency-basket-based instrument through which the IMF currently accounts for its transactions with shareholder governments. As of now, the SDR basket comprises the dollar, the euro, the Japanese yen, and the British pound. If it is to evolve into a legitimate reserve currency for the twenty-first-century world economy, the IMF needs to add the yuan to that group, perhaps offering China admission to the club as an enticement for capital account convertibility. The system would require a robust international settlement and currency swap facility so that governments can smoothly and quickly convert their SDRs into a more widely accepted currency for procurement purposes.

It would also need a mechanism through which borrowing countries can draw on the central pool of SDRs in return for paying interest. But it is not impossible to build such a thing.

Reforming the IMF. The International Monetary Fund is the one international institution positioned to manage a more coherent global financial system. We need a more centralized institution to ensure that government-owned capital can flow to where it's most efficiently put to use and is not beholden to the geopolitical interests of large nations and their powerful means of influence—whether it's the United States and its reserve currency or China with its savings pool dangling as a carrot before debtor nations. The problem is that faith in the IMF is at an all-time low. The IMF is depicted on the left, with some justification, as an insensitive taskmaster doing the bidding of financial institutions at the expense of ordinary workers, and on the right, with equal justification, as a distorter of the free market, encouraging bad behavior by bailing out spendthrift governments and their creditors. Emerging market countries, which have gone from being the most frequent recipients of IMF emergency aid to accumulating such large reserves that they now view the IMF as irrelevant, have the most to complain about. For one, the United States, which controls 17 percent of the votes on the IMF board, maintains veto power over any changes to the IMF's Articles of Agreement or the makeup of its Executive Board, both of which require an 85 percent majority. For another, there's a World War II–era anachronistic convention that a European always runs the IMF—a privilege that looks oddly outdated in light of the euro zone's bungled handling of its financial tumult—and whose corollary is that an American always heads the World Bank. The ugly episode surrounding former IMF managing director Dominique Strauss-Kahn's arrest on sexual abuse charges didn't help this image. But it was made worse when Europeans pushed through another French official, Christine Lagarde, as his replacement while emerging market countries lobbied unsuccessfully to give the job to Mexican central bank governor Agustín Carstens. Until the United States and Europe give up their own excessive control over the IMF, it won't attract the store of trust it needs to forge a more effective role in stabilizing the world financial system. As it became clear in late 2011 that the IMF would have to become the ultimate lender of last resort for the euro zone, taking over a bailout and structural reform program that the seventeen-member countries were unable to manage on their own, this lack of true international solidarity would hinder the Fund's ability to act. China and the other BRIC countries were reluctant to commit to multibillion-dollar contributions to the IMF—as was the United States—and yet without access to their vast savings pools, the IMF's resources will be insufficient to backstop an economy as big as Italy's. If the rest of the world wants the BRICs to put in more money, they will need a bigger role in running the IMF.

International financial governance. The top G20 objective has from the outset been to "rebalance" the global economy, to achieve what Bank of England governor Mervyn King calls a "grand bargain" so that countries with a large current account surplus (read: China) promote more spending, while deficit countries (read: the United States) save more. To that end, the G20 created the Mutual Assessments Process (MAP) and charged the IMF with evaluating member countries' fiscal, monetary, and microeconomic policies. The IMF would decide if they were contributing to global savings and spending imbalances and recommend changes. But after it was launched with much fanfare at the Pittsburgh summit, subsequent G20 meetings in Toronto, Seoul, Nanjing, and Paris failed to push the concept forward. The MAP inevitably ran afoul of a fundamental conflict between the desire for consensus among G20 members and the need for an enforcement mechanism. Wary of ceding such powers to the group, countries sought to narrowly define the purview of this exercise. The end result was a dismal lack of progress.

Although U.S., European, and Brazilian authorities talked at every meeting about how a revaluation in the yuan was vital for global rebalancing, China refused to accept a G20 dictate over its exchange rate. It also vetoed MAP targets for current accounts and currency reserves, rendering the program toothless. And on the other side of the "G2" relationship, Washington's unpredictable approach to fiscal management and the Fed's hyperloose monetary policy did their own damage, as China and other countries felt they were simply paying for America's profligacy and so became disinclined to cooperate with U.S. demands. Still, without rebalancing there will be a continued buildup of the savings imbalances and an uneven distribution of jobs growth, which will eventually foment another financial crisis and stoke the flames of protectionism. In a highly globalized economy of rapid financial capital flows, fully independent policy making is a luxury we can no longer afford. What's needed is give-and-take from all countries—but especially the United States and China—so that the impact of the difficult transition isn't lopsided and the burdens of job losses and economic restructuring are borne in concert with each other.

Restoring belief in government. I attended the G20 summits in Pittsburgh and Toronto. In both cities, clashes between protesters and security forces drew more headlines than the conferences themselves, but it was genteel Canada that provided the most heated battleground. The day before the meeting, while thousands of riot police took positions around a heavily barricaded security perimeter, downtown Toronto emptied out as merchants closed up shop—the smart ones boarding up windows. With dozens of checkpoints and strict rules on how we journalists could travel to and from the small selection of events to which we were invited, the city had the feel of a war zone under strict curfew. And yet it did not prevent the protests from evolving into a wild melee. Rock-throwing anarchists clashed with police, set fire to two patrol cars, and smashed storefront windows. In the end, 900 were arrested. It was if the heavy security presence served to stir up the anger of the excitable crowd even more. Yet this was more than a failure of policing. The wall of firepower installed by the state marked a deep symbolic divide between the people and the leaders who were there to represent them. In a powerful way it defined one of the world's most pressing problems: a widespread breakdown in confidence in government.

In this environment of mounting mistrust, people are inherently looking for ways to bypass the public sector and tackle their economic problems privately. Some embrace the "look after number one" mind-set that post-crisis investment advisors promote, a view that assumes the worst is to come, that fiat currencies will go the way of the Zimbabwe dollar, and that there's nothing you can do about it other than to buy gold and eschew long-term investment. As we've seen, gold has rallied on such thinking, but if everyone were to follow the same strategy, it would precipitate the very breakdown they seek to avoid. Since it's unlikely that the entire economic system will collapse into a *Mad Max*–like scenario where cash ceases to be legal tender, gold investors will ultimately be left with a horde of shiny yellow metal with no practical use. Other groups, such as the Tea Party, are lobbying for drastic cutbacks in the government presence in society. If we remove government from our lives, slash taxes, and rid ourselves of meddlesome regulations, they say, the great entrepreneurial spirit of America will return and newly unshackled businessmen will start hiring with glee. As anyone who watches U.S. television news will know, it is a passionately held view. And yet the evidence against it is compelling and comes straight from the previous decade, when unprecedented deregulation and tax cuts set the U.S. economy on a path to financial ruin.

While the excesses of pork-barrel politics and Wall Street bailouts understandably breed a desire for smaller and more efficient government, an even more important priority is that our government, the only body that stands as a collective representation of our society, is strong and imbued with the trust of its citizens. This is especially so in a globalized economic system, since individuals have few rights and powers in the international realm. Unlike large multinational banks, which enjoy the protections of de facto citizenship in various lands, we need our national governments to protect our interests offshore. Again, Argentina's unique experience with financial chaos offers a warning here. Americans who pine for a weak government might ponder how that South American country went from being the seventh richest in the world at the start of the twentieth century to experiencing one of the worst financial crises in history at the end of it. Argentina's fall from grace had zero to do with poverty—it has an enviable abundance of resources—but rather with the failure to forge a social covenant between the people and the state. It's a country without a proper banking system, where cash is used in lieu of checks, even to buy expensive apartments in ritzy parts of Buenos Aires, simply because mistrust in institutions runs so deep that people are wary of being defrauded. As Argentine social commentator Rubén Mira once explained to me, Argentines "see the state as a mafia from which we must protect ourselves." Such attitudes are a surefire way to create a dysfunctional financial system. I spent six wonderful years in Argentina, but I can say without reservation that Americans should not want their system to become like that country's. If we are to believe in ourselves, we must believe in a better society. We must believe in government and become reengaged with it.

Globalized politics. These reengaged citizens now need to steer government attention toward the oft-neglected global arena. As this book was going to print, the risk that a euro zone-led world crisis could spillover into another U.S. recession was rising at the same time that the Republican primary campaign for the 2012 presidential election was in full swing. But in their debates candidates and moderators barely mentioned the euro threat, a crisis that, if it were to come to pass, would become the defining feature of the Republican challenger's battle with President Barack Obama. Talk about missing the elephant in the room! This willful ignorance of pressing global economic issues in our political system merely leaves the door open for powerful financial interests to exploit regulatory shortfalls at the international level with minimal interference from government. It facilitates the dominance of Big Global Finance, leaving banks free to influence the reform process in their favor. We must make global economic issues matter to the electoral process.

Evicting Wall Street from Washington. Although the international nature of finance is a root problem, the starting point for reform lies in reducing its influence over national politics. In the United States, the Occupy Wall Street movement has given some impetus to this mission, as it has put people's grievances against Big Finance back into the spotlight. But despite the movement's peaceful protest and broad membership—from unions to anarchists to Ron Paul–supporting libertarians—it has to most Americans the feel of a fringe group of radicals. Still, if sleeping out under soggy tarpaulins with bongo-drum-playing students isn't their style, mainstream Americans—people like my neighbor Scott—can and should be doing something. They should be focusing their attention on the ugly underbelly of campaign finance and calling their congressmen to account on it.

Groups like Change Congress are now building awareness of such issues and encouraging individuals to attack the problem of Wall Street's far-reaching political donations through the transparency afforded by the Internet. Lawrence Lessig, the Stanford University law professor who founded this electoral reform group, quotes Henry David Thoreau to describe his organization's philosophy: "There are a thousand hacking at the branches of evil to one who is striking at the root." And indeed, money politics is the root of our problems. Through a related website and blog called Fix Congress First, Change Congress runs letter-writing campaigns and an initiative known as "rootstrikers" to expose stories about the corrupt abuses of campaign finance. Meanwhile, organizations such as Open Secrets have created comprehensive, navigable databases that detail where money is coming from and which politicians are receiving it. Reacting in part to the Supreme Court's decision in *Citizens United v. Federal Election Commission,* these groups are actively promoting legislation that would offset that ruling, which has opened the door for unnamed interest groups to spend unlimited money on issue ads that attack candidates. Comedian Stephen Colbert's personal "Super PAC" political action committee, which financed his own clever issue ads during the Republican primaries, offered another way to build awareness about the dangers of hidden political financing and of the effect of the Supreme Court ruling. And while polls show Americans continuing to support the principle of free speech that the Court sought to uphold, a majority has also said that Congress should reinstate legislative constraints on such spending. Contrary to lobbyists' arguments, money is not the same as speech, these ordinary Americans appear to be saying.

As we approach what could well be the most important presidential and congressional election for decades, voters should put these accountability issues front and center in the campaign. The spoils of victory would be sweet: legislative and executive branches that are less dependent on funding from Wall Street banks will be less accommodating of their interests. That would realign politics with the common goal of ending the implicit subsidies that go to too-big-to-fail financial institutions and their overpaid management. And if you take Wall Street out of the picture, you partly diffuse the power of other lobbyists in Washington: the health insurers, the defense contractors, the farm lobby, the steel industry, and the unions, all of whom are forced into a distracting and distorting arms race of political spending. From that base Americans could rebuild the export-driven economy that's needed to pay for its debt-laden future.

Teddy's example. Taking on Big Finance means attacking what economists Simon Johnson and James Kwak call the "American oligarchy." The term is instructive, for it's not the first time the United States economy has been dominated by a powerful clique of businessmen. A century earlier, when America was not driven by services and finance but was an industrial economy prone to different boom-and-bust patterns, the oligarchy comprised the robber barons who controlled the rail, oil, and steel industries—the likes of Cornelius Vanderbilt, John D. Rockefeller, and Andrew Carnegie. Their monopolies posed such a threat to free enterprise and competition that Theodore Roosevelt made one of the boldest moves taken by any American president when he introduced anti-trust legislation. Johnson and Kwak urge us to draw from that inspirational history now, telling us that we should "finish the job that Roosevelt began a century ago, and . . . take a stand against concentrated financial power just as he took a stand against concentrated industrial power."

Roosevelt's reforms paved the way for the American century. The 100 years that followed, a period in which no other country has fostered such rapid development, made Teddy look like a total visionary. And it wasn't the only time that a trust-busting government agency set the stage for innovation and rapid growth. The breakup of AT&T in 1983 and the subsequent Telecommunications Law of 1996, which forced the so-called Baby Bell regional companies to compete with one another in both local and long distance calling, paved the way for the Internet and mobile telephony explosions of the late 1990s and 2000s. What advances might come in the realm of consumer banking if the government were to take a similar approach to finance?

It's *our* global financial system. The financial system is a public good, much as the electricity grid or the road network is. We wrongly conceive of the financial system as a collection of privately owned banks when in fact they are merely one subset of the players in that system, the other two being customers (individuals like you and me, companies, institutional fund managers such as pension funds, and insurance firms) and the government. The financial system's proper functioning is vital to the efficient treatment of payments and receipts and for the optimal allocation of excess savings to those who will invest them most productively. Proper regulation is needed for this system to function smoothly and to prevent its abuse by one group at the expense of others. Imagine if those with the fastest and biggest vehicles convinced local authorities that speed limits, traffic lights, and other rules were creating a suboptimal road network—that to ensure speedy travel we should do away with rules and encourage everyone to drive as fast as they can. That's more or less what happened with the deregulation of banking. This is *our* financial system. We must recover control over it.

But as this book has endeavored to demonstrate, we cannot simply focus on the national financial system, for it doesn't really exist anymore.

Fixing our economy depends on global cooperation, on taking reform to the international level. Making banks accountable for their actions is only part of that. We must address the big macro problems of global imbalances, misaligned exchange rates, asymmetric savings and spending patterns, and misguided monetary and fiscal policy. Only then can we get the global financial system under control and serving our worldwide interest in human progress.

For too long we've assigned multilateral policy making to the "too hard" basket, encouraged by a history of United Nations failures, toothless treaties, and Esperanto jokes. Instead, we should remember and be inspired by some of the successes, especially the Bretton Woods agreements of 1945 and, on a smaller but no less impressive scale, the foundation and development of the European Union. It's often pointed out that such agreements were possible because they were established in the aftermath of a world war that no country wanted to repeat. Yet other integration successes have been forged in periods of peacetime and optimism: the foundation of the World Trade Organization in 1994, for example. Many other multilateral organizations—from the World Health Organization to the International Energy Agency—now play vital and highly constructive roles in the international community. They prove that when designed properly, international institutions can become trusted agents of the general public's interest. We can and must do the same for the world financial system. Globalization will continue regardless of what happens on the reform front. But when it takes place on a level playing field where the free market is protected by sensible regulation, the march of global capitalism will ultimately increase world productivity and, by extension, prosperity and general well-being. It is our duty to build the international institutions that get us to that point.

ACKNOWLEDGMENTS

If you are going to write a book about a global phenomenon, it helps to have friends in far-flung places. Thanks to the good fortune of a career that's taken me to a variety of locales, I'm lucky enough to have them. Here I hope to thank a number of those who went out of their way to help me in this project. The contributors are too many for me to name all of them, so I hope that those who go unmentioned understand the gratitude I feel.

Additionally, this book wouldn't have been possible without the candid input of numerous people who acted as primary sources for my material. They include current and present government officials, economists and other analysts and scholars, and ordinary citizens who shared their lives with me. Many of these people's names appear in these pages, while a few opted for pseudonyms (and are identified as such). To all, including those who are not mentioned, I pass on my thanks. I also add that I am solely responsible for the content of this book, including for whatever errors it may contain.

First, I'd like to give special mention to my agent Gillian MacKenzie, who again turned her intellect, energy, and enthusiasm to the conception and delivery of a compelling book proposal two years ago. At Crown, John Mahaney proved to be a creative and talented editor who softened my sometimes dull prose and overly wonky content, helping steer the manuscript toward the broad readership we were aiming for. Roger Scholl then shepherded the book into print and out into the marketplace. Publisher Tina Constable and other members of her team at Crown also deserve thanks for the professionalism and drive with which they prepared and promoted this book. That group included Tara Gilbride, Linda Kaplan, Karin Schulze, Dennelle Catlett, Meredith McGinnis, Paul Lamb, and Logan Balestrino, but there were no doubt many more involved along the way.

At Dow Jones and *The Wall Street Journal* I owe a deep debt of gratitude to my two bosses, Gabriella Stern and Jim Pensiero, who were unwavering in their support for me and for this project while they simultaneously launched a brand-new, exciting, but time-consuming news product. Before I joined Gabby and Jim's team in late 2010, I was blessed with the backing of my then editors and long-time friends Madeleine Lim and Eduardo Kaplan. I'd also like to thank Neal Lipschutz, president of Dow Jones Newswires, and Robert Thomson, editor in chief of *The Wall Street Journal,* for their support.

Many other colleagues at Dow Jones and *WSJ* newsrooms and bureaus around the world provided invaluable advice and encouragement, sharing sources and ideas that would help shape this book and assisting with vital services such as visas and translators. They include: Andy Browne in Beijing; James Areddy, Shen Hong, Summer Zhang, and Joy Shaw in Shanghai; Jeffrey Ng and Chester Yung in Hong Kong; I Made Sentana in Jakarta; Billy Mallard and Sam Holmes in Singapore; Laurence Norman in London; Santiago Pérez and Jonathan House in Madrid; Taos Turner in Buenos Aires; Geoffrey Rogow in Sydney; and Steve Wisaefski and Mark Whitehouse in New York. A special thank you must also go to my colleagues in the DJ FX Trader team for being patient with my occasional distraction in the midst of an action-packed period for the foreign exchange markets we write about.

For the translation work without which I'd have been lost in China, I was ably served by the unflappable Cleo Chen, who was introduced to me by Jennifer Cheung and Jeffrey Timmermans. In Indonesia, Tasha Tampubolon helped pack a busy schedule of interviews for me and offered good, clear translation. I'm thankful to Geoff Spencer and Orville Schell at the Asia Society in New York and to Nayan Chanda at the Yale Center for the Study of Globalization for their advice. I was given valuable introductions to debt-burdened Americans by Joan Carty and Todd Fagan at the Housing Development Fund in Connecticut and by Michael Bovee of the Consumer Recovery Network. In Peru, Hernando de Soto and his team at the Institute for Liberty and Democracy, especially Ramiro Rubio, helped arrange a fascinating tour through that country's informal mining regions and provided invaluable information on the subject. And from New York, Brent and Craig Renaud shared potentially life-saving advice, as well as some of the contacts they'd developed in Ciudad Juárez during the filming of their groundbreaking documentaries on that Mexican city's drug war.

In many of the places on my itinerary I was fortunate to count on the camaraderie of friends who also generously provided me with a place to stay along with free research assistance and advice. So a big thanks goes out to Hrefna Bachmann and Olafur Vilhjalmsson in Reykjavik, Manuela Saragosa and Steve Smith in London, Phillip and Ulrike Chambers in Barcelona (now in Rye, NY), Tim Andrew and Jane Moffat in Hong Kong, Jim Della-Giacoma and Tanya Torres in Jakarta, and Michael Poots, Jane McGrath, and Susy and Pablo Franco in Buenos Aires. Hidayat Jati opened his contact book for me in Jakarta and Linawati Sidarto in Amsterdam was also a big help with Indonesian contacts. Meanwhile, various friends in New York provided insights and advice, including Scott Robbins, Michael Ginn, and Bill Horn.

Back home in Australia, I must thank Tony Barrass and Jason Reynouf in Perth, as well as the members of my beloved family who put me up in Perth and Melbourne and provided their constant support and advice. That's my mother and father, Sally and Kevin Casey, and my siblings and siblings-in-law, Liz and Tim Lofthouse, Jenny and John Fox, Sarah Casey, Liam Ryan, Di Casey, and Amy Clarke. The same goes for my fabulous in-laws in my adopted home of New York, with a special mention for Pete, Isabel, Jennifer, and Elizabeth Carmona, and Brian Bodine.

To two very special girls, Zoe and Analia, I say thanks for making life fun, for greeting me with open arms when I'd return from trips abroad, and for helping me keep everything in perspective. But it is their mother, Alicia, to whom I owe everything. My wife of fourteen wonderful years deserves endless thanks for keeping our home running, for sticking by me during long absences and sleep-deprived nights, for her critical and sharp editing skills, and for her undying love and moral support.

NOTES

Introduction: The View from James Street

1 *There was the fact, for example:* United Nations Millennium Development Goals Report 2011, www.un.org/millenniumgoals/11_MDGReport_EN.pdf.

1 *Or there was the seven-year increase in life expectancy:* 1990–2010 data from the World Bank, http://data.worldbank.org and the UNDP Human Development Report 2010, www.beta.undp.org/content/dam/undp/library/corporate/HDR/HDR_2010_EN_Complete_reprint-1.pdf.

2 *In the United States, where inflation-adjusted data:* See 2010 Census data at www.census.gov/hhes/www/income/data/historical/index.html.

2 *The top 1 percent of earners:* Useful summaries on inequality measures based on data from the Census Bureau, the Congressional Budget Office, and the Internal Revenue Service are available at Inequality.org, www.inequality.org/inequality-data-statistics.

3 *For the first time, an April 2011 Gallup survey:* The poll, published on May 2, showed that 55 percent said such an improvement was "very or somewhat unlikely," against 44 percent who said it was "very or somewhat likely." It was the first time in a series of such polls by Gallup, CBS, the *New York Times,* and the Roper Organization that the bias had gone this way. See http://gallup.com/poll/147350/optimism-future-youth-reaches-time-low.aspx.

6 *That a China-based manufacturer:* Peter Whoriskey, "New World Trade Center's Chinese Glass Is Adding to Trade Furor," *Washington Post,* October 10, 2009.

8 *Gou grew up poor:* See http://forbes.com/profile/terry-gou.

9 *In 2010, Hon Hai Industries generated:* Frederick Balfour and Tim Culpan, "The Man Who Makes Your iPhone," *Business Week,* September 9, 2010. See also Simon Parry and Richard Jones, "He Spent £21m on a Penthouse—but Turns Lights Off to Save Money: Inside the Amazing World of Secret Billionaire Terry Gou," *Daily Mail,* June 27, 2010.

9 *C. Fred Bergsten, the director of the Peterson Institute:* Doug Palmer, "China May Be Worst Protectionist Ever: U.S. Analyst," Reuters, August 12, 2011, www.reuters.com/article/2011/08/12/us-usa-china-currency-idUSTRE77B4VB20110812.

11 *there were also hints before then that Chinese banks:* Chris Oliver, "China's Forex Drop Looks Suspicious: Analyst," *MarketWatch,* October 18, 2011.

11 *As of September 2011, China officially owned $1.15 trillion:* Treasury data from http://treasury.gov/resource-center/data-chart-center/tic/Documents/mfh.txt.

12 *Congressional Budget Office projected to reach:* Congressional Budget Office, "The Budget and Economic Outlook: An Update," August 2011, www.cbo.gov/ftpdocs/123xx/doc12316/Update_SummaryforWeb.pdf.

14 *Among the fortunes created by the young "quants":* For details on Fabrice Tourre's work and life in New York, see Kate Kelly, "Trader Seized on Mortgage-Security Boom," *Wall Street Journal,* April 17, 2010, and Jessica Pressler and Jeff VanDam, "The Fabulous Life of Fabrice Tourre," *New York Magazine,* April 23, 2010.

15 *Paulson himself took home $4 billion:* Greg Zuckerman, a reporter at the *Wall Street Journal,* dubbed Paulson's winnings "the greatest trade ever" in his book of the same name: *The Greatest Trade Ever: The Behind-the-Scenes Story of How John Paulson Defied Wall Street and Made Financial History* (Broadway Books, 2009).

16 *Industrious workers like twenty-one-year-old Xui Li:* Details of the worker's life inside Foxconn taken from interview in Shenzhen and from news accounts describing the compound. See Jason Dean, "The Forbidden City of Terry Gou," *Wall Street Journal,* August 11, 2007.

17 *But others tried to speak for them:* Cited in Jenny Chan and Ngai Pun, "Suicide as Protest for the New Generation of Chinese Migrant Workers:

Foxconn, Global Capital, and the State," *Asia-Pacific Journal: Japan Focus, 2010,* http://japanfocus.org/home. Original blog post: http://blog.sina.com.cn/s/blog_47480eca0100ikm2.html.

17 *The company staged a rally:* Gillian Wong, "Foxconn Gets Pompoms Out to Raise Morale at 'Suicide Factory,'" *The Independent,* August 19, 2010.

18 *They suffered most of the 8 million job losses:* See, for example, the data compiled by Spotlight on Poverty and Opportunity: The Source for News, Ideas and Action, www.spotlightonpoverty.org/ExclusiveCommentary.aspx?id=12f13dec-535a-4586-872a-8abf5dc1c80d.

19 *In 2007, the year before the financial crisis:* Income ratios and spending contribution taken from Bureau of Labor Statistics, www.bls.gov/cex/2007/aggregate/higherincome.pdf.

19 *Americans took on an additional $70 billion in new credit card debt:* From the Federal Reserve's monthly report on consumer credit, www.federalreserve.gov/releases/g19/Current.

19 *Among the tens of thousands of Hewlett-Packard computer components:* The details of John DeVlieger's experiences before and after the crisis come from an interview on September 12, 2011, court documents, and the prospectus for Goldman Sachs's Abacus offering: www.scribd.com/doc/30059004/30036962-Abacus-2007-Ac1-Flipbook-20070226.

20 *"bubble thinking," as Yale economist Robert Shiller calls it:* See Robert Shiller, "Animal Spirits and the Economic Outlook," speech to the National Economists Club, May 6, 2010, summary of his remarks: www.national-economists.org/gov/shiller10.html.

22 *The world was flat, declared columnist and best-selling author:* Thomas L. Friedman, *The World Is Flat: A Brief History of the 21st Century* (Farrar, Straus and Giroux, 2005).

Chapter 1: Origins of Dysfunction

31 *So, on August 5, 1971, Nixon gave a televised address:* Footage available at www.youtube.com/watch?v=iRzr1QU6K1o.

33 *Rick Perry, the governor of Texas:* See video of Perry's campaign appearance in Iowa at http://thinkprogress.org/politics/2011/08/15/296552/perry-on-bernanke-pretty-ugly-down-in-texas.

33 *Nor would there ever have been such a thing:* For the value of the Zimbabwean dollar relative to the price of eggs, see Chris McGreal, "What Comes After a Trillion?" *The Guardian,* July 17, 2008.

34 *gold has a rare and pure atomic structure:* So observes Lewis Lehrman, a persistent advocate of the gold standard. See Lewis E. Lehrman, *The True Gold Standard: A Monetary Reform Plan Without Official Reserve Currencies* (The Lehrman Institute, 2011), 15.

34 *Southern Vietnamese refugees stuffed thin 15-gram "gold leaf" bars:* The use of gold leaf bars to smuggle wealth out of Vietnam during the war in that country is described in the catalogue for an exhibition at the Bank of England Museum in 1998: www.gold.org/assets/file/pr_archive/html/bars/Categ.htm.

34 *Palestinian refugees who strapped gold chains:* Sandy Tolan, "The Palestinian Catastrophe, Then and Now," TomDispatch.com, July 10, 2006, www.tomdispatch.com/post/100409.

34 *the total amount of gold produced throughout history:* The World Gold Council estimated that 165,000 metric tons of gold had been mined through human history by 2009, which if put together would occupy "a cube of pure gold . . . 20 meters in any direction," or 8,000 cubic meters. See http://gold.org/about_gold/story_of_gold/demand_and_supply. According to the Federation Internacionale de Natacion, the average Olympic-sized swimming pool holds about 2,500 cubic meters of water (www.fina.org/project/index.php?option=com_content&task=view&id=51&Itemid=119#fr2).

35 *The economic historian Barry Eichengreen:* Barry Eichengreen, *Globalizing Capital: A History of the International Monetary System* (Princeton University Press, 2008), 30.

38 *Exports went from a healthy average annual rate:* U.S. Census data, www.census.gov/foreign-trade/statistics/historical/gands.pdf.

38 *Big U.S. exporters such as machinery producer Caterpillar:* See Edward Mozley Roche, *Managing Information Technology in Multinational Corporations* (Barraclough, 1992), 306.

40 *Mao Zedong, who had been confined to a sickbed:* Jung Chang and John Halliday, *Mao: The Unknown Story* (Anchor, 2006), 573.

44 *The global notional value of outstanding swaps:* See Simon Johnson and James Kwak, *13 Bankers: The Wall Street Takeover and the Next Financial Meltdown* (Vintage, 2011), 8, and the Bank of International Settlements' semiannual report: "Monetary and Economic Department OTC Derivatives Market Activity in the First Half of 2008," 6.

44 *In developing countries, the so-called Washington Consensus:* The term was coined by economist John Williamson of the Peterson International Institute for Economics in 1989 and was intended to describe the consensus views on development policy ideals among Washington think tanks. It was not a set of recommendations per se. Williamson's list was not entirely consistent with the

extreme laissez-faire policy prescriptions some on both right and left would later associate with the term "Washington Consensus." For example, it acknowledged the goal of redirecting public spending toward poverty alleviation via investment in education, health, and other social infrastructure.

45 *By 2000, total world merchandise trade had almost doubled from its level a decade earlier:* World trade went from $3.5 trillion to $6.45 trillion over the period. See World Trade Organization data at http://stat.wto.org/StatisticalProgram/WSDBViewData.aspx?Language=E.

46 *Reuters reporter Jim Della-Giacoma, penned a haunting personal reflection:* Taken from a draft of Della-Giacoma's unpublished memoir, provided to the author.

48 *As the country stocked up on foreign-made clothes:* Savings rate historical data from the Federal Reserve Bank of St. Louis database, http://research.stlouisfed.org/fred2/data/PSAVERT.txt.

48 *Simultaneously, the U.S. trade deficit went from:* Trade data from the U.S. Census Bureau's historical database, www.census.gov/foreign-trade/statistics/historical/exhibit_history.pdf.

49 *as* Washington Post *reporter Bob Woodward described him:* Bob Woodward, *Maestro: Greenspan's Fed and the American Boom* (Simon & Schuster, 2000).

51 *Meanwhile, mortgage buyers Fannie Mae and Freddie Mac fueled the economic distortions:* For a sound argument about the role played by the two government-sponsored enterprises in fomenting the crisis, see Russell Robert, "How Government Stoked the Mania," *Wall Street Journal,* October 3, 2008.

53 *described in a Federal Reserve–published consumer handbook:* Board of Governors of the Federal Reserve System, "Consumer Handbook on Adjustable-Rate Mortgages," April 2007.

53 *Italy's ten-year sovereign bond yields:* Lorenzo Codogno, Carlo Favero, and Alessandro Missale, "Yield Spreads on EMU Government Bonds," Economic policy.org, www.economic-policy.org/pdfs/Preliminarydrafts/37thPanel_meeting/Codognoetal.pdf.

55 *Between 2000 and 2008, some 30 percent of total world growth:* See Jim O'Neill, "BRICS at 8," Goldman Sachs, March 2010, www2.goldmansachs.com/our-thinking/brics/brics-at-8/index.html.

56 *During the twelve months ending in December 2010:* See Keith Bradsher, "China Leading Global Race to Make Clean Energy," *New York Times,* January 30, 2010; Ashlee Vance, "China Wrests Supercomputer Title from U.S.," *New York Times,* October 28, 2010; and Tom Mitchell, "Chinese Harmony Train Sets Speed Record," *Financial Times,* December 28, 2009.

57 *China's computing, telecommunications, and general networking capacity:* For China telecommunications market research, see "China—Broadband Market—Overview, Statistics and Forecasts," BuddeComm, www.budde.com.au/Research/China-Broadband-Market-Overview-Statistics-and-Forecasts.html.

57 *According to Charlene Barshefsky:* Phone interview, June 7, 2010.

59 *In 2007, economic historians Niall Ferguson and Moritz Schularick:* Niall Ferguson and Moritz Schularick, "Chimerical? Think Again," *Wall Street Journal,* February 5, 2007.

60 *A survey by the Pew Research Center:* "Americans Are of Two Minds on Trade," Pew Research Center, November 9, 2010, http://pewresearch.org/pubs/1795/poll-free-trade-agreements-jobs-wages-economic-growth-china-japan-canada.

Chapter 2: Average Joes

63 *Meet Joe Bonadio:* All the material regarding Joe Bonadio's experiences with three banks is taken from an interview on August 23, 2010, and from bank statements and other documents that Bonadio showed to the author.

70 *coincided with the loss of 1.8 million American jobs to China:* Robert E. Scott, "Costly Trade with China: Millions of U.S. Jobs Displaced with Net Job Loss in Every State," Economic Policy Institute, www.epi.org/publications/entry/bp188.

71 *It was 1967, and Fang Xiyuan:* Details on the life of Fang Xiyuan, aka James Fang, come from an interview in Shanghai, October 27, 2010.

74 *according to a report by Merrill Lynch and consulting group Capgemini:* "World Wealth Report 2010," Merrill Lynch Global Wealth Management and Capgemini, June 18, 2010.

74 Forbes *reported that China had 115 billionaires in 2011:* "The World's Billionaires," *Forbes,* March 9, 2011.

75 *Shanghai's spectacular property boom:* David Barboza, "Market Defies Fear of Real Estate Bubble in China," *New York Times,* March 4, 2010.

75 *some wealthy locals have purchased Pudong apartments for $10 million:* Ibid.

80 *in China some 221 million people:* "China's 'Floating Population' Exceeds 221 Million," People's Daily Online, http://english.peopledaily.com.cn/90001/90776/90882/7303707.html.

80 *In a few cities, Shanghai included, these rules have been relaxed:* Zhao Litao and Courtney Fu Rong, "China's Hukou Reform: The Guangdon and Shanghai Cases," EAI Background Brief No. 551, www.eai.nus.edu.sg/BB551.pdf.

85 *The most common explanation for this was one backed up by research:* See Carmen M. Reinhart and Kenneth S. Rogoff, *This Time Is Different: Eight Centuries of Financial Folly* (Princeton University Press, 2009); "2009 Market Update," Market Analysis, Research and Education, Fidelity Management and Research Co.

86 *with more than 80 percent exceeding analysts' forecasts:* See "Q3 2009 Market Update" and "2009 Market Update," Market Analysis, Research and Education, Fidelity Management and Research Co., http://claytonfsi.com/media/3q09_marketupdate.pdf; http://claytonfsi.com/media/4q09_marketupdate.pdf.

86 *David Bianco, then a Bank of America Merrill Lynch strategist:* "Outlook 2011: The New Powers of Global Growth," transcript of Merrill Lynch Wealth Management webcast, December 9, 2010, www.totalmerrill.com/publish/mkt/pdfs/Outlook-2011-RR_Transcript.pdf.

86 *it helped Wall Street make record profits of $55 billion:* Profits and bonus figures based on estimates from the New York comptroller's office, press releases, February 23, 2010, and February 23, 2011. Also see Stephen Grocer, "Banks Set for Record Pay: Top Firms Pace to Award $145 Billion for 2009, Up 18%, WSJ Study Finds," *Wall Street Journal*, January 14, 2010.

88 *Printed circuit boards, or PCBs:* Information on the printed circuit board industry, Electropac, and the lives of Raymond and Steven Boissoneau taken from interviews and materials provided at a factory tour of Electropac's premises in Manchester, New Hampshire, January 2010.

Chapter 3: Virtue and Vice

98 *Niall Ferguson has convincingly argued:* Niall Ferguson, *The Ascent of Money: A Financial History of the World* (Penguin, 2008).

99 *estimated at between 25 percent and almost 40 percent of disposable income in 2010:* Marcos Chamon, Kai Liu, and Eswar Prasad, "The Puzzle of China's Rising Household Savings Rate," VoxEU.org, www.voxeu.org/index.php?q=node/6028. The national accounts produce a higher result than China's surveys of urban and rural households, which likely stems from different definitions of what constitutes income and from the blurred distinction between business and household spending and saving activity.

99 *When you lump in the savings of businesses:* Ibid.

99 *In the year ending June 2011:* "Financial Statistics, H1 2011," People's Bank of China, www.pbc.gov.cn/image_public/UserFiles/english/upload/File/Financial%20statistics,%20h1%202011.pdf.

99 *its household savings rate is one of the lowest:* In the first decade of the new millennium, monthly readings of the U.S. personal savings rate got as low as 0.9 percent in October 2001. It briefly popped above 7.1 percent in May 2009 as households responded to the crisis by reining in spending. In the eight years before the crisis of September 2008, the rate rarely got above 4.0 percent and averaged 3.3 percent. Since then, it has averaged 4.9 percent. Data available at the Federal Reserve Bank of St. Louis's Federal Reserve Economic Data service, http://research.stlouisfed.org/fred2/graph/?s[1][id]=PSAVERT.

99 *consistently run a current account* deficit *of between 3 and 6 percent of GDP:* Data from the Bureau of Economic Analysis, www.bea.gov.

102 *There I met Wu Guoseng and Wu Xinfeng:* Interviews with both and a tour of their living premises in Zhu Hai, October 21, 2010.

103 *ten years later its annual imports from that country stood at $26.7 billion:* Robert E. Scott, "The Wal-Mart Effect: Its Chinese Imports Have Displaced Nearly 200,000 U.S. Jobs," Economic Policy Institute, www.epi.org/publication/ib235.

103 *"If Wal-Mart were a country":* Zachary Karabell, *Superfusion: How China and America Became One Economy and Why the World's Prosperity Depends on It* (Simon & Schuster, 2009), 223.

103 *Walmart's trade deficit with China alone:* Scott, "The Wal-Mart Effect."

104 *At the age of twenty, Ruan Libing:* Details of Ruan Libing's accident taken from interview at his residence in Zhu Hai, October 21, 2010, and subsequent visit to his home village, October 22, 2010.

107 *the runaway bride:* Mei Fong, "It's Cold Cash, Not Cold Feet, Motivating Runaway Brides in China," *Wall Street Journal,* June 5, 2009.

107 *"From an individual household's viewpoint":* Shang-Jin Wei, "Why Do the Chinese Save So Much?" *Forbes,* February 2, 2010.

108 *Elec-Tech relented:* "Worker's Lawsuit Challenges Inadequacies of China's Compensation System—Updated," *China Labour Bulletin,* October 20, 2010, www.clb.org.hk/en/node/100905.

109 *spokesman Kevin Gardner:* Emailed statement, October 25, 2010. Walmart ethical standards: www.walmartstores.com/ethicalstandards.

111 *rose from 8,600 in 1993 to 90,000 in 2006:* "Protecting Workers' Rights or Serving the Party," *China Labour Bulletin,* March 2009, 4.

111 *surged to 127,467 incidents in 2008:* Ibid.

111 *In the summer of 2010:* Details on Guangdong labor unrest and minimum wage hikes at "Guangdong Ponders Another Increase in the Minimum Wage," *China Labour Bulletin,* November 30, 2010.

113 *Yu Faming, director of the Employment Promotion Division:* "China needs 25 million new jobs annually in next 5 years," People's Daily Online, English Version, December 1, 2010, http://english.peopledaily.com.cn/90001/90778/90862/7217587.html.

114 *Chinese banks issued a whopping 9.6 trillion yuan:* Li Yanping and Kevin Hanlin, "China Reserves Hit Record $2.4 Trillion as Loan Growth Quickens," Bloomberg, January 15, 2010.

114 *a further 8 trillion yuan in 2010:* "Bank Loans Higher than 2010 Target," *Xinhua,* January 12, 2011.

114 *bought 13.6 million cars in 2009:* "China Car Sales 'Overtook the US' in 2009," BBC, January 11, 2010.

114 *clocked up 18 million more purchases in 2010:* Tian Ying, "China 2010 Auto Sales Reach 18 Million, Extend Lead," Bloomberg, January 10, 2011.

114 *hedge fund manager John Paulson:* Gregory Zuckerman, "Rivals Scout Paulson Assets," *Wall Street Journal,* September 28, 2011.

115 *the district of Kangbashi:* Peter Hitchens, "This Is a City Built for a Million People—but No One Lives Here," *Daily Mail,* May 29, 2011.

115 *The new Guangzhou South railway station:* Details on the construction and design of the station at "China's Super Train Station Pulls Out All Stops," Design Build Source, http://designbuildsource.com.au/china%E2%80%99s-super-train-station-pulls-stops.

116 *It has earmarked $298 billion:* Bill Powell, "China's Amazing New Bullet Train," CNN Money, August 6, 2009.

116 *"past idle steel mills and untenanted shopping malls":* "The Risk Down Under," *Grant's Interest Rate Observer* 29, no. 11 (June 3, 2011).

116 *All but one of China's twenty-two provinces:* "China by the Numbers: Understanding China's Provincial Priorities," PwC, www.pwc.com/us/en/view/issue-13/understanding-chinas-provincial-priorities.jhtml.

118 *just to pay interest on this debt, Shih says:* Victor Shih, "Looming Problem of Local Debt in China—1.6 Trillion Dollars and Rising," Elite Chinese

Politics and Political Economy, http://chinesepolitics.blogspot.com/2010/02/looming-problem-of-local-debt-in-china.html.

119 *perhaps the most prominent of the China bears:* See a video of a lecture Chanos gave at Oxford on this topic in 2010: www.youtube.com/watch?v=99HNFCn5RP8.

119 *As economist Paul Krugman predicted:* Paul Krugman, "The Myth of Asia's Miracle," *Foreign Affairs,* November/December 1994.

123 *The government announced a scheme to build 36 million:* James T. Areddy and Bob Davis, "China Pins Hope on Public Housing," *Wall Street Journal,* December 31, 2011.

124 *worth a massive $1.9 trillion as of October 2011:* Wynne Wang and Ling-ling Wei, "China Cracks Down on Informal Lending," *Wall Street Journal,* October 15, 2011.

126 *A Western doctor will prescribe pills:* Speech hosted by the Institute for International Finance, Washington, October 10, 2010.

130 *"They have a huge task ahead of them":* Interview, Shanghai, October 24, 2010.

130 *Pettis wrote in an article for* Foreign Policy: Michael Pettis, "Is China Turning Japanese," *Foreign Policy,* August 19, 2010.

Chapter 4: The Long Reach

132 *the average Argentine consumed 155 pounds of red meat:* Details on Argentine beef consumption and its decline in recent years taken from: www.argentinepost.com/2010/06/per-capita-beef-consumption-drops-to-56-kilos.html. On beef imports from Uruguay: Fernando Bertello, "Subió la importación de carne urguaya," *La Nacion,* February 17, 2010, www.lanacion.com.ar/nota.asp?nota_id=1234094.

135 *adding a further 4.6 million hectares:* According to USDA estimates and forecasts: www.pecad.fas.usda.gov/cropexplorer/default_popwin.cfm?obj_name=pecad_stories.cfm&regionid=ssa&ftype=prodbriefs.

136 *Andrés Rosenberg, who runs two farms:* Details of the Rosenbergs' experience as farmers taken from an interview with Andrés Rosenberg and tour of his farm, February 21, 2011.

138 *Gustavo Grobocopatel:* Interview, February 21, 2011.

139 *Trade with the continent grew by an average of 33 percent each year:* "China: Trade with Africa on Track to a New Record," CNN Online, October 15,

2010, http://articles.cnn.com/2010-10-15/world/china.africa.trade_1_china-and-africa-link-trade-largest-trade-partner?_s=PM:WORLD.

140 *According to* The Economist: "The Queensway Syndicate and the Africa Trade," *The Economist,* August 13, 2011.

140 *In Kenya, environmental organizations report:* Mike Pflanz, "Chinese Demand and Financial Crisis Cause Surge in Kenya Elephant Poaching," *Telegraph,* February 25, 2009.

140 *Riots in Algiers:* "Chinese Migrants in Algiers Clash," BBC, August 4, 2009.

141 *BHP Billiton's Mt. Whaleback mine:* Data on BHP's iron ore operations taken from mine visit and meetings with company representatives in October 2010.

146 *FIFO workers at Fortescue's sites start with annual salaries:* Based on author's inquiries with Fortescue representatives.

149 *Yet a closely watched housing index:* Australian Bureau of Statistics Home Price Index, www.abs.gov.au/AUSSTATS/abs@.nsf/DetailsPage/6416.0Sep%202010?OpenDocument.

150 *Qantas eventually stopped serving alcohol on FIFO flights:* Geoffrey Thomas, "Airline Staff Given Rage Alarms," *West Australian,* March 1, 2011.

150 *Researchers at Queensland University of Technology:* Kerry Carrington, Alice McIntosh, and John Scott, "Globalisation, Frontier Masculinities and Violence: Booze, Blokes and Brawls," *British Journal of Criminology,* 2010.

150 *Local media in Perth were running stories in 2010 and 2011:* See, among others, Gabrielle Knowles, "Night of Violence Across Perth," *West Australian,* May 8, 2011, and Nicole Cox, "Commissioner Says Glass Ban Won't Stop Slashing with 67 Attacks," *PerthNow,* August 12, 2010.

151 *Kelly and Anthony Curran:* Email correspondence, September 19 and 22, 2011.

152 *Western Australian manufacturers lost 17,300 jobs:* *West Australian,* November 2011.

152 *Perth-based political scientist Peter McMahon:* Interview, October 17, 2010.

156 *"The history of Western Australia has been":* Email correspondence, February 8, 2011.

156 *Ian Ashby, the managing director of BHP Iron Ore:* Details on BHP's long-range forecasts from interview with Ashby, October 15, 2010.

157 *David Robb, managing director of Iluka:* Interview, October 15, 2010.

Chapter 5: Race to the Bottom

162 *At that very moment:* Among various accounts of the crime: "Hallan a 15 decapitados," *El Universal,* Saturday, January 8, 2011.

163 *An accelerating war between rival drug gangs:* Eduardo A. Orbea, "En dos años se duplicaron las autopsias en Ciudad Juárez por la violencia del narco," UnivisionNoticias.com, February 27, 2011.

163 *the gruesome sight of a decapitated body:* "Cuelgan cuerop de decapitado en un Puente de Ciudad Juárez," *La Cronica de Hoy* (Mexico), November 7, 2008.

165 *According to the Juárez Restaurants Association:* Interview with association president Ricardo Ziga, January 8, 2011.

168 *Rocio Gallegos, a journalist from the newspaper* El Diario: Interview on January 8, 2011.

169 *In 2000, Mexico had dominated the U.S. clothing market:* See Michael F. Martin, "U.S. Clothing and Textile Trade with China and the World: Trends Since the End of Quotas," Congressional Research Service Report for Congress, July 10, 2007.

169 *But by 2008, its share had dropped to 5.3 percent:* U.S. International Trade Statistics, Value of Exports, General Imports, and Imports by Country by 6-Digit NAIC Mexico (2008), www.censtats.census.gov.

169 *In the first seven years after NAFTA:* Data from El Consejo Nacional de la Industria Maquiladora y Manufacturera de Exportación, www.cnimme.org .mx/includes/LaMaquila/Estadisticas/1a.php?title=Estadisticas.

169 *which lost out to Memphis, Tennessee:* Amos Maki, "Electrolux Coming to Memphis; Thousands of Jobs Expected," *Commercial Appeal,* December 14, 2010.

170 *twenty-nine-year-old Deissy Marquéz:* Interview, January 8, 2011.

172 *estimated to bring in $40 billion a year:* George Friedman, "Mexico: On the Road to a Failed State?" STRATFOR Global Intelligence, March 13, 2008.

173 *Mexican finance minister Ernesto Cordero:* Interview in New York offices of *Wall Street Journal,* 2011.

174 *Juárez's new mayor, Héctor Murguía Lardizábal:* Interview in New York offices of *Wall Street Journal,* 2011.

175 *according to Manuel Ochoa:* Interview in New York offices of *Wall Street Journal,* 2011.

178 *said Enorvian Ismy, secretary general of the Indonesian Textile Association:* Interview in Jakarta, November 3, 2010.

178 *Hendrik Sasmito, chairman of the PT Panarub group of companies:* Interview in Jakarta, November 2, 2010.

179 *trade minister Mari Pangestu:* Interview in Jakarta, November 4, 2010.

180 *The U.S. Office of Textiles and Apparel reports:* Martin, "U.S. Clothing and Textile Trade"; U.S. International Trade Statistics, Value of Exports, General Imports, and Imports by Country by 6-Digit NAIC Mexico (2008), www.censtats.census.gov.

180 *Ina Indrawati:* Interview in Jakarta, November 3, 2010.

182 *The incident prompted Oxfam Australia:* See Timothy Connor, "We Are Not Machines—Indonesian Nike and Adidas Workers," Oxfam Australia, March 2002, http://oxfam.org.au/resources/filestore/originals/OAus-WeAreNotMachines-0302.pdf.

182 *In October 2010, Oxfam again wrote to Adidas:* For a full account of Oxfam's communication with Adidas on various Panarub issues, see the "Talking with Adidas" links on Oxfam Australia's website, http://oxfam.org.au/explore/workers-rights/adidas/talking-with-adidas.

184 *The twenty-two-year-old, who gave her name as Dinarni:* Interview at premises of PT Panarub.

184 *According to Oxfam, only 1,500 were reabsorbed:* "Inside Adidas' Indonesian Factories," Oxfam Australia, http://oxfam.org.au/explore/workers-rights/adidas/inside-adidas-indonesian-factories#jobs.

185 *Adidas grew its sales to $12 billion in 2010:* Annual report, released March 2, 2011.

185 *For that deal, signed in 2003:* Paul Smith, "England Captain Heading for £100m Life-long Contract," *Sunday Mirror,* August 10, 2003.

Chapter 6: Global Finance Between a Rock and a Hard Place

192 *"Jefferson's legacy again demands our attention":* Simon Johnson and James Kwak, *13 Bankers: The Wall Street Takeover and the Next Financial Meltdown* (Vintage, 2011), 18.

194 *Fittingly, RBS had its beginnings:* RBS makes information about the "Darien Adventure" available in its own heritage archives: http://heritagearchives

.rbs.com/wiki/Company_of_Scotland_Trading_to_Africa_and_The_Indies, _overseas_trading_company,_1695-1707.

195 *Its December 2007 market capitalization:* "Global 500 2008," *Financial Times,* June 24, 2008.

195 *RBS was the biggest bank of them all:* "The World's Biggest Banks 2008," *Global Finance,* www.gfmag.com/tools/best-banks/2337-the-worlds-biggest-banks-2008.html#axzz1chBwJA9m.

195 *RBS ended 2007 with $3.8 trillion:* Annual results for the year ended December 31, 2007, Royal Bank of Scotland Group PLC.

198 *This had a significant impact on RBS's employees:* Annual reports (2007, 2010), Royal Bank of Scotland Group PLC.

198 *By mid-2011, RBS had lost £750 billion:* "Progress Against Business Targets," RBS.com website, https://changingthebank.rbs.com/Business_targets/KPI1.aspx.

198 *In 2011, most RBS staffers:* Kit Chellel, "Headhunters Expect RBS Exits as Project Merlin Bites," *Financial News,* February 10, 2011.

198 *The U.S. subsidiary's earnings:* Statements of Financial Condition as of June 30, 2008, and as of June 30, 2011, RBS Securities Inc.

199 *the global markets division averaged a profit of £4.6 billion:* Annual Report 2010, RBS.

199 *Now mostly owned by British taxpayers:* Avi Salzman, "Another Deal, Another Tax Break," *New York Times,* September 25, 2005; Louise Story, "R.B.S.'s Shining Star in Connecticut," *New York Times,* February 17, 2010.

199 *U.S. government bond strategist William O'Donnell:* Interviews with O'Donnell and others at RBS headquarters in Stamford, November 9, 2010.

203 *Take the case of Bruno and Lisa Miglietti:* Interview, home visit, September 14, 2010.

204 *the U.S. government owns nine out of ten new residential mortgages:* Nick Timiraos, "U.S. Gambles with Mortgage Retreat," *Wall Street Journal,* October 10, 2011.

205 *when it paid what was then a record $215 million settlement:* "Citigroup Settles FTC Charges Against the Associates Record-Setting $215 Million for Subprime Lending Victims," press release, Federal Trade Commission, September 19, 2002.

206 *The ninefold difference:* Annual financial reports, 2009 and 2010, Morgan Stanley, Goldman Sachs, JPMorgan Chase; U.S. Census 2010.

206 *now seem "quaint," he says:* Michael Lewis, *The Big Short: Inside the Doomsday Machine* (Norton, 2009), xiii.

207 *As the trio quadrupled:* Annual financial reports, 2009 and 2010, Morgan Stanley, Goldman Sachs, JPMorgan Chase.

207 *It's worth noting that almost:* See Mary Williams Walsh, "A.I.G. Lists Banks It Paid with U.S. Bailout Funds," *New York Times,* March 15, 2009.

207 *Citi was contracted to pay a bonus of $100 million:* Christopher Palmeri, "Pass the Buck: Citi Sells Phibro to Oxy," *Business Week,* October 9, 2009.

207 *Whereas JPMorgan Chase CEO Jamie Dimon and Goldman Sachs:* *Forbes* profiles, 2007, 2010.

208 *what Johnson and Kwak describe as the "financialization":* Johnson and Kwak, *13 Bankers,* 59–60.

209 *economists from the University of California, Berkeley, and the Paris School of Economics:* Thomas Piketty and Emmanuel Saez, "The Evolution of Top Incomes: A Historical and International Perspective," National Bureau of Economic Research, Working Paper 11955, January 2006.

209 *This evidence of the dangerous:* This transmission mechanism through which inequality reaches a level where it contributes to economic failure has attracted greater attention at the multilateral level in recent years. After the turn of the millennium, there was a sea change in thinking at the World Bank, such that its policy makers now recognized that excessive income disparity was not a neutral matter when it comes to economic development but a hindrance to it. The World Bank now puts considerable effort into measuring income inequality—widely publishing Gini coefficient measures to rank different countries by this standard—and actively encourages policies that pointedly attack income inequality. Since the World Bank is a U.S.-led institution, it is sobering to think that the same ideas would confront huge political obstacles in the United States, whose Gini coefficient of inequality is higher than other developed countries.

209 *Between 1978 and 2007:* The data in this paragraph, drawn from the Bureau of Economic Analysis, are cited in Johnson and Kwak, *13 Bankers,* 60.

211 *In 1988, U.S. consumer debt:* Time series from the Federal Reserve's G.19 monthly consumer credit statistical reports, www.federalreserve.gov/Releases/g19.

211 *"credit was the great equalizer," says Raghuram Rajan:* Interview, February 10, 2010.

214 *The shadow banking system's capacity to self-destruct:* The work of John Gianakopolous at Yale University has been especially instrumental, helping

central bankers conceive of measures to bring countercyclical balance to this process.

216 *Through the idea of "carried interest":* Most hedge funds work on a 20/2 system in which their fee is based on 2 percent of the clients' total investments and 20 percent of the investment gains. Most have "high-water mark" rules under which an investor's gains must be above the prior closing highest year-end value before the 20 percent performance fee kicks in. But there is no personal penalty for the hedge fund manager from losses on the fund.

219 *"Do you have a fear, like I do":* "Dimon Presses Bernanke on Impact of New Bank Rules," CNBC video, June 7, 2011, http://video.cnbc.com/gallery/?video=3000026289.

219 *Three months later, Dimon took it further:* Tom Braithwaite and Patrick Jenkins, "JPMorgan Chief Says Bank Rules 'Anti-U.S,'" *Financial Times,* September 12, 2008.

220 *Small U.S. banks were especially hard hit:* Dan Fitzpatrick and Rob Barr, "Ax Falls at Smaller Banks," *Wall Street Journal,* November 30, 2011.

221 *In putting the squeeze on the CFTC:* See, for example, the letter that Rep. Spencer Bachus (R-Ala.), who later became chairman of the House Committee on Financial Services, and Rep. Frank Lucas (R-Okla.) sent to CFTC chairman Gary Gensler and SEC chairwoman Mary Shapiro on December 16, 2010, http://online.wsj.com/public/resources/documents/bachus.pdf.

221 *"If you have a bunch of people":* Cochrane quoted in Michael Casey, "Money Talks: Bank Regulators, Put on Your Handcuffs," *Dow Jones Newswires,* November 6, 2009.

222 *"Given the danger these institutions pose":* Michael Casey, "Fed's Fisher: Too-Big-to-Fail Banks Should Be Dismantled," *Dow Jones Newswires,* March 3, 2010.

224 *says University of Texas professor James K. Galbraith:* Phone interview, April 19, 2011.

224 *The answer can be found:* See www.opensecrets.org.

225 *their political contributions for the 2012 electoral cycle were already:* Searches on individual names within www.campaignmoney.com.

225 *website describes it as being opposed to Obama administration policies:* See www.restoreourfuture.com.

226 *proposals to end the 15 percent capital gains taxation:* Congressman Sander Levin made a second unsuccessful bid at making this law in April 2009, when he reintroduced legislation he'd sponsored in the previous Congress.

226 *In total, campaign contributions from individuals and political action committees:* See www.opensecrets.org/industries/indus.php?Ind=F.

226 *saying he thinks Washington should "serve the banks":* Mary Orndoff, "Spencer Bachus Gets His Chairmanship," *Birmingham News,* December 9, 2010.

227 *We've denied them the "discipline of failure":* See Robert Johnson, "Credible Resolution: What It Takes to End Too Big to Fail," Roosevelt Institute: Project on Global Finance, March 3, 2010, http://makemarketsbemarkets.org/report/MakeMarketsBeMarkets.pdf.

228 *"We produced the dumbest socialism ever":* Lawrence Lessig, "Citizens: The Need and the Requirements," speech at TEDx San Antonio conference, October 15, 2011, http://tedxsanantonio.com/speakers/2010-speaker-lineup/lawrence-lessig.

Chapter 7: The Little Nation That Could

230 *a metaphor offered by Michael Lewis:* Michael Lewis, "Wall Street on the Tundra," *Vanity Fair,* April 2009.

232 *One passage about an early 2007 lunch party:* Armann Thorvaldsson, *Frozen Assets: How I Lived Iceland's Boom and Bust* (Wiley, 2009), 166.

234 *Reykjavik-based designer Thor Hallur:* All details from Hallur taken from interview in Reykjavik, May 14, 2010.

237 *"At thirteen years old, every kid in Iceland":* Interview, May 14, 2010.

238 *Confronted with thousands of hungry people:* Sophie Morris, "Meltdown: Iceland on the Brink," *The Independent,* January 26, 2009.

238 *"The other night, I was there for three hours":* Interview, May 14, 2010.

238 *Capturing a defining humanist objective of Ebba's group:* Interview, May 14, 2010.

239 *It read simply, "Helvitis Fokking Fokk":* Photos of protests by Joi Gunnar, November 8, 2008, http://en.flickeflu.com/set/72157609177016624.

239 A *similar message was conveyed by a customer of Islandsbanki:* Interview with Islandsbanki employee, May 14, 2010.

240 *Under the slogan "Whatever Works!":* Interview with Jon Gnarr in Reykjavik, May 16, 2010, and Michael Casey, "Comic's Party Bests Rivals in Iceland Vote," *Wall Street Journal,* May 31, 2010.

240 *"I just like the idea of giving traditional politics the middle finger,":* Interview in Reykjavik, May 16, 2010.

241 *True to form, the Best Party:* Ingibjorg Bjornsdottir, "Joke Is on Politicians in Iceland City Poll," *Sydney Morning Herald* via Agence France-Presse, June 1, 2010.

243 *The easygoing lifestyle of this gentle:* Details of Eric Graham's life taken from interview in Guernsey, May 18, 2010.

243 *As of October 13, 2011:* Data taken from Guernsey Investment Fund Association website, www.gifa.org.gg/GIFAmembers_131011.pdf, and from the "Second Quarter 2011 Investment Statistics" report of the Guernsey Financial Services Commission, www.gfsc.gg/Investment/News%5CPages/Second-Quarter-2011-Investment-Statistics.aspx.

243 *The money under these people's control filled the deposits:* Guernsey Financial Services Commission's banking statistics, updated to second quarter of 2011, www.gfsc.gg/Banking/Documents/Quarterly-Banking-statistics-Q2-2011.pdf.

244 *Cheshire sent a letter:* A copy of the letter was published on the website of the Landsbanki Guernsey Depositors' Action Group, http://info.landsbankiaction.org.gg/sites/default/files/CG%20Letter%207-Aug-2006.pdf.

244 *And Landsbanki offered a parental guarantee:* A copy of a letter affirming the guarantee was also published on the website of the Landsbanki Guernsey Depositors' Action Group, http://info.landsbankiaction.org.gg/sites/default/files/LG%20Letter%2025-Sep-2006.pdf.

244 *Eventually Deloitte and Touche LLP:* Leah Hyslop, "Government Rejects Petition by Landsbanki Guernsey Savers," *The Telegraph,* November 16, 2010.

245 *Eventually the GFSC put a stop to this unsecured upstreaming:* "GFSC Clarifies Misconceptions over Landsbanki Gsy Collapse," *Guernsey Press,* November 26, 2008.

245 *there was still an unexplained £36 million:* Rosa Prince, "Guernsey Savers Demand More Help from Treasury," *The Telegraph,* October 31, 2008.

246 *"the reason we didn't have one":* Interview, May 18, 2010.

247 *"When I put money into a bank":* Interview, May 18, 2010.

247 *Oliver Day, a forty-one-year-old project manager:* Interview, May 18, 2010.

248 *Patel, aka "Icy Chill":* See YouTube video, www.youtube.com/watch?v=3h0N3Q2qSfA.

248 *From both GFSC director Phillip Marr:* Interviews, May 18, 2010.

248 *Foot had declared that "the GFSC measured up to good practice":* "Report by Promontory Financial Group (UK) Ltd to the Guernsey Financial Services Commission (GFSC)—January 2009," published on the GFSC website, www.gfsc.gg/Banking/Documents/Promontory-Report-January-2009.pdf.

253 *When he heard the terms, David Blondal was horrified:* Interview, April 16, 2010.

254 *They did so in cinematic style:* See, for example, Archie Bland, "British Fury After Iceland Blocks £2.3bn Repayment," *The Independent,* January 6, 2010.

254 *"The one thing that people were saying":* Interview, April 16, 2010.

254 *Already, disbursements from a $10 billion:* "PM: Iceland Cannot Wait Much Longer for IMF Payout," *IceNews* via Bloomberg, September 29, 2009, www.icenews.is/index.php/2009/09/29/pm-iceland-cannot-wait-much-longer-for-imf-payout.

255 *"Insurance is the idea that the many insure the few":* Interview, April 16, 2010.

256 *Iceland's Financial Supervisory Authority:* "The Director of 'Inside Job' Replies," Charles Ferguson, Economists' Forum, FT.com, October 14, 2010.

257 *various reforms were made to the European Union agreements on deposit guarantee schemes:* Press release, "Commission Proposes Package to Boost Consumer Protection and Confidence in Financial Services," European Commission, July 12, 2010.

258 *a* Financial Times *article published one day before:* Sam Jones, Elizabeth Rigby, and Cynthia O'Murchu, "The Blue Hedge Brigade: How UK Hedge Fund Chiefs Became Top Tory Backers," *Financial Times,* December 7, 2011.

260 *The IMF projected that Ireland's:* "Fiscal Monitor—April 2011," International Monetary Fund, 127.

262 *Columbia University economist and Nobel laureate Joseph Stiglitz:* Phone interview, March 30, 2011.

262 *"This was about getting back to basics":* Comments, other details about Einarsdottir's experience taking over the Islandsbanki taken from interview, May 14, 2010.

266 *"It showed our sincerity":* Interview, May 14, 2010.

Chapter 8: PIIGS and the Systemic Crisis

271 *According to the Bank of International Settlements:* "BIS Quarterly Review," March 2009 and September 2011.

275 *A flick through the ads in* The Sentinella: *Sentinella,* Axarquia edition, May 2010.

277 *An index produced by real estate evaluation group Tinsa:* "Indice de Mercados Inmobiliarios Españoles," Tinsa, September 2011 (http://www.tinsa.es/down/IMIE/2011/IMIE_09_2011.pdf).

277 *Lorenzo Bernaldo de Quirós, a Madrid-based economist:* Interview, May 25, 2010.

277 *Mark Bellamy moved with his wife:* Interview, May 20, 2010.

278 *"They have cotton wool in their ears":* Interview, May 20, 2010.

279 *"Before the crisis, we had too much work":* Interview, May 20, 2010.

279 *Adela Díaz Pardo, who ran the bar:* Interview, May 20, 2010.

280 *A driver who also gave only his first name, Federico:* Interview, May 20, 2010.

281 *Before the boom, virtually all borrowers:* Interview with Fernando Fernández Méndez de Andes, economist at the IE Business School in Madrid, May 25, 2010.

282 *As analysts at the political risk consultancy STRATFOR:* Peter Zeihan, "Europe: The Next Strategy," *Geopolitical Weekly,* STRATFOR, December 21, 2010.

282 *Investment in the residential sector rose by 150 percent:* The European Economic Advisory Group, "Spain," *The EEAG Report on the European Economy 2011* (CESifo, 2011), 127.

282 *who were eligible for forty-five days' severance for every year they had worked:* Report on Spain by the International Labor Organization, 2007.

283 *Home prices in Dublin increased fivefold:* "Dublin House Prices Heading for 100 Times Rent Earned: Davy Stockbrokers," *FinFacts Ireland,* May 29, 2006, www.finfacts.com/irelandbusinessnews/publish/article_10005356.shtml.

283 *Iain Begg, an economist at the London School of Economics:* Interview, May 27, 2010.

285 *the ECB routinely declared:* See monetary policy decision statements among 2008 press releases at the ECB's website: www.ecb.int/press/pr/date/2008/html/index.en.html.

287 *longtime euroskeptic Martin Feldstein:* Martin Feldstein, "The Euro and the Stability Pact," Working Paper 11249, National Bureau of Economic Research, March 2005.

288 *Credit Suisse analysts:* Simon Kennedy and Jana Randow, "Trichet Seen Burying Ailing Nations with Interest-Rate Rise," Bloomberg, April 4, 2011.

298 *A* Wall Street Journal *exposé published in late December:* Marcus Walker, Charles Forelle, and Stacy Meichtry, "Deepening Crisis Over Euro Pits Leader Against Leader," *Wall Street Journal,* December 30, 2011.

304 *During my visit in May 2010:* "Zapatero's Cuts; Spain's Prime Minister Reluctantly Embraces Austerity," *The Economist,* May 20, 2010.

305 *But as of early 2011:* Jonathan House and Christopher Bjork, "Spain Pegs Cajas' Possible Problem Debt," *Wall Street Journal,* February 22, 2011.

306 *Ernesto García, twenty-three, was a sociology student:* These and other comments taken from interviews in the Plaza Dos de Mayo, May 26, 2010.

307 *"Spain is in the worst crisis of its economic history":* Interview, May 26, 2010.

308 *"The scale they are talking about":* Interview, May 27, 2010.

Chapter 9: The Global Liquidity Machine

310 *Roni Rubinov:* Details on the diamond district and Roni Rubinov's pawn shop from interview, tour of district on July 14, 2010.

313 *Bullion marketer Goldline:* Fred Thompson's TV spots for Goldline appeared frequently on Fox News and other news cable channels, as did G. Gordon Liddy's for Rosland Capital; Glenn Beck and other Fox commentators, including Mike Huckabee, also ran TV spots in favor of Goldline. The company was later hit with criminal charges for false advertising, misdemeanor, and fraud relating to claims that only minted gold coins, which price at a premium to gold bars, were a safe gold investment on the grounds that bullion could be confiscated by the government (the endorsing celebrities were not charged). See ABC News report, http://abcnews.go.com/GMA/video/goldline-facing-criminal-charges-14863908.

314 *Cash4gold.com:* See Cash4gold.com's ad at www.youtube.com/watch?v=jA3KW6Cu6-k.

314 *Mr. T, star of the* A-Team *television series:* See Mr. T's interview at www.youtube.com/watch?v=pWAu7FmKbYc.

314 *As the blurb on one promoter's website:* See http://janrgoldparties.com/index.php.

314 *And German company Ex Oriente Lux:* See the company's website: www.ex-oriente-lux.de/en.

314 *By mid-August 2011, SPDR Gold Shares:* See Mary Pilon, Liam Pleven, and Jason Zweig, "Gold Even Reigns on Stock Market," *Wall Street Journal,* August 23, 2011.

315 *For the first time in twenty-one years:* "Gold Demand Trends FY 2010," World Gold Council, February 17, 2011.

316 *which fell 17 percent on a trade-weighted basis:* See the Federal Reserve Bank of St. Louis's FRED database, trade-weighted exchange index, http://research.stlouisfed.org/fred2/graph/?s[1][id]=TWEXB.

319 *"What you want is a regulatory":* Michael Casey, "Money Talks: Don't Count on Bernanke When Regulations Fail," *Dow Jones Newswires,* September 14, 2010.

320 *Some took to labeling Bernanke:* There are numerous articles on conspiracy theorist websites about Bernanke's participation in Bilderberg conferences. One of the more prominent is Infowars.com, led by radio talk show host Alex Jones (www.infowars.com). Photos purport to show Bernanke entering the 2008 conference in Chantilly, Virginia, but there is no real evidence he ever attended any such gathering and the Fed has never responded to these claims.

324 *Hong Kong bank accounts paid virtually zero interest:* According to information on HSBC's website in November 2011, term deposits of anything less than HK$100,000 for three months or less paid annual interest of 0.01 percent. The highest rate was for twelve-month deposits of HK$1 million or more, which earned 0.2 percent.

324 *one street in Hong Kong's exclusive Peak district:* The street is Severn Road. See Tara Loader Wilkinson, "Bollinger Boulevards," *Wall Street Journal,* March 8, 2011.

324 *by September 2011 they had gained 50 percent:* Government data from the Hong Kong Rating and Valuation Department, "Property Market Statistics: Private-Domestic Rental Indices (from 1979)."

324 *Bo Bulai, the owner of Squeeze Ltd.:* Interview, October 31, 2010.

325 *By early 2011, office space in Rio de Janeiro:* According to a study by Cushman & Wakefield Inc. See Simon Packard, "Rio de Janeiro Prime Office Rents Overtake New York Rates for First Time," Bloomberg, February 18, 2011.

325 *the place was abuzz with news that a single "bungalow":* Irene Tham, "$36m Home Could Be S'pore's Most Expensive," *Straits Times,* June 13, 2010.

325 *local real estate agent Markus Tay explained:* Interview and tour of Sentosa Cove with Markus Tay, October 19, 2011.

328 *the "ultimate bubble," as George Soros called it:* Alistair Barr, "Gold Moves Pit Soros Against Paulson," *MarketWatch,* May 4, 2011.

328 *New York–based hedge fund manager John Paulson:* Hibah Yousuf, "Housing Savant Paulson Now Looks to Gold," CNNMoney.com, November 18, 2009.

328 *his personal income from the fund ran to $5 billion:* Gregory Zuckerman, "Trader Racks Up a Second Epic Gain," *Wall Street Journal,* January 28, 2011.

328 *Paulson had a much poorer year in 2011:* Kelly Bit, "Paulson's Advantage Plus Fund Drops 51% in 'Aberrational' Year," Bloomberg, January 6, 2012.

328 *He laid out his rationale for them:* As per a translation of the interview that appeared on the Zero Hedge website on April 13, 2011, www.zerohedge.com/article/presenting-john-paulsons-complete-les-echos-interview-which-he-bearish-housing-bullish-gold.

329 *Jorge Pérez was far, far removed:* Interview during visit to informal gold mines in Las Lomas region, Peru, February 27, 2011.

330 *the number of people engaged in informal mining:* "En Piura hay unos 12.000 mineros informales de oro," *Diario El Comercio,* March 1, 2011.

330 *At the entrance to the shaft:* Information on the functioning of this mine provided by workers and supervisor on-site.

332 *a clash between police and miners near Madre de Dios:* Alonzo C. Consuelo, "Violencia en Madre de Dios deja 2 muertos y al menos 37 heridos," *La Republica,* March 2, 2011.

333 *the award-winning German documentary* Tambogrande: *Tambogrande: Mangos, Murder, Mining* (2006), produced, directed, and edited by Ernesto Cabellos and Stephanie Boyd.

334 *Riofrío blamed the national government:* Interview, February 28, 2011.

334 *During the campaign against Manhattan, Arévalo Acha says:* Jorge Arévalo Acha, *El Desarrollo Esquivo: El Caso Manhattan y La Crisis Piurana* (L&L Editores/San Marcos, 2009), 18.

334 *"The informal miner makes a deal with them according to informal law":* Phone interview, March 29, 2011.

335 *De Soto has provocatively estimated to be a whopping $9.3 trillion:* Hernando de Soto, *The Mystery of Capital: Why Capitalism Triumphs in the West and Fails Everywhere Else* (Basic, 2000), 35.

335 *Worse, De Soto says, the latter group's "alienation":* Phone interview, March 29, 2011.

336 *Bill Clinton has called "the most promising":* Bill Clinton, speech at the World Congress on Information Technology, Adelaide, February 27, 2002

Chapter 10: What Is to Be Done?

338 *The incidence of violent deaths:* Steven Pinker, *The Better Angels of Our Nature* (Viking, 2011).

339 *The arguments are strong in both cases:* For a compelling argument on how various aspects of the investment practice have combined to produce unprecedented volatility in stock markets, see John Authers, *The Fearful Rise of Markets: Global Bubbles, Synchronized Meltdowns, and How to Prevent Them in the Future* (FT Press, 2010).

340 *"black swan" event, to use Nassim Taleb's term:* Nassim Taleb, *The Black Swan: The Impact of the Highly Improbable* (Random House, 2007).

340 *By mid-2011, Nouriel Roubini:* Scott Hamilton, "Roubini: Slowdown Brings Forward New Crisis," Bloomberg, September 6, 2011.

343 *Fitch Ratings sovereign analyst Richard Fox:* "China at 60% Risk of Banking Crisis, Fitch Gauge Signals," Bloomberg, March 8, 2011.

351 *"Citibank is a $1.8 trillion company":* Michael Hirsh, "The Resurrection," *National Journal,* March 28, 2011.

354 *Peterson Institute for International Economics director Fred Bergsten:* Michael Casey, "Q&A Peterson Institute's Bergsten on China's Currency," *WSJ Real Time Economics* blog, February 18, 2011.

355 *University of California at Berkeley economist Barry Eichengreen:* Barry Eichengreen, "Why the Dollar's Reign Is Near an End," *Wall Street Journal,* March 2, 2011.

361 *Lawrence Lessig, the Stanford University law professor:* Phone interview, May 9. 2011.

362 *Johnson and Kwak urge us to draw:* Simon Johnson and James Kwak, *13 Bankers: The Wall Street Takeover and the Next Financial Meltdown* (Vintage, 2011), 189.

INDEX

AAA-credit rating, 13, 52, 213, 300, 308, 322, 344
Abacus deal, 14, 20, 21
ABN-Amro, 195
Abortions, gender-based, 107
Acapulco, Mexico, 162–164
Accounting standards, 349–350
Adidas, 178, 182–185
Adjustable-rate mortgages, 53
Afghanistan, 19
Africa, trade with China and, 139–140
Agency bonds, 52
Ai Weiwei, 343
AIG, 207, 215, 220, 293
Algiers, 140
All-China Federation of Trade Unions, 111
American International Group, 203
American Recovery and Reinvestment Act, 84, 116
Ameriquest Mortgage, 19
Anti-trust legislation, 362–363
Apple Computer, 8
Arab Spring, 26, 55
Archer Daniels Midland, 136
Arévalo Acha, Jorge, 334
Argentina, 47, 132–139, 140, 170, 191, 295, 341, 359–360
Arion Bank, 236, 262
Arngrimsson, Kristjan, 240–241
Ashby, Ian, 156, 157
Asian financial crisis of 1997–98, 37, 45–48, 119, 128, 148, 154, 181, 186
Asmundsdottir, Elin (Ebba), 237–239
Association of South East Asian Nations (ASEAN), 177, 179
AT&T, 363
Australia, 343
  "Future Fund," 155
  mining industry, 141–148, 150, 154–159, 161
  Perth, 21–22, 147–153, 159, 161, 162
Australian dollar, 153–154, 160
Austria, 43, 286

Bachus, Spencer, 226
Bacon, Louis, 225
Bahamas, 192
Baht, 45
Banco Santander, 306–307
Bangladesh, 176, 314
Bank of America, 68, 70, 191, 192, 197, 203, 205, 207
Bank of Canada, 53
Bank of England, 250, 297
Bank of International Settlements, 271
Bank of Japan, 11, 322
Bank of New York Mellon, 213
Bank of Nova Scotia, 327

Bank of Spain, 305
Bankruptcy, 67, 68, 227
Banks, 189–206, 209, 211–227
in Europe, 194–196, 198–200, 202, 223, 268–271, 276, 283–284, 289, 291–298, 302, 305, 318, 340
in Guernsey, 242–250
in Iceland, 230–240, 252–257, 261–265
too-big-to-fail doctrine, 196–197, 206, 215, 216, 222, 226, 227, 269, 272, 276, 302–303, 350–352, 362
Barclays Bank, 193, 243
Barclays Capital, 327
Barings Bank, 37
Barshefsky, Charlene, 57–58, 61
Basel Committee, 197, 217, 250
Basel II accord, 217, 281
Basel III agreement, 217–219, 249, 352
Bear Stearns, 192, 197, 199
Beck, Glenn, 314
Beckham, David, 184–186
Beef, Argentinian, 132–133, 135–136
Begg, Iain, 283
Beijing, China, 116
Belgium, 3, 43, 286
Bellamy, Mark, 277–278
Bellamy, Stephanie, 277
Benchmarking, 338–339
Bergsten, C. Fred, 9–10, 354
Berlin Wall, 39, 42
Berlusconi, Silvio, 273, 298–299
Bernaldo de Quirós, Lorenzo, 277, 307
Bernanke, Ben, 33, 84, 86–88, 219, 316–317, 319–322
Bernanke Put, 318–319
Bewey, Janson, 247, 251–252
BHP Billiton, 141–147, 154–156, 158, 329
Bianco, David, 86
Bid-to-cover ratio, 200
"Big Bang" financial reforms, 41, 193, 269
Bilderberg Conferences, 320
Bjorgolfsson, Bjorgolfur Thor, 239
Black, Fisher, 37
Black-Scholes model, 37
Blankfein, Lloyd, 207
Blondal, David, 253–256
Blood House Map, 117
Blue Scope Steel, 154
BNP Paribas, 193, 243, 284
Bo Bulai, 324
Boissoneau, Raymond, 88–91, 93–95, 97, 212
Boissoneau, Steven, 88–97, 212
Bolivia, 145, 150
Bonadio, Joe, 63–71, 73, 75, 82, 97
Bond vigilantes, 270, 272, 290–291, 299, 308
Bonuses, 86, 87, 207
Boomerang (Lewis), 267–268
Brazil, 47, 54–55, 99, 134, 138, 143–145, 147, 174, 199, 201, 325, 343, 348, 354, 357
Bretton Woods system, 32, 33, 354, 364
BRICs (*see* Brazil, Russia, India, China)
Bride price, 107, 108
Brown, Don, 275
"Bubble thinking," 20–21
Budget deficit (U.S.), 50, 121
Buffett, Warren, 220, 290
Burson-Marsteller, 17
Bush, George H. W., 73
Bush, George W., 50

Calderón, Felipe, 172, 176
Caller ID with ring controller, 69, 70–71, 73–74, 76–77, 79
Cameron, David, 258, 270, 271
CampaignMoney.com, 225
Canada, 45, 53, 344, 358–359
Capgemini, 74
Capital adequacy ratio, 291, 336
Capital gains tax, 352, 353
Capitalism, 26, 39, 40, 42, 43, 45, 95, 191, 208
Cargill, 136
Carnegie, Andrew, 362
Carried interest, 216, 226, 352
Carstens, Agustín, 356
Carter, Jimmy, 38
Cash America, 314
Cash4gold.com, 314
Caterpillar, 38
CCP, 262
Center for Responsive Politics' Opensecrets.org, 224–225
Change Congress, 361
Changsha, China, 144
Channel Islands, 242–252
Chanos, Jim, 119
Chen Deming, 126
Cheshire Building Society, 244
Chicago Mercantile Exchange, 37
Chile, 145, 154

Chimerica, 7, 59
China, 2, 54–55, 64, 99, 191, 316–318, 325, 342, 348, 349, 354, 355, 357
Africa, trade with, 139–140
annual growth rate of jobs in, 112–113
Argentina, soybean imports from, 133–138, 170, 183
Australian iron ore and, 141–144, 156–158, 161
automobiles in, 114, 129
average trade surplus (2011), 10
banking crisis in 1990s, 118
broadband and cell phones in, 57
construction growth in, 116–117, 120, 123, 312
consumption in, 119–120
Cultural Revolution in, 71–72, 81
debt-to-GDP ratio in, 118
Deng Xiaoping's four modernizations, 40–41, 56
European Union and, 303
exchange rates, 7–10, 15–16, 70, 83, 120, 178, 197
exports, 9–10, 16–19, 21–22, 25, 60, 61, 120, 123, 125, 126, 311, 339, 357
five-year plan (2011), 113, 125
"floating population" of, 15, 80, 81, 145
Germany and, 288
Guangzhou, 8, 102, 110, 111, 115
high-net-worth individuals (HNWIs) in, 74
Hon Hai Industries (Foxconn), 8–10, 16–19, 110, 174
hukou residency system in, 80, 81, 108, 112, 353
Indonesia and, 177–185
iron ore industry in, 144–145
Japanese occupation of, 126
labor in, 77–83, 104–105, 108, 110–112
land expropriation in, 117
male-to-female ratio in, 107
manufacturing growth in, 55–56
Mexico and, 169, 170, 172–176, 183
minimum wage in, 83, 111
nationalist sentiment in, 125–126
Nixon's visit to, 40, 55
one-child policy in, 15, 107, 112, 183
outsourcing to, 70, 92, 94, 103–104, 346
People's Bank of China (PBOC), 7, 9–11, 52, 75, 114, 120, 122, 123, 198, 201
per capita income in, 157
railways in, 56, 105–106, 115–116
rural-to-city migration in, 15, 80, 81, 101, 106, 134, 145, 157
savings rates in, 16, 25, 59, 60, 82, 99–101, 103, 105, 107, 108, 110, 112, 113, 119, 124, 127, 169, 193, 311, 339
shadow loan business in, 124
Shanghai, 5–8, 75, 80, 81, 83, 114, 116, 118, 134
Shenzhen, 8, 9, 16, 60, 102, 109, 110, 134
slowing growth scenario, 342–344
small businesses in, 123–124
special economic zones (SEZs) in, 60, 75, 102
stimulus strategy in, 113
Tiananmen Square massacre (1989) in, 41, 72
total municipal debt in, 117–118
U.S.-China relationship, 7, 10–13, 15, 18, 55–61, 96, 322–323, 346–347
U.S. Treasury bonds and, 11, 12, 52, 61, 70, 121, 122, 202
wealth gap in, 74, 80–81
worker compensation system in, 104–105, 108, 110
World Trade Organization (WTO) and, 57–58, 134, 167, 168
Zhu Hai, 102–104, 109, 110, 134
China Investment Corporation (CIC), 292–293
China Labour Bulletin (CLB), 105
China price, 65, 83–88, 92–94, 169, 170, 185, 311
Chinese Communist Party, 71, 72, 126, 128, 129
Chinese Railway Ministry, 116
Chinese Student Protection Act of 1992, 73
Chongqing, China, 116–117
Citibank, 68, 69, 351
Citigroup, 19–20, 191, 192, 197, 204, 205, 207, 220, 222
Citizens United v. Federal Election Commission, 361, 362
Ciudad Juárez, Mexico, 22, 163–171, 173–175
Clinton, Bill, 336
Clinton administration, 50, 57
CLSA, 127
CMLTI 2006-AMC1 trust, 20

Cochrane, John H., 222
Colbert, Stephen, 241, 361
Cold War, 39, 40, 42, 43
Collateralized debt obligations (CDOs), 13–14, 18, 52, 210, 213, 214, 292, 293, 336
Colombia, 171
Commodity Futures Trading Commission (CFTC), 221, 227
Commodity prices, 317, 318, 339
Compañía de Minas Buenaventura, 329
Congressional Budget Office, 12
Connally, John, 31
Consumer Financial Protection Bureau, 227
Consumer price index (CPI), 128, 321
Consumer Recovery Network, 67, 69
Contagion, concept of, 54
Cordero, Ernesto, 173
Corzine, John, 222, 294
Costa del Sol, Andalusia, 275–280, 282
Countrywide Financial Corporation, 203, 205
Covered bonds, 219
Creative destruction, 95–96
Credit Agricole, 284
Credit card debt, 19, 67–69, 211
Credit default swap (CDS) market, 214, 215, 290, 293–294, 350
Credit Suisse, 218, 243, 288
Credy Industries, 75, 78
CSR, 144
Cultural Revolution, 71–72, 81
Curran, Kelly and Anthony, 151–152

Darien Company, 194–195
Darling, Alistair, 195–196
Day, Oliver, 247, 251
De Soto, Hernando, 334–336
Debt ceiling debate, U.S., 12, 321, 344, 345
Debt hangover thesis, 85–86
Debt settlement services, 67, 69
Dell Computer, 8
Della-Giacomo, Jim, 46
Deloitte and Touche LLP, 244
Delphi, 167, 175
Demand and supply, 24
Deng Xiaoping, 7, 40–41, 56, 72
Denmark, 286
Deregulation, 23, 44, 190, 191, 227, 269, 359, 363
Deutsche Bank, 193, 243, 327
Deutsche Bundesbank, 281, 297
Deutschmark, 36, 280
DeVlieger, John, 19–21
Díaz Pardo, Adela, 279–280
Digitization, 65
Dim sum bonds, 127
Dimon, Jamie, 207, 219, 228
Dingling Electric Company, 78–80, 82–83, 88, 184
Distressed debt funds, 302
Dodd-Frank Act, 197, 203, 220, 226, 350–351
Dollar, 31–33, 36–39, 45, 47, 51, 120–122, 127, 169, 172–173, 200, 201, 260, 315–318, 324, 338, 344, 354–355
Dongguan, China, 102
Dot.com companies, 48, 96, 158, 168
Dow Jones Industrial Average, 36, 224, 318
Drachma, 53
Draghi, Mario, 298
Dubai, 119
Dudley, Bill, 321
Dutch disease, 153

East India Company, 194
Economic Policy Institute, 70
Economist, The, 140
Efficient-market hypothesis, 43
Egypt, 55
Eichengreen, Barry, 35, 355
Einarsdottir, Birna, 262–263
El Paso, Texas, 163, 165–167
Elec-Tech International Company, 104, 105, 108, 109
Electrolux, 167, 169–170, 175
Electropac Company Inc, 88–95, 97, 98, 212
Empire State Building, New York, 6
End the Fed (Paul), 320
Enron Corporation, 119
Eton Park Capital Management, 329
Euro, 42–43, 53–54, 122, 260–261, 268, 270–272, 274, 280, 281, 286, 290, 295–296, 298, 301, 341–342, 355
European Banking Authority, 257, 292
European Central Bank (ECB), 198, 250, 272, 273, 281, 285, 288, 290, 293, 296–298, 299, 300, 341
European debt crisis, 2, 5, 12, 21, 25, 53–54, 100, 202, 213–215, 218, 219, 257, 267–273, 288–298, 302–309, 313, 340–342, 356, 360

European Economic and Financial Affairs Council (Ecofin), 286
European Economic Area, 252
European Economic Community, 36, 42, 286
European Financial Stability Facility (EFSF), 288–293, 300
European Free Trade Association, 255
European Monetary Union, 286
European Union (EU), 42–43, 54, 125, 218, 249, 252, 253, 255, 257, 259, 261, 270, 271, 273, 274, 284, 286–309, 342, 347, 349, 364
Eurostat, 286
Ex Priente Lux, 314
Exchange rates, 7–10, 15–16, 36, 38, 44, 45, 47, 70, 83, 120, 178, 197, 353–354
Exchange-traded funds (ETFs), 314, 328, 329, 338

Fang Xiyuan (James Fang), 71–78
Fannie Mae, 11, 51–52, 203, 205, 223
Federal Deposit Insurance Corporation (FDIC), 212
Federal Election Commission, 225
Federal Reserve, 32, 33, 38, 49–51, 53, 70, 84, 87–88, 121, 122, 159, 173, 190, 193, 198, 199, 202, 203, 207, 212–214, 221, 227, 250, 297, 312, 313, 315–323, 339, 355, 358
Feinberg, Kenneth, 207
Feldstein, Martin, 287
Ferguson, Niall, 7, 59, 98
Fernández, Jesús, 306
Fiat currencies, 32–33
Fidelity Investments' Market Analysis, Research and Education Group, 86
FIFO workers, 146–150, 155, 161, 331–332
Financial Accounting Standards Board, 350
Financial crisis of 2008, 2, 7, 13, 18–20, 22–26, 33, 34, 38, 44, 47, 52, 53, 59–60, 62, 64–69, 84–86, 89, 96, 100, 113, 120, 130, 152, 159, 169, 186, 192, 195, 196, 198, 203, 206, 209, 211, 213–214, 217, 220, 227, 228, 231–235, 249, 269, 272, 287, 293, 294, 339, 345, 348
Financial Services Authority (U.K.), 250, 251
Financial services tax, 349
Financial Stability Oversight Council, 221
Financial transparency, 350–351
Finland, 3, 43, 286
Fisher, Richard, 222, 320
Fitch Ratings, 214, 234, 300, 343
Fix Congress First, 361
Flextronics, 173
Floating exchange rates, 36, 353–354
Foot, Michael, 248
Forbes magazine, 8, 15, 74, 107, 225
Foreclosures, 18, 20, 85, 203, 228, 321
Foreign Investment Review Board (Australia), 159
Foreign Policy, 130
Forrest, Andrew "Twiggy," 143, 154
Fortescue Metal Group, 143–146, 148, 154
Fortress Paper, 341
Foshan, China, 102
401(k) accounts, 48
Fox, Richard, 343
Fox, Vicente, 175
Foxconn (Hon Hai Industries), 8–10, 16–19, 110, 174
France, 42, 193, 197, 259, 261, 269–271, 283–287, 289, 303, 349
Franco, Francisco, 306
Franken, Al, 241
Freddie Mac, 11, 51–52, 203, 205, 223
Free market system, 23, 24, 26, 43
Free trade, 2, 97, 177, 179
Freeport-McMoran, 329
French franc, 280, 295
Friedman, Thomas, 22, 23
FTSE 100 index, 36

Galbraith, James K., 224
Galileo Galilei, 5
Gallegos, Rocio, 168
Gallup survey (2011), 3
García, Ernesto, 306
Gardner, Kevin, 109
GATT (General Agreement on Tariffs and Trade), 57
Geithner, Timothy, 207
General Electric Company, 93
General Motors Corporation, 167
George I, King of England, 195
Germany, 3, 42, 53, 61, 193, 197, 259, 261, 267–271, 274, 276, 280, 283–290, 297, 298, 303, 341, 347
Ghea Panggabean, 179
Gillard, Julia, 154
Gillibrand, Kirsten, 226

Glass-Steagall Act, 41, 43, 190, 212, 220, 352
Glitnir Bank, 230–231, 234–236, 239, 256, 261, 262
Gnarr, Jon, 240–241
Gold, 31–37, 156, 190, 251–252, 310–315, 317, 325–331, 336, 359
Goldline International, 313–314
Goldman Sachs, 14, 15, 86–87, 192, 207, 220, 225, 227
Gou, Terry, 8–9, 16, 17–18
Graham, Eric, 243, 245–247
Grant, Jim, 116
Great Depression, 2, 84, 131, 190, 209, 228, 256, 321, 347
Great Moderation, 39
Greece, 3, 12, 21, 24, 35, 53–54, 197, 218, 259, 261, 267–269, 271–274, 281, 283, 284, 286, 288, 289, 292, 293, 295, 298, 299, 301–302, 308, 340, 341, 345, 346, 347
Green Bullion Financial Services, 314
Greenspan, Alan, 49–50, 52, 318
Greenspan Put, 318, 319
Greenwich Capital, 199
Grimsson, Olafur Ragnar, 254, 255
Grobocopatel, Gustavo, 138
Group of 20 (G20), 26, 176, 308, 348, 351, 354, 357–358
  Financial Stability Board, 349
Growth and Stability Pact of European Monetary Union, 286
Guangzhou, China, 8, 102, 110, 111, 115
Guangzhou-to-Wuhan bullet train, 56, 105–106, 144
Gudmundsdottir, Sigurbjorg Alda, 238
Gudmundsson, Magnus, 265
Guernsey, 242–252
Guernsey Financial Services Commission (GFSC), 244–247, 250, 251
Guernsey Investment Fund Association, 243

Haarde, Geir, 240
Hadco, 91
Hall, Andrew J., 207
Hallur, Thor, 234, 236–237, 263
Hamilton, Alexander, 190
Harris, Chris, 147
HBOS PLC group, 196, 197
Hedge funds, 192, 201, 207–208, 210, 223, 225, 226, 312, 352
Heritable Bank, 245
Hewlett-Packard, 8, 19
High-net-worth individuals (HNWIs), 74
High-speed trading, 223–224, 338
Hoenig, Thomas, 320
Home Affordable Modification Program, 204
Hon Hai Industries (Foxconn), 8–10, 16–19, 110, 174
Honda, 110
Honduras, 180
Hong Kong, 102, 127, 323–325
Housing and Urban Development, U.S. Department of, 52
HSBC, 243, 327
Hu Jintao, 126, 129
Huang Rong, 102–103
Hukou residency system, 80, 81, 108, 112, 353
Humala, Ollanta, 329
Hunan Valin Iron and Steel Group, 144

IBM Corporation, 91
Iceland, 3, 228–242, 249, 252–266, 268
Iceland Air, 262
Iceland Group, 262
Icelandic Central Bank, 235–236
Icelandic Depositors' and Investors' Guarantee Fund, 252
Icelandic Financial Supervisory Authority, 235, 256
Icesave, 233, 244, 245, 247, 252–255, 257, 264
Iluka, 157
Income inequality, 2, 23, 206–211
InDefence, 253, 254, 314
Index-based exchange-traded funds, 224
India, 54–55, 99, 107, 143–145, 147, 326, 348, 357
Indonesia, 45–47, 82, 176–186, 191, 343–344
Indrawati, Ina, 180
Industrial Revolution, 189
Infant mortality, 1
Inflation, 33, 36–39, 48, 85, 121, 122, 130, 170, 281–282, 288, 312, 316, 317, 324, 328, 343, 344
Innes, Brian, 156
Institute for Liberty and Democracy (ILD), 335
Institute of International Finance (IIF), 301–302
Integrated-circuit microprocessors (IC chips), 76–78

Intel, 8, 77, 90
Intellectual property, 77
Interest-only mortgages, 65, 66
Interest rates, 12–13, 16, 25, 44, 50, 51, 60, 83, 121–124, 127, 169, 178, 203, 281, 303, 315, 316, 344
International Accounting Standards Board, 350
International Energy Agency, 364
International Monetary Fund (IMF), 26, 32, 46, 54, 118, 125, 157, 236, 254, 259, 260, 274, 284, 290, 293, 299, 303, 315, 327, 342, 351, 354–357
International Swaps and Derivatives Association (ISDA), 293
Internet, 2, 48, 56
Inventory cycle, 85
Iran, 314
Iraq war, 19, 51, 163
Ireland, 3, 12, 21, 43, 53–54, 160, 197, 218, 258–262, 268, 269, 271–274, 283, 284, 286, 288, 289, 292, 308, 346
Islandsbanki, 239, 262–263
Isle of Man, 246, 249
Ismy, Enorvian, 178
Italy, 21, 24, 43, 53–54, 197, 268, 271–273, 283, 286, 287, 289, 292, 293, 295, 296, 298–299, 345, 357
Ivory trade, 140

Japan, 38, 40, 65, 193, 201, 232, 303, 342, 347
  economy in, 84, 130, 131
  foreign reserves of, 131
  occupation of China, 126
  steel demand and, 156
  U.S. Treasury bonds and, 52
Jefferson, Thomas, 190, 192
Jersey, 246, 249
JF Technical Developing Company, 73
Jiang Qing, 71, 72
Johnson, Robert, 227
Johnson, Simon, 192, 208, 319, 362–363
Jones Lang Lasalle, 130
Jonsson, Gunar, 238
JPMorgan Chase, 68, 69, 192, 197, 199, 207, 213, 219, 223
Just-in-time inventory management systems, 56–57

Kangbashi, China, 115
Karabell, Zachary, 103
Kaupthing Bank, 230–231, 234–236, 246, 256, 261, 262, 265
Kedaung Group, 179
Kenya, 140
Keynes, John Maynard, 87, 215, 294, 322
King, Mervyn, 357
Kirchner, Cristina, 137–138
Kirchner, Néstor, 135, 137
Kissinger, Henry, 40
Klibaner, Michael, 130
Krona, 230, 231, 235, 236, 262
Krugman, Paul, 119
Kwak, James, 192, 208, 362–363
Kynikos Associates, 119

Lagarde, Christine, 356
Landsbanki Guernsey, 242, 244–248, 250, 252
Landsbanki Guernsey Depositors Action Group, 246–248, 251
Landsbanki of Iceland, 230–231, 233–236, 239, 244, 252, 253, 256, 257, 261
Lanning, Hugh, 308–309
Leeson, Nick, 37
Lehman Brothers, 64, 84, 98, 113, 192, 194, 196, 215, 233, 234, 269, 308, 313, 339, 340
Lessig, Lawrence, 228, 361
Leverage cycle, 214
Lewis, Michael, 206, 230, 261–262
Leyzaola, Julián, 174
Li Keqiang, 128
Liar's Poker (Lewis), 206
Libya, 55, 140
Life expectancy, 1
Liquidity trap, 322
Lira, 53, 280, 295
Literacy rates, 1–2
Liu Xiemei, 106–107
Lloyds Banking Group, 196, 197
London Gold Market Fixing Ltd., 327
London riots (2011), 308
Long-Term Capital Management (LTCM), 37
Long-term refinancing operation (LTRO), 296, 297
Louvre Accord, 39
Luxembourg, 43, 286
Lyublinsky, Michael, 200

Ma Peijun, 71–75, 78
Ma Ren Yuan, 78, 82, 83

Maastricht Treaty, 42, 286–288, 299, 300, 304
Macias, Miguel, 165
Maggie Ma, 78
Manhattan, New York, 6–8
Manhattan Minerals, 333–335
Mannish, Michael, 275
Mantega, Guido, 199–200, 316
Mao Zedong, 40, 55, 72, 80, 106, 126, 144
Maquiladora industry, 165, 167–172, 175
Marquéz, Deissy, 170–171, 174–177
Marr, Philip, 248
Marxism, 126
Mauritius, 180
McCormick, Terry, 275
McMahon, Peter, 152, 153
McMansions, 51
Medicare, 344
Merkel, Angela, 290, 298
Merrill Lynch, 66, 70, 74, 82, 192, 197, 207
Merton, Robert, 37–38
Mexico, 45, 162–177, 180, 181, 185, 347
MF Global, 221, 222, 294
Microsoft, 8
Middle East uprisings, 26, 55, 317
Midterm elections (U.S.) of 2010, 60, 225
Miglietti, Bruno and Lisa, 203–204, 206
Mindich, Eric, 329
Mining
  in Australia, 141–148, 150, 154–159, 161
  in Peru, 329–335
Mira, Rubén, 360
Mizuno, 178
Monoculture farming, 137
Monsanto Corporation, 133
Monti, Mario, 298
Moody's, 214, 234, 300
Moore, George, 90
Moore Capital, 225
Moore's law, 90
Morgan, J. Pierpont, 189
Morgan Stanley, 192, 207
Mortgages, 14–15, 19, 20, 44, 53, 65, 66, 204–205, 213, 281–282
  subprime, 14, 24, 52, 70, 159, 192, 195, 207, 264, 284, 285
Multiple-currency reserve system, 355
Mutual Assessment Process (MAP), 357

NAFTA (*see* North American Free Trade Agreement [NAFTA])
Napolitano, Giorgio, 298
Nasdaq index, 50
National People's Congress, 108
National Westminster Bank, 195
Natural disasters, 317
Negative amortization loan, 204
Negative equity, 263–264
Negative gearing, 159
Neocolonialism, 140
Neoliberalism, 23, 24
Netherlands, 3, 43, 195, 233, 252, 254–256, 266, 268, 286
New Balance, 178
New Economy, 49, 158
New York Estate Buyers, 310–311
New York Liberty Pawnshop, 310–311
Nixon, Richard, 31–32, 35, 36, 40, 51, 128
Nixon Shock of 1971, 32, 34, 36, 55
No-till farming, 133
Nomura, 193
North American Free Trade Agreement (NAFTA), 44–45, 167–169, 173, 174
Northwest Shelf Natural Gas project, 149, 153
Norway, 154

Obama, Barack, 113, 221, 225, 227, 265, 292, 313, 360
Obama administration, 84, 204, 223–225, 321
Obrador, Andrés Manual López, 176
Occidental Petroleum, 207
Occupy Wall Street movement, 2, 3, 26, 209, 361
Ochoa, Manuel, 175
Oddsson, David, 235–236
O'Donnell, William, 199, 200
Offshoring, 56, 91
Oil, 36, 139, 140, 317
Olafsson, Ragnar, 254
One-child policy, 107, 112, 183
O'Neill, Jim, 54
Open Market Committee (Federal Reserve), 193
Open Secrets, 361
Opium Wars, 41, 126

Options, 37–38
O'Reilly, Bill, 314
Organisation for Economic Cooperation and Development, 174
Organization of Arab Petroleum Exporting Countries (OAPEC), 36–37
Output gap, 85, 86
Outsourcing, 49, 56, 65, 70, 87, 92, 94, 103–104, 346
Over-the-counter swaps, 44
Oxfam Australia, 182, 184

Pangestu, Mari, 179
Papademos, Lucas, 299
Papandreou, George, 289, 299
Paradox of thrift, 215, 294
Patel, Sailesh Carlyle, 248
Paul, Ron, 190, 320, 361
Paulson, John, 14–15, 20, 21, 114, 225, 328, 329
Paulson & Company, 14–15, 225
Paulson, Hank, 227
Pawnshops, 310–314
Pearl River Delta, China, 83, 102, 103
Pension funds, 18, 201, 203, 283, 302, 353
People's Bank of China (PBOC), 7, 9–11, 52, 75, 114, 120, 122, 123, 198, 201
Perón, Eva, 132, 135
Perry, Rick, 33, 320
Perth, Australia, 21–22, 147–153, 159, 161, 162
Peru, 328–336
Peseta, 53, 280
Peso, 169, 172–173
Peter G. Peterson Foundation, 345
Peterson Institute for International Economics, 9–10
Pettis, Michael, 16, 119, 130–131
Pew Research Center, 60
PIIGS (*see* Portugal, Ireland, Italy, Greece, and Spain)
Plaza Accord, 39
Plosser, Charles, 320
Portugal, 3, 12, 21, 43, 53, 197, 218, 261, 268, 271, 283, 284, 286, 288, 289, 292
Pound sterling, 36, 276, 278, 355
Presidential election (U.S.)
  1992, 226
  2008, 225, 226
  2012, 3, 60, 225, 345, 346, 349, 360, 362
Primary dealers, 193, 200, 202
Printed circuits boards (PCBs), 88–97, 140
Privatization, 23, 44, 114
Project Merlin plan, 198
Promontory Financial Group U.K., 248, 249, 251
Protectionism, 4, 96, 97, 256, 347
PT Panarub group, 178, 181–185
Punt, 53

Qantas Airlines, 146, 150
Quantitative easing (QE2), 199–202, 315, 316, 318, 319, 325
Quantum Fund, 329

Rajan, Raghuram, 211
Rajoy, Mariano, 305
Reagan, Ronald, 42, 72
Recession (1981), 38
Reebok, 184
Reinhart, Carmen, 85
Reksono, Wiwih, 180
Renouf, Jayson, 148, 149
Reserve Bank of Australia, 159
Restore Our Future Inc., 225
Rhodes, William, 302
Rio Tinto, 143–145, 154, 156, 161
Riofrío, Francisco, 333–334
Robb, David, 157
"Robin Hood" tax, 270
Robo-signing scandal, 203
Rockefeller, John D., 362
Rodríguez, Armando "El Choco," 168
Rodriguez, Ruth, 170, 171
Roosevelt, Theodore, 362–363
Rosenberg, Andrés, 136–138
Rosland Capital, 314
Rothman, Andy, 127
Roubini, Nouriel, 340
Royal Bank of Scotland (RBS), 194–196, 198–200, 202, 223
Ruan Kaigui, 106–107
Ruan Libing, 104–108, 110, 112
Ruan Xiaolu, 105, 106, 109–110
Rubinov, Roni, 310–313, 315, 326
Rudd, Kevin, 154
Rueda, Sandra, 306
Rupiah, 45
Russia, 47, 54–55, 99, 314, 348, 357

S&P 500 index, 86, 210
Salomon Brothers, 206

Sanmina-SCI, 91
Sanyo, 110
Sasmito, Hendrik, 178–179, 181–183
Savings and loan crisis (U.S.), 39
Savings rates
in China, 16, 25, 59, 60, 82, 99–101, 103, 105, 107, 108, 110, 112, 113, 119, 124, 127
in U.S., 48, 59, 99–100, 183
Scholes, Myron, 37–38
Schularick, Moritz, 59
Schumer, Charles, 226
Schumpeter, Joseph, 95
Schwarzenegger, Arnold, 241
Securities and Exchange Commission (SEC), 14, 15
September 11 terrorist attacks, 6, 50, 89
Shadow banking system, 124, 213, 214, 223, 319
Shang-Jin Wei, 107
Shanghai, China, 5–8, 75, 80, 81, 83, 114, 116, 118, 134
Shantou, China, 102
Shenzhen, China, 8, 9, 16, 60, 102, 109, 110, 134
Shih, Victor, 118
Shiller, Robert, 20–21
Shinco, 79
Sigfusson, Steingrimur, 266
Sigurdardottir, Johanna, 240, 253, 265
Sigurdsson, Hreidar Mar, 265
Singapore, 325
Slim, Carlos, 174, 176
Smith, Adam, 2
Social Security, 344
Société Générale, 284, 327
Sony, 8
Soros, George, 328–329
South Korea, 45, 47, 65, 76, 201, 302, 344
Sovereign wealth funds, 154, 156
Soviet Union, 24, 40, 42
Soybeans, 133–138, 140
Spain, 12, 21, 43, 53–54, 160, 197, 261, 268, 271–282, 284, 286–289, 292, 293, 295–297, 299, 304–307
SPDR Gold Shares, 314
SPDR S&P 500 ETF, 314
Special Drawing Rights (SDRs), 355
Special economic zones (SEZs), 60, 75, 102, 112
Special investment vehicles (SIVs), 117–118
Sports shoe industry, 180–186
Standard & Poor's, 12, 214, 234, 300, 308, 321–322, 344
State Statistical Bureau (China), 128
Stem cell research, 5
Stiglitz, Joseph, 262
Stock market crash (1987), 39
STRATFOR, 174, 282
Strauss-Kahn, Dominique, 356
Subprime mortgages, 14, 24, 52, 70, 159, 192, 195, 207, 264, 284, 285
Sudan, 140
Suharto regime, 45, 46, 178, 180
Svavarsson, Eirikur S., 254
Swiss francs, 231, 232, 323
Switzerland, 193, 218, 232
Systemic risk, 196, 271–272, 294, 351, 352

Tail risk, 37
Taiwan, 40, 76, 201, 344
Taiwan Semiconductor Manufacturing Company, 77
Taleb, Nassim, 340
Tariffs, 4, 44, 60, 96
Tarullo, Daniel, 218, 219
Tax code, simplification of, 352–353
Tax havens, 192
Tax reforms of 2001, 216, 359
Tay, Markus, 325
Tchenguiz, Robert and Vincent, 265
Tea Party movement, 3, 26, 264, 322, 359
Technological change, 4–5
Telecommunications Law of 1996, 363
Telefónica, 306–307
Thailand, 45, 47, 314
Thatcher, Margaret, 41, 42, 193, 308
Thompson, Paul, 161, 162
Thoreau, Henry David, 361
Thorvaldsson, Armann, 231–232
Tiananmen Square massacre (1989), 41
Tianhe-1A computer, 56
Tianjin, China, 8, 117
Tinsa, 277
Too-big-to-fail doctrine, 196–197, 206, 215, 216, 222, 226, 227, 269, 272, 276, 302–303, 350–352, 362
Toshiba, 77
Tourre, Fabrice, 14, 15, 20, 52
Toyota, 110
Trade deficit (U.S.), 31, 38, 48
Trade sanctions bill (2011), 126
Transparency, financial, 350–351

Trichet, Jean-Claude, 298
Trott, Lyndon, 246, 249
Troubled Asset Recovery Program (TARP), 196, 207, 223
Tunisia, 55
Turkey, 295

UBS, 124, 193, 199, 218
Unemployment, 37, 49, 85, 87, 95, 232, 237, 238, 243, 259, 282, 305–306, 308, 321, 322
United Kingdom, 3, 41–42, 193–198, 218, 223, 233, 241, 242, 245–250, 253–258, 261, 266, 269–271, 274, 284–286, 300, 301, 308, 349
United Nations, 307, 364
  Millennium Development Goal, 1
U.S.-China relationship, 7, 10–13, 15, 18, 55–61, 96, 322–323, 346–347
U.S. debt ceiling debate, 12, 321, 344, 345
U.S. Foreign Trade Zone, 167
U.S. Treasury bonds, 11–13, 52, 61, 70, 84, 121, 122, 127, 154, 193, 199–202, 316, 320, 323, 338, 345, 347
Uruguay round of trade, 44
Utopianism, 26

Vale, 143, 144
Value at risk (VaR) model, 217
Vanderbilt, Cornelius, 362
Vázquez López, Juvéncio, 164–165
Venezuela, 174
Ventura, Jesse, 241
Vietnam, 76, 111, 177, 184, 185
Vietnam War, 31
Virgin Atlantic Airways, 146
Volcker, Paul, 38, 39, 220
Volcker Rule, 220

Walmart, 48, 103–105, 108–109, 143
Wang Shen Ju, 79, 81, 82, 184
Warren, Elizabeth, 227
Washington Consensus, 44
Wasilenkoff, Chad, 341
Waterman, Toni, 278
Wealth disparities, 2, 23, 206–211
Wealth effect, 203, 210–211
Wen Jiabao, 126, 128, 303
Western Texas Intermediate oil contract, 317
Wimo, 180
Won, 45
Woodward, Bob, 49
Woolley, Paul, 353
World Bank, 307, 356
World Gold Council, 315
World Health Organization, 364
World Trade Center, New York, 6, 7, 50
World Trade Organization (WTO), 4, 26, 44, 57–58, 134, 167, 168, 180, 348, 364
World War II, 126
Wu Guoseng, 102–103
Wu Xinfeng, 102, 103
Wu Yi, 58
Wuhan, China, 115

Xi Jinping, 128–129

Yellen, Janet, 321
Yen, 36, 39, 231, 232, 323, 338, 355
Y2K, 88, 92
Yu Faming, 113
Yuan, 9, 10, 21, 25, 47, 60, 120–123, 125–129, 169, 173, 201, 260, 303, 311, 323, 347, 357

Zapatero, José Luís Rodríguez, 304–305
Zero Hedge, 117
Zhao Ziyang, 72
Zhou Xiaochuan, 126
Zhu Hai, China, 102–104, 109, 110, 134
Zhuhai Raysharp Tech Company, 102–103
Ziga, Ricardo, 166
Zycon, 91